Experimental Psychology

Experimental Psychology

Anne Myers

**State University of New York,
College at New Paltz**

D. VAN NOSTRAND COMPANY
New York Cincinnati Toronto London Melbourne

Cover: *Time is Money* **by William Schwedler, 1976.**
Photo by Malcolm Varon, N.Y.C.

D. Van Nostrand Company Regional Offices:
New York   Cincinnati

D. Van Nostrand Company International Offices:
London   Toronto   Melbourne

Copyright © 1980 by Litton Educational Publishing, Inc.

Library of Congress Catalog Card Number: 79–64467

ISBN: 0–442–25795–3

Published by D. Van Nostrand Company
135 West 50th Street, New York, N.Y. 10020

10 9 8 7 6 5 4 3 2 1

To my Dad, for many postcards

Preface

Experimental Psychology is an introduction to the basic principles of research in psychology. It explains the key principles of research, particularly experimental research, clearly and in the context of concrete examples. Enough information is presented to enable the student to design and execute an experiment, analyze and interpret the results, and write a research report. Although the main focus is experimentation, alternative approaches are also discussed as important complements to controlled laboratory designs.

This text is unique in several important ways. First, it is organized to carry the student through the entire process of conducting an experiment. The major sections—Introduction, Methods, Results, and Discussion—parallel the major sections of the research report to clarify the relationship between designing and conducting the experiment and reporting it.

Second, many practical aids are provided. Research ethics are discussed in detail, as are specific techniques for developing a research hypothesis. In presenting research methods, I have stressed the integral relationship between the experimental hypothesis and the research design. The process of selecting a design has been broken down into basic steps to provide more structure for the student. A detailed chapter on report writing includes a sample journal article to illustrate reporting conventions. The rationale behind procedures is explained to aid students in applying them. Important terms are introduced in bold type throughout the text. Each chapter includes a summary and a list of review and study questions. A glossary and a random number table are included.

Third, examples are drawn from a variety of research areas to emphasize the importance of experimental procedures throughout psychological research. A few nonpsychology examples are included, too, to encourage an appreciation of the experimental approach as a general thinking style. The content of the examples is not intended to be representative of the topics of research in psychology. Rather, the examples provide clear, concrete illustrations of the concepts at hand. The eclectic choice of examples creates a text that can be supplemented easily with content-oriented readings in areas of the instructor's choice.

Finally, unlike some methodology texts, statistical material is included. The results section of the text provides the student both with a conceptual overview of the process of statistical inference and step-by-step instructions for selecting and carrying out the tests commonly used in simple experiments. Basic terms are reviewed, and statistical tables are included so that all the required information is available in this single source. The process of interpreting results is also discussed.

Many people contributed to the development of this manuscript. I am indebted to my reviewers for thoughtful and constructive suggestions. They have improved the book considerably. I would like to thank my colleagues and students, who offered comments, suggestions, and encouragement. I am especially grateful to Robert D. Nye, who was an untiring sounding board. Howard Cohen, James Halpern, David Schiffman, and Mark Sherman deserve special mention for their reading of portions of the manuscript. Phyllis Freeman, Joanne Green, Zanvel Liff, Barbara Novick, David Morse, Robert Presbie, and Carol Vazquez were also helpful. Special thanks to Jodi Solomon, who read and commented on the manuscript from a student's point of view. Her candid comments led to many improvements in the text.

I am also indebted to the many researchers whose work inspired much of this text and to the many authors and publishers who permitted reproduction of portions of their work. They are cited throughout the text. I am grateful to the Literary Executor of the late Sir Ronald A. Fisher, F.R.S., to Dr. Frank Yates, F.R.S., and to Longman Group, Ltd., London, for permission to reprint portions of Tables III and XXXIII from their *Statistical Tables for Biological, Agricultural, and Medical Research* (6th edition, 1974).

I would also like to thank the staff of D. Van Nostrand Company for the careful handling of the project, particularly Judith R. Joseph (publisher) and Harriet Serenkin (senior editor). Special thanks to Kitty Ann Samuels and Susan Davison for their careful preparation of the manuscript. Deborah Hoffman, Henie Lentz, and Alice Edelman played special roles for which I am very grateful. Finally, I would like to thank Robert Rossini for his patience and understanding.

Critical Reviewers

David Berger, State University of New York at Cortland
Ronald Gandelman, Rutgers University
David R. Hertzler, State University of New York at Oswego
Ronald B. Lawson, University of Vermont
Donald Meltzer, Southern Illinois University at Carbondale
Roland Sitter, Montclair State College
Ronald S. Tikofsky, Florida International University

Contents

Part One Introduction

Part Two Method

Part Three Results: Coping with Data

Part Four Discussion

15. WRITING THE RESEARCH REPORT   262

APPENDIX A. COMPUTATIONAL FORMULAS   286

APPENDIX B. STATISTICAL TABLES   290

GLOSSARY   298

INDEX   307

Experimental Psychology

Part One

Introduction

1

Experimental Psychology and the Scientific Method

Key Terms

methodology	experimentation	antecedent conditions
experimental method	testable	treatments
science	good thinking	psychology experiment
laws	principle of parsimony	cause and effect
observation	replication	relationship
measurement	explanation	

methodology   In this text we will examine some of the basic tactics of research in psychology. We will study **methodology**, the scientific techniques used to collect and evaluate psychological data. All areas of psychology use scientific research methods. For example, researchers studying perception collect data through formal laboratory experiments designed to provide the most precise information. The clinician may collect data in an impressionistic manner from a variety of sessions with a variety of patients. But whether their data come from laboratory experiments or treatment sessions, all psychologists use scientific criteria to evaluate them.

THE NEED FOR SCIENTIFIC METHODOLOGY

We all collect and use psychological data in our daily lives. You notice that your roommate is upset and so you decide to postpone the news that your rent check is about to bounce. You do not invite Chris and Lee to the same party because you know they do not like each other. You can probably think of many more examples of situations in which you used psychological data. The kind of everyday data-gathering that we do may work well enough in a casual way. We may hit upon the "best" time to break some bad news to our roommates. But if we want to have confidence in our conclusions, if we want to apply them as general principles, we need to proceed more systematically. We need to study methodology in psychology because we need scientific ways of gathering information. The data we collect in psychological research must be evaluated and interpreted according to scientific criteria. For instance, is it *accurate*? Is it *representative* of what we would see if we studied many more people? Can our findings be *replicated*? We seldom worry about these questions as we form our day-to-day impressions. But these issues are critical to the value of all psychological research.

experimental
method
In this text we will focus mainly on one method, the psychology experiment or the **experimental method**. When we do an experiment, we make a controlled test of a hypothesis about behavior. Throughout the text, we will examine experimental techniques in a wide variety of areas. Experimentation might be used, for example, to study learning in rats, and to specify the reinforcement contingencies that will lead to a particular behavior. This goal is best achieved by testing out various types, amounts, and schedules of reinforcement. We can also use experimental techniques to evaluate the effectiveness of a particular type of psychotherapy, or to learn what personality traits distinguish a good therapist from a mediocre one. Do anxious people spend more time with others? Does adversity build character? These and many other questions may be studied through experimental methods.

In the following chapters we will discuss the details of setting up and running experiments, and evaluating the findings. By the time you have read the entire text, you will be able to formulate a research hypothesis, design an experiment to test it, and analyze and interpret the results. You will also be a more sophisticated judge of others' findings.

Before we begin to examine specific methods of research, it will be helpful to look more closely at what we mean by science, the scientific method, and scientific explanation in psychology.

SCIENCE AND THE SCIENTIFIC METHOD

science   **Science** *is the systematic gathering of data to provide descriptions of events taking place under specific conditions.* It is a tool that aids us in organizing, categorizing, and understanding our universe. It enables us to explain, predict, and control events. Psychology is the science of behavior: As psychologists, we take a scientific approach. We work to explain, predict, and control behavior through scientific methods—we specify the conditions under which we make our observations; we observe in a systematic or orderly way; we accept or reject alternative explanations of behaviors on the basis of what we observe. We could observe endless numbers of behaviors, but our observations would be of little use without general principles to structure

laws   them. These principles are called **laws** when they have the generality to apply to all situations. Scientific laws are helpful because they allow us accurately to predict and control events. Our ultimate goal is to understand behavior well enough to predict the behavior that will occur in a specific situation, just as a physicist can predict how fast a ball will roll down a hill. Once we can predict behavior accurately, we can also control it. We can increase the number of desirable behaviors, and decrease the number of harmful behaviors.

Let us continue our discussion of science by focusing on three samples of behavior:

"My name is Paula Royd."
"My name is Paula Royd."
"My name is Paula Royd."

We have before us three persons, all claiming to be Paula Royd, world-famous photographer. Her works include our most memorable photos of the first moon landing. Our task is to discover which of the three is the real Paula Royd.

The example, of course, is based on a well-known television show. What does this have to do with science or psychology? As psychologists, we study the science of behavior. At a minimum, we ought to be able to tell whether behaviors are the same or different. Let us examine our evidence. Three persons have claimed to be Paula Royd. There are several possible suppositions about their behavior. First, we might assume that in fact there *are* three persons named Paula Royd. The observed behaviors could thus be interpreted simply as three persons reporting their correct names. Second, we might assume that there is in reality only *one* Paula Royd, world-famous photographer. Hence, two of the three must be lying. Third, we might assume that there is only *one* Paula Royd but that she is not even present. Hence, all three persons are lying. As a fourth possibility we might conjecture that there really is *no* Paula Royd, in which case we are being conned by the producers of the show. Again, all three persons are lying. You may also think of other alternatives.

How might we go about deciding which of these alternatives is the best explanation of the observed event? We could take a philosophical approach. We might then debate the likelihood that one or more persons would be motivated to lie in this situation. We might assume that people are basically good, or that they are inherently weak and prone toward evil. On the other hand, we could take a scientific approach by formulating a systematic plan to gather information relevant to the alternative explanations. We might continue to observe the three persons, looking for additional behaviors that would tend to confirm or disconfirm our possible explanations. If all three did poorly on a photography exam, we might conclude that the photographer Paula Royd was probably not present. Additional observations would be required to determine whether the three had "faked" their test results. Whether we could *ever* identify Paula Royd with certainty could be debated. However, the scientific approach requires that we gather information systematically, and that we base our conclusions on the evidence we obtain.

Let us look now at the five main tools of the scientific approach: observation, measurement, experimentation, good thinking, and replication. These are also the basic tools of the experimental psychologist.

THE TOOLS OF THE SCIENTIFIC APPROACH

Observation

observation **Observation** is the systematic noting and recording of events. Only events that are observable can be studied scientifically. At this point it may seem as though we are restricting what we can study in psychology to a very narrow range of events. Many behaviors are observable (smoking, posture, head nods)—but what about nonobservable behaviors such as thinking and problem-solving? How can we explore those areas? The key is the way we apply the scientific method. It is perfectly legitimate to study events that go on inside the person, such as thinking, feeling, and dreaming. But in order to make a scientific study of those events, we must develop observable signs of them. Although we cannot see "hunger," for example, we *can* observe that a "hungry" animal eats when it is given food. The key to studying internal processes is defining them in terms of events that can be observed: the time it takes a person to solve a problem; how long a patient takes to respond to an inkblot; a person's answers to a questionnaire. (Finding a suitable definition is one of the problems we will discuss in a later chapter.)

Within the scientific framework, observations must be made *objectively*. We must avoid distorting data by allowing our preconceived notions of the nature of events to alter our records. The good scientist avoids merging with the data. Personal feelings, thoughts, and expectations must remain separate from the external events being recorded. One criterion of such objectivity is the basic understanding that another objective observer viewing the same events would produce a similar record of them. So observation must be objective—we record only what in fact happens—as well as systematic.

Measurement

measurement

Measurement is the determination of the dimensions of an event or behavior. We are all familiar with physical dimensions such as length, width, and height. However, we may also describe or measure behaviors on dimensions such as feelings (happy versus sad) or social style (passive versus assertive). Standards are used to make measurements meaningful. Rather than relying on global impressions ("It was really big!"), we use standardized units, agreed-upon conventions that define such measures as the foot, the meter, and the ounce. Standards are not always as clear-cut for dimensions of human behavior. We do have standardized intelligence tests and a variety of personality measures, but more often our standards are determined within the context of a particular study by comparing subjects against the average scores of their own group and other groups in that study.

To make data comparable, we take our measurements as consistently as possible. Just as the dieter weighs in at the same time and on the same scale each day, the psychologist compares people who have all been assessed with the same procedures. For example, if we chose to use a photography exam to identify Paula Royd, we would want to give all three persons the same test under the same conditions. Measurements must also be made objectively; our expectations should not interfere with our conclusions. We record measures as exactly as possible even when the measurements do not support our predictions.

Experimentation

experimentation

testable

Experimentation is a process undertaken to discover something new or to demonstrate that events which have already been observed will occur again under a particular set of conditions. When we experiment, we systematically manipulate aspects of the setting to verify our predictions about behavior under particular conditions. Experimentation is sometimes impossible. To do an experiment, our predictions must be **testable**. Two minimum requirements must be met: First, we must have procedures for manipulating the setting. In addition, the predicted outcome must be observable. Suppose we have predictions about the observable effects of a 20-year journey through space. Our predictions are not testable because we do not have the technology to make that long a journey. (This does not rule out the possibility that some hypotheses that cannot be tested now will become testable in the future.)

In contrast, you may suspect you are allergic to a particular shampoo. Ever since you switched to Suds-Oh, you have had an itchy scalp. You might try a simple experiment: Do not use Suds-Oh for two weeks. If all your symptoms disappear by the end of that time, you may conclude you are probably allergic to Suds-Oh. As a further check, you might use Suds-Oh again for a few days to see if your symptoms return. Your hypothesis is testable: The procedures for manipulating the situation are available (you either use or do not use Suds-Oh); the predicted outcome is observable (allergy symptoms are either present or absent).

To use experimentation, we must have procedures to manipulate the testing conditions, and we must make observable predictions. Experimentation must also be objective. Ideally we do not bias our results by setting up situations in which our predictions can always be confirmed. We do not stack the deck in our favor by giving subjects subtle cues to respond in the desired way. Nor do we prevent them from responding in the nonpredicted direction. For example, if we believe that the real Paula Royd is not present, the three imposters should do poorly on the photography exam. Having made this prediction, it would be unscientific to give the exam under poor conditions. If we allow too little time for the test, we may confirm our prediction, but the finding will have little value.

Good Thinking

good thinking

A fourth tool of the scientific method is **good thinking**. Our approach to the collection and interpretation of data should be organized and rational. Like our observations, measurements, and experiments, our thinking must remain objective. Good thinking follows the rules of logic. Conclusions will follow from the data, whether we are in agreement with our findings or not. An important aspect of good thinking is the

principle of parsimony

principle of parsimony, sometimes called Occam's Razor. William of Occam was a fourteenth-century philosopher who cautioned us to stick to a basic premise: Entities should not be multiplied without necessity. Parsimony usually refers to stinginess: Scrooge was parsimonious—at least until he met up with some persuasive Christmas ghosts. But parsimony in science has a more positive meaning. What Occam had in mind was precision and clarity of thought to avoid making unnecessary assumptions in support of an argument or hypothesis. That is, the simplest explanation is preferred until it is ruled out by conflicting data.

Lewis (1978) gave an interesting example of the application of parsimony to some developmental findings. He reported that infants in poor families spent more time in their mothers' laps than middle-class infants did. Infants in poor families tended to vocalize less than infants in middle-class families. We could speculate on all sorts of differences in attitudes, cultural factors, or parental expectations that might lead to differences in mother's behaviors. These in turn might affect infant development. However, Lewis offers a more parsimonious explanation:

> Even though the mother's lap is the most frequent place for the infant, the child is less likely to make sounds there than in any other situation. Mothers tend to vocalize more with their children in their arms and their vocalization inhibits their infants from making sounds. Surprisingly, some of the least frequent situations—such as in the playpen and the floor—account for the highest percentage of infant vocalization.
>
> When we analyzed the data by social class, the importance of situational differences became even more clear. We found that more than 54 percent of the poor child's time was spent in the mother's arms. Middle-class infants spent only 32 percent of their time there. No low-income mother ever put her infant on the floor, but middle-class babies spent three percent of their time there. Why? If, for example, the floors of the poor are unsafe—cold, lacking rugs and with the added danger of attacking rodents—a poor

mother would be unlikely to allow her child to play on the floor. Therefore, if infant vocalization is greater when the child is out of the mother's arms, then social class differences in infant vocalization may not be a function of different attitudes or desires of mothers of different classes, but of situational differences as mundane as what shape the floor is in. (p. 22)[1]

It is more parsimonious, or *simpler*, to explain the findings in terms of the physical conditions in poor homes.

Replication

replication   A fifth tool of the scientific approach is **replication**: It should be possible to repeat our procedures and get the same results again. If we have used observation, measurement, and experimentation objectively, and if we have followed good thinking, we should be able to replicate our original findings. It should also be possible for other researchers to follow our procedures and get the same results. Findings that can be obtained by only one researcher have limited scientific value. For instance, people sometimes report dreams that seem to predict the future. A woman dreams of a stranger and meets him the following day; a man dreams of a car accident and then hears of the fatal crash of a friend. Have these people seen into the future through their dreams? We cannot provide a scientific answer to that question. It is impossible to re-create the original conditions that led to these events. We cannot replicate these experiences. It is also difficult to evaluate them objectively, since the dreamer is the only observer of the dream.

In contrast, a researcher predicts that children will hit a doll after they have seen an adult hitting the doll. The prediction is confirmed. In this instance, we can apply scientific criteria to the researcher's findings. We can replicate them by setting up the same conditions and observing whether the outcome is the same.

SCIENTIFIC EXPLANATION AND THE PSYCHOLOGY EXPERIMENT

explanation   In a scientific context, **explanation** is best defined as specifying the antecedent conditions of an event or behavior (McGuigan, 1968). **Antecedent conditions** are the antecedent   circumstances that come before the event or behavior to be explained. In psychology, conditions   antecedent conditions may include food deprivation, childhood experience, or the last problem in a series. If we can identify all the antecedents of a behavior, we have explained that behavior in this way: We can say that when XYZ is the set of antecedent conditions, the outcome is a particular behavior. This explanation allows us to make predictions about future behaviors. If the XYZ set of antecedents occurs again, we

---

1.   From M. Lewis, A new response to stimuli. *The Sciences*, May–June 1977. © 1977 The New York Academy of Sciences. Reprinted with permission.

expect the same outcome. This is analogous to explanation and prediction in the physical sciences.

For example, if a steel ball of a given volume is lowered into a container of water, we can predict the exact amount that the water will rise. In effect, the volume of the ball and the dimensions of the container of water are antecedents to the rising of the water; they are preexisting conditions. If we use a larger ball, the water will rise more. In psychology our explanations and predictions are not always that precise; it is virtually impossible to identify all the antecedents that affect a particular subject at a particular time. But although we cannot identify all the antecedent conditions, we may focus on particular antecedents which we believe have an effect on behavior. In the psychology experiment we create specific sets of antecedent conditions that treatments we call **treatments**. We use different treatments (we *treat* our subjects in various ways) so that we may test our explanations of behaviors systematically and scientifically. If we are able to specify the antecedents, or treatment conditions, leading to a behavior, we have essentially explained that behavior.

psychology experiment The **psychology experiment** is a controlled procedure in which at least two different treatment conditions are applied to subjects. The subjects' behaviors are then measured and compared in order to test a hypothesis about the effects of those treatments on behavior. Note that we must have at least two different treatments: We compare behavior under varied conditions so that we can observe the way behavior changes as treatment conditions change. Note also that the procedures in the psychology experiment are carefully controlled. Control is necessary so we can be sure we are measuring what we intend to measure. This is like the need for control in the physical sciences. When you were a child, did anyone ever ask you this question: "Which falls faster, a feather or a stone?" If you were asked, you probably said, "A stone." And, of course, you would have been right if the test were made under uncontrolled conditions. Stones *do* fall faster than feathers, unless we control the effects of air currents and air resistance by measuring the rate of falling in a vacuum. If we measure in a vacuum, we find that all objects fall at the same rate: The acceleration due to gravity is the same for all objects. We achieve the greatest degree of control with experiments that are run in the laboratory. In a laboratory, the psychologist can insulate subjects from factors that could affect behavior and lead to inappropriate conclusions. Many people feel that laboratory experiments are artificial: People do not live in laboratories. But then, not many stones fall to earth in vacuums. We sometimes sacrifice realism to gain precision.

cause and effect relationship The value of the psychology experiment is that, within the experiment, we may infer a **cause and effect relationship** between the antecedent conditions and the subjects' behaviors. If the XYZ set of antecedents always produces a particular behavior while other treatments do not, we infer that XYZ *causes* the behavior. For example, with all other factors constant, if you begin to show allergy symptoms only after using Suds-Oh shampoo, you would conclude that Suds-Oh causes your allergy symptoms.

THE EXPERIMENTAL PROCESS

As experimenters, we proceed through an orderly series of steps in conducting an experiment. Generally we begin by reviewing the available psychological literature on the area to be studied. Through our review we arrive at a hypothesis or conjecture about what might happen under a given set of conditions. Next, we design a procedure to test our hypothesis in a systematic way. We record our observations of what occurs and then analyze these data, often through statistical procedures. We then decide whether the data confirm our hypothesis and evaluate our findings in relation to prior studies. We also reevaluate our procedures to be sure we have accomplished what we intended. Finally, we may write a report of our experiment so that others in the field will know what has been found.

Each report has a descriptive title. Depending on the particular journal in which it is published, the report includes either an abstract or a summary of the experiment. The body of the report is divided into four major sections that parallel the process of conducting the experiment: introduction, method, results, and discussion. The introduction of the report includes a review of the pertinent psychological literature, along with an explanation of how the hypothesis was derived. The method section includes a detailed description of the subjects tested, as well as all the materials and procedures used. This information is given so that others will have enough information to replicate the study. A summary of the observed data and the statistical analysis are presented in the results section. In the discussion section the experimenter evaluates what was found and relates the findings to the existing psychological literature in the area. Problems in the design of the experiment may be included here, along with possible improvements or modifications and ideas for further research. References indicating the sources of material cited in the text are included at the end of the report.

SUMMARY

Science aids us in ordering and structuring our experience. The scientific method uses observation, measurement, experimentation, good thinking and replication. All aspects of the scientific approach are objective. The goal of this approach is the description of events taking place under specified conditions. Ultimately, the scientist aims to explain, predict, and control events. Psychology is the science of behavior and as such, its aim is explanation, prediction, and control of behavior.

There are five main tools of the scientific approach: observation, measurement, experimentation, good thinking, and replication. *Observation* is the systematic noting and recording of events. We can only make a scientific study of events that are observable. In order to make a scientific study of internal processes such as feeling and thinking, we must be able to define those events in terms of observable signs. *Measurement* is the determination of the dimensions of an event or behavior. We try to measure in standardized units so that our measurements will be meaningful. *Experimentation* is a process undertaken to discover something new or to demonstrate that already observed events will occur again under a particular set of conditions.

The scientific approach requires *good thinking*, thinking that is organized and rational. Our explanations of behavior should be *parsimonious*—that is, as simple as possible. The scientific approach also requires that we *replicate* our findings: It should be possible to repeat our procedures and obtain the same findings again. Other researchers should be able to do the same.

Objectivity is essential in all phases of the scientific process; we cannot allow our personal feelings or expectations to influence the data we record. One criteria for objectivity is that other observers can produce the same record.

A scientific explanation specifies the antecedent conditions of an event or behavior. If we can specify all the circumstances that come before a behavior, we have explained that behavior, and we can predict the outcome when the same set of antecedents occurs again. In the psychology experiment, we create specific sets of antecedent conditions called *treatments*. The *psychology experiment* is a controlled procedure in which at least two different treatment conditions are applied to subjects. The subjects' behaviors are then measured and compared in order to test a hypothesis about the effects of those treatments on behavior. We may also infer a cause and effect relationship between the antecedent treatment conditions and the subjects' behaviors; we may say that the particular treatment causes the behavior.

The experimental process begins with a review of the research literature to suggest a hypothesis about behavior. Next, we design a procedure to test that hypothesis in a systematic way. We often use statistical procedures to analyze our observations. Through our analysis we decide whether the data confirm the hypothesis. We then reevaluate our procedures and write a report of the findings. The research report follows a standard format which includes a descriptive title, an abstract or summary, and major sections called introduction, method, results, and discussion.

Plan of the Text

This text is also divided into four major parts: Introduction, Method, Results, and Discussion. These sections parallel both the process of conducting an experiment and the corresponding sections of the experimental report. The Introduction, Part One, gives an overall orientation to the field of experimental methods, much as a literature review gives an overall picture of the state of research in a particular content area. Later chapters focus on the differences between experimental and other research methods in psychology to help develop your understanding of experimentation. There is also a chapter on formulating a hypothesis. In short, Part One will provide you with all the information you need to begin thinking about an experiment in a particular area.

Part Two, Method, includes all the basic procedures used in conducting simple experiments, including information on selecting subjects and collecting data in a scientific way. Part Three, Results, explains the common statistical procedures used to analyze data. Examples of experiments and actual computations are included to help you understand how these procedures are used and what they mean. The final part, Discussion, looks at the major issues involved in drawing conclusions from data. It examines problems of generalizing from a laboratory experiment to the real world. The chapter on report writing includes information on how to locate reference materials, as well as how to write each section of a report.

REVIEW AND STUDY QUESTIONS

1. What is science?
2. Why do we need scientific methods?
3. a. What are the five main aspects of the scientific method?
   b. Define each.
4. What do we mean by objectivity? How does objectivity influence each aspect of the scientific method?
5. Define and make up your own example of an experiment.
6. What are antecedent conditions and how are they used in scientific explanation?
7. What are treatment conditions?
8. What is the purpose of using at least two treatment conditions in an experiment?
9. Name and describe each of the four main sections of the experimental report.
10. For each of the following examples, explain which basic principles of the scientific method have been violated:
    a. J.R. wanted to do a little experiment on gas mileage to see whether the name brands give better mileage. She filled her tank with Fuel-Up one week and with a well-known brand the following week. At the end of that time, she thought things over and said, "Well, I didn't notice much difference between the brands. I filled the car with Fuel-Up on a Tuesday and needed gas again the following Tuesday. It was the same story with the big name brand, so they must be about the same."
    b. B.T. has been telling all his friends that his 2-year-old son Joe can read. One evening B.T. invites some of his friends over for coffee and offers to give a demonstration of his son's remarkable skill. Joe then appears to read a small storybook that B.T. keeps on the coffee table. One of the friends is not convinced and asks the boy to read a page from a different but equally simple storybook. Joe remains silent. B.T. explains Joe's behavior by saying, "He's just shy with strangers."

REFERENCES

Lewis, M. A new response to stimuli. *The Sciences*, May–June, 1977, The New York Academy of Sciences. In *Readings in psychology 78/79*, Annual Editions. Guilford, Conn.: The Dushkin Publishing Group, 1978.

McGuigan, F. J. *Experimental psychology* (2nd ed.). Englewood Cliffs, N.J.: Prentice-Hall, 1968.

2

Alternatives to the Experimental Approach

Key Terms

phenomenology	unobtrusive measure	direct relationship
case study	correlational study	negative correlation
deviant case analysis	correlation	inverse relationship
naturalistic observation	positive correlation	ex post facto study
field study		

In the psychology experiment, we create specific sets of antecedent conditions, or treatments, to test a hypothesis concerning their effect on behavior. The experimental approach is especially useful when we have a specific hypothesis about which of several antecedent conditions have the most influence on behavior. However, in a variety of situations we may not need or may not be able to obtain data in the rigorous fashion required by the experimental approach. At these times, we may wish to gather data in other ways.

The alternatives to the experimental method are used in situations where an experiment is not required or is not feasible. Each provides useful data, but it is important to understand the scope of these approaches as they are applied in psychological studies. We will discuss six major nonexperimental approaches in this chapter: (1) phenomenology, (2) case studies, (3) naturalistic observation, (4) field studies, (5) correlational studies, and (6) ex post facto studies. We will look at examples of how they are used and compare them to the experimental approach.

PHENOMENOLOGY

phenomenology

So far we have discussed the scientific method in terms of observing and recording events that are assumed to be external to the observer. The phenomenological approach is an important supplement to the scientific method. **Phenomenology** is the description of one's own immediate experience. Rather than looking out at behaviors in the world, we begin with our own experience as a source of data. Much early work in psychology was based on the phenomenological approach. Boring (1950) cites Purkinje as a good example of the phenomenologically based researcher. Purkinje was interested in the physiology of vision. He noticed that colors seemed to change as twilight deepened: Reds appeared black, while blues retained their hue. This observation (now called the Purkinje phenomenon) eventually led to our understanding of the spectral sensitivity of the rods and cones of the eye.

William James also used the phenomenological approach. In his *Principles of Psychology* (1950, original 1890) James dealt with basic psychological issues, including habits, consciousness, and the stream of thought. Many were approached from the perspective of his own experience. One of his most appealing passages deals with his own difficulty in getting up in the morning. He pointed out that our resistance to getting up inhibits our movement. While we concentrate on the pleasure of warm sheets and the dread of a cold floor, we are paralyzed. Said James, "If I may generalize from my own experience, we more often than not get up without any struggle or decision at all. We suddenly find that we have got up" (p. 524). Thus if we do *not* resist, we ought to be able to rise without effort.

The phenomenological approach precludes experimental manipulation: comparison of behaviors under different treatment conditions is *not* required. When using this approach, we simply attend to our own experience. As Boring (1950) explained: "Since phenomenology deals with immediate experience, its conclusions are instantaneous. They emerge at once and need not wait upon the results of calculations derived from measurements. Nor does a phenomenologist use statistics, since a frequency does not occur at an instant and cannot be immediately observed" (p. 602).

Thus, the phenomenological approach is applied to a small sample of subjects—a sample of one. We cannot be sure that the process we are observing in ourselves is not altered in some way by our attention to it. Since the observer is also the person whose process is observed, we may not able to achieve the degree of accuracy and

Figure 2.1 William James (1842–1910). National Library of Medicine, Bethesda, Maryland 20014.

objectivity through phenomenology that we might achieve through other methods. Also, our private experience is not publicly observable; it will be difficult for others to replicate our experiences and apply scientific criteria to our findings. Since comparisons of subjects under different conditions are *not* made, the phenomenological approach does not permit us to make cause and effect statements about our experience. Purkinje could not know absolutely that his experience of altered color was due to an external change (a change in the amount of light) which would affect all observers in a similar manner. Had he not been a scientist, he might have explained his experience in terms of a demon that had taken possession of his sense organs. In the absence of further evidence, one explanation would have been as good as the other.

Although phenomenology does not yield cause and effect statements, it is a useful source of information that may lead us to formulate hypotheses suitable for experimentation. Experimentation is required to determine *which* antecedent conditions produce the behavior or experience. It is also necessary since, as James noted, it may not be legitimate to generalize from one's own experience to everyone else's. If Purkinje had been colorblind, his experience at sundown would have been very different from that of most people. We may wish to experiment to discern whether other people report the same experience under the same or different conditions.

Phenomenology may lead us into areas of dicovery that might otherwise go unnoticed. We will return to phenomenology again when we discuss means of formulating a hypothesis for an experiment.

CASE STUDIES

case study   Like phenomenology, the case study method is used to study individuals. The **case study** is a descriptive record of an individual's experiences and/or behaviors that may be used in a variety of ways: to make inferences about developmental processes, the impact of life events, a person's level of functioning, and the origin of disorders. Such a record may be produced by systematically recording experiences and behaviors as they occur over time. The exact procedures used will depend on the purpose of the study. Sometimes, as in the clinical case, we may work from a record made after the fact: The client or other knowledgeable source provides information concerning events in the client's life, the client's reactions, and behaviors. An excerpt from a clinical case is presented in Box 2.1 to illustrate the kind of information that may be found in a case study.

This information may be used in a variety of ways. First, we may use a case study to make inferences about developmental processes: We may observe whether progressive changes in functioning occur as the person ages. This approach provided the first systematic data on the development of children's motor and linguistic abilities. By making extensive records of the behaviors of individual children, early researchers such as Velten (1943) arrived at descriptions of normal developmental sequences. Psychodynamic development may be inferred from case studies. Freud's case of Hans (Freud, 1962) is an example of the way in which an individual case may suggest a developmental process. Hans was afraid of horses. Freud's analysis of Hans' conversations with his father and the dreams he reported suggested that the fear of horses was a symbol for Hans' fear of his father and castration. Such case studies led to Freud's formulation of the theory of the Oedipus complex.

The case study provides information from which we may draw conclusions about the impact of significant events in a person's life. We may evaluate whether changes occurred in the individual's adjustment following critical events such as the loss of a job or the birth of a child. Knowledge about these events may lead to a better understanding of the psychodynamics of experience. For example, the fact that an early loss, (such as the death of a parent), is associated with depression in later life is indicated by many cases (Jacobs, 1971). As we understand the impact of such events more fully, we may be able to devise more appropriate treatment techniques, as well as preventive measures.

In addition, the case study is used to evaluate an individual's overall level of functioning. We compare our case against some hypothetical standard of "normal" behavior. Based on this comparison, we may suspect some form of psychopathology. We may then compare our case against other cases to assess the degree of similarity

Box 2.1 **Case Study: An Example of Involutional Paranoid Reaction**

A. S. was admitted to the hospital at the age of 59. The patient was born in Latvia. Little is known concerning her childhood experiences and the emotional climate of the home. She came to the United States at the age of 19 to marry a man who had preceded her to this country. She and her husband returned to Latvia, where the husband took over his father's farm and attained considerable success and status. At this point the farm buildings were destroyed by fire, and the patient was so seriously burned that she required hospital care for three months. They returned to the United States and the husband established an upholstering business in which the patient assisted until this business failed. The husband then began to drink, and he committed suicide by hanging, a casualty discovered by the patient.

When she was approximately 54 years of age, the patient began to complain that people were talking about her, that her son-in-law was maritally unfaithful, that nearly all persons, especially the clergy of a different religious faith, were sexually immoral. She expressed a fear that she would be "signed away for experimental purposes." She stated that a physician who had treated her at the menopause had given her cancer. Finally, after having complained to the police on several occasions that her food was being drugged and that a "society of science" was plotting against her, she was committed.

Following the patient's admission to the hospital, her daughter, in describing her mother's personality pattern, reported that she had always been a meticulous, hard-working person who was critical, suspicious, stubborn, uncompromising and domineering. The daughter described her mother as an immaculate housekeeper who also did "beautiful sewing."

On arrival at the hospital, her sensorium was clear, and she was fully oriented. She was suspicious, and when her abdominal reflexes were tested, she asked if the physician was going to operate on her. At times she became quite agitated and hostile and insisted that she be permitted to leave. Someone, she said, was trying to secure possession of her home and to kill her; she must therefore appeal to the police to help her. She complained that the nurses were trying to compel her to perform unpleasant tasks because they were members of a religious organization that was persecuting her.

Because of an electrocardiogram suggestive of coronary involvement and myocardial damage, it was decided not to give the patient electroshock treatment. After seven months of hospital residence, the patient became much less tense, was pleasant and cooperative, and was regarded as one of the most faithful and capable workers in the hospital cafeteria. Within a year after her admission, she was given freedom of the hospital grounds and was to spend weekends with friends. Unless questioned, she expressed no delusional ideas. Upon inquiry, however, it was found that there had been no fundamental change in her paranoid ideation. Fifteen months after her admission the patient was permitted to leave the hospital. A year later her employer wrote: "Mrs. S. is cheerful and pleasant and I am very satisfied with her work."

So little is known about this woman's emotional relations with parents and siblings during childhood and any early traumatizing experiences that it is not easy to construct a desirably complete genetic-dynamic formulation of her psychotic personality disturbance. Her daughter's report that the patient was a meticulous, critical, suspicious, stubborn, dominating, and un-compromising person suggests that, because of a basic feeling of insecurity, she had developed these personality characteristics to serve as defenses. In spite of a long series of threats, these defenses proved adequate for many years until the involutional period, with its various accompanying psychological factors, became so menacing that life-long traits were no longer able to control anxiety-producing threats. As a further defense, therefore, the patient resorted to projection to a reality-sacrificing, or psychotic, degree.

Although the problems that the patient had found too difficult to meet must remain a matter of speculation, one suspects, in view of the nature of her personality traits and the character of her delusions, that a deeply seated hostility, the fear of economic insecurity, and a weakening in the repression of instinctive sex drives may have been important ones.[1]

1. From L. C. Kolb, *Modern clinical psychiatry*. Philadelphia: Saunders, 1973, pp. 365–366. Reprinted with permission.

or difference. This is the process underlying diagnosis. Diagnostic categories reflect groupings of many case histories of many different patients. Clinicians have noted similarities among different patients that permit their problems to be classified into groups. Thus, the records of schizophrenics presumably have certain important similarities. In making a diagnosis, the clinician can compare the behaviors of an individual patient with those of other patients who have displayed similar behaviors.

deviant case analysis   The **deviant case analysis** (Robinson, 1976) is an extension of the evaluative case study in which deviant individuals are compared with those who are not. By examining the histories of these different types of individuals, we may be able to isolate the significant variations between them. These variations may have implications for the etiology, or origin, of the deviance in question. We may then wish to experiment to determine whether these variations have a cause and effect relationship to the behavior. This is the procedure being used by Sarnoff Mednick to study the etiology of schizophrenia. He found that autonomic nervous system functioning differed between schizophrenic and normal children (Mednick, 1969). Now a study in progress is designed to test whether these differences may be used to predict which children will become schizophrenic.

Clearly the case study is a useful source of information. It is especially useful when we cannot experiment because of practical or ethical reasons. We would not subject an individual to a stressful life experience such as widowhood simply to observe the outcome. However, this approach has limitations that make it undesirable in situations where experimentation is possible. First, since we are working with only one or perhaps a few subjects, we cannot be sure the people we are evaluating are representative of the general population: We would obtain a very distorted picture of language development if we studied one exceptional child. Second, if we are not able to observe the individual directly all the time, we cannot be sure that we are aware of all the relevant aspects of the individual's life. This is especially true when we are working with a record made after the fact. Such a record is apt to be inaccurate because people may not remember all that happened at a particular point in time.

They may also neglect to mention points they believe are irrelevant, or embarrassing. Furthermore, since we have not specified the antecedent conditions, we cannot make cause and effect statements about the behaviors we observe. For instance, we cannot say that an early loss causes later depression, but merely that there seems to be a relationship between them.

NATURALISTIC OBSERVATION

naturalistic observation

Naturalistic observation is the technique of observing events as they occur in their natural setting. It is descriptive: Like phenomenology and the case study method, it involves no manipulation of antecedent conditions. This method has been used most extensively in animal research, but it may be applied to human behavior as well. During naturalistic observation, the observer remains unobtrusive (for example, behind a duck blind) so that the behaviors observed are not contaminated by the presence of the observer. Every attempt is made to keep the setting as natural as possible, so that the naturally occurring events will not be altered in any way.

At times it may be necessary to compare laboratory findings against behavior in natural settings to confirm the utility of the laboratory setting for a particular research topic. Some behaviors may be distorted by bringing them into the laboratory setting. Such behaviors are best observed where they occur naturally. Naturalistic observation remains important even when experimentation is possible. According to Miller (1977), naturalistic observation may augment experimentation in five ways: (1) studying nature for its own sake; (2) in using nature as a starting point from which to develop a program of laboratory research; (3) in using nature to validate or add substance to previously obtained laboratory findings; (4) in obtaining information about species differences that will subsequently increase the efficient use of animals in the laboratory; and (5) in using the field as a naturalistic "laboratory" to test some hypothesis or theoretical concept.

Naturalistic observation will be more useful in some situations than others. For example, if we are interested in the mating behavior of wild ducks, naturalistic observation is a sensible way to proceed. However, the data we obtain are descriptive. Through naturalistic observation we could obtain a good description of mating in ducks, but we would not know why ducks mated. We would be unable to separate out the effects of different aspects of the environment that govern mating behavior. Suppose we observed a courtship dance, a display of feathers, and an unusual call. We would not be able to tell which of these behaviors is required for mating to occur. In other words, we would not be able to specify the relevant antecedent conditions that affect mating. Hence we would not able to make cause and effect statements concerning the behavior we have observed. As Miller suggests, naturalistic observation provides a description of the behaviors and the setting in which they occur, and may be used as the starting point for a series of experiments to test hypotheses about these behaviors. In the laboratory, we might choreograph a puppet duck to do a courtship dance without a display of feathers and without a mating call. This would enable us to see whether the dance alone would elicit mating behavior from other ducks.

A further limitation of naturalistic observation is that we are dealing with particular samples of time which may or may not contain the behaviors we wish to observe. We must wait for mating, fighting, or any other behavior of interest to occur within our viewing range. If we bring our study into the laboratory, we may be able to create conditions to elicit the behavior of interest within a circumscribed time and space. When we do bring our subjects into the laboratory, we must be aware of the possibility that their behaviors in the artificial setting may not be the same as they are in the wild. Particularly with human subjects, we may find that behaviors become very different when the subjects know they are being watched. We may even find that subjects attempt to guess the purpose of the experiment so that they may either confirm the researcher's expectations, or sabotage the results. (We will discuss these issues further in later chapters.)

FIELD STUDIES

field study **Field studies** are conducted in the field, or real-life setting. Many field studies include naturalistic observation as one source of data. However, other techniques are also used. The clearest difference between the two approaches is that in the field study the researcher will often interact directly with the subjects of the study. The researcher may observe the subjects initially, then interview them to get their opinions. In other situations, the researcher may choose not to observe behaviors at all, but to make inferences about behaviors solely from interview or survey data. The researcher may also make inferences about behavior from observations of aspects of the environment.

A study by Bechtol and Williams (1977) is a good example of the field study approach. Bechtol and Williams were interested in California litter. They noted that unregulated coastline areas attract large numbers of beachgoers, even though the supervised state beaches are considerably cleaner. They set out to determine who were the users of the unregulated beaches, whether there was a pattern to the littering that occurs on such a beach, and how users of the beach feel about playing in the midst of debris. They employed a number of different techniques used in field studies.

Bechtol and Williams spent two years observing activities on a beach in southern California. They used naturalistic observation to determine who used the beach: They simply watched and recorded what sorts of people appeared. They saw that unobtrusive young people were the principal users of the beach. An **unobtrusive measure** was measure used to assess the pattern of littering: Bechtol and Williams collected and counted all the cans left on the beach. By using an unobtrusive measure, they assessed behavior without their subjects' knowledge. From the number of cans in the sand, they inferred that people litter the beach. There was no need to see anyone litter. As we might expect, Bechtol and Williams found that littering was greatest during the summer, when beach use was greatest.

In addition to observation, Bechtol and Williams approached people on the beach and asked them how they felt about the condition of the beach. Here we see the clearest deviation from naturalistic observation. Instead of remaining inconspicuous, the researchers interviewed people to get their views. The interview and survey are important aspects of field research. Particularly when dealing with covert phenomena like feelings and attitudes, observation may not always suffice. Bechtol and Williams found that users of the beach were disturbed about its condition. All the people interviewed reported that they always took their own trash with them when they left, although in two years of observation the researchers never saw a single person do so. This is a good example of why interview and survey data should be supplemented with objective observations, including unobtrusive measures, whenever possible.

Like the other approaches we have discussed so far in this chapter, the field study does not involve any direct manipulation of conditions. Behaviors are observed and recorded as they occur in the natural setting. Subjects are interviewed in the "wild," where the contaminating effects of a laboratory setting are absent. It is a useful way of gathering many types of data, particularly when the researcher is studying behaviors like littering, which we might not see in the laboratory. Note that a field study is not the same as a field experiment. A field experiment is simply an experiment done *outside* the laboratory.

CORRELATIONAL STUDIES

correlational
study

correlation

Unlike naturalistic observation, field studies, and most case studies, a correlational study may be conducted in the laboratory or in the field. **A correlational study** is one that determines the correlation, or degree of relationship, between two or more traits, behaviors, or events. First, the traits or behaviors of interest are measured. The degree of relationship, or **correlation**, between them is then determined through statistical procedures. In the correlational study, the researcher measures events without attempting to alter the antecedent conditions in any way; he or she is simply asking how well the measures go together. Once the correlation is known, it can be used to make predictions. If we know a person's score on one measure, we can predict that person's score on another measure that is highly related to it. The higher the correlation, the more accurate our prediction will be.

Suppose a researcher wonders whether there is a relationship between the length of people's fingernails and the size of their vocabulary. The researcher would conduct a correlational study to determine whether such a relationship exists. First, he or she would devise an objective measure of vocabulary. Either a standardized test or an improvised procedure might be used. For instance, the researcher might ask subjects to go through a dictionary and check off all the words that are familiar. One approach might be preferred to another depending on time, resources, and the subjects' patience. The researcher would also carefully measure the length of each subject's fingernails. The degree of relationship between the two measures would then be assessed through statistical procedures. The Pearson Product Moment Correlation Coefficient (r) is the most commonly used procedure. You'll see it reported in most correlational studies. The values of r can vary between -1 and $+1$. The sign (plus or minus) tells us the direction of the relationship; the absolute value of r (the unsigned value) tells us the strength of the relationship. When r is computed, three general outcomes are possible: a positive relationship, negative relationship, or no relationship.[1] These are illustrated for you in Figure 2.2.

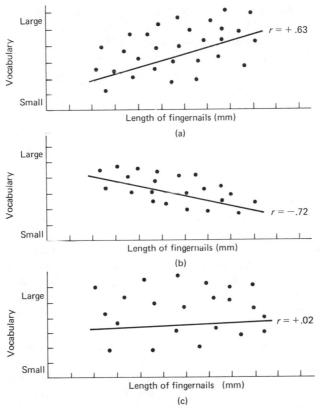

Figure 2.2 Some hypothetical relationships between size of vocabulary and length of fingernails. (a) A positive (direct) relationship; (b) a negative (inverse) relationship; (c) no strong relationship.

1.   This discussion is limited to linear (or straight-line) relationships. The Pearson r does not measure nonlinear relationships.

positive correlation

direct relationship

When the computed value of r is positive, there is a **positive correlation** between vocabulary and length of fingernails: The larger your vocabulary, the longer your fingernails. This is also called a **direct relationship**. The absolute (unsigned) value of r tells us how strong the relationship is. If $r = +1$, we have a perfect positive correlation. When $r = +1$, we can predict the value of one measure with complete accuracy if we know a subject's score on the other measure. Positive values of r that are less than +1, (for example, +.52) tell us there is a direct relationship between our two measures, but we cannot predict the value of one from the other with complete accuracy because the relationship between them is imperfect. If the value of r is relatively small (for example, +.02), our prediction may be no more accurate than any other educated guess. In that event, the correlation would not be very useful.

negative correlation

inverse relationship

A second possibility is a **negative correlation** between vocabulary and length of fingernails (that is, r is negative). This would mean that the longer your fingernails, the smaller your vocabulary. This is also called an **inverse relationship**. We could predict vocabulary just as well from a negative correlation as from a positive one— provided that the strength of the relationships was the same. The strength of the relationship is indexed by the absolute (or unsigned) value of r. A correlation of $r = -.34$ actually represents a stronger relationship than $r = +.16$. The sign merely tells us whether the relationship is direct or inverse; the absolute value tells us how strong it is. As the absolute value gets larger, we can make a more accurate prediction of a person's score on one measure when we know the person's score on the other. A third possibility is, of course, *no* relationship between vocabulary and length of fingernails (r is near zero). In that event, we would not learn anything about vocabulary by looking at a person's fingernails.

When we are dealing with correlational data, we cannot make causal inferences: Correlation does not prove causation. In other words, although a relationship exists between two measures, we cannot say that one causes the other, even when such a statement appears reasonable. The fact that two measures are related does not prove that one is responsible for the occurrence of the other. Over the last thousand years, there has probably been a correlation between the number of automobiles and the number of airplanes in the world. But we would not want to say that automobiles *cause* airplanes, or vice versa. More likely, their relationship is mediated by some third dimension, such as the growth of industrial technology. Similarly, there probably *is* a positive relationship between length of fingernails and vocabulary because both measures are related to a third factor, age. Younger subjects, notably infants, have very short fingernails. They also have small vocabularies. Older subjects, with longer fingernails, have larger vocabularies.

In an experiment, we establish causality by setting up at least two different treatment conditions and evaluating their effect on behavior. If we can specify exactly the conditions that will lead to a particular behavior, we have explained that behavior and may say that a particular set of conditions *caused* that behavior. This is not possible in the correlational study because we do not manipulate the conditions under which we are testing; we simply measure what occurs and ask whether two dimensions are related to each other. Like the other nonexperimental methods we have discussed, correlational studies aid us in setting up hypotheses suitable for experimental study. They suggest meaningful explanations of behavior. We will return to correlation again in our discussion of formulating an experimental hypothesis.

EX POST FACTO STUDIES

ex post facto
study

Often researchers are interested in the effects of traits, behaviors, or events that cannot or should not be manipulated: age, intelligence, widowhood, the loss of a limb. In those cases, the researcher may choose to do an **ex post facto study**, a study in which the researcher looks at the effects of selected traits, events, or behaviors systematically but without actually manipulating them. The researcher studies the effects of differences that already exist between subjects. *Ex post facto* means after the fact. In effect, the researcher capitalizes on changes in the antecedent conditions that occurred *before* the study. Preexisting differences are used as the basis for forming different treatment groups in the study: Tim's father died last year, and so Tim is placed in a group of subjects who have experienced the loss of a parent. Subjects come into a study with traits that already differ from one subject to another. The differences are used as the basis for separating them into groups (extroverts, introverts), and the researcher then looks for differences in behavior that are related to group membership.

The ex post facto approach has some special advantages. Like the correlational study, it deals with things as they occur. There is no manipulation of the conditions that interest the researcher. However, the ex post facto study allows a researcher to zero in on those occurrences in a more systematic way. Instead of studying the whole range of people along a particular dimension (extremely introverted to extremely extroverted), the focus can be on a carefully chosen subset. Typically the ex post facto researcher studies the extremes, the subjects who rank highest and lowest on the dimension of interest. This increases the likelihood that the researcher will be able to see the effects of changes along that dimension more clearly.

In addition, ex post facto studies are generally done with many of the same rigorous control procedures used in experiments. The researcher makes a prediction in advance and attempts to test it in the most objective way. We may think of the ex post facto approach as a bridge between the nonexperimental and the experimental approaches. The ex post facto researcher systematically forms treatment groups based on preexisting conditions such as the subjects' age or sex. However, from that point on, the procedures are virtually the same as in any experiment. In fact, many researchers combine the ex post facto approach and experimentation in the same study. They may look at one dimension through the ex post facto approach while manipulating another dimension experimentally.

Zanni, Saylor, and Ferguson (1978) used the ex post facto approach to study the way in which neurotic styles influence memory. A style is a characteristic way of functioning. We sometimes comment on a person's actions by saying, "That's just her style." Neurotic styles (Shapiro, 1965) are ways of functioning that seem to be associated with neurotic conditions. Zanni et al. zeroed in on two neurotic styles, the obsessive-compulsive and the hysteric. One contrast between these two styles can be illustrated with a simple example. Shapiro suggests that when asked to give a description of someone, the obsessive-compulsive provides many factual details: The obsessive-compulsive has a "sharply focused, technical apprehension of the world" (p. 110). The hysteric is apt to answer by giving overall impressions: "She's terrific." Such impressions lack the clarity and detail of the obsessive-compulsive response. Shapiro adds this enlightening vignette:

> Once, for example, in taking a case history from an exceedingly hysterical patient, I made repeated efforts to obtain a description of her father from her. She seemed, however, hardly to understand the sort of data I was interested in, and the best she could provide was, "My father? He was wham-bang! That's all—just wham-bang!" (p. 111).

Given the apparent contrasts between these styles, Shapiro suggested that people with the obsessive-compulsive style have better memories than people with the hysterical style.

As you can probably guess, we cannot study a trait like neurotic style in a strictly experimental manner. How would we go about manipulating each person's neurotic style to create the tendencies we want to study? If we *could* devise procedures that would accomplish that goal, would we want to use them? The issue becomes even clearer if we consider another condition—cancer. It is obviously better to study groups of people who already have this disease, rather than trying to produce it in healthy people. Zanni et al. did not create neurotic styles in the subjects they studied; they used differences that already existed. They gave the subjects a standardized written test to measure obsessive and hysterical tendencies. On the basis of their test scores, subjects were divided into three groups of 12: those who displayed the most extreme obsessive-compulsive tendencies, those who displayed the most extreme hysterical tendencies, and a third group who showed no clear tendencies toward either style. All the subjects were shown a film and then tested on their ability to recall the details of the film. "Did you see a fire hydrant?" was a typical question on the memory test. As predicted, the group showing obsessive-compulsive tendencies scored significantly higher on the memory test than the other groups.

The ex post facto approach enables us to explore many dimensions, like neurotic style, which we could not study experimentally. For that reason, it is a very useful source of information. However, there are difficulties in interpreting the results of ex post facto studies. The researcher is not actually manipulating the antecedent conditions of the study. You could say that the subjects assign themselves to the various "treatment" groups of the experiment: The characteristics they bring with them establish their group membership. This limits our ability to make cause and effect statements about the outcome of an ex post facto study. We can make cause and effect statments *if* we can specify a set of antecedent conditions that will always lead to a predicted outcome. In the ex post facto study, we would like to be able to say that the dimension on which we grouped our subjects was responsible for the pattern of results we observe. However, when we group subjects according to a characteristic they already have, such as age, we may be setting up groups that differ from one another in other ways too. Hysterics and obsessives might have certain other characteristics that affect the way they remember things. With a factor such as age, the problems become even more apparent: People of different ages vary in many respects. Age is a crude index of differences in life experiences, education, and often nutrition and prenatal care as well. If we say that age "caused" differences in our subjects' behavior, we are on shaky ground. You can easily think of similar problems that arise when we group people by sex, race, or socioeconomic status.

Despite its limitations, the ex post facto approach is a useful technique which allows us to demonstrate that certain predictable relationships exist. We can establish, for instance, that age, or neurotic style, or sex are associated with particular patterns of behavior. In some respects, ex post facto studies are more useful than certain kinds of experimental studies because they provide more realistic data. However, when it is possible to experiment, the experiment is preferred because it allows us to draw conclusions about cause and effect that we cannot make on the basis of ex post facto data.

The nonexperimental approaches are largely descriptive; they focus on naturally occurring events. No attempt is made to systematically manipulate or control antecedent conditions. Subjects are not observed under carefully specified treatment conditions. This can make replication difficult. For these reasons, the nonexperimental approaches cannot be used to establish cause and effect explanations of behavior. When we wish to confirm cause and effect relationships, experimentation is required. Despite their limitations, these approaches are important adjuncts to experimentation. Without attention to our own experience and the ongoing activities around us, we would miss a great deal of relevant psychological data. The nonexperimental approaches lack the artificiality that is sometimes criticized in experimental research. In fact, they are often used as the sources of experimental hypotheses that lead to further research. We will return to some of them again in our next chapter, which deals with formulating a hypothesis.

SUMMARY

We have looked at six major nonexperimental approaches to data collection: phenomenology, case studies, naturalistic observation, field studies, correlational studies, and ex post facto studies. Although these approaches differ in detail, they share certain features that distinguish them from the experimental approach.

Phenomenology is the description of one's own immediate experience. Rather than looking out at behaviors in the world, the phenomenological approach requires that we begin with our own experience as a source of data. Phenomenological data are limited in two main respects: Since we do not compare subjects under different conditions, we cannot make cause and effect statements about our experience. We also have no way of knowing whether attending to our experience alters it. What we observe may not be completely accurate, or objective.

The *case study* is also used to study individuals. It is a descriptive record of an individual's experiences and/or behaviors that may be used in several ways: to make inferences about developmental processes, the impact of life events, a person's level of functioning, and the origin of disorders. The record may be made systematically over a period of time, or after the fact, as is often the case in clinical practice. This approach enables us to study a variety of life events we would not study experimentally.

Naturalistic observation is the technique of observing events as they occur in their natural setting. It is a descriptive method. During naturalistic observation, the observer remains unobtrusive so that the behaviors are not distorted by the presence of an intruder. This approach allows us to study behaviors that would be distorted or absent in the laboratory. It also gives us the chance to verify the accuracy of findings that were obtained in the laboratory.

Field studies are studies done in a real-life setting; they may include a variety of techniques of collecting data. In addition to observing behaviors, the researcher may interact with the subjects of a field study. Interviews may be conducted. Various *unobtrusive measures* may be used to assess behavior without subjects' knowledge. Like naturalistic observation, the field study allows us to explore behavior that we probably would not see in the laboratory. But it shares the same limitations. We cannot make inferences about cause and effect relationships on the basis of a field study because we do not manipulate the conditions.

Correlational studies may be run in the laboratory or in the field. A correlational study is done to determine the correlation, or degree of relationship, between two or more traits, behaviors, or events. First, the factors of interest are measured; then, the degree of relationship between them is established through statistical procedures. When two measures are correlated, we can predict the value of one if we know the value of the other. But we cannot infer cause and effect from a correlation.

Ex post facto studies are a bridge between the nonexperimental and the experimental methods. In an ex post facto study, the researcher uses preexisting characteristics to separate subjects into groups. The researcher then looks for differences in behaviors as a function of group membership. Typically the ex post facto study involves factors that cannot or should not be studied experimentally. Predictions are made and tested through many of the same techniques that are used in experiments.

REVIEW AND STUDY QUESTIONS

1. Describe each of the nonexperimental approaches and give an example of how each might be used: (1) phenomenology, (2) case study, (3) naturalistic observation, (4) field study, (5) correlational study, (6) ex post facto study.

2. What are some of the advantages and disadvantages of the nonexperimental approaches?

3. For each of the following research topics, indicate the type of nonexperimental approach that would be most useful, and explain why. (You may find more than one approach potentially useful for some topics.)
   a. Pushing ahead in line.
   b. Daydreaming.
   c. Locating the most popular painting in an art gallery.
   d. Finding whether warm weather is associated with good moods.
   e. Studying whether first-born children are more aggressive than later-borns.
   f. Determining whether a particular patient has improved with psychotherapy.
   g. Predicting the outcome of an election.

4. For each of your answers to question 3, explain whether or not an experiment would generate more useful information than the nonexperimental method you selected. Would it be possible to set up experiments to explore all these problems? If not, why not?

5. What are unobtrusive measures?

6. Devise an unobtrusive measure to establish each of the following:
   a. Which juke box selection is the most popular?
   b. What are the most popular library books?
   c. Do people prefer to sit on the left or the right side when they go to the movies?
   d. If people find addressed letters with stamps on them, will they mail them?

7. Explain the meaning of the statement "Correlation does not prove causation."

8. Jack just computed the Pearson Product Moment Correlation Coefficient for two sets of data. He got $r = +2.3$. Jack is thrilled, marveling at what a large relationship he found. What can he conclude from his findings?

9. A college administrator has located a new aptitude test that is correlated with academic achievement ($r = -.54$). The admissions committee of the college now uses a screening test also correlated with academic achievement, but the correlation is $r = +.45$. Which test would be a better choice if the admissions committee is interested in predicting how well prospective students would do at the school?

REFERENCES

Bechtol, B., and Williams, J. California litter. *Natural History*, 1977, *86*, No. 6, 62–65.

Boring, E. G. *A history of experimental psychology* (2nd ed.). New York: Appleton-Century-Crofts, 1950.

Freud, S. Analysis of a phobia in a five-year-old boy (1st ed., 1909). In *The complete psychological works of Sigmund Freud*, Vol. X. London: Hogarth, 1962.

Jacobson, E. *Depression*. New York: International Universities Press, 1971.

James, W. *Principles of psychology* (1st ed., New York, Holt, 1890). New York: Dover, 1950.

Kolb, L. C. *Modern clinical psychiatry* (8th ed.). Philadelphia: Saunders, 1973.

Mednick, S. A. A longitudinal study of children with a high risk for schizophrenia. In M. Zax and G. Stricker (Eds.), *The study of abnormal behavior*. London: Macmillan, 1969.

Miller, D. Roles of naturalistic observation in comparative psychology. *American Psychologist*, 1977, *32*, No. 3, 211–219.

Robinson, P. W. *Fundamentals of experimental psychology*. Englewood Cliffs, N.J.: Prentice-Hall, 1976.

Shapiro, D. *Neurotic styles*. New York: Basic Books, 1965.

Velten, H. V. The growth of phonemic and lexical patterns in infant language. *Language*, 1943, *19*, 281–292.

Zanni, G. R., Saylor, K., and Ferguson, J. Recall and neurotic styles: A test of David Shapiro's theory. *Psychiatric Spectator*, 1978, *11*, No. 3, 6 ff. East Hanover, N.J.: Sandoz Pharmaceuticals, D. J. Publications, Inc.

3

Formulating the Hypothesis

Key Terms

experimental hypothesis	testable	deductive model
synthetic statement	inductive model	Galilean model
analytic statement	Aristotelian model	serendipity
contradictory statement	theory	intuition

The term "hypothesis" has appeared a number of times in the preceding chapters. You now know that the psychology experiment is designed to test hypotheses about the effect of different treatment conditions on behavior. In this chapter, we will focus on the hypothesis in detail. We will look at its characteristics and discuss several ways of arriving at hypotheses suitable for experimental study: induction, deduction, building on prior research, serendipity, and intuition.

The hypothesis represents the end of the long process of thinking about a behavior, discarding improbable explanations of it, and proposing one particular explanation that seems plausible. It is a tentative explanation of an event or behavior. Some nonscientific synonyms are "inkling," "conjecture," and "hunch." The **exper-** experimental hypothesis **imental hypothesis** is a statement of a potential relationship between at least two

experimental
hypothesis

31

variables—the specific antecedent conditions and the behaviors to be measured. The hypothesis is the thesis, or main idea, of the experiment. Once it has been formulated, the researcher's task is to set up an experiment that will test it appropriately.

THE CHARACTERISTICS OF AN EXPERIMENTAL HYPOTHESIS

Suppose you began to make a list of all the conditions that could affect a particular behavior. Say the behavior is the speed at which you are reading this book. The factors that affect your reading speed include the style in which this text is written, and your average reading speed. Your pace might also be affected by the amount of noise outside the window, the amount of light in the room, and whether or not you have eaten lunch. Perhaps it is even affected by the number of people who are now singing in Tibet, and by the number of shrimp in the ocean. Clearly an enormous number of factors might affect your behavior at any given time. Before doing an experiment to determine which factors were critical to your reading speed, we would want to narrow down the possibilities.

Things far removed from one another are not likely to be causally related. Thus, we would not consider the shrimp population as a likely explanation for reading speed. Similarly, we would not spend much time on the people in Tibet. However, factors such as writing style, your normal reading speed, lighting, and so on, probably *do* determine your speed. If you have not had lunch, your images of food will certainly reduce your speed.

This process of whittling away at the number of possible factors affecting your reading speed is the key to formulating a hypothesis. Now that we have selected out a small, finite number of possibilities, we are ready to propose an explanation for your reading speed. We are ready to state a hypothesis.

synthetic statement

analytic statement

contradictory statement

The experimental hypothesis must be stated in such a way that it can be either true or false; it must be a **synthetic statement.** Other kinds of statements are analytic or contradictory. The **analytic statement** is a statement that is always true, such as "I am in Denver *or* I am not in Denver." Since this statement covers all possibilities, it is always true. **Contradictory statements** are statements that are always false, such as "I have a brother *and* I do not have a brother." If we propose hypotheses in the form of analytic or contradictory statements, our experiments will provide no information. Since analytic statements are always true and contradictory statements are always false, we do not need to conduct experiments to test them. The experimental hypothesis must be a synthetic statement so that there is some chance that it is true, and some chance that it is false. "Hungry students read slowly" is a synthetic statement that can be confirmed or disconfirmed. An experiment designed to test it will provide information useful in deciding between the two possibilities; it will add to our knowledge.

In order to ensure that a hypothesis is a synthetic statement, we must evaluate its form. A hypothesis meets the definition of a synthetic statement if it can be stated in what is known as the "If . . . then" form. The "If . . . then" form is another way of expressing the potential relationship between the antecedents and the behaviors to be measured: "*If* you look at an arousing photograph, *then* your pupils will dilate," is such a hypothesis. It expresses a potential relationship between a particular antecedent condition (being shown an arousing photograph) and a behavior (pupil dilation). The statement can be true or false. Perhaps the content of a photograph has no effect on the pupils. Similarly, consider the saying, "Adversity builds character." This might be considered a hypothesis concerning the way in which life experiences affect character development. Is this a synthetic statement? In its present form, no. But this statement can be easily translated into the "If . . . then" form: "If you have experienced difficult life circumstances, then you will have character." Again this statement may be true or false. Bad experiences do not necessarily guarantee good growth.

testable An experimental hypothesis must also be **testable.** That is, the means for manipulating antecedent conditions and measuring the resulting behavior must exist. The hypothesis should be *parsimonious*. You will recall from Chapter 1 that parsimony means that the simplest explanation is preferred. Thus, a simple hypothesis is preferred over one that requires many supporting assumptions. The hypothesis, "If you look at an arousing photograph, then your pupils will dilate," would be preferred over "If you look at an arousing photograph, then your pupils will dilate if it is a warm Saturday in June."

Ideally, a hypothesis is also fruitful, that is, it leads to new studies. It is often difficult to know in advance which hypotheses will be the most fruitful. An example of a fruitful hypothesis is Watson and Rayner's 1920 study of classical conditioning. They hypothesized that fear of otherwise neutral objects could be acquired through learning. Their hypothesis might be stated in the "If . . . then" form as follows: If a child, Albert, is repeatedly exposed to a loud cry-inducing noise in the presence of a harmless furry animal, then Albert will begin to cry at the sight of the animal alone. This hypothesis and its confirmation led to a multitude of studies on classical conditioning in human subjects that still continue.

We have considered what may seem like an awesome number of criteria for a good hypothesis. The good hypothesis is a synthetic statement of the "If . . . then" form. It is testable, parsimonious, and fruitful. With so many criteria and so many areas of research, how does an experimenter ever arrive at a hypothesis? According to Bertrand Russell (1945), "As a rule, the framing of hypotheses is the most difficult part of scientific work, and the part where great ability is indispensable. So far, no method has been found which would make it possible to invent hypotheses by rule" (p. 545).

A number of general approaches describe the way in which hypotheses are most often formed. Although there are no rules that can be used to generate hypotheses, an understanding of these approaches will help you to think about the psychological issues you might like to study experimentally.

THE INDUCTIVE MODEL

inductive model

Aristotelian
model

The **inductive** or **Aristotelian model** of formulating a hypothesis, the process of reasoning from specific cases to more general principles, is often used in science and mathematics. By examining individual instances, we may be able to construct an overall classification scheme to describe them. Such a descriptive scheme may then suggest what will happen in new instances.

Has something like this ever happened to you at a party? A stranger comes over to you and says: "You must be a Libran. I can tell by your beautiful clothes, your meticulous grooming, and the birthstone ring you're wearing." The stranger has tried a somewhat overworked opening—but it illustrates the basics of inductive thinking. He or she has taken certain specific facts about you, your style of dress, and your manner and fit them into a more general classification scheme—namely, the signs of the zodiac. People of different signs are said to have different personality traits which are dependent on the sign of birth, as well as the positions of the planets at the exact time of birth. A person familiar with astrology may take certain specific facts about you and arrive at a hypothesis about your birth sign through induction. Given the classification scheme, predictions can be made about the personality of a person who is unknown except for date and place of birth. The adequacy of the scheme can be assessed by comparing the accuracy of predictions based on the scheme to the accuracy we would achieve by simply guessing.

B. F. Skinner is a convincing advocate for inductive research in psychology. Skinner studied operant conditioning in rats and pigeons extensively. In operant conditioning, the organism is reinforced or rewarded when it produces a particular response, such as bar pressing, which has been selected by the experimenter for reinforcement. Skinner studied many variations of the basic operant procedures, keeping careful records of what happened to behavior under various conditions. He tried giving reinforcement on some but not all occasions when the animal emitted the required response. He tried new reinforcement contingencies based solely on the number of responses emitted—one pellet of food for each three bar presses— or on the elapsed time—one pellet of food per minute for one or more bar presses. He tried withholding reinforcement after the response was well established. Out of numerous experiments, Skinner developed the concepts of partial reinforcement and extinction, along with reliable descriptions of the way intermittent reinforcement alters behavior (Ferster and Skinner, 1957). Concepts essential to understanding the learning process grew out of Skinner's inductive approach and suggested many new hypotheses and applications of the concepts outside the laboratory.

theory

Induction is the basic tool of theory building. A **theory** is a set of general principles that can be used to explain and predict behavior. Through induction, researchers construct theories by taking bits of empirical data and forming general explanatory schemes to accommodate those facts. For instance, Bowlby (1969) developed a theory of mother-infant attachment based on observations of animal behaviors. The theory explains mother-infant attachment in terms of instinctive attachment behaviors. The process of induction then, involves these steps: Observe events. Try to organize them into a classification scheme. Look for patterns and relationships that suggest other as yet undiscovered events that will confirm as well as enlarge the scheme.

THE DEDUCTIVE MODEL

deductive
model

Galilean model

The **deductive** or **Galilean model** of formulating a hypothesis is the converse of the inductive approach. Deduction is the process of reasoning from general principles to predictions about specific instances. The deductive model is most useful when we have a well-developed theory with clearly stated basic premises. Then it is possible to deduce predictions about what should happen in new situations where the theory would apply. Testing such predictions provides a test of the value of the theory.

The best example of the deductive method in psychology is the work of Clark Hull. Hull (1884–1952) was an American behaviorist whose goal was to provide a comprehensive theory that would explain learning. Hull valued precision and laid out much of his theory in the form of mathematical equations that could be used to predict behavior. The theory is too complex to explain in any detail here, but we will look at one simplified example of the way in which Hull used deduction to formulate new hypotheses.[1]

If we are reinforced (or rewarded) after doing something, we are more likely to do that thing again. The more times we are reinforced, the more likely that behavior becomes. In Hull's terms, reinforcement increases *habit strength*. We are more likely to behave in ways that have been reinforced because those behaviors have greater habit strength. However, other factors are also important. Hull (1943) assumed that *drive* activates habit strength. Drive (for example, hunger) increases the odds that a particular behavior will be emitted. Hull represented the relationship between drive and habit strength in a mathematical equation. Drive and habit strength interact to determine the value of $_sE_R$, the *reaction potential*, the likelihood that a particular behavior will appear.[2] Reaction potential is a function of drive and habit strength:

$$_sE_R = f(_sH_R) \times f(D)$$

Given that this relationship exists, certain other predictions follow: If we increase the habit strength of a behavior by increasing the number of reinforced trials, then that behavior should occur more often. An increase in drive should increase the odds

1. For a more detailed discussion, see E. R. Hilgard and G. H. Bower, *Theories of Learning.*
2. The formula presented here is an early statement of reaction potential. Hull later revised this formula to incorporate more variables.

Box 3.1   **Dmitri Mendeleyev and the Periodic Table**

The work of Dmitri Mendeleyev illustrates the use of induction to generate scientific hypotheses. Mendeleyev was a nineteenth-century chemist interested in devising a meaningful classification scheme for all 66 elements known at that time. He reviewed the atomic weight (the weight of a single atom as compared to a standard) and the typical properties of all the elements. Mendeleyev saw a pattern, a general relationship now known as the periodic law: When arranged according to their atomic weights, the elements show a periodical change in properties. From the patterns he observed, Mendeleyev was able to predict the discovery of a number of new elements, as well as their properties (Partington, 1964). Although his classification scheme has been revised to incorporate new elements (there are now 105 in all), Mendeleyev's basic work remains a cornerstone of chemistry and physics.

Although we have discussed Mendeleyev as an example of an inductive thinker, his work also illustrates the complementary nature of induction and deduction. Mendeleyev saw a pattern in the atomic numbers of the elements and their properties. However, he also saw that some elements did not exactly fit this pattern. Having arrived at the general pattern through induction, Mendeleyev deduced that some of the atomic numbers on record were inaccurate. The probable course of Mendeleyev's thinking is represented schematically by Figure 3.1.

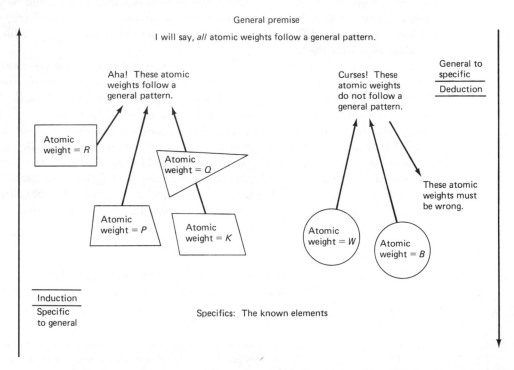

Figure 3.1   Schematic representation of Mendeleyev's thinking on atomic weights.

of that behavior also. We can design experiments to test these predictions—we can manipulate habit strength and drive and observe the effects on behavior. Through such experiments we can verify the accuracy of the initial premises. We might find, for example, that drive does not interact with habit strength, so a different premise would be necessary to explain behavior. This example is an extremely simplified illustration of Hull's approach. However, to understand induction and deduction more fully, let us use it to contrast the two approaches.

If he had proceeded inductively, Hull would have begun by observing many examples of learning and looking for an organizing classification scheme. He might have noticed that hungry rats learn more than satiated rats. Thus he might have said that there are two classes of animals—the learners (hungry animals) and the non-learners (stuffed animals). Based on this classfication scheme, he could predict which animals would learn and which would not. In contrast, Hull began by stating a number of basic premises he believed could explain learning. These premises were stated in precise mathematical terms. By stating his assumptions explicitly, Hull enabled other researchers to make and test predictions from his theory. Such tests produced data that did not always conform to Hull's model. These conflicting data led to more and more supporting assumptions and the eventual collapse of the theory. The tests of the predictions made from Hull's basic premises showed that the theory was an inadequate explanation of learning.

We have looked at induction and deduction as two separate approaches to formulating a hypothesis. In practice, these approaches are not so neatly separated. As you might imagine, a theorist like Hull does not make up grand premises without some reference back to specific cases. Hull was certainly familiar with specific studies on learning that were being done in his own as well as other laboratories. Thus, his premises could have been formed initially through induction from specific cases. Later tests of the premises were based on predictions derived from the premises through deduction. Box 3.1 illustrates the importance of these processes in the work of the chemist Dmitri Mendeleyev.

Both induction and deduction are important in research. Both are useful in formulating hypotheses for study. Through induction we devise general principles and theories that can be used to organize, explain, and predict behavior until more satisfactory principles are found. Through deduction we rigorously test the implications of those theories.

BUILDING ON PRIOR RESEARCH

So far we have discussed global approaches that can be applied to a variety of research topics. Now we will look at how the researcher narrows down the field of possibilities enough to formulate a single hypothesis. The most useful way of finding hypotheses is by working from research that has already been done. The nonexperimental studies discussed in Chapter 2, for example, are a good source of ideas for experimentation. Each of these approaches may lead to tentative explanations of behavior. However, the information we obtain through these studies does not allow us to make cause and effect inferences. Since nonexperimental studies do not include manipulation of the antecedent conditions, there is no way to identify which antecedents produce the behaviors observed. In order to make cause and effect inferences, we must experiment—that is, we must manipulate the antecedents and observe the resultant change in behavior. Nonexperimental studies often suggest cause and effect explanations that can be translated into experimental hypotheses. We will look briefly at two examples of the way in which this might be done.

The Bechtol and Williams (1977) study of California litter was a field study. Bechtol and Williams observed the people on an unregulated beach in California to see who would litter. They concluded that everyone littered. Since the litter problem was more serious on this unregulated beach than on the state-operated beaches, we can ask a number of experimental questions about littering. The fact that everyone on the unregulated beach left trash suggests two possibilities. First, perhaps the people who choose to use unregulated beaches are systematically different from people who do not. Perhaps they are more rebellious, and hence more likely to flaunt convention by littering. Through their interviews Bechtol and Williams found that the users of the nonregulated beach were there because they could do things, such as drink and make bonfires, that were prohibited in the regulated areas. Thus we may state a hypothesis in the "If . . . then" form: "If people have rebellious personalities, then they will litter." We can study different sets of antecedents through an ex post facto study. We can select two groups of people varying in personality. One group would have rebellious personalities, the other group would be conformists. If we took these groups to the beach, we would expect to find that those in the rebellious group litter more than those in the conformist group. We would then conclude that the antecedents (the personality differences) are associated with differences in littering behavior. Notice that the Bechtol and Williams study suggests this explanation. Our ex post facto study clarifies the existence of the relationship. However, a true experiment (that is, creating rebellious and conformist subjects) is required to establish a cause and effect relationship.

Another explanation for littering suggested by Bechtol and Williams is that there were no trash baskets on the unregulated beach. From this observation, we may state another hypothesis about littering: "If there are no trash baskets, then people will litter." In this case, we can set up different antecedent conditions to test the hypothesis experimentally. We set up one beach with trash containers, and an identical beach without trash baskets. Let us assume that the people who use the two beaches are comparable. Given our hypothesis, we would expect to find less litter on the beach that has trash baskets. If trash baskets have no effect on littering, we would find the same amount of litter accumulating on both beaches. If there is the predicted difference in litter for the two beaches, we conclude that the lack of trash baskets causes littering.

The other nonexperimental approaches may also lead to experimental hypotheses. One very important example is the research on cigarette smoking and cancer. At first, only correlational data were available. Researchers noted a positive correlation between smoking and lung cancer: People who smoked cigarettes had higher rates of lung cancer than people who did not smoke. This suggested the hypothesis that smoking causes cancer. Stated in the "If . . . then" form: "If people smoke, then they will get cancer." Experimenters test the hypothesis under controlled conditions. Because of ethical issues, the subjects in these experiments are usually animals rather than humans; if smoking really does cause cancer, scientists would not want to expose human subjects to smoking. The experiments begin with the creation of different antecedent conditions—groups of rats are exposed to varying amounts of cigarette smoke. If rats who "smoke" develop higher rates of cancer than rats that do not, the conclusion is that smoking causes cancer. Again, the systematic manipulation of the antecedent conditions permits us to make cause and effect inferences that cannot be made on the basis of correlational data alone.

It is also possible to get ideas for new hypotheses from prior experimental research. If you do not already have a specific hypothesis in mind, you will find the experimental literature useful in focusing your thinking on important issues. As you read more and more studies in an area, you may begin to see points that other researchers have missed or disregarded. These may form the basis for new experiments. By reading prior studies, you will also see the kinds of problems others have had in researching a topic. This will help you to anticipate difficulties you might not have thought of alone. A good review of the literature available on your topic is important in designing a good experiment, and in writing an effective report. You will also avoid duplicating someone else's work.

SERENDIPITY AND THE WINDFALL HYPOTHESIS

All the approaches we have looked at so far are purposeful; the experimenter is usually looking for a new hypothesis on which to base an experiment. However, at times discoveries have been made where none was intended. Such discoveries may be attributed to serendipity. The word comes from the eighteenth-century tale of "The Three Princes of Serendip" by Horace Walpole, which describes the adventures
serendipity   of the three princes who found many valuable things they were not seeking. **Serendipity** is the knack of finding things that are not being sought. Discoveries through serendipity have been made in the physical sciences as well as in psychology.

An element of serendipity appeared in the work of Ivan Pavlov, a Russian physiologist whose main interest was the digestive glands (Figure 3.2). His studies involved feeding dogs and observing the changes that occurred in their stomach secretions. Through his work, Pavlov became interested in salivation. He asked such questions as, "If I feed the dog, how long will it be before the dog begins to salivate?" The questions seemed straightforward enough until Pavlov began to notice some

Figure 3.2   Ivan Pavlov (1849–1936). National Library of Medicine, Bethesda, Maryland 20014.

distracting things. As the dogs became familiar with the bread Pavlov fed them, they began to salivate even before they were actually fed. Seeing the food seemed to produce salivation. Indeed, in a short while the dogs began to salivate as soon as he entered the room. Pavlov found these observations so interesting that he began to study the "psychic secretions" which he hypothesized were the result of the dogs' mental activity. His unplanned observations pulled him in a most unexpected direction.

What Pavlov observed was the phenomenon of classical conditioning. Initially, salivation was elicited only by eating the food. After repeated pairings, the sight of the food, as well as the sight of Pavlov, also elicited salivation. Pavlov won the Nobel Prize for his work on digestion, but he also made an unplanned contribution to the psychological study of learning.

Are such happy accidents really achievements? Didn't animal trainers and many parents know about conditioning already? Couldn't *anyone* have made the same contribution as Pavlov, if not with salivation, then with some other response? The answer is probably "No." What distinguishes a scientist like Pavlov is that he was able to differentiate between a commonplace incident and something of great importance. Another person might have abandoned the salivation research as hopeless. Pavlov continued his research, performing many new experiments and offering unique interpretations of his findings. Serendipity can be useful in generating new hypotheses only when we are open to new possibilities. The good scientist takes note of all potentially relevant observations, and analyzes and evaluates them: Are they interpretable? Do they explain something which was previously unexplained? Do they suggest a new way of looking at a problem? Serendipity is not just a matter of luck; it is also a matter of knowing enough to use an opportunity.

INTUITION

Intuition is the last approach we will discuss in this chapter. It is an approach not discussed in most experimental psychology texts. Psychology is a science. As such, it should be governed by formal, logical rules. But using intuition is not necessarily unscientific; rather, the inferences drawn from intuition often violate scientific criteria.

intuition   **Intuition** may be defined as knowing without reasoning. As such, it is probably closest to phenomenology. We acquire phenomenological knowledge simply by attending to our own experience. However, intuition may take us beyond mere apprehension of our own experiences. We may feel by "intuition" that a close relative has died. Because what the feeling is cannot be specified in observable, quantifiable terms, it seems out of place in a scientific context.

Although it is difficult to be concrete about what we mean by intuition, intuition is probably a very common basis for experimentation. We have a hunch about what might happen in a particular situation, so we set up an experiment to test it. Intuition guides what we choose to study. Of course, our experiments are still conducted in the context of prior research. We review the experimental literature to avoid carrying out experiments that are futile given what is already known. For example, we may believe intuitively that dogs can see colors, but a review of the prior work on perception shows that they cannot.[3] Knowing this, we would not begin a new series of tests to check color vision in dogs.

We must be careful to remain within the bounds of science when we use our intuition. By intuition, we may have a tentative explanation for behavior or events. But such an explanation is truly tentative; it cannot be accepted as valid until it has been translated into a hypothesis and subjected to empirical tests. Intuition is just that—and it should not be confused with fact. If we were going on vacation and knew only by intuition that the plane leaves at noon, it would be risky to go to the airport

3. Dogs are able to discriminate brightness. Such discriminations sometimes appear to be based on color, but dogs do not have color vision.

without first checking to verify the flight schedule. Furthermore, intuition should not destroy objectivity. Even though we believe intuitively that something is true, we must be prepared to change our thinking if the experimental evidence does not confirm our belief. Unless we find flaws in the experiments that would account for the incongruity, the observable data take precedence over intuition.

WHEN ALL ELSE FAILS

If you are reading this text as part of a course requirement, you may also be required to design an experiment of your own. You realize by now that you must have a hypothesis. Perhaps you also realize that our discussion of the ways in which others derive hypotheses has not been particularly helpful. As Russell said, there are no rules that can be used to generate hypotheses. If you feel completely at sea, here are some suggestions that have helped other students.

You are least likely to come up with a hypothesis by trying to think about everything you know about psychology. Begin by focusing on one or two broad areas that interest you. Perhaps you like learning and memory. If so, that is the place to start.

Once you select your broad areas of interest, take out a general psychology text and re-read the sections on these areas. You may now be able to narrow down the number of possible topics even further. Perhaps you are most interested in the work on learning lists of words. Now locate the latest research that has been done in this area. You may have to do quite a bit of reading before you can derive a hypothesis of your own. Try to structure your reading in terms of the approaches we have discussed. Do you find any specific instances that suggest general principles? Is there a study that sets out a theory leading to deductions that are testable? Were there nonexperimental studies that can be redone as experiments to test cause and effect inferences? You may hit upon something by accident, or you may develop a hunch about what might happen in a slightly new experimental setting.

Since there are no rules, it is usually impossible to predict how long it will take to develop a good hypothesis. Remember that the work you will do in a single course will probably not alter the course of psychology too much. Set realistic goals for yourself. Work from hypotheses that can be tested in the time frame you have available. You will probably need all the time you can get, which means that it is not a good idea to wait until the last minute to begin thinking about a hypothesis.

SUMMARY

Every experiment is designed to test a hypothesis about the effects of different treatment conditions on behavior. Every experiment must have a hypothesis. The hypothesis represents the end of the process of thinking about a behavior and zeroing in on one particular explanation that seems plausible.

The *experimental hypothesis* has several characteristics. First, it must be a synthetic statement. A hypothesis meets the definition of a synthetic statement if it can be stated in the "If . . . then" form. Second, the experimental hypothesis must be testable. The means for manipulating the antecedent conditions and measuring the resulting behavior must exist. The hypothesis must also be parsimonious: The simplest hypothesis is preferred until it is ruled out by conflicting evidence. Ideally, the hypothesis is also fruitful and will lead to new research.

Hypotheses may be found through induction, deduction, serendipity, or intuition. *Induction* is the process of reasoning from specific cases to more general principles. *Deduction* is the process of reasoning from general principles to predictions about specific instances. In practice, induction and deduction are often used together. Through induction we may devise general principles or *theories* that may be used to organize, explain, and predict behavior until more satisfactory principles are found. Through deduction, we may rigorously test the implications of a premise or theory. Regardless of which method we use, we are generally building on prior research. Ex post facto and other nonexperimental studies may suggest experiments to test cause and effect relationships. We may also experiment to replicate prior findings and to test new predictions that follow from them.

Hypotheses occasionally grow out of *serendipity*, the knack of finding things that are not being sought. Researchers occasionally make unexpected observations that lead them in surprising directions. *Intuition*, may also lead to hypotheses. We may have a hunch that something is true, and carry out an experiment to test that notion. Hypotheses may also arise out of systematic searches through the research in specific areas of interest.

REVIEW AND STUDY QUESTIONS

1. What is a hypothesis?
2. What are the characteristics of a good hypothesis?
3. Which of the following are synthetic statements? Why?
   a. If I am cold, then it is December.
   b. Out of sight, out of mind.
   c. Virtue is its own reward.
   d. John is my brother and my nephew.
   e. A statement that is always true is always true.
4. For each of the statements in question 3, decide whether the statement can be transformed into the "If . . . then" form.
5. Explain what is meant by induction and deduction. How are they different?
6. What is serendipity?
7. Is a discovery made through serendipity just a matter of luck?
8. a. What is the role of intuition in research?
   b. Is intuition scientific?

9. Before you set up an experiment, you should make a review of the research literature. What is the purpose of such a review?

10. Dr. P has just completed a study which shows a correlation between the amount of time children watch television and their attention span. Assume the correlation was $-.34$. State an experimental hypothesis based on this finding, and devise a simple procedure for testing it.

11. Explain the way in which an ex post facto study could be used to generate an experimental hypothesis.

12. Mary is lost: she just can't think of a hypothesis. Can you give her any advice on how to proceed?

13. Select one of the following research areas. Review some of the prior work in that area and formulate a new experimental hypothesis based on your review:
    a. Paired-associate learning
    b. The influence of a set in problem-solving
    c. Solving anagrams (scrambled words)
    d. Bystander apathy
    e. The exposure effect

REFERENCES

Bechtol, B., and Williams, J. California litter. *Natural History*, 1977, 86, No. 6, 62–65.

Bowlby, J. *Attachment and loss (Vol. 1). Attachment.* New York: Basic Books, 1969.

Ferster, C.B., and Skinner, B.F. *Schedules of reinforcement.* New York: Appleton-Century-Crofts, 1957.

Hilgard, E. R., and Bower, G. H. *Theories of learning.* New York: Appleton-Century-Crofts, 1966.

Hull, C. *Principles of behavior.* New York: Appleton-Century-Crofts, 1943.

Partington, J. R. *A history of chemistry*, Vol. IV. London: Macmillan, 1964.

Pavlov, I. *Conditioned reflexes.* Translated by G. V. Anrep. London: Oxford University Press, 1927.

Russell, B. *A history of western philosophy.* New York: Simon and Schuster, 1945.

Watson, J. B., and Rayner, R. Conditioned emotional reactions. *Journal of Experimental Psychology*, 1920, 3, 1–14.

Part Two

Method

The Basics of Experimentation

Key Terms

independent variable	reliability	experimental condition
subject variable	validity	experimental group
dependent variable	face validity	control condition
operational definition	content validity	control group
experimental operational definition	predictive validity	extraneous variable
measured operational definition	internal validity	confounding
hypothetical constructs	external validity	

Once you have formulated a hypothesis, you will want to set up an experiment to test it. To review briefly, the psychology experiment has these main features: We manipulate the antecedent conditions to create at least two different treatment conditions. At least two treatments are required so that we can make statements about the impact of different sets of antecedents. If we used only one treatment, there would be no way to evaluate what happens to behaviors as the conditions change. We expose subjects to different treatment conditions so that we can measure the effects of those conditions on behavior. We record the responses or behaviors of subjects under various conditions and then compare them. We can then assess whether our predictions are confirmed.

Doing an experiment allows us to draw causal inferences about behavior. If behavior changes as the antecedent conditions change, we may say that the differences in antecedent conditions *caused* the difference in behavior. However, such an inference is justified only when a carefully controlled test of our predictions has been made. The chapters in this section of the text deal with the basic methods and problems involved in planning a good experiment. By the end of this chapter, you will be familiar with the basic components of experiments: the independent variable, the dependent variable, operational definitions, and control groups. We will examine these concepts in the context of particular experiments. We will also discuss some issues involved in evaluating definitions and experiments: reliability, validity, and confounding. The concepts presented in this chapter are fundamentals of experimental design; we will return to them again and again throughout the book.

INDEPENDENT AND DEPENDENT VARIABLES

A hypothesis states a potential relationship between two variables. Variables are things that vary, things that can take on different values along some dimension. To be more precise, the experimental hypothesis expresses a potential relationship between two kinds of variables, the independent and the dependent variable.

independent
variable

The **independent variable** in an experiment is the antecedent condition (the treatment) that the experimenter deliberately manipulates to assess its effect on behavior. The experimenter alters the antecedents systematically to see whether behavior changes as the conditions change. The independent variable is simply the particular condition the experimenter chooses to vary. It is "independent" in the sense that its values are set by the experimenter; they are not affected by anything else that happens in the experiment. The researcher decides what the particular treatment conditions will be. Because we must have at least two different treatment conditions to meet the definition of an experiment, each independent variable must have at least two values.

In a broader sense, the independent variable is also the main variable of interest. In an ex post facto study, the researcher studies the way behavior changes as a subject variable

function of changes in variables outside the researcher's control. These are typically **subject variables**, characteristics of the subjects themselves (age, sex) that cannot be manipulated experimentally. It is common for researchers to refer to these variables as "independent variables" too. Although they are not manipulated by the researcher, they are often "independent" in the sense that the researcher selects the particular values that will be included in the study. For instance, Zanni et al. (1978) selected subjects who most clearly showed obsessive and hysterical tendencies.

dependent variable

The **dependent variable** is the variable measured to determine whether the independent variable had an effect. The dependent variable is the particular aspect of behavior that we expect our independent variable to alter. If the hypothesis is correct, different values of the independent variable should produce changes in the dependent variable. The dependent variable is "dependent" in the sense that *its* values are assumed to depend on the values of the independent variable: As the independent variable changes value (as we look at behavior under different treatment conditions), we expect to see corresponding changes in the value of the dependent variable.

Selecting an appropriate dependent variable is an important part of setting up an experiment. We could rely on our overall impression of whether the independent variable has some effect. However, we need more precision than that in a scientific study. We also need an objective measure of the effect of the independent variable. We do not want the evaluation of the outcome of the experiment to depend on our subjective judgment, which might be somewhat biased. In addition, our findings will have more widely understood meaning if they are presented in terms of an observable dimension that can be measured again and again. By clearly defining the way we are measuring the effect of the independent variable, we make it easier for others to replicate our research.

Some Research Examples

Schachter.   Consider this hypothesis, tested by Schachter (1959): If people are anxious, then they will want to affiliate, or be with others. Put another way, misery loves company. The hypothesis states a potential relationship between two variables, anxiety and affiliation. To test the hypothesis, Schachter did the following experiment. Subjects were brought into a room with an experimenter wearing horn-rimmed glasses and a white laboratory coat. The experimenter introduced himself as Dr. Gregor Zilstein of the Departments of Neurology and Psychiatry. He explained that this was an experiment on the effects of electric shock. The subjects were split into two groups. One group was shown some elaborate electrical equipment and led to expect painful shocks: "These shocks will hurt, they will be painful. As you can guess, if, in research of this sort, we're to learn anything at all that will really help humanity, it is necessary that our shocks be *intense*" (p. 13). The other group received instructions leading them to believe they would feel no pain: ". . . do not let the word 'shock' trouble you; I am sure that you will enjoy the experiment. . . . I assure you that what you feel will not in any way be painful. It will resemble more a tickle or a tingle than anything unpleasant" (p. 13).

Thus both groups were told that they would receive electric shock, but one group expected pain while the other did not. The group that expected pain was assumed to be more anxious than the group that did not. The experimenter then explained that there would be a delay while the experiment was being set up, and asked the subjects to indicate on a questionnaire whether they preferred to wait for the next part of the experiment alone, with other subjects, or had no preference. Based on the hypothesis, those subjects who were more anxious would be more likely to want to wait with others. This was the end of the experiment. The real purpose of the study was then explained, and no one ever actually received electric shock.[1]

In his hypothesis, Schachter stated a potential relationship between two variables, anxiety and affiliation: If subjects are anxious, then they will want to affiliate with others. The hypothesis expresses the relationship between the independent and the dependent variable.

The *independent variable* in any experiment is the antecedent condition (the treatment) deliberately manipulated by the experimenter in order to assess its effect on behavior. Schachter manipulated anxiety by giving his subjects varying instructions leading them to believe that they either would or would not be exposed to painful shock; anxiety was the independent variable in this experiment. It was "independent" in the sense that its values were set by Schachter. It was not affected by anything that occurred in the experiment.

The *dependent variable* is the variable measured to determine whether the independent variable had an effect on behavior. It is "dependent" in the sense that its values are assumed to depend on the values of the independent variable. In Schachter's experiment, the dependent variable was affiliation. According to the hypothesis, whether subjects choose to wait alone or with others depends on how anxious they are: Anxious subjects will be less likely to want to wait alone. If anxiety has no effect on affiliation, all the subjects, whether anxious or not, will be equally willing to wait alone. In fact, Schachter found that subjects who expected painful shocks were less likely to want to wait alone.

Hess.   Let us look at another hypothesis based on Hess' (1975) work: Large pupils make people more attractive. There is popular support for this notion. Women once used the drug belladonna to make themselves more beautiful. One of the effects of belladonna is dilation (widening) of the pupils. Candlelight dinners seem to flatter everyone. Aside from masking minor imperfections, dim light also causes pupils to dilate.

---

1.   Although no one was ever shocked in Schachter's experiment, the ethics of the procedure may be questioned by some psychologists. We will return to this experiment when we discuss the ethics of research in the next chapter.

To test his hypothesis, Hess asked male subjects to rate four photographs of two women. The photographs were retouched so that each woman had small pupils in one photograph and large pupils in another. Thus the two photographs were identical except for pupil size (examples of Hess' photographs are shown in Figure 4.1). Subjects were asked to select which woman in a series of pairs of these photographs appeared to be more friendly, charming, and so on.

The independent variable in this experiment was pupil size. Hess deliberately varied the size of the pupils in order to test the effects of pupil size. He used two different values or levels of the independent variable: large and small pupils. The dependent variable was attractiveness. If the hypothesis is correct, measures of attractiveness should depend on size of pupils. In fact, Hess found that his subjects were likely to attribute more of the positive traits to the women with large pupils.

Identifying Variables

You will have little difficulty identifying the independent and dependent variables in an experiment if you take the time to think about what the experimenter did. Ask yourself the following questions: What did the experimenter manipulate? Is this what I am calling the independent variable? What was used to assess the effect of the independent variable? Is this what I am calling the dependent variable? Suppose we are designing an experiment to test our own hypothesis. How will we identify the independent and dependent variables? Since the experiment has not been done, we cannot examine the procedures that were used. There is no simple rule for deciding which variable is the independent variable in a hypothesis. To make this determination, we must think about the hypothesis and the way we would go about testing it.

When you are working with your own hypothesis, you must ask the same types of questions you ask about an experiment that has already been done: What conditions will you manipulate or vary to test the hypothesis? (This is your independent variable.) What will you measure to find out whether your independent variable had an effect? (This is your dependent variable.) Keep in mind that if you do not need to manipulate the antecedent conditions by creating different treatment conditions (if you will simply measure behaviors as they occur), you do not have an experimental hypothesis.

Suppose this is your hypothesis: People learn words faster when the words are written horizontally than when they are written vertically. You have come to this hypothesis through your review of research on the effects of practice. Since English-speaking people customarily see words printed horizontally, you suspect that words presented vertically might seem more unfamiliar and so be harder to learn. What are the independent and dependent variables in this hypothesis?

First, what will be manipulated? To test the hypothesis, you must manipulate the way the words are presented. You must present some words vertically, and some horizontally. The independent variable is word position. You could run the experiment with two treatment conditions, horizontal and vertical presentation. What will

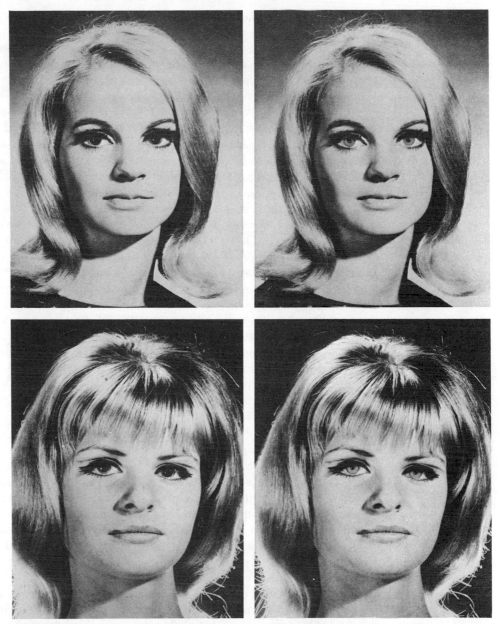

Figure 4.1 Photographs of two women retouched so that each woman had large pupils in one photograph and small pupils in the other. From E. Hess, "Role of pupil size in communication." *Scientific American*, 1975, *233*, No. 5, 111. Reprinted by permission of Eckhard E. Hess and *Scientific American*.

you measure to evaluate the effect of word position? According to the hypothesis, the position of the words will affect the rate of learning. Rate of learning is the dependent variable. If the hypothesis is correct, subjects will learn words faster if they are presented in the horizontal position. You are predicting that the rate of learning depends on the way the words are presented.

The independent variable in one experiment may function as the dependent variable in another. Whether a particular variable is an independent variable, a dependent variable, or neither depends on the particular hypothesis being tested. In Schachter's experiment, the independent variable was anxiety and the dependent variable was affiliation. Schachter found that subjects who were made anxious wanted to wait for the next part of the experiment with others. Based on Schachter's findings, we might suggest a new hypothesis: Perhaps people want to be with others when they are anxious because being with others causes them to become less anxious. How would we go about testing this hypothesis? We might place subjects in one of two conditions. In one condition, subjects are asked to spend 20 minutes alone in a room; in another condition, they are asked to spend 20 minutes waiting in a room with another person. At the end of the waiting period, the subjects' anxiety level is measured. If the hypothesis is correct, subjects who wait alone should be more anxious than subjects who wait with another person. The independent variable in this experiment is affiliation. We manipulate affiliation by assigning subjects to wait either alone or with others. The dependent variable is anxiety. According to the hypothesis, anxiety level depends on whether subjects wait alone or with another person. In Schachter's original experiment, anxiety was the independent variable, and affiliation was the dependent variable. As you can see, we changed the status of these variables when we turned to another hypothesis.

OPERATIONAL DEFINITIONS

The definition of the variable itself may change from one experiment to another. When we run an experiment, we naturally want to be sure that others will understand what we have done. Many concepts have more than one meaning, and those meanings are often vague. If we study variables without defining them exactly, the meaning of our findings will be unclear. As scientists, we also want to be sure that our procedures are stated clearly enough to enable other researchers to replicate our findings.

operational definition

In order to avoid confusion about what we did in an experiment, we use operational definitions. An **operational definition** specifies the precise meaning of a variable within an experiment: It defines a variable in terms of observable operations, procedures, and measurements. We include operational definitions in written reports of experiments so that other researchers will understand exactly what was done and will be able to replicate it. Operational definitions are sets of instructions that tell others how to carry out an experiment. They are statements of the operating procedures.

Operational definitions are quite different from ordinary dictionary definitions: A dictionary may define "kindness" as "the quality of being kind, or sympathetic and friendly." "Learning" may be "acquiring skill or knowledge." Although both definitions may be adequate for our everyday use of these terms, neither will do in the context of an experiment. With these definitions, we do not know how to produce different levels or values of these variables. They do not give us procedures we could follow to make people feel kind or unkind, or to have more or less learning. Similarly, they contain no information on how to measure or quantify these variables. How would we determine who has more kindness or more learning? Operational definitions include both types of information.

Defining the Independent Variable: Experimental Operational Definitions

experimental operational definition

We can distinguish between two kinds of operational definitions, experimental operational definitions and measured operational definitions (Kerlinger, 1973). **Experimental operational definitions** explain the meaning of independent variables; they define exactly what was done to create the various treatment conditions of the experiment. An experimental operational definition includes all the steps that were followed to set up each value of the independent variable. Schachter gave experimental operational definitions of high and low anxiety. The high-anxiety condition was defined in terms of the electronic equipment set up in the room, the ominous behavior of Dr. Zilstein, and the explicit statement that the subjects should expect painful shocks. The low-anxiety condition was defined by the absence of equipment, Dr. Zilstein's more relaxed manner, and explicit statements that the shocks would not be painful. If we were to replicate Schachter's experiment, we would be able to follow all these procedures in setting up each of the two treatment conditions. Note that if Schachter had merely said, "I set up a high-anxiety condition and a neutral condition," we would not know how to go about repeating his experiment. We would also have difficulty interpreting his findings, since we would have no way of judging just how "anxiety-producing" his conditions may have been.

Defining the Dependent Variable: Measured Operational Definitions

measured operational definition

Dependent variables are defined by measured operational definitions. A **measured operational definition** describes what we do to measure a variable. Measured operational definitions of the dependent variable describe exactly what procedures we follow to assess the impact of different treatment conditions. They include exact descriptions of the particular behaviors or responses recorded. They also explain how those responses are scored. If we are using scores on a standardized test to measure our dependent variable, we identify the test by name: "scores on the Wechsler Adult

Intelligence Scale"—not simply "scores on an intelligence test." If our measure is not standardized, we describe it in enough detail to allow other researchers to repeat our procedures. In Schachter's experiment, the dependent variable, affiliation, was given a measured operational definition. Schachter scored the desire to affiliate by having subjects check off their preferences on a questionnaire. The questionnaire is described in detail in his report. Again, it would be easy to replicate his procedures for measuring affiliation: We would simply administer the same questionnaire in the same way.

Defining Constructs Operationally

hypothetical
constructs

The need for operational definitions is apparent when we zero in on variables, such as anxiety, that are actually hypothetical constructs. **Hypothetical constructs** are processes postulated to explain behavior. Constructs cannot be observed directly. We infer their existence from behaviors that we can observe: An ordinarily good student panics and does poorly on an important exam. An actor has "stage fright" and forgets his lines. From these observations, we infer the existence of "anxiety." Now, we could say that "anxiety" is a peculiar feeling of queasiness that inhibits behavior. Unfortunately, that definition also neatly fits my first experience of eating raw clams. I was *not* anxious. But I was definitely queasy, and I have not eaten clams since. Furthermore, what we mean by "anxiety" may be quite different if we are talking about a person's experience before taking a test compared to waiting in line for a roller coaster ride.

Typically, several different definitions may be formulated for the same construct. Schachter's experiment illustrated one definition. In effect, Schachter said that "high anxiety" is the feeling experienced in a particular kind of situation—namely, one in which the person expects pain. In the "low anxiety" condition, the subjects saw no equipment and did not expect pain. By definition, the feeling they experienced in this setting is "low anxiety." You may or may not agree with Schachter's decision to define anxiety in this way, but you do know what definitions apply in this particular experiment.

Similarly, there are many possible measured operational definitions of anxiety. We need a measured operational definition when anxiety is a dependent variable. One such definition might be "a heartbeat in excess of 120 beats per minute following five minutes rest on a sofa." This definition could be used to explain what we mean by "anxiety" in a particular experiment. Notice that the components of the definition are observable dimensions; we can readily determine a person's pulse. We would expect to get good agreement on whether or not a person is "anxious" according to this definition.

We can also define anxiety by a score on a written test such as the Taylor Manifest Anxiety Scale (Taylor, 1953). This test includes a variety of items that are assumed to index different degrees of anxiety. The test includes items dealing with the frequency of nightmares, fear of spiders, worries about work, and so on. In using the test we assume that people who express many of these concerns are more anxious than those who express few of them. We use predetermined cutoff scores to determine who is anxious and who is not. Again, we have an objective, observable set of measures (the subjects' responses to a series of test items) to define anxiety. To say that anxiety is "feeling queasy" is not acceptable. We cannot observe queasiness directly, nor can we be sure that subjects will know what we mean if we simply ask them whether they are "anxious."

Learning is also a construct. Like anxiety, it cannot be observed directly; it must be operationally defined by objective criteria. We can define learning in terms of performance on a written test, in a maze, or on a bicycle. We can count up the number of correct responses or errors. The time taken to complete a task may also be used as an index of learning. Although the operational definitions vary, they all specify learning in observable terms. We cannot measure learning directly, but we can infer its occurrence from these objective measures. We can state our procedures clearly enough to permit other researchers to measure learning in the same way.

Defining Nonconstruct Variables

It is easy to see why operational definitions are required when we are dealing with constructs. Something that cannot be seen must be defined by observable dimensions before we can deal with it scientifically. However, operational definitions are equally important when we are working with variables that can be observed more directly. Suppose we wish to test the effects of lighting on newborn babies. We may wish to compare crying among babies in light rooms versus crying in dark rooms, as did Irwin and Weiss in 1934. The comparison seems straightforward enough, but before it can be made we must operationally define what we mean by "light" versus "dark" rooms. Is a "light" room as bright as a sunny day? Is a "dark" room light-tight, or one in which the shades are drawn? To make a legitimate comparison, we must define what we mean by "light" and "dark" as objectively as possible, ideally by the use of a photometer or light meter. The dependent variable, crying, must also be defined in such a way that independent observers agree on its occurrence. Do intermittent sounds constitute "crying" or must the sound be sustained? Is a whimper also a cry? These decisions must be made before the experiment is conducted. Otherwise, the results may not mean anything to anyone except the experimenter.

EVALUATING OPERATIONAL DEFINITIONS

Since there may be many definitions for the same variable, how is it possible to know which definition is the best? There are no hard and fast answers to this question. As with many other aspects of experimentation, what works well in one experiment may simply not be appropriate in another. Our definition must be objective and precise so that others can duplicate the procedures. In addition, there are more general criteria. We can group these under the general headings of reliability and validity.[2]

Reliability

reliability   **Reliability** means consistency and predictability. Good operational definitions are reliable: If we apply them in more than one experiment, they ought to work in similar ways each time. Suppose we have specified all the operations that must be performed to create two treatment conditions, hungry and not hungry. If our operational definition is reliable, every time we apply the definition (each time we create these two conditions), we should obtain similar consequences. Subjects in the "hungry" condition should consistently show signs of hunger—increased activity, food-seeking, or a verbal report of hunger if our subjects are people. If our "hungry" subjects show signs of hunger only occasionally, our operational definition is not reliable. The procedures we have specified to define the various levels of the independent variable work haphazardly: Sometimes we produce hunger, and sometimes not. Better definitions are needed.

Measured operational definitions should also be reliable. If we took several sets of measurements according to our operational definition of the dependent variable, we should get the same results each time. When possible, we select measuring devices, such as standardized tests, that are known to be reliable. Otherwise, we make sure our procedures are clearly and simply defined. The more accurate they are, the more likely they are to be reliable. There are several procedures for checking the reliability of measures. One is simply having different observers taking measurements of the same responses (for example, several raters score subjects' essays for "assertiveness"). If there is little agreement between them, the chances are good that the measuring device is not reliable.

Validity

validity   A second important problem in formulating operational definitions is stating definitions that are valid. Valid definitions are sound; they can withstand criticism. More specifically, **validity** in experiments refers to the principle of studying the thing that actually interests us. We can formulate precise, objective definitions. They may even be reliable. But if they are not valid, we have not accomplished the goals of our experiment.

Often several procedures have been used to manipulate the same variable. Construct variables such as hunger, for example, can be approached in a variety of

---

2.   These issues also affect our ability to make statements that go beyond the experiment we did. We will return to them in a later chapter.

ways. Is one definition more valid than another? We may define hunger in terms of hours of food deprivation: an animal that has been without food for 24 hours is hungry. We can also define it in terms of body weight: an animal maintained at 90 percent of its normal body weight is hungry. Other definitions, such as stimulating appropriate parts of the brain, may also be used. But which is the most valid? Which represents what we want to call "hunger"?

One approach to the problem is a comparison of the consequences of the various procedures. If all of them produce "hunger," they should all lead to the same signs of hunger we looked for in evaluating the reliability of a manipulation. Hungry animals will be more active, will eat foods they refuse when they have a choice, and so on. Researchers make these kinds of comparisons to develop the best procedures. Comparing all the available procedures is not always feasible, particularly in the course of a single experiment. However, it should be clear that we need to evaluate the validity of our experimental manipulations. We must ask whether we *really* manipulated what we intended to manipulate.

Face Validity.   Validity of operational definitions is least likely to be a problem with variables that can be manipulated and measured fairly directly. For instance, in studying the effects of pupil size, it is reasonably easy to know whether we are using a valid experimental operational definition of pupil size. We simply use a standard measuring device, such as a ruler, to define the treatment conditions. Defining pupil

face validity size by the marks on a ruler has **face validity.** The procedure is self-evident; we do not need to convince people that a ruler measures width. Face validity is a minimum requirement.

Similar issues arise in evaluating definitions of the dependent variable. The validity of a measured operational definition centers around the question of whether we measured what we intended to measure. As with experimental definitions, there should be some consensus that our procedures yield information about the variable we had in mind when we started the experiment. At a minimum, our procedures should have face validity. Aside from using common sense in selecting appropriate measures, two other kinds of validity are important as we develop measures: content validity and predictive validity. Measures that appear to have face validity do not necessarily meet these criteria.

content validity *Content Validity.*   **Content validity** depends on whether we are measuring what we intended to measure. When we evaluate content validity, we are asking this question: Does the content of our measure reflect the content of the thing we are measuring? The questions students might raise about an exam are often questions of content validity. An exam is supposed to measure what students have learned. However, students may sometimes feel an exam includes only questions about the things they did not understand: the content of the exam is not what they learned. Winston Churchill had the same feeling when he wrote:

I had scarcely passed my 12th birthday when I entered the inhospitable regions of examinations, through which, for the next seven years, I was destined to journey. These examinations were a great trial to me. The subjects which were dearest to the examiners, were almost invariably those I fancied least. I would have liked to be examined in History, Poetry, and writing essays. The examiners, on the other hand, were partial to Latin and Mathematics. And their will prevailed. Moreover, the questions which they asked on both these subjects were almost invariably those to which I was unable to suggest the satisfactory answer. I should have liked to be asked to say what I knew. They always tried to ask what I did not know. When I would willingly have displayed my knowledge, they sought to expose my ignorance. This sort of treatment had only one result: I did not do well in examinations.[3]

Whether a particular measure has content validity is often a matter of judgment. Teachers and students sometimes disagree on whether particular tests or particular questions are fair representations of the course material. However, for experimental purposes, we try to obtain some consensus on the content validity of our measures.

Suppose you have devised a questionnaire to measure racial attitudes. You have a series of questions about whether people would live in integrated neighborhoods, whether they would help a person of another race who was in trouble, and so on. You could simply administer the questionnaire. However, you would have a better idea of whether your questionnaire has content validity if you obtained ratings of the items from objective judges. Each judge would be asked to rate each item for whether it measures racial attitudes. You would then have the opportunity to include items that are most representative of that variable, according to the raters' judgments. If the raters do not agree on the items, the questionnaire will have to be reworked.

The degree of content validity we can achieve depends on the particular variable we want to measure. The more specific the variable, the easier it will be. Clearly, it would be relatively easy to define weight gain in a way that would have high content validity. Measuring the size of a mental image poses more difficult problems.

Predictive Validity.   We can also ask whether our measures of the dependent variable have **predictive validity.** Do our procedures yield information that enables us to predict what subjects will do in another situation? They should, if we are measuring what we intend to measure. Schachter defined the desire to affiliate in terms of subjects' responses to a questionnaire. They were asked to indicate whether they preferred to wait alone, with others, or had no preference. This definition has face validity. It seems to have something to do with people's desire to be together. It seems to have content validity too; part of the desire to affiliate is a wish to be with other people. When we raise the question of predictive validity, however, we are asking this: Can we use people's responses to this questionnaire to predict a particular behavior? If people have the desire to affiliate, it is reasonable to predict that they will stay near others when they have the opportunity. In Schachter's study, we could

predictive validity

3.   Winston Churchill, *My early life.* New York: Scribner's, 1930. Reprinted with permission.

evaluate the predictive validity of the affiliation measure by changing the procedures slightly. Instead of telling subjects that the experiment was over after they completed the questionnaire, we could take them all into a large waiting room. If the affiliation measure has predictive validity, the subjects who said they wanted to wait with others will seat themselves closer together and perhaps talk to each other more than subjects who preferred to wait alone. If we do not observe these overt signs of the desire to affiliate, we may have to conclude that the written measure does not have predictive validity: it does not predict what people will do.

EVALUATING THE EXPERIMENT: INTERNAL VALIDITY

So far we have focused on the notion of validity in connection with operating procedures. We want to develop procedures that define our variables in valid ways. However, a more general evaluation is also required: Is the experiment valid? Can we make valid statements about the effects of our independent variable? We can talk about two kinds of validity when we are looking at the experiment as a whole. The

internal validity   first is **internal validity,** the soundness of the procedures within the experiment. Later in the book we will discuss **external validity**, how well the findings of the

external validity   experiment apply to situations that were not tested directly (for example, real life).

When we set up an experiment, we plan procedures to measure the effects of various treatment levels. We are trying to assess the impact of the independent variable. We can ask whether we have achieved that goal in the context of the experiment: An experiment is internally valid if we can be sure that the changes in behavior observed across the treatment conditions of the experiment were actually caused by the independent variable (Campbell, 1957). If other explanations are possible, the experiment is not valid; we cannot identify the impact of the independent variable with certainty. We cannot make any correct generalizations from an experiment that is not internally valid. In the following sections, we will look at three important concepts that are tied to the problem of internal validity: control groups, extraneous variables, and confounding. These factors affect our ability to understand the effects of our treatment conditions.

Control Groups

In order to assess the impact of the independent variable, we must have at least two different treatment conditions so that we can compare the effect of different values of the independent variable. We cannot draw valid conclusions about the effect of the independent variable without this comparison.

In the simplest experiments, we have only two treatment conditions. Usually, one condition is an experimental condition, and the other is a control condition. In

experimental   the **experimental condition,** we apply a particular value of our independent variable

condition   to the subjects and measure the dependent variable. The subjects in an experimental

experimental group

control condition

control group

condition are called an **experimental group**. The **control condition** is used to determine the value of the dependent variable without the experimental manipulation. The subjects in a control condition are called a **control group**. In the control condition, we carry out exactly the same procedures that are followed in the experimental condition, except for the experimental manipulation. In a sense, the control condition is a "no treatment" condition. We simply measure subjects' responses without trying to alter them in any way. We need the control condition so that we know how subjects ordinarily perform on the dependent measure. The control condition gives us a standard that makes the responses under the experimental conditions interpretable: We can compare subjects' performance in the experimental condition, to see whether they did better, worse, or the same as subjects who were not exposed to our experimental manipulation. Without the control group, we cannot say whether the experimental subjects did better or worse than usual.

Suppose we plan an experiment on the effects of drinking coffee on productivity. Everyday experience tells us that some people simply cannot function without a morning cup of coffee. Our hypothesis, then, is that a cup of coffee in the morning enhances productivity. Coffee drinking is our independent variable; productivity is the dependent variable. A cup of coffee will be operationally defined as one teaspoon of Instant Maxwell House dissolved in one cup of boiling water. The operational definition here is important. The proportion of coffee to water is critical, since the strength of the coffee probably determines its effect. There may be subtle differences between the effects of brewed versus instant coffee which might need to be explored in the future. The particular brand might also make a difference. Whether we allow subjects to use cream and sugar is another issue. If some subjects used sugar and others did not, that might make a difference because sugar is a source of quick energy. For simplicity, we will require our subjects to drink the coffee without cream and sugar. Now that we have settled on an operational definition of the independent variable, let us turn to the dependent variable, productivity. Again for simplicity, let us operationally define productivity as the number of "o's" a subject crosses out on a page of newsprint in 10 minutes.

Assume that we have actually run this experiment and the data are as follows: The average number of "o's" crossed out per subject was 362.14. The subjects were extremely productive, since the total number on the page was 289. Some subjects were so productive that they crossed out the same "o" more than once, perhaps out of boredom or despair. We conclude that coffee enhances productivity.

Is this a valid conclusion? No. It should be clear from the example that we cannot make any valid inference about the relationship between coffee drinking and productivity from this study. We have no basis for the conclusion that coffee drinking "enhanced" productivity. Since we used only one value of the independent variable, drinking a cup of coffee of one set of proportions, we cannot draw any conclusions about whether or not the coffee altered behavior from what it would have been if the subject had not drunk coffee. This experiment requires a control group.

The control group would receive no coffee, but would be given the same instructions for the productivity task, the same amount of time to complete the task, and so on. The control group is used to establish a standard against which to compare the experimental group. If the groups are identical except for the fact that one (the experimental group) drinks coffee and the other (the control group) does not drink coffee, any differences in productivity must be due to the effects of the coffee. If we observe differences in performance, we might then suspect that coffee drinking enhanced (or reduced) productivity. A statistical test would be required to verify our impression. But without this comparison, we *cannot* evaluate our data. Without a control group, there is no way of knowing whether drinking coffee had any effect on productivity, and we do not have a valid experiment. Box 4.1 illustrates the application of these principles in an actual study.

Box 4.1 A Research Example

Doob, Carlsmith, Freedman, Landauer, and Tom (1969) were interested in the effect of the initial selling price of an item on final sales. Manufacturers will often introduce new products at special low prices, and provide free samples or coupons to induce consumers to try the products. The hope is that shoppers will continue to buy the product. Doob et al. tested this notion by introducing new products at low prices in a chain of discount houses. The initial low prices were later raised to the regular selling prices. If the marketers' notion is correct, shoppers should continue to buy the product after the price increases. A variety of items was tested, including mouthwash, toothpaste, aluminum foil, and light bulbs. In most cases the researchers found that, predictably, sales dropped off after the price increase but continued at a reasonable level. On the surface it seems that the low price was a useful device to encourage people to try the products, since at least some buyers continued to use them.

Nevertheless, as you can see, the experiment requires a control group. In order to establish normal sales for each product, Doob et al. introduced the products at their regular prices in another comparable set of stores. That is, they included a control condition in which there was no price reduction. This is an essential part of the experiment. Without knowing what sales are when the initial price is the regular price, we cannot say whether the lower price affects sales at all. Some buyers will try any new product regardless of its price. Thus, initial sales might be explained by curiosity. Since a product usually has some merits, at least some buyers will remain after the price increase. In fact, Doob et al. found that the low initial selling price actually reduced overall sales of the products. After periods ranging from 4 to 20 weeks, depending on the product, they found that in stores where the initial price was the usual selling price, sales were higher than in stores where an initially low price was later increased to the normal selling price. They explain their paradoxical findings in terms of cognitive dissonance theory: When customers pay more for a product, they must come to like it more in order to reduce their dissonance, or conflict, over buying something at that price. On the other hand, a cheap item does not need to be as good to be worth the price; there is little need to justify buying it.

Experiments without Control Groups

In some cases a valid experiment may be conducted without a control group. These experiments also require at least two experimental conditions, because we must always have data to evaluate behavior under different values or levels of our independent variable.

Holloway and Hornstein (1976) carried out a well-designed experiment without a control group. They suggested that the news influences our view of human nature. In one experiment, they tested the effect of hearing good or bad news. Subjects were brought into a waiting room one at a time. They thought they were waiting for the experiment to begin, but in reality it had already started. While they were in the waiting room, a radio played music for a time. The music was then interrupted by the voice of a newscaster who read one of two "news items." Half the subjects heard the report of a man whose life would be saved because of a kind donor who would provide the organ needed for an emergency kidney transplant. The remaining subjects heard a very different story. This one reported the murder of an elderly woman. The murderer was identified as a respected clergyman and neighbor of the victim. After these reports, the radio returned to music until one of the researchers casually turned it off and ostensibly began the experiment.

In the next part of the experiment, subjects were asked to make ratings concerning human nature. They were asked such questions as "What percentage of people try to apply the Golden Rule even in today's complex society?" Holloway and Hornstein found that "The people who heard the tale of the woman's murder thought much less of their fellows than those who heard the good news about the kidney donor. The former estimated that *fewer* members of their community were decent, honest, and altruistic" (p. 76.).

In this experiment, the independent variable was news (good versus bad). The dependent variable was the opinion of humankind—that is, how honest, decent, and upright the subjects rated other people. The experiment had only two groups of subjects, those who heard "good news" and those who heard "bad news." Good news was operationally defined as a news story in which one person helps another. Bad news was operationally defined as a news story in which one person harms another. The dependent variable was operationally defined in terms of subjects' answers to a series of questions about the morals and attitudes of others.

The Holloway and Hornstein experiment is a well-designed experiment that has no control group. All subjects heard some news, either good or bad. Holloway and Hornstein concluded: "The good news produces more favorable views of humanity's general moral disposition than bad news does—despite the fact that the news deals only with certain special cases and not at all with human nature on the grand scale" (p. 76). The conclusion is worded carefully. Since there was no group which received *no* news at all, Holloway and Hornstein could only make statements about the relationship between the different values of the independent variable that were actually tested—good and bad news.

Still, it is possible that hearing *any* news will alter people's attitudes or feelings.

Folklore tells us, "No news is good news." Does this mean that even good news might produce some negative effects? Perhaps the highest ratings of humanity would be obtained from subjects who heard no news at all. Indeed, we might speculate that although the "good" news story in the Holloway and Hornstein experiment has a "happy" ending, it is not a particularly good story at all. Both men must endure the pain and risk of major surgery; each will have to function for the rest of his life with only one kidney. This story could cause some subjects to focus on human frailty, which in turn might cast doubt on others' ability to resist temptation and abide by ethical and moral standards. Of course, there is no way of verifying any of these speculations without a control group. *The conclusions that may be drawn from an experiment are restricted by the scope and representativeness of the treatment conditions.*

As you design your own experiments, you will want to focus on the hypothesis you are testing. You must decide in advance which and how many treatment conditions will be necessary to make an adequate test of your hypothesis. Since Holloway and Hornstein focused on the differences produced by good versus bad news, the absence of a control group does not invalidate their study. In general, though, using a control group increases the amount of information about the effect of the independent variable.

Extraneous Variables and Confounding

From an experiment we can draw a causal inference about the relationship between the independent and dependent variables. If the value of the dependent variable changes significantly as the independent variable changes, we may say that the independent variable *caused* changes in the dependent variable. But this inference is justified only when the experiment is well controlled. Many things other than the independent and dependent variables may be changing throughout an experiment — time of day, the experimenter's level of fatigue, the particular subjects who are being tested. Variables other than the independent and dependent variables in an exper-

extraneous variable iment are called **extraneous variables**, factors which are not the main focus of the experiment. They are neither intentionally manipulated as independent variables, nor dependent variables which are measured as indexes of the effect of the independent variable. They can include differences among subjects, equipment failures, inconsistent instructions—in short, anything that varies. In a well-controlled experiment, the variation in the independent variable is the only systematic variation that occurs across treatment conditions. All aspects of the experiment remain constant except for the independent variable, which the experimenter intentionally manipulates, and the dependent variable, which is used to measure its effect. *If extraneous variables are not controlled or held constant, we may not be able to tell whether changes in the dependent variable were caused by changes in the independent variable or by extraneous variables which also changed value across conditions.*

When the value of an extraneous variable changes systematically across the

confounding

conditions of an experiment (that is, when it changes along with the independent variable) we have a situation known as **confounding**. A good experiment is free of confounding. When there is confounding, experimental results cannot be interpreted with certainty. Causal relationships between the independent and dependent variables may not be inferred. In effect, confounding sabotages the experiment because the effects we see can be explained equally well by changes in the extraneous variable or in the independent variable; our experiment is not internally valid. Boxes 4.2 and 4.3 present some hypothetical experiments in which confounding is a problem. In subsequent chapters, we will study some of the basic techniques used to avoid confounding.

Box 4.2   Confounded Experiment A

With the increasing concern about food additives, we might hypothesize that the average consumer would now be more likely to select a product with fewer food additives than a similar one with more additives. Suppose we set up an experiment to be conducted in a local supermarket.

We approach every third customer who enters the market and ask that person to participate in a study of consumer preferences. We show the subject two containers of potato chips. The first ("Gumshoe Potato Chips") lists the following ingredients: potatoes, oil, salt. The second container ("Crunchy Chips") lists these ingredients: potatoes, oil, salt, monosodium glutamate, calcium silicate, disodium inosinate, disodium guanylate, polymorphospervosinate, artificial flavor, and artificial color. We now ask our subjects to examine both packages and select the one they would be more likely to buy, assuming the price of the two items is equal.

Suppose that of the 236 shoppers who agreed to participate, 232 select the second as the product they would be most likely to buy. May we conclude that, contrary to our original hypothesis, shoppers prefer products with more additives? Definitely not.

This experiment contains a confounding variable. The independent variable is the number of additives listed on a food package. The dependent variable is desirability, measured by the subjects' reports of which product they would be more likely to purchase. There are two conditions in the experiment—a control condition in which the product has no additives and an experimental condition in which the product has many additives. Do subjects prefer the experimental food that contains many additives? Based simply on reported preferences, we might be tempted to conclude that shoppers actually prefer foods that contain more ingredients. However, in addition to the number of additives, the names of the products also varied across conditions. The name "Crunchy Chips," which suggests a crispy product, may be more appealing than "Gumshoe Potato Chips." Since the names of the products as well as the ingredients are different, we cannot conclude with certainty that subjects chose one product over the other because of the ingredients and not the names.

In order to establish that subjects prefer one product over another on the basis of ingredients, we must eliminate the names of the products.[4] We might relabel both products simply "Potato Chips." We would also want to be sure that no other extraneous variables influenced the subjects' decisions. Thus, we would also want to use two containers of the same color and size, keep the price of the two items constant, and refrain from smiling as subjects examine the first label. With all other factors held constant across conditions, if subjects still showed a clear preference for one product over the other, we *might* then conclude that subjects preferred one to the other because of the ingredients.

4. In a later chapter you will learn about a more complex design in which it is possible to explore the effects of *both* the names and the ingredients at the same time.

Our goal is always to set up the experiment in such a way that the independent variable is the only variable (besides the dependent variable) which changes value across conditions. In order to draw causal inferences about the effects of the independent variable, we must be sure that no extraneous variables are changing along with the independent variable.

Box 4.3   Confounded Experiment B

Suppose I am interested in testing the effectiveness of holding discussion periods during each class session. For one class I allow 15 minutes toward the end of each class during which students may ask questions about the material covered. In the other class, I spend the last 15 minutes of class reading aloud from the textbook. At the end of the semester I compare the performance of the two classes on a standardized test. My hypothesis is that students in the experimental group which participated in class discussion will perform better than students in the control group who did not participate in discussion. Assume the average grade on the standardized test is 78.3 for the experimental group and 79.2 for the control group. Although not identical, the performance of the two groups is not significantly different. In effect, one group did about as well as the other. Should I conclude that the use of discussion as a teaching tool has no effect?

Before I would be justified in making such an inference, I would probably want to do further research. Many confounding variables may have affected the outcome of the experiment. One is the time of each class. I neglected to tell you that the experimental class (with discussion) met at 8 A.M. The control class (no discussion) met at 11 A.M. Since the sleepy experimental class hardly ever participated in "discussions," the impact of this variable was probably negligible. This is comparable to testing the effect of a drug but finding later that subjects didn't take it because they didn't like its taste. Other factors must also be considered. For instance, students who register early are more likely to get into the popular 11 A.M. classes. Students who like to take classes at 8 A.M. may be quite different from those who register for courses later in the day. The style of the instructor may also vary with the time of day. Thus, in a seemingly straightforward comparison of two classroom procedures we have several possibly confounding variables. We might explain the results by saying that the discussion approach is ineffective, but the results may also be due to differences in the makeup of the class, whether the class is awake or asleep, whether the instructor is lively or dull, and so on.

It is difficult to control all the sources of possible confounding in an experiment. Whenever we test two different groups of subjects, there will be differences between them. We must often compromise in setting up our experimental design by focusing on the variables most likely to affect the dependent variable we are measuring. For example, in a study of learning in the classroom, we would be more concerned about finding classes of comparable intelligence than classes containing equal numbers of brown- and blue-eyed students. Just as we narrow down the number of possible independent variables we want to explore, we narrow down the number of extraneous variables we choose to control. The rule of thumb is to control as many variables as possible. If a variable may be held constant in the experiment, it makes sense to do so even when any impact of that variable on the results may be doubtful. However, we often find that as we control one variable, another changes value and is out of control (see Figure 4.2). For example, in our teaching experiment, we may find two comparable classes meeting at 11 A.M. But obviously these two classes will have two different instructors. We must make a choice about which variables are most critical for good control. Complete control is never possible: Many of the design problems you will face can be described as "finding the least worst alternative."

"We couldn't imagine what was producing this extraordinary effect. Then we recalled last spring's brief, periodic inseepages of tear gas."

Figure 4.2 Drawing by Ed Fisher; © 1970. The New Yorker Magazine, Inc.

SUMMARY

In this chapter we have examined a number of basic experimental concepts. The *independent variable* is the antecedent condition (the treatment) that is deliberately manipulated by the experimenter to assess its effect on behavior. We use different values or levels of the independent variable in order to determine how changes in the independent variable alter the value of the dependent variable, our index of behavior. The dependent variable is an indicator of change in behavior. Its values are assumed to depend on the values of the independent variable.

Both independent and dependent variables must be defined operationally. An *operational definition* specifies the precise meaning of a variable within an experiment: it defines the variable in terms of observable operations, procedures, and measurements. Operational definitions establish what operations and procedures constitute each of the different values needed to test the effect of the independent variable. They also specify the procedures used to measure the impact of the independent variable. These definitions are developed according to criteria of reliability and validity. Reliable procedures have consistent and predictable outcomes. Valid definitions are sound and sensible. If our definitions are valid, we will be manipulating and measuring the variables we intend to study. *Face validity* is a minimum criterion for judging validity. We may also evaluate the *content* and *predictive* validity of our dependent measures.

An experiment is *internally valid* if we can be sure that the changes in behavior which occur across treatment conditions were caused by the independent variable. To make valid statements about the effect of the independent variable, we must use at least two treatment conditions. One may be a control condition that tells us how subjects do on the dependent variable when the independent variable is not manipulated. Other conditions are experimental conditions in which different values of the independent variable are applied.

Ideally, the independent variable is the only variable that changes value in the different treatment conditions of the experiment. However, sometimes we find that *extraneous variables*, variables that are neither independent nor dependent variables in the experiment, also change across conditions. When extraneous variables change value from one treatment condition to another along with the independent variable, we have a situation known as *confounding*. When there is confounding, we cannot say for sure whether the changes we see in the dependent variable from one condition to another were caused by the changes in the values of the independent variable, or by an extraneous variable which was also changing: The experiment is not internally valid.

REVIEW AND STUDY QUESTIONS

1. Define each of the following terms:
   a. Independent variable
   b. Dependent variable
   c. Extraneous variable

2. Identify the independent and dependent variables in each of the following hypotheses:
   a. Absence makes the heart grow fonder.
   b. It takes longer to recognize the person in a photograph seen upside down.
   c. People feel sadder in rooms painted blue.
   d. Smoking cigarettes causes cancer.

3. What is an operational definition?

4. Formulate an experimental operational definition for each of the independent variables in question 2.

5. Formulate a measured operational definition for each dependent variable in question 2.

6. For each hypothesis in question 2, discuss three extraneous variables that might interfere with making a valid test of that hypothesis.

7. Define and give an example to illustrate each of these terms:
   a. Validity
   b. Reliability
   c. Content validity
   d. Predictive validity

8. a. Discuss the requirements of a good operational definition.
   b. What specific criteria are applied to measured operational definitions?

9. What is internal validity? Why is it important?

10. An ambitious graduate student wanted to collect all the data for his thesis in one day. His project involved subjects' ability to solve word problems. The student began by testing all the subjects in his experimental group first, beginning at noon. Unfortunately, the testing took far longer than he had expected. By the time he finished testing the first group of subjects, it was nearly midnight. But he didn't let that stop him. He knocked at dormitory doors and woke the occupants. Before the drowsy student could protest, the experiment was completed according to the procedures of the control condition. Without knowing more about the experiment, what can you say about any conclusions this researcher might draw?

11. A researcher wanted to test the effect of riding the subway on mental health. She formed two groups of subjects, an experimental group and a control group. The experimental group rode the subway for 60 minutes every morning. The control group jogged for an equal period of time. At the end of one month, both

groups were measured on a scale of adjustment and well-being. The control group was found to be better adjusted than the experimental group. Do you accept the conclusion that riding the subway damages mental health? Why or why not?

12. How could you change the study described in question 11 to set up an experiment that would be internally valid?

REFERENCES

Campbell, D. T. Factors relevant to the validity of experiments in social settings. *Psychological Bulletin*, 1957, *54*, 297–312.

Doob, A. N., Carlsmith, J. M., Freedman, J. L., Landauer, T. K., and Tom, S. Effect of initial selling price on subsequent sales. *Journal of Personality and Social Psychology*, 1969, *11*, 345–350.

Hess, E. Role of pupil size in communication. *Scientific American*, 1975, *233*, No. 5, 110 ff.

Holloway, S. M., and Hornstein, H. A. How good news makes us good. *Psychology Today*, 1976, *10*, 76 ff.

Irwin, O. C., and Weiss, L. A. Differential variations in the activity and crying of newborn infants under different intensities of light: A comparison of observational with polygraph findings. *University of Iowa Studies in Child Welfare*, 1934, *9*, 139–147.

Kerlinger, F. N. *Foundations of behavioral research* (2nd ed.). New York: Holt, Rinehart and Winston, 1973.

Schachter, S. *The psychology of affiliation*. Stanford, Calif.: Stanford University Press, 1959.

Taylor, J. A. A personality scale of manifest anxiety, *Journal of Abnormal and Social Psychology*, 1953, *48*, 285–290.

5

Subjects: Ethics and Recruitment

Key Terms

informed consent	sample of subjects	random number table
population	random selection	significant difference
sample		

So far we have focused on the basic principles for setting up an experiment to make the best possible test of the relationship between the independent and dependent variables. But any research project also involves decisions concerning the subjects who will participate in the study. In this chapter we will discuss the ethics of the relationship between researcher and subjects, and the researcher's responsibilities. We will also consider some more practical aspects, such as how to go about recruiting and selecting subjects.

RESEARCH ETHICS

The researcher's foremost concern in recruiting and using subjects is treating them ethically and responsibly. Whether we work with animals or human subjects, we must consider their safety and welfare. Responsible psychological research is not an attempt to satisfy idle curiosity about other people's innermost thoughts and experiences. Responsible research is aimed at advancing our understanding of feelings, thoughts, and behaviors in ways that will ultimately benefit humanity. But the well-being of the individual subject is no less important than the search for general knowledge: Research that is harmful to subjects is undesirable even though it may add to the store of knowledge. For instance, early experience is an important aspect of child development—but we would not raise children in isolation just to assess the effects of deprivation. There is no way we can justify such a study, no matter how important the knowledge we might gain.

A researcher is legally responsible for what happens to the subjects of a study. He or she is liable for any harm that comes to subjects, even if it occurs unintentionally. This means a researcher could be sued for damages if an experiment hurt someone, whether the injury was physical or psychological, intentional or accidental.

In order to protect the subjects of psychological research, a number of specific legal and ethical guidelines have been formulated. From a legal standpoint, human subjects are protected by a federal law [Title 45, Section 46.106(b)]. This law requires that each institution set up a review committee to evaluate every proposed study. The review committee must ensure that the safety of the subjects is adequately protected, that any risks to the individual are outweighed by potential benefits or the importance of the knowledge to be gained, and that each subject gives informed consent to participate.

informed
consent

Informed consent means that the subject agrees to participate after receiving full information concerning the nature and purpose of the study. Several aspects of informed consent are particularly relevant to psychological research. First, the person must be exercising free will in deciding to participate in the experiment. Consent must be given without the use of force, duress, or coercion. The person must also be free to drop out of the experiment at any time. Second, subjects must receive a full explanation of the procedures to be followed, and an offer to answer any questions about the procedures. Third, the potential risks and benefits of the experiment must be made clear. If there is any possibility of pain or injury to subjects, this must be explained in advance so that subjects know what they are getting into. Consent should be given in writing. When the subject is a minor or is impaired, consent should be obtained from a parent or legal guardian. Even in these cases, however, subjects should still be given as much explanation as they can understand, and they should be allowed to refuse to participate, even though permission has been given by the parent or guardian.

THE AMERICAN PSYCHOLOGICAL ASSOCIATION GUIDELINES

Although the law contains specific provisions for the way research is to be conducted, questions may still arise in actual situations. For this reason, the American Psychological Association(APA) has published its own set of ethical principles. The code applies to psychologists and students who assume the role of psychologists by engaging in research or practice. The APA principles include the same general requirements for ensuring the subjects' welfare as in the law, as well as help in evaluating specific cases. The ten APA principles are reproduced in Box 5.1.[1]

1.   You may obtain a copy of the booklet, *Ethical Principles in the Conduct of Research with Human Participants*, by sending a request to the American Psychological Association, 1200 Seventeenth Street N.W., Washington, D.C. 20036.

Box 5.1   The Ethical Principles of the American Psychological Association

The decision to undertake research should rest upon a considered judgment by the individual psychologist about how best to contribute to psychological science and to human welfare. The responsible psychologist weighs *alternative* directions in which personal energies and resources might be invested. Having made the decision to conduct research, psychologists must carry out their investigations *with respect for the people who participate and with concern for their dignity and welfare*. The Principles that follow make explicit the investigator's ethical responsibilities toward participants over the course of research, from the initial decision to pursue a study to the steps necessary to protect the confidentiality of research data. These Principles should be interpreted in terms of the context provided in the complete document offered as a supplement to these Principles.

1. In planning a study the investigator has the personal responsibility to make a *careful evaluation of its ethical acceptability,* taking into account these Principles for research with human beings. To the extent that this appraisal, weighing scientific and humane values, suggests a deviation from any Principle, the investigator incurs an increasingly serious obligation to seek ethical advice and to observe *more stringent safeguards to protect the rights of the human research participant.*

2. Responsibility for the establishment and maintenance of *acceptable ethical practice* in research always remains with the individual investigator. The investigator is also responsible for the ethical treatment of research participants by collaborators, assistants, students, and employees, all of whom, however, incur parallel obligations.

3. Ethical practice requires the investigator to *inform the participant of all features of the research that reasonably might be expected to influence willingness to participate* and to explain all other aspects of the research about which the participant inquires. Failure to make full disclosure gives added emphasis to the investigator's responsibility to protect the welfare and dignity of the research participant.

4. *Openness and honesty are essential characteristics* of the relationship between inves-

tigator and research participant. When the methodological requirements of a study necessitate concealment or deception, the investigator is required to *ensure the participant's understanding of the reasons for this action* and *to restore the quality of the relationship with the investigator.*

5. Ethical research practice requires the investigator to *respect the individual's freedom to decline to participate in research or to discontinue participation at any time.* The obligation to protect this freedom requires special vigilance when the investigator is in a position of *power* over the participant. The decision to limit this freedom increases the investigator's responsibility to protect the participant's dignity and welfare.

6. Ethically acceptable research begins with the establishment of a *clear and fair agreement* between the investigator and the research participant that clarifies the responsibilities of each. The investigator has the obligation to honor all promises and commitments included in that agreement.

7. The ethical investigator *protects participants from physical and mental discomfort, harm, and danger.* If the risk of such consequences exists, the investigator is required to *inform* the participant of that fact, secure consent before proceeding, and take all possible measures to minimize distress. A research procedure may *not* be used if it is likely to cause *serious* and *lasting harm* to participants.

8. After the data are collected, ethical practice requires the investigator to provide the participant with a *full clarification of the nature of the study* and to remove any misconceptions that may have arisen. Where scientific or humane values justify delaying or withholding information, the investigator acquires a special responsibility to assure that there are *no damaging consequences* for the participant.

9. Where research procedures may result in *undesirable consequences* for the participant, the investigator has the responsibility to *detect* and *remove* or *correct* these consequences, including, where relevant, *long-term after effects.*

10. Information obtained about the research participants during the course of an investigation is *confidential.* When the possibility exists that others may obtain access to such information, ethical research practice requires that this possibility, together with the plans for protecting confidentiality, be explained to the participants as a part of the procedure for obtaining informed consent.[2]

2. These principles were written by the Committee on Ethical Standards in Psychological Research. Copyright 1973 by the American Psychological Association; reprinted by permission. Emphasis added.

The guidelines require that whenever there is any question concerning the ethics of an experiment or procedure, the researcher should *seek advice from others and employ all possible safeguards for the subjects* (principle 1). Institutions engaging in research are required by law to have a research review board that makes decisions on each study. (Check with your instructor or supervisor to clarify the procedures that apply in your institution. Always obtain approval for an experiment from an instructor or review committee *before* you begin.)

Even after procedures have been approved, *the individual researcher has the final responsibility for carrying out the study in an ethical way* (principle 2). Obtaining informed consent is especially important. *Subjects are free to refuse to participate, or to discontinue participation, at any time* (principle 5). The responsibilities of both subject and experimenter must be agreed upon in advance, and the experimenter must honor all commitments made to subjects (principle 6). Commitments include such things as promises to pay subjects and to share the results of the study with them.

Deception and Full Disclosure

The relationship between researcher and participants should be open and honest (principle 4). In many psychological studies, however, the true purpose of the study is disguised. For instance, Holloway and Hornstein (1976) did not tell subjects that the experiment began as soon as they came into the waiting room. Subjects sat and listened to a radio that broadcast music and a fictitious news report. Whether subjects heard good news or bad news was the main focus of the study. Subjects later rated others on traits such as honesty. The purpose of the experiment was to determine whether good news would make subjects rate others more favorably. In fact, it did. Holloway and Hornstein clearly used deception in their experiment; subjects had no way of knowing that the experiment began in the waiting room or that the reports they heard were contrived to test the effects of news on attitudes.

When we consider the principles concerning full disclosure of experimental procedures, we must also consider the impact of disclosure on the outcome of the study. If Holloway and Hornstein had told subjects the news reports were fictitious, would they have responded in the same way? There is no way to be sure without actually running such an experiment. But it is possible that the impact of the reports would have been different if subjects had known they were phony. Similarly, in Schachter's (1959) study of anxiety and affiliation, subjects probably would not have become anxious if they had known they would not actually be shocked; they probably would have behaved differently.

Sometimes a small omission, or outright deception, seems necessary to make an appropriate test of the experimental hypothesis. How can this be reconciled with the principles of informed consent? The APA principles give us some guidance: "Ethical practice requires the investigator to inform the participant of all features of the research that reasonably might be expected to influence willingness to participate, and to *explain all other aspects of the research about which the subject inquires*" (principle 3). In other words, if the subjects are misled, the deception must be such that subjects would not refuse to participate if they knew what was really happening. For instance, it would not be ethical to recruit subjects for a learning experiment without telling them we intend to punish their incorrect responses by exposing them to the sound of scratching nails on a blackboard. Since many subjects might decline to participate in such a study, our deception would be unethical. In contrast, as far as we know, Holloway and Hornstein's subjects would probably have consented to hearing a fictitious newscast, just as Schachter's subjects would have agreed to be in a study in which they would not be shocked. Furthermore, in both studies the researchers adhered to the principle of full disclosure by completely debriefing subjects at the end of the experiment—that is, by explaining the nature and the purpose of the studies (principles 4 and 8).

Debriefing, however, can mean other risks. We assume that debriefing will undo the effects of the deception. Is this assumption justified? Is it possible that an explanation of what was done may not relieve subjects' fears? Bramel's (1963) study of projection is an example of a study in which debriefing may have been insufficient. Bramel was interested in studying attributive projection. Attributive projection is the process of projecting traits onto another person. The traits projected are traits the person is consciously aware of having. This makes it different from the classical projection Freud described. In classical projection, the traits projected are those the person is not consciously aware of possessing. In order to ensure that subjects had a consciously possessed trait they might project, Bramel employed a procedural deception. Male subjects were shown photographs of males in various stages of nudity. Subjects were given false feedback about their degree of arousal to the pictures which led them to believe they possessed homosexual tendencies. Bramel then tested the subjects for projection of arousal onto others. He asked them to estimate how aroused other people would be when they saw the pictures. Bramel found that subjects projected arousal onto people who were similar to themselves (other students), but not onto people who were unlike themselves (criminals).

Of course Bramel debriefed all his subjects at the end of the experiment: He told them the feedback had been false: there was no indication of homosexual tendencies in their responses, since this was not even being measured. Was the explanation sufficient? It is possible that for subjects who had doubts about their sexual identity the bogus feedback aroused considerable anxiety and discomfort. It is also possible that subjects may have doubted Bramel's final full disclosure. If he admitted deceiving them about the feedback, perhaps he was also deceiving them about their real responses. At the very least, subjects may have felt cynical about research and perhaps foolish at having been duped by the experimenter. *Whether the effects of deception can ever be fully reversed by debriefing remains a serious ethical question.* Regardless of any later explanation, the subjects' anxiety and discomfort during the experiment are real. Once done, these experiences cannot be undone.

Consider this example of an experiment concerning classical conditioning and extinction in human subjects. Campbell, Sanderson, and Laverty (1964) established classical conditioning in a single trial through the use of a traumatic event. Classical conditioning, first studied in Pavlov's laboratory, involves the pairing of an initially neutral conditioned stimulus (CS) with an unconditioned stimulus (UCS) that always leads to a specific unconditioned (unlearned) response (UCR). After repeated pairings, the originally neutral conditioned stimulus (CS) will lead to a response that resembles the unconditioned response. This response is known as the conditioned response

(CR), since its occurrence is dependent upon the success of the conditioning procedure. Campbell et al. used a drug, succinylcholine chloride dihydrate ("Scoline") to induce temporary paralysis and cessation of breathing in their subjects. Although the paralysis and inability to breathe were not painful, according to subjects' reports the experience was "horrific." "All the subjects in the standard series thought they were dying" (p. 631). The effect of the drug (UCS) led to an intense emotional reaction (UCR). The drug was paired with a tone (CS). Subjects became conditioned to the tone in just one trial. After a single pairing of the tone with the drug, the tone alone was sufficient to arouse emotional upset (CR) in most subjects. The emotional reaction persisted (that is, failed to extinguish) and actually *increased* with repeated presentations of the tone. Whether debriefed or not, these subjects went through a very upsetting experience.

Since we cannot always reverse our experimental effects, it makes sense to avoid procedures that are potentially harmful, painful, or upsetting to subjects (principle 7). In addition to their dubious ethical standing, such procedures often add little to our understanding of behavioral processes. For instance, we know that high anxiety has debilitating effects on many behaviors. What does it add to our understanding of the thinking process to find that subjects learn rhymes, solve riddles, or do anything else less efficiently when they are made anxious? When experimental procedures lead to undesirable consequences for subjects, the experimenter has the responsibility to correct these consequences (principle 9). This could mean holding additional debriefing sessions, or providing continuing counseling or psychotherapy to correct the upset.

Anonymity and Confidentiality

One final consideration is the importance of maintaining anonymity and confidentiality (principle 10). The researcher has the responsibility to protect subjects' privacy. When possible, data should be given anonymously and identified only by code numbers. Thus subjects would indicate only a number on a questionnaire, not names. Data collected are confidential. They may not be used for any purpose not explained to the subject. They do not become items of gossip to be shared with friends. When shared with colleagues, data must also be treated with discretion and subjects' identities protected. Fictitious names or code numbers should be used. Identifying details should be disguised if there is a chance that a subject will be identifiable.

Protecting the Welfare of Animal Subjects

The principles governing informed consent, anonymity, and confidentiality are clearly important aspects of ethical research involving human subjects. However, additional standards must be applied to research involving animals. Guidelines on the care and use of animals are also published by the American Psychological Association.[3] We will review the most important points here.

3. See the *American Psychologist*, 1972, *27*, 337.

Animals do not have the understanding of human subjects, so the notion of informed consent is irrelevant. Animals cannot give consent and they cannot walk out on procedures. Most animal research is done with animals raised in laboratories so they will be available for study. The animals are typically raised in cages and are totally dependent on the experimenter or lab assistant for food, water, and healthy conditions. When using animals for study, the experimenter is responsible for providing adequate care. The animals must be sheltered in clean cages of adequate size. Except when food or water deprivation is a variable for study, they must receive sufficient nourishment. When surgical procedures are required, the animals should be anesthetized and given good postoperative care to ensure the minimum amount of pain and discomfort. If it is necessary to sacrifice an animal, the procedure should be done by a researcher trained to carry it out in a humane fashion. As with human subjects, our concern is to avoid any unnecessary pain or risk to the subject. Research involving any procedure that might be painful to the animals, such as surgery, drug use, or shock, must be closely supervised by a researcher specially trained in the field.

SELECTING SUBJECTS

Populations and Samples

population

Selecting subjects is an important part of any experiment, regardless of its design. First, the researcher must decide who or what the subjects will be. The type of subject needed will depend on what is being studied. If we are doing an experiment on the attitudes of college students, we will obviously want to use college students as subjects. To study the effects of a drug, rats or monkeys might be more desirable. Ideally, when we conduct an experiment we should include all members of the population we wish to study. The **population** consists of all people, animals, or objects that have at least one characteristic in common. All undergraduates form one population; all jelly beans form another.

sample

sample of subjects

Before making statements about "students," "baboons," or "fathers," we ought to examine all the individuals who belong to these populations. But in practice this is rarely possible: An experiment on adult human learning would go on forever if we tried to test all adult humans. It would also be enormously expensive—and what if we missed some people? Would the results be invalid? Because of these problems, the researcher usually tests only a **sample**—a part of something assumed to be representative of the whole. Manufacturers sometimes distribute samples of new products. A small portion of the product gives us an idea of what the product is like so that perhaps we will buy a larger size later. A **sample of subjects** is a group that is a part of the population of interest. The researcher uses a sample of subjects to get an idea of how all members of the population would behave. Data collected from a sample of subjects may be used to draw inferences about a population without examining all its members. In this way pollsters such as Gallup are able to make predictions about the outcome of important elections. Not everyone in the country is questioned in the poll, but we get an idea of how the voting will go on the basis of the responses of those who are sampled.

The way in which the sample is selected is important. Different samples may produce very different data. *The less the sample resembles the whole population, the less likely it is that the behavior of the sample mirrors that of the population.* We could be very wrong about the percentage of votes going to a candidate if we based our predictions on a preelection sample that included only Democrats. The representativeness of a sample poses problems for the way in which we will interpret the results of an experiment. Can we *generalize* the findings to the entire population? Suppose the sample does not reflect what is true of the population; the data we collect may give us an inaccurate picture of the effect of the experimental treatments. We will return to this issue when we discuss the interpretation of experimental results in later chapters. For now, let us look at some sampling problems.

Random Selection

random
selection

In order to obtain the most representative sample, we must select subjects at random. By **random selection** we mean that all individuals in the population being studied have an equal chance of being selected to participate in the experiment. A truly random sample is formed in such a way that there is no bias in favor of selecting one member of the population over another. Also, the selection of one individual should not influence the selection of any other individual. How do these principles apply in practice?

Suppose we want to do an experiment on the use of learning strategies among elderly people. Such research with children (for example, Wolff and Levin, 1972) indicates that learning is better when the researcher provides the child with a strategy for remembering. Would this procedure benefit the elderly, who sometimes have difficulty recalling information? The population we are interested in studying is the population of elderly people, which we might operationally define as all people over age 65. Clearly we cannot study the entire population; what we want is a sample representative of the population. In practice we often find that even this goal cannot be achieved. We may, for example, have access to the residents of one nursing home. Thus the "population" available for study is already a select group. Although we would ultimately like to make statements about the general population of all elderly people, our sample must be taken from this smaller group. Suppose we have access to the 32 residents of a local home for the aged, and our experiment requires only 20 subjects. Assuming that all the residents are willing to participate in the experiment, how do we decide which 20 will take part?

We could simply ask everyone to report to the testing room and allow the first 20 arrivals to be in the study. But some residents may arrive at the testing room later than others for a variety of reasons. Those who are new to the home might not know their way around the grounds and might take more time to find the correct room. General health may be a factor. Individuals who do not feel well may not want to walk to the testing room. Furthermore, there may be significant personality differences between those who get up early and those who sleep late. Thus, a sample of subjects based on arrival time may not be representative of the group as a whole. It would be biased to include a disproportionate number of healthy early-risers who know their way around the building.

Suppose, instead, that we simply test the 20 people who happen to be sitting in the solarium at a given moment. We have now restricted our sample of nursing home residents to the entire group of people in one room. This approach also poses problems. People who sit in the solarium may be different from those who do not. The solarium may provide more opportunity for conversation; residents who stay in their rooms may be more introverted than those who choose to come out. Such a difference could affect the outcome of our experiment. Perhaps extroverted subjects are more likely to develop rapport with the experimenter and use the suggested strategies. The behavior of introverted subjects might be quite different. A bias in favor of including only extroverted subjects would limit our ability to make statements about nursing home residents or elderly people in general because we would expect to find both introverts and extroverts in these populations.

Techniques for Random Selection.   We can get a fairly good random sample of subjects if we write all the prospective subjects' names on small pieces of paper, put them into a hat, mix well, and draw them out one by one until we have as many as we need. To simplify the procedure, we can assign numbers instead of using names. The hat method is usually adequate, but it is not foolproof: A small variation in the size of the papers may bias the selection. The papers may not be mixed enough, so you draw out only names beginning with "X," or only the last numbers you wrote.

If you need many subjects, you may not want to spend your time drawing numbers out of hats. For this reason you should become familiar with the random number table (see Appendix). A **random number table** is a table of numbers generated by a computer so that every number to be used (in this case 00 to 99) has an equal chance of being selected for each position in the table. Unlike the hat method, the computer-generated table is totally unbiased.

random number
table

How do we use the random number table? We begin by assigning code numbers to all members of our subject pool. At the nursing home, we might simply number the subjects in the order they appear on an alphabetical list. If there are 32 people available, we assign them numbers 1 through 32. If we need only 20 subjects, we go through the random number table in an orderly manner (such as by reading vertically down each successive column of numbers) to find the first twenty numbers between 1 and 32 that appear in the table. Look at Appendix Table B1. In the first column, we find the numbers 03, 16, and 12. All are between 1 and 32. So, subjects 3, 16, and 12 will be in our sample. The numbers 97 and 55 also appear in the first column, but since they are greater than 32, we ignore them. We continue going through the table systematically until we have a total of 20 subjects. This group of 20 is a random sample of the 32 people available for the experiment.

To form this group of 20 we arbitrarily began with the first number in the first column. To avoid using the same subject numbers over and over again in our experiments, we start at a different point in the table for each study. The starting point for each study should be decided in a blind manner. For instance, you might close your eyes and put your finger on a part of the table. You would begin your selection there.

Practical Limits.　　Ideally, when we take a random sample, every individual in the population has an equal chance of being selected. In practice, this ideal is rarely achieved. Our samples must be drawn from subsets of the population, such as the residents of one nursing home. Typically we do not have access to all college students. We can sample only the airline passengers at the terminal nearest us. Our nursing home example dealt with a situation in which we have more individuals available than are needed. Unfortunately, this is not always the case[4]: People are often reluctant to participate in an experiment because they feel it will take too much time. Unfortunately, they are also often wary of psychological research. At times individuals seem fearful that the experimenter will uncover very private information. This attitude stems partly from the popularization of Freud's ideas, especially the idea that every action contains an important hidden meaning known only to the trained psychologist. This makes it especially important that we follow ethical guidelines and keep subjects informed of what we are doing.

As you recruit subjects, you may find that you have to use procedures that do not guarantee a random sample. You may have to recruit all your subjects from a single class or location. Students in my classes have found that the lobby of our college library is sometimes a good place to find willing subjects. In desperation, they have also resorted to asking their friends to participate. However, asking friends to be subjects is risky on three counts. First, it can dissolve a friendship. Second, friends may not be totally naive about the purpose of an experiment that you have been talking about for two weeks. They may also be sensitive to subtle cues to behave in particular ways. These cues may influence the way they respond in the experiment and may lead to erroneous data. Third and most important, they may feel obliged to participate. This raises ethical questions concerning free choice. But even when we have the time, energy, and resources to do extensive sampling, another difficulty remains. Since it is unethical to coerce people into participating in an experiment, there is no way of knowing whether those who choose to participate are essentially different from those who do not. Perhaps we would obtain very different data if we tested everyone regardless of personal choice. Without resorting to coercion, there is no way we can ever guarantee a truly random sample.

4.　I recall scouting for subjects to take part in a brief on-the-spot perception experiment that lasted about a minute. Prospective subjects often provided elaborate explanations of why they had no time to participate. Their stories usually lasted longer than the actual experiment.

Reporting Procedures

In reporting an experiment, researchers pay special attention to selection of subjects. Usually, it is not enough to say that a sample was randomly selected; the report must give enough information to enable another researcher to replicate the experiment. The details of the type of subject and the selection process are important parts of the procedure.

The way a sample is chosen also affects what can be concluded from the results. The report must explain recruitment procedures so that the experiment will be interpretable as well as replicable. We need to tell the reader exactly how the sample was obtained. This includes identifying the specific population sampled (for example, college students), as well as an exact description of where and how subjects were obtained (for example, "The subjects were 60 undergraduates [30 males and 30 females] at the University of Oregon who responded to an ad in the college newspaper").

Any details that might have influenced the type of subject participating in the study must be included. If subjects were paid for participating, that fact should be noted. If subjects were recruited from a class and their participation fulfilled a course requirement, readers should be told that too. In our nursing home example, we might say: "The subjects were 20 (8 male and 12 female) randomly selected residents of the Valley Nursing Home in Elmtown, Ohio. Subjects ranged in age from 67.2 years to 73.4 years. The average age was 69.3 years." Note that this statement immediately tells readers that although we are discussing learning in the "elderly," our subjects are drawn at random from a very small pool—namely, the residents of a single nursing home. It also tells readers that we tested both males and females who fell within a particular age range.

Any limitations on who could participate should also be noted. For instance, of the people who responded to the newspaper ad, we may choose to include only those with 20/20 vision, or only those over age 18. We must report whatever restrictions we imposed so that readers know exactly what sorts of subjects we tested. Occasionally some subjects who are selected are not included in the report: they dropped out, their data were discarded because they could not follow the instructions, and so on. These facts should also be reported.

How Many Subjects?

How many subjects are enough for an experiment? 10? 100? There is no simple answer to this question: in later chapters we will discuss experiments that require only one or two subjects, and others that require many more. Usually we want to have more than one or two subjects in each treatment condition. Remember that we use samples of subjects to make inferences about the way the independent variable affects the population. Too small a sample can lead to erroneous results. For instance, if we wanted to know the height of the "average" American adult, we would want a large sample. Samples of two or three people would probably be inadequate even if they were randomly selected. We would hesitate to make statements about millions of people on the basis of such a small sample. Similarly, in an experiment we might hesitate to make great claims for our independent variable on the basis of a few subjects.

Of course, if everyone behaved exactly the same way, if everyone were exactly the same, we could use samples of one or two subjects with confidence. We would know that the results reflect what we would find if we tested everyone in the population. But we know that, in reality, subjects are not all the same. Different subjects will get different scores. Our independent variable may affect different subjects in different ways. The more responses vary, the harder it is to get a sample that reflects what goes on in the population. If individuals in the population are all very similar to one another on the dependent variable, small samples are adequate. However, when individuals are likely to be quite different, larger samples are needed. If we take larger samples, we are more likely to obtain individuals who represent the full range of behaviors on the dependent variable—some people who score high, some who score low, and some who score in between. Thus, a larger sample is more likely to mirror the actual state of the population.

Typically, we get slightly different responses from different subjects in an experiment because of individual differences. Subjects' scores should also differ because of the treatment conditions. We expect the behavior of subjects under different treatment conditions to be noticeably different. We use statistical tests to make comparisons between the behavior of subjects under different treatment conditions. When we discuss test results (Part Three), you will see exactly how these procedures work. As we choose our samples, though, certain general characteristics of these procedures shape our decisions. The statistical procedures we will discuss in this text require computing averages of the results under different treatments. In effect, we ask whether, *on the average*, our independent variable had an effect. We evaluate the effect in terms of the amount of fluctuation we would expect to see among *any* samples measured on our dependent variable. We are not especially interested in the performance of individual subjects in the experiment; we know that individual scores will differ. The question is whether or not we see more of a difference if we look at responses obtained under different treatment conditions.

significant
differences

We use statistical procedures to decide whether the differences we see between responses under different treatment conditions are **significant**: Are they more extreme than the differences we would probably see among *any* groups that we measure on the dependent variable? From a statistical standpoint, it is much harder to show that differences between treatment groups are significant when we use a small number of subjects. This is especially true when individual responses are apt to vary a great deal from one subject to another under any circumstances. For that reason, we usually try to have a reasonably large number of subjects in each treatment group. If the effects of the independent variable are strong, we should be able to detect them with about 10 to 20 subjects per group. A moderately strong effect should show up with about 20 to 30 subjects per group. Weaker effects may be detected through larger groups. Of course, these are only rough estimates. Other factors besides the number of subjects and the impact of the independent variable influence the outcome; a larger sample is no guarantee that an experiment will turn out as you expect.

Practical considerations also affect the total number of subjects to be used. You may plan to have 50, but if you can only get 30 that may have to do. If the experiment requires lengthy individual testing sessions, it may not be feasible to run large numbers of subjects. You can use the review of prior research as a guide. If other researchers have had success with 20 subjects, that is a reasonable number. As a rule of thumb, it is advisable to have at least 10 subjects in each treatment group. Smaller numbers make it very difficult to detect an effect of the independent variable unless it is enormous.

SUMMARY

A well-planned experiment includes careful selection and treatment of the subjects who participate. Today, some aspects of psychological research are regulated by federal law. An institution must, for example, have a review board to approve each study. Many of the law's provisions are reflected in the ethical guidelines of the American Psychological Association. Most important is the *informed consent* of all those who will be subjects in an experiment. This consent must be given freely, without force or coercion. The person must also understand that he or she is free to drop out of the experiment at any time. In addition, subjects must be given as much information about the experiment as possible so that they can make a reasonable decision about whether or not to participate.

Sometimes, however, a researcher may need to disguise the true purpose of the study so that subjects will behave naturally and spontaneously. In experiments that require some deception, subjects must be debriefed. But because simply debriefing subjects does not guarantee that we can undo any upset we caused them, researchers try to avoid exposing subjects to any unnecessary pain or risk. When possible, data should be given anonymously and identified only by code numbers. Data collected are confidential; they may not be used for any purpose not explained to the subject. When they are reported, data should be identified by code number or fictitious names to protect subjects' identities.

Additional ethical principles apply in research with animals. Since animals have no choice about being subjects, researchers have a special responsibility to look out for their welfare. They must receive adequate physical care to keep them healthy and comfortable. If drugs, surgery, or any potentially painful procedures are involved, they must be closely supervised by a researcher who is specially trained in the field.

All experiments pose the problem of how to select subjects. The first decision is what population to study. Depending on what we are studying, one population will be more suitable than another. Since we cannot usually study every member of a population, we must take a *sample*. We try to obtain the sample by selecting subjects at random—by using objective, unbiased selection procedures such as a *random number table*. If our samples are not random, they may not be good reflections of the whole population.

There are no hard and fast rules for deciding exactly how many subjects to use in an experiment. Usually we want to have more than one or two subjects so that the sample will reflect the range of behaviors we would see in the population as a whole. Statistical tests are needed to show whether the differences between behaviors under the different treatment conditions are *significant*—more extreme than the differences we would expect to see among *any* samples measured on the dependent variable. Larger samples are often preferred because it is much harder to show that the independent variable had an effect if the sample of subjects was small.

REVIEW AND STUDY QUESTIONS

1. What is informed consent?

2. What is the principle of full disclosure?

3. At the end of the semester, all students in one section of a general psychology course are told they will not receive credit for the course unless they take part in the instructor's research project. Students who refuse to participate are given Incompletes and do not get credit for the course. Is this approach unethical? Which principles of the APA guidelines have been violated?

4. An experimenter studying the effects of stress gave subjects a series of maze problems to solve. The subjects were led to believe that the problems were all quite easy. In fact, several had no solution. Some of the subjects were visibly upset by their inability to solve the problems. At the end of the study, the experimenter gave no explanation of the procedures. What ethical principles apply in this case? What *should* the experimenter have done?

5. In a study of sexual attitudes, a student experimenter finds that Pat, a friend's spouse, has responded "Yes" to the question "Have you ever had an extramarital affair?" The student is sure that the friend is unaware of Pat's behavior. The student decides to show Pat's answers to the friend. What ethical principles have been violated? How could this situation have been avoided?

6. Have you ever been a subject in a research project? If so, how were ethical principles applied in that study?

7. What ethical principles apply when we do research with animals?

8. Define each of the following terms:
   a. Population
   b. Sample
   c. Random selection

9. Why do we need to select subjects at random?

10. Evaluate each of the following as a technique for obtaining a random sample.
    a. An experimenter obtains subjects by asking every third driver stopping at the light on Hollywood and Vine to be in an experiment.
    b. A researcher places an ad in a local paper asking for volunteers for a psychology experiment.
    c. An experimenter calls every fourth number in the phone book and asks for volunteers for a research project.
    d. A wealthy graduate student posts signs on the university bulletin boards offering $5 per hour for participating in a two-hour perception experiment.
11. What is a random number table?
12. Using the random number table in the back of the book, select a random sample of 10 subjects from a subject pool of 20.

REFERENCES

Bramel, D. Selection of a target for defensive projection. *Journal of Abnormal and Social Psychology,* 1963, *66,* 318–324.

Campbell, D., Sanderson, R. E., and Laverty, S. C. Characteristics of a conditioned response in human subjects during extinction trials following a single traumatic conditioning trial. *Journal of Abnormal and Social Psychology,* 1964, *68,* 627–639.

Holloway, S. M., and Hornstein, H. A. How good news makes us good. *Psychology Today,* 1976, *10,* No. 7, 76 ff.

Schachter, S. *The psychology of affiliation.* Stanford, Calif.: Stanford University, Press, 1959.

Wolff, P., and Levin, J. R. The role of overt activity in children's imagery production. *Child Development,* 1972, *43,* 537–548.

6

Basic Experimental Designs

Key Terms

experimental design	two-group design	random assignment
between-subjects design	two independent groups design	two matched groups design

experimental design

In order to test an experimental hypothesis, a researcher must develop a basic plan or design for the experiment. The **experimental design** is the general structure of the experiment. As we discussed various examples in earlier chapters, you may have noticed that some experiments resembled others in their overall structure. For instance, both Schachter's experiment on anxiety and affiliation and the Holloway and Hornstein study of good and bad news included two groups of subjects and two values of the independent variable. Experiments that test different hypotheses may have the same design. On the other hand, the same hypothesis may sometimes be approached through more than one design. The design is the general structure of the experiment, *not* its specific content. It is made up of such things as the number of treatment conditions and whether the subjects in all conditions are the same or different individuals. The particular design used in an experiment is determined mainly by the nature of the hypothesis. However, prior research, the kind of information the researcher is seeking, and practical problems in running the experiment also influence choice of design.

Although there is an infinite variety of potential hypotheses, a few basic designs may be used for the majority of research questions. Three aspects of the experiment play the biggest part in determining the design: (1) the number of independent variables, (2) the number of treatment conditions needed to make a fair test of the experimental hypothesis, and (3) whether the same or different subjects are used in each of the treatment conditions. We will look at basic research designs in terms of these dimensions. In this chapter, and the next, we will look at designs in which different subjects take part in each condition of the experiment. These are called **between-subjects design** **between-subjects designs.** The name is based on the fact that we draw conclusions from between-subjects experiments by making comparisons between the behavior of different groups of subjects. In Chapter 8, we will look at within-subjects designs in which the same subjects take part in more than one treatment condition of the experiment.

ONE INDEPENDENT VARIABLE: TWO-GROUP DESIGNS

The simplest experiments are those in which there is only one independent variable. As you know, an experiment must have at least two treatment conditions: The independent variable is manipulated in such a way that at least two levels or treatment conditions are created. When only two treatment conditions are needed, the experimenter may choose to form two separate groups of subjects. This approach is **two-group design** known as the **two-group design.** Usually, but not always, one group is a control group, which receives the "zero value" of the independent variable (for example, no drug). The other group, the experimental group, is exposed to a nonzero value of the independent variable. Both groups are then measured on the dependent variable and their behavior compared. If the independent variable has an effect, there should be differences between the two groups on the dependent variable.

There are two variations of the two-group design: One is the two independent groups design, the other is the two matched groups design. Both use two treatment conditions, but they differ dramatically in the way the researcher decides *which* subjects will take part in each treatment condition.

TWO INDEPENDENT GROUPS

two independent groups design In the **two independent groups design,** randomly selected subjects are placed in each of two treatment conditions through random assignment. The first step is to choose subjects through unbiased selection procedures. We may draw names out of a hat or use the random number table to decide which individuals will be in the experiment. Ideally, each member of the population we study should have an equal chance of being selected for our experiment. However, since a two-group design involves two treatment conditions, we also need to make decisions about which individuals will take part in each treatment condition. We do that by using another procedure, random assignment.

Random Assignment

random
assignment

The independent groups design requires that in addition to being selected at random, our subjects are also assigned to the two treatment conditions at random. **Random assignment** means that every subject has an equal chance of being placed in any of the treatment conditions. When we use an independent groups design, we use the same unbiased procedures for assigning subjects to groups that we used in choosing them for the experiment in the first place. Putting subject 3 in the control group should not affect the chances that subject 4 will also be assigned to that group. In an independent groups design, the groups are "independent" of each other. The makeup of one group has no effect on that of the other.[1]

If subjects are not assigned at random, confounding may occur. We may inadvertently put all our witty subjects in the control group, and so distort the outcome of the experiment. Random assignment gives us a better chance of forming groups that are roughly the same on all the extraneous variables that might affect our dependent variable. Assigning subjects at random controls for the differences that exist between subjects before the experiment. In short, it controls for subject variables. When there are two treatment conditions, as in the two independent groups design, assignment may be made by simply flipping a coin. When there are more than two conditions, we may use the random table. These methods eliminate bias; they reduce the chances that our experiment will be confounded because treatment groups are already different when we start the experiment.

Remember that random selection and random assignment are two separate procedures. It is possible to select a random sample from the population, but then assign the subjects to groups in a biased way. The reverse is also possible. Suppose we start out with a nonrandom, biased sample of subjects. We can randomly assign those subjects to our treatment groups. But the original sample is still biased and may not represent the population we are trying to study. Nonrandom selection affects the external validity of an experiment, how well the findings can be applied to the population and other situations. Random assignment, however, is critical to internal validity. If subjects are not assigned at random, confounding may occur. The experiment will not be internally valid because we will not be sure that the independent variable caused the differences observed across treatment conditions. It could be that the differences we see were created by the way we assigned the subjects to the

---

1.   Sometimes we may have to deviate from this ideal plan. For practical reasons, we may want to have equal numbers of subjects in all treatment groups. That may mean that we have to throw our last few subjects into one particular group to even up the numbers. We call this *random assignment with constraints*. The assignment is random, except for our limitations on number per group, equal numbers of males and females per group, and so on.

groups. Box 6.1 describes a two-group experiment in which the researcher failed to assign subjects at random.

Even though the researcher tries to assign subjects at random, however, without objective aids, the assignments may be biased in subtle ways. For instance, without being aware of it, the experimenter may put all the subjects she dislikes into the control condition because it is the most tedious. The treatment groups would then be different even before the experiment begins. If the groups are already different at the start, it might look as though the experimental manipulation is having some

---

Box 6.1   Ulcers in Executive Monkeys

Brady's (1958) study of ulcers in "executive" monkeys has received a great deal of publicity. The monkeys were divided into two groups. An "executive" group was given control of a button connected to an apparatus that produced electric shock. The "executive's" task was to prevent a painful electric shock by hitting the control button at least once every 20 seconds. Each "nonexecutive" was coupled (or yoked) with an executive. If the executive failed to hit the button in time, the nonexecutive would also receive a shock. The nonexecutives had no control over the shock; only the executives could prevent it.

The independent variable in Brady's experiment was control over the shock. The executives had control; the nonexecutives had none. The dependent variable was the development of gastrointestinal ulcers. Brady hypothesized that monkeys which had the responsibility of remaining vigilant and preventing the shock would be more apt to develop ulcers. In other words, their "executive" responsibilities in the experiment would be stressful; they would develop ulcers just as a hard-driving human executive might. After the experimental phase of the experiment ended, Brady sacrificed the monkeys and studied their tissues for signs of ulcers. As predicted, the "executives" had many ulcers; the "nonexecutives" did not.

On the face of it, his experimental procedure appears sound. Brady devised a controlled task that would presumably be more stressful to one treatment group than the other. Executives and nonexecutives were coupled together so that both received the *same* total number of shocks. The only difference was the degree of control the monkeys had over the shocks. Nevertheless, the study has been severely criticized. Weiss (1968) pointed out that Brady's treatment groups were not formed at random. Brady had used a pretest to determine which monkey in each pair could learn to avoid the shock more quickly, and this monkey was then made the executive. The study was not internally valid. The way the treatment groups were formed introduced a confounding variable. We cannot be sure that the requirements of the "executive" job produced ulcers. The "executive" monkeys may have been more sensitive to the shock, or they may have differed in other ways from the nonexecutives before the experiment began. They may, for example, have been more prone to ulcers under any circumstances. In fact, in another study using rats as subjects, Weiss (1968) demonstrated that lack of control over the shocks was apt to be more stressful than being in charge of things—if subjects were assigned to the treatment conditions *at random*. The number of coping attempts and the amount of appropriate or "relevant" feedback were also identified as important variables.

effect, even if it is not. The opposite can also happen. Differences in the treatment groups can mask the effect of the independent variable. Either way, the experiment leads to *false conclusions* about the effects of the independent variable.

Randomization was also important in a classic study by Kelley (1950). Kelley was interested in the effects of people's expectations on their impressions of others. He carried out a two independent groups experiment. General psychology students were given one of two descriptions of a guest lecturer before he came to class. Half the students were told the visitor was "warm," half were told he was "cold." Kelley was careful to hand out the descriptions of the lecturer at random. The guest came and led a 20-minute class discussion. After that, students were asked to report their impressions of him. Their ratings differed in ways which indicated that students who expected the lecturer to be warm reacted more favorably to him.

Why was it important to hand out the descriptions of the lecturer at random? What might have happened if, say, all the "warm" descriptions were given out first? For one thing, students who sit in different parts of the classroom might be different. If we gave out all the "warm" descriptions first, they might go to all the students who sit in the front of the class. Perhaps these students sit up front because they are more interested in the material, or because they arrive earlier. In any case, their reactions to the class may be different from those of people who sit in the back. When it comes time to rate a guest speaker, these attitudes could alter the ratings as much as the descriptions that were given. Again, differences between subjects could confound the results of the experiment.

Forming Independent Groups

Let us look a little more closely at the randomization procedures used to form two independent groups in an experiment.

Zajonc, Heingartner, and Herman (1969) tested the hypothesis that cockroaches would run faster through a simple maze when other roaches were present than when they had to run alone. The hypothesis is based on the principle of social facilitation: in the presence of an audience, the performance of some behaviors improves. Cockroaches should do better in some mazes when other roaches are present. We can test this hypothesis using two independent groups.[2] One group, the experimental group, runs through the maze in the presence of an audience. The control group runs alone. The dependent variable is the average time it takes each group to run the maze. The subjects must be assigned at random to each condition.

We begin by assembling our roaches for the experiment. As we take each roach out of its cage, we flip a coin to decide whether it goes into the experimental or the control group. By assigning subjects at random, we hope to create two groups that

---

2.   Zajonc's actual experiment had a more complicated design to include a test of the effect of drive level as well as the presence of an audience.

are roughly equivalent on important subject variables that could influence the out-come of the experiment. One important subject variable that could affect our results is the weight of each individual subject; heavy subjects might run more slowly than light ones under any circumstances. Weight, then, is a potential source of confounding in this experiment.

Table 6.1 shows the hypothetical weights of subjects assigned at random to the two treatment conditions. As you can see, the weights of individual subjects differ. We would expect this, since subjects differ from one another. If we look at the groups on the whole, however, we find that their *average* weights (represented by $\overline{X}$) are about the same. Even though individual roaches in each group weigh different amounts, the average weight of the groups is about equal. If we chose to, we could evaluate whether the small difference between the groups is statistically significant. We would find that although the groups are not identical, the difference between them is not significant—that is, it is not enough to merit concern. We can accept the groups as equivalent enough for our purposes. Assigning our subjects to the groups at random, we create two groups that are equivalent on an important subject variable. We will not have confounding due to weight in this experiment.

TABLE 6.1   COCKROACHES RANDOMLY ASSIGNED TO TREATMENT CONDITIONS: HYPOTHETICAL WEIGHTS

EXPERIMENTAL GROUP		CONTROL GROUP	
Subject Number	Hypothetical Weight (gm)	Subject Number	Hypothetical Weight (gm)
S_1	1.59	S_6	3.52
S_2	1.26	S_7	1.57
S_3	1.34	S_8	2.31
S_4	3.68	S_9	1.31
S_5	2.49	S_{10}	1.18
$N = 5$		$N = 5$	
$\overline{X}_E = 2.072$		$\overline{X}_C = 1.978$	

Note: Randomization produced two groups of very similar average weight. ($\overline{X}_E$ is about the same as $\overline{X}_C$).

When we assign subjects at random, we expect to form groups that are roughly the same on any subject variables that could affect our dependent variable. This is important because we may not always be aware of every variable that should be controlled. Sometimes we are aware of variables but do not have the tools, the time, or the resources to measure them. Assigning subjects at random controls for differ-ences we have not identified, but which might somehow bias the study.

When to Use a Two Independent Groups Design

How do we decide whether the two independent groups design is appropriate for an experiment? We begin by looking at the hypothesis. If there is only one independent variable, the two independent groups approach may work if the hypothesis can be tested with two treatment conditions. In an experiment like the one on cockroaches, two groups made sense. We simply wanted to see whether cockroaches would run better with (condition 1) or without (condition 2) an audience. When we run the experiment, we carefully assign subjects to the treatment conditions at random.

When we use the two independent groups design, we assume that randomization is successful. We assume that when we start the experiment, the treatment groups are about the same on all the extraneous subject variables that might affect the outcome. Unfortunately, this is not always the way things turn out.

In our cockroach experiment, we assigned subjects to the treatment groups at random. As you saw in Table 6.1, the random assignment produced two groups of very similar average weight. But suppose we do the experiment again. We again take the roaches from their cages and flip a coin to decide which group to put them in. The hypothetical weights of these new groups are shown in Table 6.2 What is wrong? We assigned our subjects at random, but the control group looks much heavier than the experimental group. How can this be? Well, you know that random assignment means every subject has an equal chance of being assigned to either treatment condition. There is always a chance that treatment groups will end up being very different on some subject variables. Here, our random assignment did not work. The control group turned out to be quite heavy compared to the experiment group. Since the dependent variable in this experiment is running speed, the difference in weight may contaminate the results. The way things turned out here, the weight of the two groups is a confounding variable. If there is a difference in the

TABLE 6.2   COCKROACHES RANDOMLY ASSIGNED TO TREATMENT CONDITIONS

EXPERIMENTAL GROUP		CONTROL GROUP	
Subject Number	Hypothetical Weight (gm)	Subject Number	Hypothetical Weight (gm)
S_{10}	1.18	S_4	3.68
S_2	1.26	S_6	3.52
S_3	1.34	S_8	2.31
S_9	1.31	S_5	2.49
S_7	1.57	S_1	1.59
$N = 5$		$N = 5$	
$\overline{X}_E = 1.332$		$\overline{X}_C = 2.718$	

Note: Randomization produced two groups of very different weight.

running speed of the two groups, we cannot be sure whether it is due to the audience or to the difference in weight. The difference in running speed can be explained equally well by either variable.

TWO MATCHED GROUPS

two matched groups design

Randomization does not guarantee that treatment groups will be comparable on all the relevant extraneous subject variables. Researchers therefore sometimes use the second of the two-group procedures, the **two matched groups design.** In this design there are also two groups of subjects, but the researcher assigns them to groups by matching or equating them on a characteristic that will probably affect the dependent variable. The researcher forms the groups in such a way that they are sure to be comparable on an extraneous variable which might otherwise produce confounding.

Matching before and after an Experiment

In order to form matched groups, subjects must be measured on the extraneous variable that will be used for the matching. Table 6.3 shows the way our cockroaches might be divided into two groups matched on weight. Once the roaches have been weighed, we divide them into pairs. The members of each pair are selected so that they have similar weights. For instance, the first pair is made up of subjects 2 and 10. Subject 2 weighs 1.26 grams; subject 10 weighs 1.18 grams. Although they are not exactly equal in weight, they are closer to each other than to any other roaches in the sample. *When it is not possible to form pairs of subjects that are identical on*

TABLE 6.3 COCKROACHES ASSIGNED TO TWO GROUPS MATCHED ON WEIGHT

Pair	EXPERIMENTAL GROUP		CONTROL GROUP	
	Subject Number	Hypothetical Weight (gm)	Subject Number	Hypothetical Weight (gm)
a	S_2	1.26	S_{10}	1.18
b	S_3	1.34	S_9	1.31
c	S_1	1.59	S_7	1.57
d	S_8	2.31	S_5	2.49
e	S_6	3.52	S_4	3.68
	$N = 5$ $\overline{X}_E = 2.004$		$N = 5$ $\overline{X}_C = 2.046$	

Note: The matched groups have very similar average weights ($\overline{X}_E$ is about the same as $\overline{X}_C$). *Within each pair*, the members are assigned to the treatment conditions at random. One member of each pair is randomly chosen to be in the control group; the other member is placed in the experimental group.

the matching variable, the researcher must decide how much of a discrepancy will be tolerated. A difference of .08 grams might be acceptable, but a difference of 2 grams might not. According to Underwood (1966), the decision is arbitrary. However, we obviously want to make good enough matches to ensure that our groups are not significantly different on the matching variable. If there is no suitable match for an individual in the sample, that individual must be eliminated from the study. After all the pairs have been formed, we randomly assign one member of each to the experimental condition. We can do this by simply flipping a coin. It is very important to put the members of each pair into the treatment conditions at random. If we do not, we may create a new source of confounding—exactly what we are trying to avoid.

In this example, the matching is done before the experiment is run. In some experiments, it may not be feasible to do the matching beforehand. Suppose we need to match our subjects on intelligence. We may not be able to give an intelligence test, score it, match and assign subjects to groups, and run the actual experiment in a single block of time. Since we must know the test scores before we can do the matching, we might need a separate testing session just to give the test. In these situations, we may proceed differently. We make the initial assignment to conditions at random and run the experiment with two randomly assigned groups of subjects that may or may not be comparable on our matching variable. Our subjects take part in the treatment conditions as usual. However, we also give them the intelligence test (that is, we measure them on the matching variable). When the experiment is over, we use the intelligence test scores to match them across the two groups, discarding those subjects in each group that cannot be matched. This process is summarized in Table 6.4. As you can see from the table, matching after the experiment is run may create problems. We cannot be sure there will be a suitable match for each subject in our sample. Some subjects will have to be discarded if no match is available. The net result is that the total number of subjects available for analysis may be smaller than we had planned. Having less data reduces the chance of detecting

TABLE 6.4   MATCHING SUBJECTS AFTER THE EXPERIMENT: PAIRING OF SCORES ON THE MATCHING VARIABLE, INTELLIGENCE

EXPERIMENTAL GROUP		CONTROL GROUP	
Subject Number	IQ	IQ	Subject Number
S_1	109	91	S_6
S_2	94	100	S_7
S_3	116	111	S_8
S_4	102	(63)	S_9
S_5	(133)	115	S_{10}

Note: Connecting lines represent final pairs of subjects. Subjects 5 and 9 must be discarded because there are no suitable matches for them in the sample.

the effect of the independent variable. For this reason, matching before running the experiment is preferable to matching after it.

When to Use Two Matched Groups

Whether to match at all is another question. The advantages are clear: By matching on a variable that is likely to affect the dependent variable, we eliminate one possible source of confounding. We do not need to *assume* that our treatment groups are comparable on an important extraneous variable; we can make them comparable through matching. When we match we also use statistical procedures that differ from those used with randomly assigned groups. We will look at these procedures in some detail in Part Three of the book; it is enough to say here that the matched groups procedure allows us to make comparisons based on the differences between the members of each of our matched pairs of subjects. Because some of the effects of individual differences are controlled within each pair, the impact of the independent variable is clearer. We are able to compare the responses of rather similar subjects who were tested under different treatment conditions. Procedures for randomly assigned groups require that we pool our data and make comparisons between group averages. This makes it somewhat harder to detect the effect of our independent variable: We are forced to look at treatment effects along with the effects of individual differences. If our independent variable has an effect, we are more likely to detect it in our data if we have used matching.

Matching procedures are especially useful when we have very small numbers of subjects because there is a greater chance that randomization will produce groups that are dissimilar. The risk is not so great when we are working with large numbers of subjects. The larger the groups, the better the chances that randomization will lead to similar groups. For example, if we have only two subjects, one heavy and one light, there is no chance at all of forming similar groups. We will always have one heavy "group" and one light "group." As we add additional subjects, the odds are better that random assignment will produce similar groups.

Since there are advantages in using the matched groups design, why not always use it? By matching on a variable such as weight, we can guarantee that our treatment groups will be similar on at least one extraneous variable. Unfortunately, there are potential disadvantages in this procedure too, disadvantages related to the statistical techniques used to analyze the data from two-group experiments. *When we match, it is essential that we match on the basis of an extraneous variable that is highly related to the dependent variable of the experiment.* In an experiment on weight loss, it would make sense to begin by matching subjects on weight. Subjects who are already heavy may be more likely to lose weight during the experiment. It would not make sense to match subjects on weight in an experiment on how to teach spelling to 12-year-olds because it is difficult to see any clear connection between weight and spelling ability. It would be more appropriate to match on another variable such as intelligence; intelligence *does* affect the ability to spell. We would want to match on intelligence to avoid getting two groups of different IQ who would learn spelling at different rates regardless of the teaching method. Unfortunately, it is not always easy to know what variables are the best to use for matching. If we match on a variable that is not highly correlated with the dependent variable, it will be more difficult to detect the effect of experimental manipulations. Box 6.2 summarizes the guidelines for setting up two-group designs.

Box 6.2   **Using a Two-Group Design: Guidelines**

Use a two-group design whenever two values of the independent variable are needed to test a hypothesis. Usually, but not always, one condition will be a control condition in which you administer the zero value (no manipulation) of the independent variable. The second condition will be an experimental condition in which you use a nonzero value of the independent variable. In addition to selecting subjects at random, you must assign your subjects to the treatment conditions at random: Each subject must have an equal chance of being assigned to each of the two conditions. If subjects are not assigned at random, there may be confounding in the experiment: The two treatment groups may be different before the experiment begins. If they are different to start with, you will not be able to tell whether differences in the dependent variable across conditions are due to the experimental manipulation or to the initial difference between the groups.

   To avoid confounding because of subject variables, you may want to form matched groups of subjects. Matched groups are used when we do not want to assume that randomization alone was enough to produce two equivalent groups. We form matched groups by first measuring subjects on the variable that will be used for matching. Then we divide the subjects into pairs. The pairs are formed so that the members are roughly the same on the matching variable (for example, subjects with similar personalities). Then we randomly assign one member of each pair to the experimental condition; the other member of each pair is placed in the control condition. This guarantees that the final groups of subjects are about the same on the matching variable. If we cannot do the matching before the experiment, we can randomly assign the subjects to the treatment conditions first. Then we carry out the experiment and measure the subjects on the matching variable. After the experiment, we form our pairs and discard the data of subjects that have no suitable match in the sample. We can lose data this way, so it is a good idea to do the matching before the experiment begins.

SUMMARY

The *design* of an experiment is its general structure, the experimenter's plan for testing the hypothesis. Design is the general structure of the experiment, not its specific content. The design of an experiment is decided mainly on the basis of three factors: (1) the number of independent variables in the hypothesis, (2) the number of treatment conditions needed to make a fair test of the hypothesis, and (3) whether the same or different subjects are used in each of the treatment conditions.

Between-subjects designs are designs in which different subjects take part in each condition of the experiment. The name comes from the fact that we draw conclusions from between-subjects experiments by making comparisons between the behavior of different groups of subjects. We have looked at two main types of between-subjects designs: *two independent groups* and *two matched groups*.

The two independent groups design is used when one independent variable must be tested at two treatment levels or values. Usually one of the treatment conditions is a control condition in which the subjects receive the zero value of the independent variable. The other condition is an experimental condition in which the subjects are given some nonzero value of the independent variable. The independent groups design is based on the assumption that subjects are assigned at random. If treatment groups are different on a variable related to the dependent variable of the experiment, the result may be *confounding*. When we use an independent groups design, we assume that randomization was *successful*. Sometimes, however, especially when the total number of subjects is small, we do not want to rely on randomization. Even with random assignment, sometimes treatment groups start out being different from each other in important ways. These differences can affect the dependent variable, and we may not be able to separate the effects of the independent variable from the effects of the initial differences between the groups.

Instead of relying on randomization, we may want to use the *matched groups approach*. In a matched groups design we select a variable that is highly related to the dependent variable and measure subjects on that variable. For a two-group experiment, we form pairs of subjects having similar scores on the matching variable, and then randomly assign one member of each pair to the experimental condition. The other member of each pair is placed in the control condition.

Matching is advantageous because we can guarantee that groups start out the same on variables that matter. However, there are also disadvantages: We do not always know what we should use as our matching variable. Because of the statistical tests used for matched groups, we have to be sure that our matching variable is really related to our dependent variable. If it is not, we will have less chance of showing whether or not the independent variable had an effect.

REVIEW AND STUDY QUESTIONS

1. What is the design of an experiment?
2. What features of the experimental hypothesis affect the choice of a design?
3. Explain random assignment.
4. How does random assignment differ from random selection?
5. Why is it important to assign subjects to each treatment condition at random?
6. Describe a matched groups design. How is the matching done?

7. A watched pot never boils. What design can you use to test this notion? How many treatment conditions do you need?

8. You are planning an experiment to test whether students learn better *with* or *without* a radio playing while they study.
   a. What will be your independent and dependent variables?
   b. How will you define them operationally?
   c. What type of design will you use?
   d. Is more than one design possible?
   e. What subject variables will you need to control?

9. A skeptical student tells you that it's silly to bother with two groups of subjects. After all, you're really only interested in what the experimental group does. How would you convince the student otherwise?

10. A researcher would like to match subjects on weight for an experiment on weight control. Below are the weights of each subject in the sample. Match them into pairs and form one experimental and one control group by using random assignment.

Subject Number	Weight	Subject Number	Weight
S_1	115	S_9	122
S_2	185	S_{10}	160
S_3	163	S_{11}	159
S_4	122	S_{12}	154
S_5	165	S_{13}	143
S_6	183	S_{14}	143
S_7	184	S_{15}	138
S_8	115	S_{16}	137

11. As you formed pairs for question 10, you may have found you had to accept "matches" that were not perfect. How much of a discrepancy did you tolerate within each pair? What requirements of the matching procedures did you consider as you made your decisions?

REFERENCES

Brady, J. V. Ulcers in "executive" monkeys. *Scientific American*, 1958, *199* (4), 95–100.

Kelley, H. H. The warm-cold variable in the first impressions of persons. *Journal of Personality*, 1950, *18*, 431–439.

McGuigan, F. J. *Experimental psychology: A methodological approach*, 2nd. ed. Englewood Cliffs, N.J.: Prentice-Hall, 1968.

Weiss, J. M. Psychological factors in stress and disease. *Scientific American*, 1972, *226* (6), 104–113.

Zajonc, R. B., Heingartner, A., and Herman, E. M. Social enhancement and impairment of performance in the cockroach. *Journal of Personality and Social Psychology*, 1969, *13*, 83–92.

7

Experiments with More Than Two Groups

Key Terms

multiple-group design

multiple independent groups design

factorial design

factor

two-factor experiment

main effect

interaction

higher-order interactions

In the last chapter we saw how we can test a variety of hypotheses by using two groups of subjects. We run subjects through two sets of treatment conditions so that we can see how their behavior differs when the independent variable has different values. We can use groups of subjects who are assigned to the treatment conditions at random, or matched on a relevant subject variable. In this chapter we will look at two additional types of designs, multiple-group and factorial designs. Like the two-group designs, they can be carried out using the between-subjects approach: Different groups of subjects participate in the different treatment conditions of the experiment. But we use these designs when two conditions are not enough to tell us what we want to know.

MULTIPLE-GROUP DESIGNS

multiple-group
design

multiple
independent
groups design

Sometimes it takes more than two treatment conditions to make a good test of a hypothesis: In an experiment to test the effectiveness of a new drug, we might need to test several different dosages. A simple comparison between the presence or absence of the drug would be too crude to assess its effects adequately; the amount of a drug makes a difference in how well it works. In situations where the amount or degree of the independent variable is important, we usually need a **multiple-group design**: a design in which there are more than two groups of subjects and each group is run through a different treatment condition. Usually one of the treatment conditions is a control condition in which subjects receive the zero value of the independent variable. The most commonly used multiple-group design is **multiple independent groups,** in which the subjects are assigned to the different treatment conditions at random. It's also possible to use multiple groups and match subjects. The basic procedures are the same as those used in the two matched groups design, except that there are more than two treatment conditions. Because most researchers use the randomized approach, we will do the same here.

Do you remember the experiment on coffee drinking and productivity from Chapter 4? In the initial experiment, we compared the performance of an experimental group that drank one cup of coffee with a control group that drank no coffee. We concluded that coffee drinking apparently had a positive effect on productivity. If one cup of coffee is beneficial, perhaps two or more might be even better. We could now repeat the experiment, expanding it to include more values or levels of the independent variable. Suppose we conduct the experiment again with three groups of subjects, one control group and two experimental groups. The control group (C) drinks no coffee. The first experimental group (E_1) drinks one cup; the second experimental group (E_2) drinks two cups. Assume that the hypothesis is confirmed again: The more coffee subjects drink, the more productive they are. The hypothetical results are illustrated in Figure 7.1, which reflects a gradual increase in productivity as the amount of coffee consumption increases.

By now we may be fairly convinced that coffee enhances productivity. But let us try just one more experiment. This time we will have four groups, one control and three experimental groups. The hypothetical outcome of this experiment is illustrated in Figure 7.2. Again we see that moderate amounts of coffee appear to enhance productivity. However, something different seems to be happening to group E_3. Group E_3 received the largest amount of coffee, but productivity for this group is *low* relative to the other groups. Although the smaller amounts of coffee seems to increase productivity, the larger amount seems to inhibit it. These fictitious results

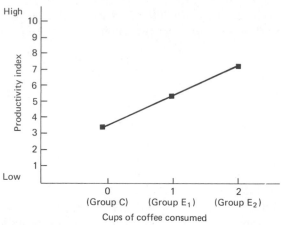

Figure 7.1   Productivity as a function of the amount of coffee consumed (fictitious data).

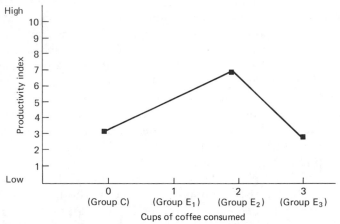

Figure 7.2   Productivity as a function of the amount of coffee consumed (fictitious data).

resemble some actual research findings. Broadhurst (1959), for example, reported that subjects perform best on complicated tasks when they have a moderate amount of drive (that is, motivation). This is paradoxical: When we have little motivation, we do not accomplish much. But too much motivation interferes with performance. Think about taking a test: A little anxiety stimulates you and helps you to do better. But if you are extremely anxious, you may not remember anything; your mind goes blank and you do not do very well.

Because different values of the same independent variable can produce different effects, researchers often test *more* than two levels of an independent variable. By using more than two conditions, they can often get a better idea of how the independent variable operates. They need to test such variables across a wide range of values to get an understanding of how they work.

Choosing Treatments

What if we decide that we need more than two treatment conditions? How do we know how many to use? Some variables have an infinite number of possible values; we could not test them all even if we wanted to. We might be able to create many different conditions, but using all of them might not make sense. Let us look at an actual experiment by Lassen (1973) which illustrates how an experimenter can zero in on the appropriate number of conditions.

Lassen (1973) was interested in what happens during a patient's initial interview with a therapist. In particular, she thought that seating arrangements might affect the amount of anxiety patients showed during their first session. Lassen used a multiple-group design to test the hypothesis that patients would show more anxiety with increasing distance from the therapist. Three groups of patients were randomly assigned to each of three experimental conditions. In the first condition, patients were seated 3 feet away from the therapist. In the second condition, patients were seated 6 feet away, and in the third condition they were 9 feet away. The sessions were tape-recorded. Later the tapes were used by raters who evaluated the amount of anxiety displayed by each of the patients during the sessions. Lassen found that patients seated 3 feet away from the therapist showed less anxiety than patients in the 6-feet condition. Patients who were seated 9 feet away showed the most anxiety. The therapists who ran the sessions, however, unanimously preferred the 6-feet condition, although they adapted to the 3-feet condition "unless a patient was particularly flirtatious, hostile, odorous, or fat" (p. 231). They were less comfortable in the 9-feet condition, feeling out of touch.

Lassen's independent variable, the distance between patient and therapist, can take on an infinite number of values. Some, of course, are obviously inappropriate for this experiment. We could seat patients and therapists in the same chair. A distance of a mile would be even more ridiculous. Still, there are many other real possibilities. Lassen could have placed patients at 1 foot. She could have used 18 or even 100 feet. Why did she restrict the conditions to 3, 6, and 9 feet? Let us try to imagine some of the thinking that might go into the choice of these three condtions:

I want to see the effect of different distances between patient and therapist in the first session. I know there are an infinite number of possible distances. Which ones make the most sense? Well, in our culture strangers usually don't stand too close to one another to have a conversation. Most people think it's rude for a stranger to come very close to ask a question. We prefer to have a little distance between us. From what I've seen of people's behavior, 3 feet seems to be about as close as people want to stand when they are talking to someone they don't know very well. Patients and therapists would rarely want to get closer than this. If we look at the way that furniture is arranged in therapists' offices, the closest chairs seem to be about 3 feet apart. So it makes sense to use 3 feet as the smallest distance I will test.

Now about the greatest distance. I can eliminate distances over about 20 feet because patient and therapist would probably have difficulty hearing each other if they were that far apart. Anyway, most consultation rooms aren't that large. People seem to feel that much distance isn't appropriate. What about 20 feet? Even that seems too great. It's just not comfortable to talk to someone that far away. The chairs in consultation rooms seem to be placed no more than 10 feet apart. Since I've decided to use 3 feet as my smallest distance, I'll use 9 feet as my largest distance. That way I'll have two conditions that are proportional to one another: Nine feet is exactly three times as far as 3 feet.

I'd also like to test a distance in between these two extremes so that I'll have a better idea of how distance affects patients' behavior. I could use several conditions between 3 and 9 feet, but one is probably enough to give me a good idea of how distance affects anxiety. So I'll use one more condition. Since my extremes are 3 and 9 feet, I'll make the middle condition 6 feet. That way I'll have three conditions that are all proportional to one another. Six feet is twice as far as 3 feet, the smallest distance. Nine feet is three times as far as the smallest distance.

Actually, if you consult Lassen's article, you will find that her decisions were dictated by prior research. She cites Hall's (1966) space dimensions as the source of her choices. Hall described a number of space categories, including personal distance–far ($2\frac{1}{2}$ to 4 feet), social distance–close (4 to 7 feet), and social distance–far (7 to 12 feet). As you can see, Lassen set up her treatment conditions to fit these categories.

But notice that Lassen chose conditions that are proportional to one another. Given Hall's categories, she could have used distances of 3, 5, and 12 feet. Instead she chose to use 3, 6, and 9 feet. Why? You will find that research involving quantitative variables is usually done this way. You may see an experimenter using drug doses of, say, 5, 10, and 15 mg. You are less likely to see one in which the experimenter uses randomly chosen doses such as 2, 9, and 14 mg. It is possible to do experiments with conditions that are selected at random rather than planned. Sometimes that is the only possible way. However, many researchers prefer to be able to make statements about conditions that are proportional. For instance, Lassen could see very clearly from her study whether doubling the distance between the patient and the therapist also doubled the patient's rated anxiety.

When you think about using a multiple-group design, always think in terms of the hypothesis you are testing. The principal question you should ask is this: *What will I gain by adding these extra conditions to the experiment?* Lassen was interested in evaluating the usefulness of Hall's categories. Since there were several categories, it made sense for her to use more than two treatment conditions. It is also reasonable from a commonsense viewpoint. The effect of distance, like stimulation, might be complex. Instead of simply increasing as the distance increases, the patient's anxiety might increase to a point and then decline. For instance, at a very great distance, patients might feel out of touch and uninvolved with their sessions. Using three conditions gave Lassen a better idea of *how* distance of the therapist works within its usual range of values.

Let us return to another experiment in which the researchers decided *not* to use the multiple-group approach. Instead of using only "good" and "bad" news stories, Holloway and Hornstein (1976) could also have used "super," "very good," "not so good," "very bad," and "horrid." However, these additional levels may have added little to our understanding of the effects of news. Holloway and Hornstein used only those levels that were critical to their hypothesis. Since the hypothesis dealt with the effects of good versus bad news, it was appropriate to test only these contrasting levels. Notice that the levels chosen were at *opposite* ends of the continuum. Researchers try to use extreme values of a variable. They do this to maximize the possibility of seeing a change across conditions. The effects of "good" versus "very good" stories might be about the *same*. If we test values that are further apart, we are more likely to find a difference if one exists. Sometimes the difference in extreme values is all we are interested in. Then it is more economical to use a two-group design, even though a multiple-group design is possible. As a general rule of thumb, select the simplest design that will make an adequate test of your hypothesis.

Practical Limits

As you set up experiments, you will make decisions about which comparisons will provide the most appropriate test of the hypothesis. An experiment that includes several levels of the independent variable can often yield more information than one which includes only two groups. However, practical considerations also affect choice of design. The multiple randomized groups procedures assume that treatment groups are formed by random assignment. Thus, there will be as many different treatment groups in the experiment as there are levels of the independent variable. If you have five levels of the independent variable, you will need five groups of subjects. It may be difficult to find enough subjects to make this design feasible. Running additional levels also takes more time. The statistical procedures are a little more complicated than those used with the two-group design. Thus, it makes sense to think through all the advantages and disadvantages of the multiple-group design before you begin your experiment. A review of the experimental literature in the area should guide you. If prior researchers have consistently used two-group designs to compare only the most extreme values of the independent variable, you may want to do the same. However, if others have used additional levels to gather information, this may be the most appropriate strategy.

MORE THAN ONE INDEPENDENT VARIABLE: FACTORIAL DESIGNS

All the designs we have looked at so far had only one independent variable. But in real life, variables rarely occur alone. It often seems most appropriate to look at more than one variable at a time. Suppose we wanted to see whether talking to plants actually makes them grow better. Like any other hypothesis, this one would have to be tested in a rigorous, controlled fashion. We could set up a simple experiment in which talking is the independent variable. But we might also want to know whether music is beneficial to plants. We could run another experiment in which music is the independent variable. This approach is very inefficient: We may need twice as many plants, and perhaps twice as much time to carry out two experiments rather than one. It also has another disadvantage. There may be a relationship between the effects of music and talking. Perhaps plants that get conversation do not need music. Maybe they prefer music to conversation. There is no way to look for these kinds of relationships if we study music and conversation separately. We need another kind of experimental design, one that enables us to look at the effects of more than one

factorial design   independent variable at a time.

factor   Designs in which we study two or more independent variables at the same time are called **factorial designs.** The independent variables in these designs are called **factors.** The simplest factorial design has only two factors; it is called a **two-factor**

two-factor   **experiment.**

experiment   The data we get from a factorial experiment give us two kinds of information. First, they give us information about the effect of each independent variable in the experiment. These are called main effects. Second, they enable us to ask this question: How does the operation of one independent variable affect the operation of another in the experiment?

Looking for Main Effects

main effect   **A main effect** is the action of one independent variable in an experiment. When we measure a main effect, we are asking: How much did the changes in this independent variable across treatment conditions change subjects' behavior? When we look more closely at statistical tests, we will look at this definition again in a more quantitative way. However, keep in mind that a main effect is simply changes in behavior associated with changes in the value of *one* independent variable. It is the effect that interests us—what happened because of our experimental manipulation.

When we have only one independent variable in an experiment, we do not usually talk about main effects, although we could. There is only one main effect in an experiment with one independent variable. When there is more than one independent variable, there are as many main effects as there are independent variables. These main effects may or may not be statistically significant. To tell whether they are, we need to carry out statistical tests. When we do those tests, we evaluate the impact of each independent variable in the experiment. We test whether each main effect is statistically significant.

Looking for Interactions

Factorial designs are useful because they allow us to look at the effects of more than one independent variable at a time. This is more efficient than running several different experiments, but it also has another advantage. The factorial design gives us the chance to test for relationships *between* independent variables. Earlier we posed the notion that plants that get conversation might not need music. This is one interaction

example of how two (or more) variables might affect each other. When this kind of relationship exists, we say we have an **interaction**.

An interaction is present if there is a change in the effect of one independent variable when *another* independent variable in the experiment changes value. For instance, we could suppose that music might be helpful to plants that are always ignored. But the same music might have no effect on plants exposed to speech. In other words, there could be an interaction between these two variables. Let us look at a more realistic example. A few drinks at a party can make you feel relaxed and happy. If you are upset or anxious, a sleeping pill may help you to sleep. By themselves, alcohol and sleeping pills in moderation may not be especially harmful. But take the two together, and you may end up dead or in a coma. There is an interaction between these two substances: the effect of the two together is different from the effect of each taken alone.

The number of possible interactions depends on the number of independent variables in the experiment. When there are two independent variables, there is usually only one possible interaction.[1] The two independent variables may interact with each other. When there are more than two independent variables, the picture might be more complex. We can get **higher order interactions** that involve more than two variables at a time. For instance, in a three-factor experiment, it is possible to get an interaction between all three independent variables: The action of each independent variable could be influenced by the values of the other two.

higher-order
interactions

Like main effects, we measure interactions quantitatively through statistical tests—we evaluate their significance. It is possible to run an experiment and find that an interaction between variables is significant even though the main effects are not. We may also get significant main effects with no significant interaction. All possible combinations of outcomes can occur. We will look at some at these possibilities more closely in our discussion of statistical procedures. Box 7.1 presents an actual research problem that can be approached through factorial designs.

Box 7.1   **Dichotic Listening: A Factorial Approach**

To understand the nature of the problem, try to imagine this situation: You are at a party. It is a large party and the room is crowded. On every side of you, people are carrying on conversations. But in spite of all the noise and confusion, you are able to follow one voice saying, "Hi. I'm Chris. I'm a silversmith. Didn't I see you at the Crafts Fair last week?" Cherry (1953) called this the "cocktail party phenomenon." In spite of all the distracting noises, voices, and competing messages, we are able to select just one voice to listen to. Cherry's observations led him and other researchers into the study of *selective attention*, the process by which we take in some of the available input and reject the rest.

The technique Cherry developed for studying this phenomenon is called *dichotic listening*: The subject listens with both ears, but each ear gets a different verbal message. It's a bit like

---

1.   The picture is more complicated when we have the same subjects in more than one treatment condition of the experiment.

trying to listen to two telephone conversations at the same time. Most of us are not able to do that very well, so we listen on one line and put everyone else on "hold."Of course, we need an objective measure to judge how well subjects can separate incoming messages in the dichotic listening task. We do not want to rely on subjects' general impressions of how well they do. Cherry asked his subjects to "shadow" one of the two messages, to repeat one of the messages as it was presented. How accurate a subject is in shadowing one message is a clear indication of how well that subject is able to separate the two messages that are presented.

Many variables may affect our ability to separate two incoming messages. Anne Treisman, noted for her work in this area, explored the effects of a number of physical and linguistic variables. (See, for example, Treisman, 1964.) Our example is based on some of her work.

One thing that we want to know about dichotic listening is whether the voices that carry the messages are important. Is it easier to separate two messages spoken by dissimilar voices? It seems likely that it would be. It might be harder for subjects to disentangle words spoken by similar voices—say, two deep male voices. We can explore changes in the speaker's voice as an independent variable: We simply manipulate the speaker's voice in a two-group experiment. For half the subjects, two similar incoming messages are spoken by similar voices. For the remaining subjects, the messages are spoken by two voices that differ along specified dimensions—say, the sex of the speaker. We have two levels of our voice variable, similar and different.

We may also want to study the effects of the content of the nonshadowed message. The content of the message is probably important. (How often has your attention shifted from one speaker to another when you heard your name mentioned?) If both messages have similar content—that is, they deal with the same subject matter—will it be harder for subjects to separate them? Now, we could run a second two-group experiment to test this notion. One group of subjects would hear two messages that have similar content—perhaps passages from the same story. The other group would hear two messages that have different content—perhaps passages from different stories. We would measure our dependent variable (shadowing) to assess the effect of changing the message content.

As you can guess, this may not be the most efficient way to handle our questions about these variables. Two experiments can be time-consuming. Also, if we run two experiments, we cannot answer any questions about the relationship between the two variables. After all, in reality, the speaker's voice and the content will often change together. Does the effect of the speaker's voice make a difference depending on whether the content of the messages is the same or different? Will the content be more critical when the voices are similar? In short, do these variables interact with each other in some way? We can only assess the way our variables operate together if we do one experiment that enables us to study the impact of both variables at the same time. To do this, we need a factorial design.

Laying Out a Factorial Design

We can use a factorial design to approach the research problem outlined in Box 7.1. We can study the effects of speaker's voice and message content on shadowing in the same study. Speaker's voice is one factor; message content is another. We will use only two levels (values) of each factor, testing the effects of extreme values. It helps to look at our design graphically as we set it up. If you can translate your thinking about an experiment into a simple diagram, you will find it easier to understand what you're testing and what kind of design you're using.[2] Figure 7.3 illustrates our two-factor experiment. Your diagram will be more complex if you are working with more than two factors, or more than two levels of each factor.

We begin by diagramming the basic components of the design, the two factors (1). Notice that we label each factor with a number. These numbers may be used later as a shorthand way of referring to the factors in the final report. We are planning to use two levels of the voice factor. Our question about the effect of the voice at this point is simply whether or not it has *any* effect on shadowing. It makes sense to use "similar" and "dissimilar" as the two levels of this factor. We can always explore

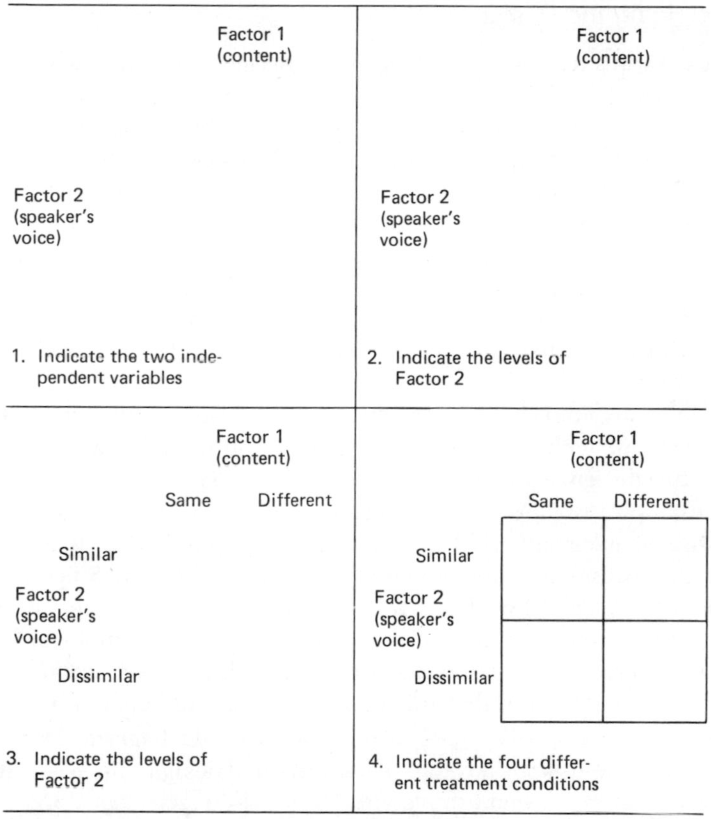

Factor 1
(content)

Factor 1
(content)

Factor 2
(speaker's
voice)

Factor 2
(speaker's
voice)

1. Indicate the two inde-
   pendent variables

2. Indicate the levels of
   Factor 2

Factor 1
(content)

Same   Different

Factor 1
(content)

Same   Different

Similar

Factor 2
(speaker's
voice)

Dissimilar

Similar

Factor 2
(speaker's
voice)

Dissimilar

3. Indicate the levels of
   Factor 2

4. Indicate the four different treatment conditions

Figure 7.3 Diagramming a two-factor design.

2. You can also use the diagram later as you do the appropriate statistical tests. Values of the dependent variable, say the percentage of words correctly shadowed, would be recorded in the cells. (See also Part Three.)

more subtle differences in future studies. This is exactly what we would do if we were setting up a two-group design with speaker's voice as our independent variable. We may indicate the two levels of the voice factor in the diagram simply by "similar" and "dissimilar" (2). We predicted that the content of the messages has an effect. Since we want only two values of the content variable, we can use "same" and "different" as treatment levels, just as we would in a two-group design. Again we indicate "same" and "different" in our diagram (3). We now draw in the four separate cells that represent the four treatment conditions needed in the experiment (4). If we assign our subjects to the conditions at random, each cell also represents a different group of randomly assigned subjects. Some subjects will hear similar voices speaking the same content; others will hear similar voices speaking different content, etc.

Describing the Design

We know this is a two-factor experiment because there are two independent variables. However, there is another common way of describing factorial designs. It is a shorthand method which actually gives us more information. The design we are looking at here is called a "2 × 2 factorial design" (read as two by two factorial design). This notation tells us several things about the experiment it describes. First, the numbers tell us the number of factors involved. Here there are two numbers (2 and 2). Each number refers to a different factor. Hence this experiment has two factors. The value of each number tells us how many levels each factor has. If we have a 2 × 2 design we automatically know there are 2 levels of each of the 2 factors of the experiment. We also know that the experiment has four different conditions (the product of 2 × 2).

Although our example involves only two factors, it is possible to design factorial experiments with any number of factors. The number of factors will determine the way the design is labeled—an experiment involving three independent variables, for example, is called a three-factor experiment. The numerical notation indicates additional information. If an experiment is referred to as a "2 × 2 × 3 factorial design," we immediately know several things about it. Since three digits are mentioned (2, 2, and 3) we know this experiment involves three independent variables. The numerical value of each digit also tells us the number of levels of each of the factors. We know that the first factor has 2 levels; the second has 2; and the third has 3. We also know that this experiment has 12 separate conditions (the product of 2 × 2 × 3). Figure 7.4 (p. 113) presents a sample diagram of a 2 × 2 × 3 experiment. Box 7.2 presents another example of a factorial design, one based on a real experiment in which there was an interaction.

Box 7.2   *An Experimental Interaction*: Depression and Reinforcement

Miller and Seligman (1973) were interested in the relationship between depression and the way people perceive reinforcement. They suggested that depression is similar to learned helplessness, a condition seen in animals that have been treated in particular ways. In the early studies of learned helplessness (for example, Seligman, Maier, and Solomon, 1969), dogs were placed in cages with electrified grids and given shocks at varying intervals. The shocks were not dependent on anything the dogs did. In effect, shocks occurred at random. The dogs could not avoid the shocks or escape them. Following these experiences, the animals were unable to learn to escape or avoid shock even when they had the opportunity to do so. They seemed to accept shock passively. They had learned to be helpless. Their behavior contrasted sharply with the quick learning of escape and avoidance behaviors seen in animals that had never received inescapable shock. Miller and Seligman proposed that just as the "helpless" animals learned that their behavior is unrelated to the shock they receive, depressives have learned that their behavior is unrelated to the rewards they receive. Thus if depressed and nondepressed subjects receive reinforcement, the impact of reinforcement should be different for the two groups.

The researchers hypothesized that when nondepressed subjects receive reinforcement on a task that involves skill, they raise their expectations of success on future tries. After hitting the bullseye on a dart board, a nondepressed person should raise his or her estimate of the odds of doing the same on the next attempt. For depressed subjects who fit the model of learned helplessness, the predictions are different: Depressed subjects will alter their expectations less than subjects who are not depressed. After hitting a bullseye, the depressed person may continue to believe that the chances of hitting it are near zero. Put another way, depressed subjects tend to ignore past reinforcement when they predict how well they will do on a task that involves skill: they view reinforcement as unrelated to their own behavior. A depressed baseball player with a .354 batting average may expect to strike out every time he comes to the plate; one who is not depressed might be more optimistic. On tasks that involve chance rather than skill, such as rolling snake eyes, reinforcement (that is, success) really is unrelated to behavior. Miller and Seligman predicted that the expectations for success on these tasks would not change much for depressed or nondepressed subjects following reinforcement.[3]

We can structure our example in a more systematic way if we look at it in terms of the concepts we have discussed so far. First, we know that every experiment has a hypothesis. What is the hypothesis of this experiment? If you review Miller and Seligman's predictions, you will find their hypothesis really has two parts: First, depressed and nondepressed subjects respond differently to reinforcement. Second, the type of task (skill versus chance) determines whether reinforcement will alter estimates of future success.

What is the independent variable in this experiment? What must be manipulated to test the experimental hypothesis? First, subjects who are depressed must be compared with subjects who are not depressed. The first independent variable is type of subject. Notice, however, that this is an ex post facto variable. The "manipulation" of this variable is simply the selection process. Miller and Seligman measure depression and then assign subjects to the two conditions (depressed and nondepressed) on the basis of these measurements. They do not actually depress anyone, nor would they want to for ethical reasons. The researchers also made a prediction about differences in expectations for depressed vs. nondepressed subjects when they receive reinforcement for performance on tasks that are either skilled or chance tasks. The type of task must vary so that both predictions can be tested. Type of task is a second independent variable,

3.   The picture is more complicated if we try to take into account the "gambler's fallacy." If we have not rolled snake eyes for a long time, we tend to think it is more likely to come up. Given your knowledge of randomness, can you explain why this does not actually happen?

one that *is* manipulated directly by the experimenters. Miller and Seligman varied the type of task to see whether the effect of reinforcement differed when subjects knew that reinforcement was under their control (skill) versus not under their control (chance). Since one independent variable was manipulated directly by the experimenters and the other was an ex post facto variable, this experiment follows the mixed model we discussed in Chapter 2. Since more than one independent variable was studied, we are also looking at a factorial design. This is a two-factor experiment, since there are two independent variables.

At this point you may be wondering why reinforcement is not also an independent variable in this experiment. The reason is simple. Miller and Seligman controlled reinforcement so that everyone received exactly the same amount. Since reinforcement was the same for all subjects in all conditions, it is not a variable. Controlling reinforcement was necessary in order to avoid confounding. If some subjects happened to be very good at the skill task, they would have received much more reinforcement than subjects who were not very good at it. If we observed changes in the subjects' estimates of future success, those estimates could simply reflect differences in how successful the subjects had already been in the experiment. They might tell us nothing about the impact of depression. Controlling reinforcement involved a slight deception. Subjects thought their success on the skill task depended only on performance. However, the apparatus, a wooden platform which had to be raised without knocking off the steel ball on it, was rigged with a magnet so that all the subjects were sucessful 50 percent of the time. The chance task, a guessing game, was also set up so that the chance of success was 50 percent.

The dependent variable in this experiment was subjects' expectations. The experimenters used subjects' estimates of success on future tries to measure the effects of both type of subject and type of task. If type of subject makes a difference, expectations will change differently for different subjects. If type of task makes a difference, expectations will change differently for different tasks. Miller and Seligman actually predicted an interaction between the type of subject and the type of task. They predicted that the way subjects alter expectations depends on both type of task and type of subject. Their findings are represented graphically in Figure 7.5. You can see from the graph that the results differ for different types of subjects. Nondepressed subjects alter their success estimates on tasks that involve skill; depressed subjects keep their estimates about the same during both types of task.

CHOOSING A BETWEEN-SUBJECTS DESIGN

As you begin planning your first experiments, you will probably experience the temptation of trying to do everything in one experiment. You may try to set up studies with as many as five or six different factors. But if you try to do too many things at once, you may lose sight of what you are trying to accomplish. A simple set of hypotheses that zeroes in on the most important variables is better than a more elaborate set which includes everything from astrological sign to zest for life. Keep your first experiment simple. Although the factorial designs make it possible to look at many different variables at a time, do not get carried away. Focus on the variables

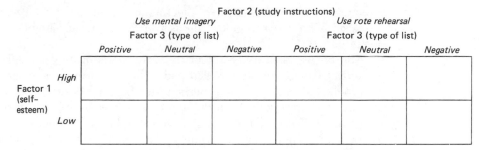

Figure 7.4   Diagram of a 2 ×2 ×3 factorial design. The diagram represents an experiment in which there are three independent variables: self-esteem, study instructions, and type of word to be learned. The hypothesis of this experiment is as follows: Subjects with high self-esteem will remember a list of words with positive connotation better than lists of negative or neutral words, but only under the imagery condition. Subjects with low self-esteem will remember words with negative connotations better, but only under the imagery condition.

that are critical. Once again, a review of the experimental literature will be a helpful guide. If other researchers have simply controlled time of day by testing all their subjects together, there is no need to vary time of day in your study so that you can include it as an independent variable—unless you have strong reasons for doing so. You will develop a better understanding of the experimental process by starting with simple designs and working up to more complex ones.

There are several practical reasons for keeping factorial designs simple. First, subjects are usually assigned to each of the treatment conditions at random. This means you will need as many groups of subjects as you have treatment conditions. It is not always easy to find subjects. Also, more treatment conditions means more time to run the experiment and more time to do the statistical analysis. It is just not

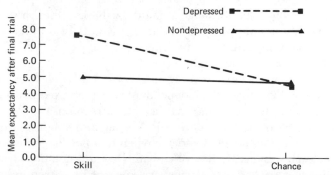

Figure 7.5   Depressed and nondepressed subjects' estimates of success on the next trial following a series of practice trials. From W. Miller and M. Seligman, Depression and the perception of reinforcement. *Journal of Abnormal Psychology*, 1973, *82*, 62–73. Copyright 1973 by the American Psychological Association. Reprinted by permission of the American Psychological Association and W. R. Miller.

practical to include unnecessary factors and conditions. Use your review of prior research in the area to guide you as you decide what variables and what levels to include.

So far we have covered four different kinds of between-subjects designs. We looked at two-group designs that had either independent or matched groups. We also looked at multiple-group designs and factorial designs. You may still feel a bit uneasy about trying to select the appropriate design for your own between-subjects experiment. To make things easier, you should always begin with some basic questions. Your design will be determined to a large extent by the number of independent variables you have and by the number of treatment conditions needed to test your hypothesis. You should also use your literature review to get an idea of the kinds of designs others have used for similar problems. To help make your search more systematic, the basics of the decision-making process are summarized in Figure 7.6. Simply begin at the top and work down, answering the questions in terms of your experiment.

SUMMARY

In between-subjects designs, a comparison of two values of the independent variable is sometimes not enough; we need more than two treatment conditions to test an experimental hypothesis. A *multiple-group design* serves this purpose. In a *multiple independent groups design*, there are more than two levels of the independent variable and subjects are assigned to treatment conditions at random. With several treatment conditions, researchers can look at the effects of several different values of the independent variable and see whether low, medium, and high values of a variable produce increasing changes in the dependent variable. They can also detect more complex patterns. For instance, some variables may produce little change at extreme values but a lot of change at middle values. Although we can get additional information from a multiple-group design, it is not always practical or necessary to do so. For many experimental hypotheses, a comparison of just two values of the independent variable is sufficient.

Another between-subjects design is the *factorial design*, one that has more than one independent variable. The independent variables are called *factors*. By studying more than one factor at a time, we can measure *main effects*, the action of each independent variable in the experiment. We can also measure *interactions*: a change in the effect of an independent variable when *another* independent variable changes value. Factorial designs are described with standard notation. If we are told that an experiment has a $3 \times 2 \times 4$ design, we know it has three independent variables because three numbers are given. The value of each number tells us how many levels each factor has. The first factor has 3, the second has 2, and the third has 4 levels or values. We also know there are 24 treatment conditions, the product of $3 \times 2 \times 4$.

There are practical limitations on using factorial designs. They often require

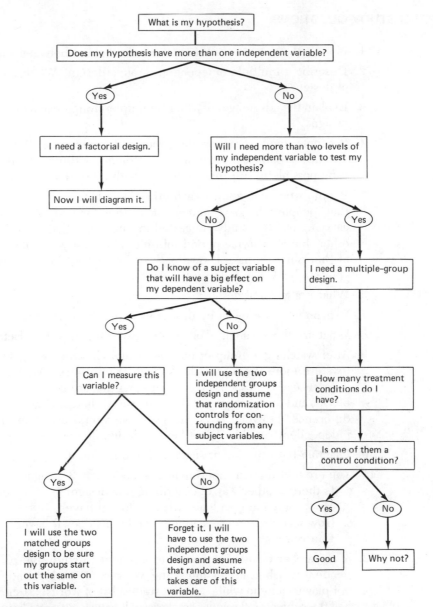

Figure 7.6 Questions to ask in designing a between-subjects experiment (start at the top and work down).

many subjects. They can be time-consuming and they require more complicated statistical procedures than the other designs we have discussed. However, they also provide valuable information other types of experiments cannot provide.

REVIEW AND STUDY QUESTIONS

1. Review the meaning of these terms: design and between-subjects design.

2. Describe a multiple independent groups design. When do we need this type of design?

3. Explain the advantages of using a multiple-group design rather than a two-group design.

4. If people stand closer together, they will communicate better. How would you test this hypothesis? How many treatment conditions would you need? Would it be possible to test this hypothesis with more than one design?

5. People who have known each other for a long time may communicate better than people who have known each other for a short time. Imagine you are carrying out the study suggested in question 4. All your subjects know each other, but for varying periods of time. How can you make sure that the length of time subjects have known each other will not be a confounding variable in your study? What design is needed?

6. What is a factorial design?

7. Explain what we mean by the terms *main effect* and *interaction*.

8. What are the advantages of running experiments with a factorial design?

9. After watching a group of nursery school children, we get the idea that some toys are more popular with children than others. We would like to test the difference in time spent playing with toys that are used for building (for example, blocks) and toys that are not (for example, stuffed animals). Since there are many differences between boys and girls, we would also like to look at sex as an independent variable. What kind of design do we need?

10. Diagram the experiment suggested in question 9.

11. You are told that an experiment has a $3 \times 3 \times 3$ design.
    a. Is there another way of describing this design?
    b. How many independent variables does it have?
    c. How many different treatment conditions does it have?
    d. Can you make a diagram of it?

12. A researcher decides to run an experiment to study the effects of three independent variables on learning. She will vary (1) background noise by playing or not playing a radio while subjects study a list of words; (2) she will vary smoking: half the subjects (all regular smokers) will have a cigarette before the experiment, and half will not; and (3) she will vary the length of the list to be learned: half the subjects will try to learn a long list, half will try to learn a short list in the same amount of time. The dependent variable is the percentage of words recalled. Take this hypothetical experiment and do the following:
    a. Describe this experiment using shorthand notation for factorial designs.
    b. Diagram the experiment.

      c. In addition to defining the subject population as "regular smokers," what other subject variables might be important to the outcome of this study? How can they be controlled?

      d. Identify three nonsubject variables you think might affect the outcome of this study.

13. A new student in class says: "I'm not going to bother thinking about the design of my experiment in advance. I'll just go ahead and run it and then figure out what it is later." How would you convince this student that his approach will not work?

14. What features of an experimental hypothesis are important in selecting a design?

REFERENCES

Broadhurst, P. L. The interaction of task difficulty and motivation: The Yerkes-Dodson Law revived. *Acta Psychologica*, 1959, *16*, 321–328.

Cherry, E. C. Some experiments on recognition of speech, with one, and with two ears. *Journal of the Acoustical Society of America*, 1953, *25*, 975–979.

Hall, E. T. *Hidden dimensions*. Garden City, N.Y.: Doubleday, 1966.

Lassen, C. L. Effect of proximity on anxiety and communication in the initial psychiatric interview. *Journal of Abnormal Psychology*, 1973, *81*, 226–232.

Miller, W., and Seligman, M. Depression and the perception of reinforcement. *Journal of Abnormal Psychology*, 1973, *82*, 62–73.

Seligman, M., Maier, S., and Solomon, R. Pavlovian fear conditioning and learned helplessness. In R. Church and B. Campbell (eds.), *Aversive Conditioning and Learning*. New York: Appleton-Century-Crofts, 1969.

Treisman, A. M. Verbal cues, language, and meaning in selective attention. *American Journal of Psychology*, 1964, *77*, 206–219.

8

Within-Subjects Designs

Key Terms

within-subjects design	small N design	generalizing
baseline	large N design	ABA design

Up to now, we have looked at four main types of designs: two independent groups, two matched groups, multiple groups, and factorial designs. All our examples of these designs had one underlying assumption—that the subjects in each of the different treatment conditions were *different* randomly selected individuals. We assumed that each subject would be in only one treatment condition. Such designs are called between-subjects designs. Conclusions are based on comparisons between different subjects (that is, the different groups of the experiment). This approach usually works well, but only in certain cases. Others call for a different type of design, as the following example illustrates.

When I was a student I was interested in memory. One of the problems I worked on was whether we remember things better when they are seen with things we like. I was planning a controlled experiment to test the notion that people would remember numbers better if they were paired with the names of the people they liked. I made up a list of well-known people—artists, writers, politicians. My plan was to have a group of raters judge their reactions to the names on a scale from "very positive" to "very negative." I could then pair the names with numbers and make up two lists, one of "positive pairs" and one of "negative pairs."

As the raters made their judgments, my simple plan folded. The raters did not agree at all. One's reaction to sculptor Alexander Calder was "very positive"; another charitably rated his reaction "slightly negative," although he later confessed that he places all modern art in the same category as old newspapers. Other raters had never heard of Calder. The only name that generated any consistent reaction was Adolf Hitler; nobody liked him. Then other problems arose. Different raters varied a great deal in the intensity of their reactions. Some felt very mildly about all the names; others used only the extremes of the scales. Would it make sense to compare different subjects whose reactions to the names might vary just as much?

A between-subjects design would not work well for my experiment. My raters' reactions to the names were inconsistent, and I expected my subjects to be just as unpredictable. I could not make comparisons between different subjects because I knew their reactions to the names would be too dissimilar: What was a "positive" pair to one subject might be "negative" or "neutral" to someone else. The answer

within-subjects design
was a **within-subjects design**. In a within-subjects design, each subject serves in more than one condition of the experiment. In my case, I asked subjects to make their own ratings of the names. I formed "positive" and "negative" pairs of numbers and names based on each subject's own ratings. Then I compared how much subjects remembered of their own positive pairs with how much they remembered of their own negative pairs. The same subjects were in both conditions of the experiment. This enabled me to see how different conditions led to different behaviors *within the same subjects.*

A WITHIN-SUBJECTS EXPERIMENT: OPTICAL ILLUSIONS

We can set up a variety of within-subjects designs for several subjects. The basic principles remain the same: Each subject takes part in more than one condition of the experiment. We make comparisons of the behavior of the same subjects under different conditions. If our independent variable is having an effect, we are more likely to find it if we use a within-subjects design. In a between-subjects design, the effects of our independent variable can be masked by the differences between the groups on all sorts of extraneous variables. A comparison within-groups is more precise. If we see different behaviors under different treatment conditions, the differences are more likely to be linked to our experimental manipulation. Remember that the whole point of an experiment is to set up a situation in which the independent variable is the only thing that changes systematically across the conditions of the experiment. In a between-subjects design, the independent variable changes—but the subjects also change. We can usually assume that randomization controls for extraneous variables that might affect the dependent variable. We have better control with a within-subjects design because we use the same subjects over and over.

Coren and Girgus (1972) used a within-subjects design to study optical illusions, configurations like those in Figure 8.1. They are figures that are deceptive; we see things in them which do not really exist. For instance, in the Müller-Lyer illusion, the two horizontal lines are actually the same length, but the one with the wings pointing in appears shorter.[1] Coren and Girgus wanted to see whether the amount

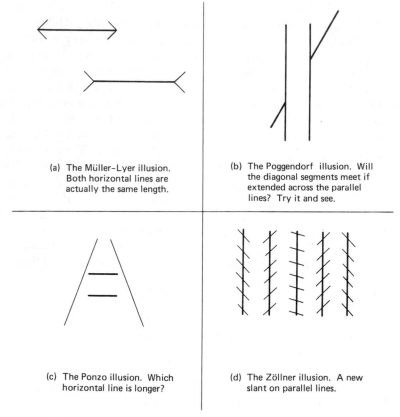

(a) The Müller–Lyer illusion. Both horizontal lines are actually the same length.

(b) The Poggendorf illusion. Will the diagonal segments meet if extended across the parallel lines? Try it and see.

(c) The Ponzo illusion. Which horizontal line is longer?

(d) The Zöllner illusion. A new slant on parallel lines.

Figure 8.1 Examples of optical illusions.

1. Recently, Favreau (1977) showed that in many textbook illustrations of the Müller-Lyer illusion, one line actually *is* shorter than the other. Textbook figures are often drawn to maximize the illusion. Favreau postulates the existence of a conspiracy to disillusion beginning psychology students, but you can try drawing your own honest Müller-Lyer figure using identical lines. You will find that even without exaggeration, the illusion is powerful.

of illusion people saw would change if they looked at the figures several times. They suggested that our perceptions correct themselves as we become more familiar with the figures.

The amount of illusion subjects see in a figure varies. One sees very little distortion; another reports a large effect. Thus it would be hard to see whether several exposures to the illusion figures made a difference if we compared data from different subjects. We stand a better chance of detecting the effect of repeated exposures if we compare the reports of the same subjects as they see the figures again and again. Coren and Girgus did exactly that. They used a within-subjects design to measure the changes in the illusions over a series of trials. Each subject saw each of the illusion figures several times. The more times the subjects saw the figures, the less illusion they saw. The effect of repeated exposures probably would have been muddled if Coren and Girgus had done the experiment with a between-groups design. The within-subjects design works better when there are large individual differences in the way that subjects react to treatment conditions. Changes in the responses of different subjects across different conditions could be caused by the independent variable, differences between the subjects, or both. By getting responses from the same subjects again and again, Coren and Girgus got a more accurate idea of how their independent variable worked. They made their data more precise by comparing responses of the same subjects under different conditions, eliminating the error from differences between subjects. The responses of the same subjects are likely to be more consistent from one measurement to another. If responses change across conditions, the changes are more likely to be caused by the independent variable.

ADVANTAGES OF WITHIN-SUBJECTS DESIGNS

In within-subjects experiments we use the same subjects in our different treatment conditions. This is a big help when we cannot get many subjects; we can actually run an entire experiment with only one subject if we have to. If we have four treatment conditions and want ten subjects in each condition, we need only ten subjects if we run the experiment within-subjects. Each of the ten subjects runs through all four conditions. However, if we run the same experiment between-subjects, we need 40 subjects, 10 in each of the four conditions.

A within-subjects design can also save us time when we are running the experiment. If being a subject requires training, it is more efficient to train each subject for several conditions instead of one.

If our subjects are Harry, Mike, and Marie, they will all be in more than one of the conditions of our experiment. This gives us good control over subject variables, the ways in which subjects differ from one another. Harry, Mike, and Marie have a lot in common at different times. If we test them at different times, their responses will overlap. Their responses will be more different from the ones Susan, Ruth, and Mark give. That is what we see when we test subjects. Different subjects act in very different ways. The less overlap there is between subjects' behavior, the more we need a within-subjects design. When we run an experiment, we usually do not care much about how individual subjects differ from one another. We really want to see whether the different values of our independent variable created differences in behavior.

We usually have the best chance of detecting the effect of our independent variable if we compare the behavior of the same subjects under different conditions. The within-subjects design controls for subject variables. That way, if we see differences in behavior under different conditions, we know that they are not likely to be simply the differences that occur because Susan, Ruth, and Mark do not act like Harry, Mike, and Marie.

From a statistical standpoint, that means we have a better chance of detecting the effect of our experimental manipulation if we use a within-subjects design. The reasons parallel the reasons we discussed in connection with the matched-groups procedures. Since we are looking at the responses of the same people under different conditions, we expect their responses to be about the same—unless our treatment conditions affect their behavior. If we have the same subjects in all our conditions (or matched subjects who are also somewhat similar), any differences in behavior produced by the experimental intervention will be more apparent. They will not be buried among the variability that is created by testing different subjects.

In a within-subjects experiment, we can also get an ongoing record of subjects' behavior over time. This gives us a more complete picture of the way the independent variable works in the experiment. We have both practical and methodological gains with this approach. Since there are so many advantages to a within-subjects design, why not always use it?

DISADVANTAGES OF WITHIN-SUBJECTS DESIGNS

Practical Limitations

There are several reasons why within-subjects designs do not always work. Sometimes they actually are not practical. Within-subjects designs generally require each subject to spend more time in the experiment. For instance, the various conditions of an experiment might be several stories that subjects read and evaluate. A researcher may need to schedule several hours of testing if this experiment is run with a within-subjects design: each subject would spend several hours reading and scoring several stories. The same experiment might be run in an hour with a between-subjects design: each subject spends just one hour reading and evaluating one story. If a procedure involves testing each subject individually, a great deal of time can be lost resetting equipment for each subject for each condition. That could mean many extra hours. If it is a perception experiment that requires calibrating several sensitive electronic instruments for each condition, the researcher is in for some tedious testing sessions.

Experiments often become tedious for subjects too. A subject who is expected to perform many tasks may begin to get restless during the experiment. That can lead to inaccurate data. A subject may begin to make hasty judgments in the hope that the experiment will be over. For the most part, these limitations are really just inconveniences. We can spend an additional 10, 20, or even 100 hours testing subjects if it is essential to the value of the experiment. Sometimes it is, and experimenters may spend hours or even days testing each subject. But there are more serious problems that limit the within-subjects approach. These are problems linked to the independent variable.

Interference between Conditions

Often each subject can be in only one condition of the experiment. Taking part in more than one condition would be either impossible or useless. Imagine that we are doing a study on brain functioning. We want to see whether damage to the hippocampus causes violent behavior in cats. We operate on the cats and surgically damage the hippocampus of each one. After surgery, we look for changes in the cats' behavior. If they start acting mean, we might be tempted to conclude that what we did to their brains affected their behavior. But the changes might be due to the anesthesia we used, the trauma of surgery, or postoperative care. The only way to get good control of this experiment is by using two groups of animals. We need a control group that goes through the entire surgical procedure *except* for the damage to the brain. The

baseline   control group gives us our **baseline** of behavior; it tells us how cats behave when they have had surgery but have not had their brains damaged. We then compare the control group with the experimental group. If we see differences, we might be able to say that damage to the hippocampus causes violent behavior.

You can see that it would be impossible to put all the cats through both conditions of this experiment. We could begin by collecting some baseline data. We could operate and then look for the changes in behavior. But we could not reverse the damage and make the cats like new again. We could not check out whether some routine part of the surgery caused behavior changes. We could not get very good control of this experiment if we used a within-subjects design. If one treatment condition precludes another, as it does in this kind of experiment, we will do better with a between-subjects design.

Sometimes it is possible to run all subjects through all treatments, although it does not make sense to do that. What if we want subjects to learn a list of words? In one condition we tell the subjects to learn the words by forming mental pictures (images) of them. In the other condition, we ask subjects to repeat the words over and over. We want to use the same list in both conditions so that the difficulty of the list will not be a confounding variable. But once the subjects have practiced the list in one condition, they will recall it more easily in the next condition. If they formed pictures of elephants sitting on flagpoles, they will remember elephants and flagpoles. Bower, a well-know researcher in the field of memory, knew that and used between-subjects designs in similar experiments (Bower, 1972).

The interference between different conditions of an experiment is the biggest drawback in using within-subjects designs. If the treatments clash so badly that we cannot give them to the same subjects, we need a between-subjects design. Even in less extreme situations, we use special control procedures to offset some of the interference between conditions. We will look at those procedures in detail in the next chapter.

SMALL *N* DESIGNS

small *N* design

Since subjects get more than one treatment condition in a within-subjects experiment, we can run experiments with very few subjects. The clearest examples of the within-subjects approach are experiments with only one subject. The basic idea for these experiments was developed and used extensively by B. F. Skinner. Skinner thought there was often more to gain by looking closely at the behavior of a single subject, rather than using statistical tests to compare data obtained from different groups of subjects. Skinner's approach is called a **small *N* design**. (*N* stands for the number of subjects needed in the experiment.) A small *N* design is a special case of a within-subjects experiment. In a small *N* design we use just one or two subjects. This approach is very useful in exploratory research; if we see that a variable affects the behavior of one subject, we can expand the research to larger groups later. Running an experiment with one subject requires special procedures. Let us look at them in a simple hypothetical experiment.

A Small *N* Design: Talking to Plants

large *N* design

We want to test the notion that talking to a plant makes it grow better. Of course, we want to approach this hypothesis in a rigorous, scientific way. As you know, we can set this up as a two-group experiment. We can compare different groups of plants—we talk to one group, but not to the other. We measure their growth and see how the groups compare. Instead, we might plan a multiple-group experiment and use varying amounts of talking as our treatment conditions. We might even choose to look at a second variable (such as music) and set up a factorial design. These designs, which require groups of subjects, are usually called **large *N* designs**.

If we do not have a greenhouse, we can use a small *N* design to do our experiment on talking to plants. First, we carefully choose our subjects. Cactus grows too slowly to be of much use; bamboo grows very quickly but needs a tropical climate. After some library research, we settle on the hardy *ficus elastica*, better known as the rubber plant. We begin with the control condition of the experiment (condition A). For a time we do not talk to the plant at all. During this period, say three months, we simply chart its growth. This establishes a baseline of behavior without the experimental manipulation. In the second phase of the experiment, we introduce the experimental manipulation (condition B): For the second three-month period we talk to the plant for two hours a day. "Talking" is operationally defined as reading aloud from Euell Gibbons' *In Search of the Wild Asparagus*. We continue to chart the plant's growth throughout this phase of the experiment. If talking aids growth, the plant should grow more during the second part of the experiment. If talking has no effect on growth, the plant should continue to grow about as much as it did in the baseline condition.

So far this procedure looks very much like what we do when we carry out a two-group design: we use a control group to establish a baseline of behavior; we compare behavior in the experimental condition with what we see in the control condition. The procedures are similar in this respect, but there is also an important difference. Since we are using only one subject, we are looking at that subject at different points in time. Our rubber plant is three months older by the time we finish the first set of observations. The season has changed. The plant now gets a different amount of light each day. The humidity has probably changed too. Of course, some of these extraneous variables can be controlled. We can raise our plant in a laboratory, where light, temperature, and moisture are always the same. But we cannot discount the fact that the plant has aged. Any differences in the amount of growth we see during the experimental manipulation *might* be due to natural changes in the growth cycle of this plant. In other words, we may have confounding. For this reason, the small *N* design includes one additional, crucial step. After completing the experimental manipulation, *we remove the independent variable and return to the original control condition (A)*. We do not talk to the subject at all in this last phase of the experiment; we simply continue to monitor its growth.

We verify the effect of our independent variable in the small *N* experiment by returning to the original baseline condition. Our hypothesis is that talking to a plant makes it grow faster. Suppose that our plant *did* grow faster in the second phase of the experiment: Compared to the baseline condition, the plant grew faster when we talked to it. If the change in growth rate was produced by some extraneous variable such as maturation, the growth rate probably will not change much after we stop talking to the plant. On the other hand, if talking caused the plant to grow faster, we might expect a decline in the growth rate after we stop. Under some circumstances, the change in behavior caused by an experimental manipulation may persist even after the experimental manipulation has been discontinued. If the target behavior does not return to the baseline level, we cannot automatically rule out the effect of the independent variable. One problem is that no matter how hard we try, we may not be able to re-create the original baseline conditions perfectly. This is especially true in experiments outside the laboratory. In these cases, replication is essential. We can return to the baseline condition and reapply the experimental manipulation many times if we wish. Often we need to do that several times to make sure our findings were not produced by some chance variation in the testing situation.

When to Use Small *N* Designs

Like all within-subject designs, the small *N* design is appropriate *when we want good control over subject variables*. It is also appropriate when we are interested in the behavior of a particular subject. The small *N* design is applied to many behavior modification problems, which often concern a single person (see Box 8.1). We have focused on the importance of returning to the baseline conditions to verify the impact of our independent variable. However, in many behavior modification studies researchers choose *not* to return to the control condition. This is often true in experiments done to modify self-injurious behaviors. Suppose you were working with a disturbed child who hit his head against the wall, kicked himself, and punched himself with his fists. Tate and Baroff (1966) reported their work with just such a boy. When the boy, Sam, harmed himself, Tate and Baroff stopped talking to him and stopped holding his hands. With these and other interventions, Sam's self-destructive behaviors decreased.

How do we know that not talking to Sam and not holding his hand actually caused the change in behavior? Perhaps the change was just a coincidence. Would we want to find out? Would we want to return to an original set of conditions that might make Sam hurt himself again? No. Even though the experimental procedures require a return to the baseline conditions, psychologists sacrifice some scientific precision for ethical reasons. When we make an intervention we hope will be therapeutic, our goal is helping the patient. If we succeed in changing his or her behavior to something more adaptive, we have accomplished that goal.

Box 8.1   A Behavior Modification Experiment: Picking Up after Jim

Hall (1971) reports on the case of a new bride who was having a problem with her husband: "According to the wife, Jim's jacket was a permanent fixture on the back of the couch and his shoes could usually be found close by. Occasionally he would decorate the back of the chair with a sweater." (p. 43). The bride did not want to pick up after Jim, or continue nagging him to put his clothes away. The solution was found through a simple behavior modification experiment. In behavior modification experiments researchers try to change behaviors by applying various rewards and punishments as the independent variable. Rewards and punishments are presented as a *consequence* of the target behaviors to be modified. Researchers often use small *N* designs to do this. How did a small *N* design get a husband to pick up his clothes?

First, of course, the experimenters needed a baseline of behavior. We need to know how often the husband left his clothes in the living room under the usual circumstances. Records were made of how many items of clothing remained in the living room for more than 15 minutes; the average was two per day. During the experimental phase of the study, husband and wife agreed that whoever left more clothing in the living room during the week would have to do the dishes the following week. Leaving clothing in the living room then had a specific consequence. The husband could avoid that consequence by putting his clothes away. During the two-week experimental period, the husband left no clothing in the living room. (Presumably the tidy wife did the same, so it is not clear who actually did the dishes during that time.)

Did the threat of doing the dishes (the independent variable) really produce the change in behavior? Perhaps the husband just became more aware of his wife's concern for the appearance of the house. The wife thought the problem was solved. She let her husband know that the threat of dishwashing was lifted; nothing more would happen if he left his clothes in the living room. The outcome is illustrated in Figure 8.2. The husband went back to leaving his clothes in the room when the threat of doing the dishes was removed. It seemed that the threat really did affect his behavior. Still, you can see from the figure that he did not leave quite as many clothes around as before. It may be that second "baseline" period was not exactly identical to the first. For instance, if the weather had warmed up, Jim's jacket may have stayed in the closet during that time. This story had a happy ending. As you can see from the figure, after additional training (doing dishes contingent$_2$), Jim put his clothes away.

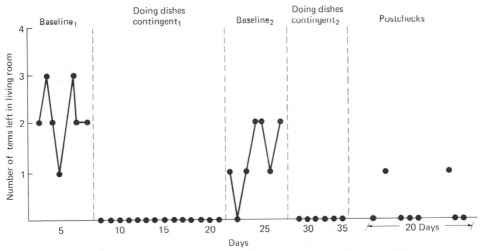

Figure 8.2 A record of the number of clothing items left in the living room by a newlywed husband. Copyright 1971 by H and H Enterprises. Reprinted by permission of R. Vance Hall, Sandy J. Alley, and Lois Cox, and H and H Enterprises.

The small *N* design is appropriate when studying a particular subject, such as one disturbed child. It is also useful when very few subjects are available. You can actually carry out an entire experiment with just one subject. Usually though, we do not want to stop with one subject. When we do experiments, we want to be able **generalizing** to **generalize** from our results—we want to be able to make statements about people or rats that were not actually subjects in an experiment. Many researchers prefer to do large *N* studies because they believe that they can then generalize from their results more successfully. All other things being equal, an experiment with more subjects has greater generality.

In a large *N* study we may form separate groups of subjects for each treatment condition. The subjects run through their assigned conditions, and we then measure them on the dependent variable. We pool data from each group and evaluate it statistically to see if the groups behaved differently. In a small *N* experiment, we watch one or two subjects over an extended period of time. We record baseline data. We introduce the experimental intervention and monitor the changes in the dependent variable throughout the experimental condition. Typically we take several measurements. We can see whether the effect of the experimental intervention is instant or whether it builds over time. We continue to measure after the intervention is removed. We can verify that the independent variable causes changes in behavior because we can see what happens when that variable is removed. In short, we may get a more complete and accurate picture from a small N study than from a large N study that tests the same hypothesis. Usually the impact of the independent variable is so apparent in small N studies that statistical tests are not needed to evaluate the results.

Then why not use a small N design for every experiment? We would certainly save a lot of time recruiting subjects and doing statistics. But is it safe to generalize from a small N study? Many researchers say "Yes," because we can evaluate how "typical" our small sample is. We can compare the behavior of our rat with the many records of other rats in the research literature. If our rat seems to behave about the same as other rats, we assume it is a typical subject. However, even if the subject behaves typically in our baseline conditions, we still cannot be sure this particular subject is not unusually sensitive to the independent variable. We also cannot be sure that the results are not due to some unseen accident. For instance, our plant study could be contaminated by a well-meaning cleaning person who gives fertilizer to our subject just at the time we begin talking to it. For these reasons, it is especially important to replicate the findings of a small N experiment.

It is impossible to say whether small or large N studies always have greater generality. All things rarely are equal. A large N study with a badly biased sample may tell us little about behavior in the population. The findings of a well-controlled experiment with a single subject might be replicated again and again. By gathering baseline data, applying the experimental manipulation, and then returning to the baseline condition, we can get a very clear idea of the impact of the independent variable.

ABA DESIGNS

ABA design   The small N designs we have discussed are also called **ABA designs.** *ABA* refers to the order of the conditions of the experiment. *A* (the control condition) is presented first, followed by *B* (the experimental condition). Finally we return to the control condition (*A*) to verify that the change in behavior is linked to the independent variable. Most small N designs are *ABA* designs. Some are variations of the *ABA* format (for example, *ABAB*). If we want to use several experimental conditions in a small N experiment, we can extend the *ABA* format. We can proceed as follows: AB_1 AB_2 AB_3 and so on. What is important is that we collect baseline data before any experimental intervention, and that we return to the baseline (control) condition after each experimental treatment.

Instead of looking at the behavior of a single subject across conditions, we can also look at the behavior of a single group across conditions. We can study changes in the group without much concern for how individual subjects change. The *ABA* within-subjects design enables us to do this. The basics of this design are the same as the *ABA* small *N* design; the only difference is that we test a group rather than one or two subjects. The main limitation of this approach is that the experimental treatment must be reversible: we must be able to return to the control condition. If treatment conditions are not reversible, we cannot use an *ABA* design. (We will look at some alternative procedures in the next chapter.) However, when we can use an *ABA* design, it is advantageous because it requires few subjects and because we can usually evaluate the data without statistical tests.

Pedalino and Gamboa (1974) wanted to study the behavior of workers in a large manufacturing and distribution center. Very simply, they wanted to see how they could get more people to come to work regularly. They hypothesized that attendance would improve if people were rewarded for coming to work regularly. Their independent variable was reinforcement; their dependent variable was absenteeism. How would we test this hypothesis with a between-subjects design? The obvious choice is a two-group design. We would begin by taking a random sample of workers. We would randomly place half our sample in the control condition, their usual work situation. The other half would be in the experimental condition—they would receive reinforcement for coming to work regularly. Can you foresee any problems with this approach?

Of course, various workers may have very different work environments. Kathy has Ms. Merkle as her supervisor. Ms. Merkle is known as a tyrant. She stands over people's desks and points out their errors as they work. John is supervised by Mr. Albert, who is equally irritating. Both Kathy and John get frequent headaches and often find themselves unable to come to work. On the other hand, Robert and Joan work with Mr. Solomon. His philosophy is that people really want to do a good job, and they will if you encourage them. Ms. Murphy feels the same. She and Mr. Solomon praise their staff whenever they do well. Besides having different supervisors, our subjects may also be different ages. If absenteeism is related to age, that could make a difference. Of course we assume that randomization takes care of things like age, supervisors, and other subject variables. Our randomly formed groups should be about the same age, the same general health, have supervisors who are equally awful, and so on. If we are especially concerned about any of these variables, we can form matched groups.

But there are still other disadvantages in using two or more separate groups. We may not be able to get as much control over the experiment as we can with a within-subjects design. If our random groups are spread over several offices, we may not be able to monitor all the changes in working conditions that occur during our experiment: Supervisors are rotated; workers get raises; some quit and others take their places. We also do not have the chance to see what happens to the same workers before, during, and after the experimental intervention. The *ABA* design gives us that chance. We can nail down the effect of our independent variable by observing the same group before, during, and after the experimental treatment.

For these reasons, Pedalino and Gamboa tested their hypothesis using an *ABA* within-subjects design. First they collected baseline data: They measured the amount of absenteeism under the usual working conditions. The experimental condition was a lottery poker game. During this condition, each employee was allowed to pick a card from a deck of playing cards on each day he or she came to work on time. At the end of the five-day work week, the employee with the best poker hand won $20. During the time the lottery was in effect, absenteeism dropped 18 percent. When the lottery was stopped, people began skipping work more often. Pedalino and Gamboa concluded that the lottery poker game had reduced absenteeism.

You can see that switching back to the baseline condition was essential. Something else might have happened about the same time the lottery was started. Maybe everyone had just gotten a raise and felt better about coming to work. Maybe the flu season ended. But we know that the lottery produced a change in attendance because absenteeism rose again when the lottery ended. As a further check, Pedalino and Gamboa started up the lottery again, and absenteeism dropped.

HOW CAN YOU CHOOSE?

How do you decide whether to use a within-subjects or a between-subjects design? First, as always, think about the hypothesis of the experiment. How many treatment conditions are needed to test the hypothesis? Would it be possible to have each subject in more than one of these conditions? If so, you may be able to use a within-subjects design. Do your treatment conditions interfere with one another? Yes? Then you ought to use a between-subjects design. Can you reverse your experimental treatment? You may want to consider an *ABA* design.

Consider the practical advantages of each approach. Is it simpler to run the experiment one way or the other? Which will be more time-consuming? If you can get only a few subjects, the within-subjects design may be better. Remember that there is a tradeoff: The longer the experiment takes, the harder it may be to find willing subjects.

You can control subject variables best in a within-subjects design. If there are likely to be large individual differences in the way subjects respond to the experiment, the within-subjects approach is usually better.

Remember to review the research literature. If other experimenters have used within-subjects designs for similar problems, it is probably because that approach works best.

If all other things seem equal, use the within-subjects design. It is better from a statistical standpoint; you will maximize your chances of detecting the effect of the independent variable with a within-subjects design.

SUMMARY

Within-subjects designs are designs in which each subject takes part in more than one condition of the experiment. These designs are advantageous because they enable us to compare the behavior of the same subjects under different treatment conditions. We can often get a more precise picture of the effects of the independent variable from a within-subjects design than we can from a between-subjects design. Subject variables are better controlled in the within-subjects experiment. We eliminate the error produced by differences between subjects and thus make a more precise assessment of the impact of the independent variable.

The *small N design* is used to study the behavior of only one or two subjects at a time. This approach requires very careful control over the conditions of the experiment. A typical small N experiment begins with observing and recording the subject's behavior under the control conditions. This is the *baseline*. The experimental intervention is then introduced and the subject's behavior is monitored throughout the experimental period. The subject's behavior during the experimental period is then compared with the baseline records. To rule out the possibility of coincidence, there is a return to the original control condition. Because many conditions can change over time, small N experiments should be replicated.

Most small N studies are also *ABA designs*. ABA refers to the order of the treatment conditions. We can use the *ABA* approach or some variation in many experiments with groups of subjects as well as individuals. The main limitation on this approach is that we can use it only with experimental treatments that are completely reversible.

Whether to choose a within-subjects or a between-subjects design depends on several factors. Practical and methodological considerations come into play. A within-subjects design requires fewer subjects. It is less time-consuming when each subject requires extensive training. It controls well for subject variables. Statistically, a researcher stands a better chance of detecting the effect of the independent variable using a within-subjects design. We cannot use within-subjects designs if experimental conditions will interfere with one another, as in various learning tasks. Sometimes they are also impractical because they take longer to run than a corresponding between-subjects experiment.

REVIEW AND STUDY QUESTIONS

1. What is a within-subjects experiment? How is it different from a between-subjects experiment?

2. Discuss three advantages of using a within-subjects design.

3. Discuss three disadvantages of using a within-subjects design.

4. What is a small N design?

5. Discuss the relative advantages and disadvantages of small N versus large N designs.

6. Outline an experiment to test this hypothesis: Children who are given weaponlike toys (for example, toy guns and knives) become more aggressive.
   a. What are your independent and dependent variables?
   b. How will you operationalize "aggression"?

c. How would you test this hypothesis using a small *N* design?

d. What are the disadvantages of using a small *N* design for this experiment? Would another within-subjects approach be possible?

7. Mary Johnson is very excited about the within-subjects approach. "Now I'll never need to run large numbers of subjects again," she says. What has she forgotten?

8. For each of the following dependent measures, evaluate the pros and cons of using a within-subjects approach.

a. The taste of a new toothpaste.

b. The cavity-preventing properties of a new toothpaste.

c. The readability of a new typeface.

d. The impact of good and bad news.

9. One student is still looking for shortcuts. He says: "Running through the control condition of an experiment twice is silly. I'll just run through *A* and *B* and draw my conclusions from that." What would you say to him to convince him that carrying out the entire *ABA* design would be a better idea?

10. Explain how the levels of your independent variable can influence your decision to use a within- or between-subjects design.

11. What requirements must be met to make the within-subjects approach feasible?

12. Ms. Perkins, a school principal, is interested in this question: Does having breakfast improve children's school performance? She would like to gather some scientific data on this question. You are invited in as a consultant because Ms. Perkins is not sure how to proceed. Help her out by doing the following:

a. Identify the independent and dependent variables for her.

b. Formulate a workable operational definition for each variable.

c. Outline two different approaches to this research question, one a between-subjects approach, one a within-subjects approach.

d. Explain to Ms. Perkins the relative advantages and disadvantages of these approaches for her problem.

e. Which approach would you recommend and why?

f. What potential problems can you anticipate in carrying out this study?

REFERENCES

Bower, G. H. Mental imagery and associative learning. In L. W. Gregg (ed.), *Cognition in learning and memory*. New York: Wiley, 1972.

Coren, S., and Girgus, J. Illusion decrement in intersecting line figures. *Psychonomic Science*, 1972, *26*, 108–110.

Favreau, O. E. Psychology in action: Disillusioned. *American Psychologist*, 1977, *32* (7), 568–571.

Hall, R. V. *Managing behavior. 3: Applications in school and home*. Lawrence, Kansas: H and H Enterprises, 1971.

Pedalino, E., and Gamboa, V. Behavior modification and absenteeism: Intervention in one industrial setting. *Journal of Applied Psychology*, 1974, *59*, 694–698.

Tate, B. G., and Baroff, G. S. Aversive control of self-injurious behavior in a psychotic boy. *Behavior Research and Therapy*, 1966, *4*, 281–287.

Controlling Extraneous Variables: Physical Variables

Key Terms

physical variable	counterbalancing
elimination	within-subjects counterbalancing
constancy of conditions	between-subjects counterbalancing
balancing	complete counterbalancing
order effects	partial counterbalancing
practice effects	randomized counterbalancing
progressive error	carryover effect

One of your main goals as an experimenter is to set up experiments in which there is no confusion. When we experiment, we want to create treatment conditions that will let us see the effects of the independent variables clearly. Experiments should be internally valid. Ideally, only the independent variable should change systematically from one condition to another. In the last two chapters, you saw how we can control for some subject variables that might lead to confounding: We can use random assignment, match subjects on variables that are related to the dependent variable, or run the experiment using a within-subjects design. In this chapter and the one that follows, we will look closely at some other techniques for handling three types of extraneous variables: physical, personality, and social. Each poses special problems in an experiment. Many can be controlled by the same procedures, but some require special procedures just for them. In this chapter we will look at the first type, the physical variables.

PHYSICAL VARIABLES

Poor Janice Johnson was trying to run an experiment on riddles. Her riddles were tricky and they made a person think. On her first day of testing, Janice recruited subjects in the library and tested them on the spot in a quiet reading room. The next day she came back to run the rest of the experiment. To her dismay, Janice found that the reading room was closed. The only place she could test her subjects was in the lobby of the building. It was fairly quiet there, but people walked by now and then, talking and laughing. Janice cried, "Good grief, these testing conditions will confound my experiment! Why did I run all my control subjects yesterday?"

physical variable
The testing room, the noise, the distractions are all **physical variables**, aspects of the testing conditions that need to be controlled. Janice was in trouble because she ran all her control subjects on the first day. The control group was therefore tested under quiet conditions. The experimental group had to be tested in a different place with more noise and interruptions. There was confounding in Janice's experiment: the testing conditions changed along with the independent variable. Her problems could have been avoided by using one of the three general techniques for controlling physical variables: elimination, constancy of conditions, and balancing. We cannot possibly identify all the extraneous variables that influence the outcome of a study—but we try to find as many as we can. By using control techniques, we increase the chances of an internally valid experiment.

Elimination and Constancy

elimination
To make sure that an extraneous variable does not affect an experiment, we just take it out—we **eliminate** it. If noise might confound the results, we test in a soundproof room. If we do not want interruptions, we hang a sign on the door saying "Do not disturb. Test in progress."

Ideally, we would like to eliminate all extraneous variables from an experiment. But this, of course, is easier said than done. Sometimes there is no soundproof room. Things like the weather, the lighting, and the paint on the walls are just there. We cannot eliminate them. Instead, we use the second control procedure, constancy of conditions.

constancy of conditions
Constancy of conditions means simply that we keep treatment conditions as nearly similar as possible. If we cannot eliminate a variable, we make sure that it stays the same in all treatment conditions. We cannot take the paint off the walls,

but we can test all subjects in the same room. That way we make sure that the pea-green walls offend all subjects equally in all conditions. The same goes for lighting, the comfort of the chairs, the mustiness of the drapes; all stay the same for all the subjects. We also try to keep the mechanics of the testing procedures the same. For instance, it is helpful to write out instructions to subjects before beginning the experiment. The written instructions are then *read* to subjects to guarantee that all subjects in each condition get the same directions. Exactly the same amount of time is allowed for each subject to complete each task—unless time is the independent variable.

Many physical variables like time of testing, testing place, and mechanical procedures can be kept constant with a little effort. An experimenter may end up controlling some variables that would not have affected the results anyway, but it is better to use the controls than to regret it later. If someone can punch holes in the results simply by pointing out that the experimental group had lunch but the control group did not, the experimenter will have a hard time making a strong case for the effects of the independent variable.

Balancing

Sometimes neither elimination nor constancy can be used. Perhaps some variables cannot be eliminated. For example, we would like to test in a soundproof room but we do not have access to one. We would like to test all subjects together at the same time, but only some subjects can come at any one time. What can we do in these situations? Confounding occurs when something in the experiment changes systematically along with the independent variable. If we cannot eliminate extraneous variables or keep them constant throughout an experiment, we can still make sure that they do not confound the results. The key to the problem is the *way* the variables change. If they change in an orderly way, we are in trouble. If we test experimental subjects in one room and control subjects in another, we have created an orderly change in many of the variables that make up testing conditions. We will not be able to tell for sure whether the independent variable caused changes between groups. The control group might do better if it is tested in the same sunny room as the experimental group. The key to controlling variables that cannot be eliminated or held constant is the third technique for physical variables, balancing.

balancing

We know that ideally we should not test subjects in two different rooms. But perhaps we have no choice; it is two rooms or nothing. We want to be sure testing conditions do not change in a way that is related to the independent variable. We can do this through **balancing**, distributing the effects of an extraneous variable across the different treatment conditions of the experiment. A way we might do this with room assignment is shown in Table 9.1.

We begin by randomly assigning half the subjects to the first testing room. The other half will be tested in the second room. Next, we randomly assign half the subjects *in each room* to the experimental condition; the remaining subjects will be

TABLE 9.1   BALANCING THE EFFECTS OF THE TESTING ROOM ACROSS TWO TREATMENT
CONDITIONS, CONTROL (C) AND EXPERIMENTAL (E)

Green Testing Room: Subjects	Pink Testing Room: Subjects
C_1	C_4
C_2	C_5
C_3	C_6
E_1	E_4
E_2	E_5
E_3	E_6

Note: Half the subjects are randomly assigned to each testing room. Half the subjects in each room are then randomly assigned to the control condition, half to the experimental condition.

in the control condition. Notice that we have not wiped out the differences between the two testing rooms; they are just as different as ever. However, the effects of the rooms are the same or balanced for both treatment conditions. For every control subject tested in the green room, there is also an experimental subject tested in that room. For every control subject tested in the pink room, there is also an experimental subject tested in that room.

Janice could have salvaged her riddle experiment by using balancing. Instead of testing all control subjects on the first day, she should have randomly assigned each subject to either the experimental or the control condition. Then, by chance she would have tested roughly half the control subjects in the quiet reading room, along with roughly half the experimental subjects. On the second day, she would have continued assigning subjects to the two treatment conditions at random. She then would have tested about half the control subjects and half the experimental subjects in the noisy lobby. Notice that she still would have had subjects who were tested under two different testing conditions. But the effects of these conditions would have been about the same for the two treatments in the experiment. Testing conditions would not have confounded the results of her experiment.

We can use balancing for many other variables as well. For example, if we cannot test all subjects at the same time, we can arrange things so that we test equal numbers of experimental and control subjects before and after lunch. Many physical variables will be balanced across conditions automatically as we assign our subjects to treatment conditions at random. Time of testing, weather conditions, and the day of the week are typically controlled in this way. Usually we do not even think about these sorts of extraneous variables. As long as there is no systematic change in an extraneous variable, things are fine. If we assign subjects to treatment conditions at random, we can be reasonably sure that we will not accidentally test all control subjects on a cool, comfortable day and all experimental subjects on a hot, muggy day.

At this point you may be wondering whether there is a limit on the number of extraneous variables that must be controlled. There may indeed be many possibilities, but you can set up a reasonably good experiment by taking precautions. Get rid of the variables that you can eliminate. Keep treatment conditions as similar as possible. Balance out the effects of other variables such as the testing room by making sure that the effects are distributed evenly across all treatment conditions. As always, be sure to assign individual subjects to treatment conditions at random. The experimental literature will also aid you in planning strategy. If other experimenters have carefully controlled the size of the testing room, you will want to be more cautious with that variable than some others, like the day of the week. If you can avoid it, do not let extraneous variables change along with the independent variable. You can never completely rule out the possibility of confounding if you let that happen.

CONTROLLING WITHIN-SUBJECTS DESIGNS

The procedures we have discussed so far—elimination, constancy of conditions, and balancing—are needed in most experiments. However, there are special problems in using a within-subjects design. The fact that subjects take part in more than one condition of the experiment leads to some snags that we do not get when we test different subjects in each condition. The problems that arise can be grouped into two categories: order effects and carryover effects.

Controlling for Order Effects: Counterbalancing

Suppose we want to do some market research on a new brand of cola. We know that people differ a great deal in the way they rate things like foods and beverages, so we decide to use a within-subjects design. We would like to get people to compare their present brand of cola with our new brand. We will get ratings on how good our cola tastes compared to the old brands. That information will tell us whether we can expect the new product to compete with well-known brands. Our hypothesis is that our new cola will get better ratings than the old brands.

We recruit cola-drinkers and bring them to our testing center. For 2 hours prior to the taste test, we keep them in a lounge where they can relax and read magazines—but they cannot eat or drink. Then we give a glass of the new cola to each subject. We give each person time to drink it and then ask him or her to indicate on a rating scale how much he or she liked the taste. Since we want to compare subjects' ratings of the new cola with their ratings of their regular brands, we carry out a second condition. We ask the subjects to drink a glass of their favorite cola. After, we get subjects to rate their own drinks on the rating scale. Now we have ratings of the two types of colas, new and old. We can compare the average ratings and see how our product competes.

Would it surprise you to learn that the average rating of our new brand was much higher than the average rating of the old brands? Why not? What is wrong with this experiment? You can imagine that any cola might taste good after you have not had anything to drink for a couple of hours—especially if you have been waiting in a hot, dry place. Your first cola will taste better than your second. In this experiment, we varied the brand of cola people were asked to drink. There were two conditions, New Brand and Old Brand. Unfortunately, in addition to varying the brand of cola, we changed an important extraneous variable. We created confounding by always giving subjects the new cola first. Subjects might have rated New Brand higher because it really is delicious, but the ratings were probably distorted because subjects had not had anything to drink for a full 2 hours before they tasted the new product. The subjects may have given the old brands lower ratings because they had just had something else to drink and were no longer thirsty. In this experiment, we see that the *order* in which we presented the treatment conditions (that is, the different colas) may have changed the subjects' responses; we have confounding due

order effects   to **order effects**, the changes in performance that occur when a condition falls in different places in a series of treatments.

Order effects are important in within-subjects experiments. The within-subjects design requires that each subject be in more than one condition, so that naturally subjects will receive some treatments before others. If the order of the treatments alters their effects, we can get some very distorted data. Two kinds of changes occur when subjects run in more than one condition: (1) Performance can decline as the experiment goes on. Subjects get tired. As they solve more and more word problems, for instance, they may begin to make mistakes. They may also become bored or irritated by the experiment and merely "go through the motions" until it is over.

practice effects   (2) Other factors may lead to improvement as the experiment proceeds—to **practice effects**. As subjects become familar with the experiment, they may relax and do a little better. They get better at using the apparatus, develop strategies for solving problems, or even catch on to the real purpose of the study.

progressive   All these changes, both positive and negative, are called **progressive error**: As
error   the experiment progresses, results are distorted. The changes in subjects' responses are not caused by the independent variable; they are order effects produced when we run subjects through more than one treatment condition. We control for any extraneous variable by making sure it affects all treatment conditions in the same way. We can do that by eliminating the variable completely, by holding it constant, or by balancing it out across treatment conditions. In a within-subjects experiment, we cannot eliminate order effects or hold them constant. But we *can* balance them out or distribute them across the conditions so that they affect all conditions equally.

Think about the cola experiment. We did a poor job of setting it up because we let the order of the colas stay the same for all subjects. Everyone tasted the New Brand first. How could we redo the experiment so that progressive error would affect the results for both kinds of colas in the same way? We want to be sure that subjects' ratings reflect accurate taste judgments, not merely a difference between the first and second glass of cola. Suppose we modify our procedures a little. We run the first condition the same as before; subjects do not eat or drink for 2 hours. Then they drink a glass of New Brand cola and give their ratings. But instead of having them drink the Old Brand immediately, we have them return to the lounge for another 2 hours. At the end of that time, we give them the Old Brand cola and get the second set of ratings. Does this help? We avoid the problem of having subjects drink New Brand after 2 hours in the lounge and Old Brand when they are not as thirsty. However, our data may still be contaminated by the order of the conditions. When the subjects drink New Brand, they have been in the lounge a total of 2 hours. When they drink Old Brand, they have spent 4 hours in the lounge. By this time, they may be tired of hanging around. They may be getting hungry. They have also had practice filling out the rating scale, as well as time to think about what they said before.

counter-
balancing

Fortunately, researchers have worked out several procedures for controlling for order effects. These procedures are called **counterbalancing** and they all have the same function: to distribute progressive error across the different treatment conditions of the experiment. By using these procedures, we can guarantee that the order effects which change results in one condition will be offset or counterbalanced by the order effects operating on other conditions.

Let us assume that we can actually graph the effects of progressive error in our cola experiment. With each subject, error accumulates. Subjects get better at filling out the rating scale, they develop criteria for evaluating taste, and so on. Figure 9.1 illustrates what progressive error in this experiment might look like. You can see that it is low in the early part of the experiment and increases gradually as the experiment continues. If everyone tastes New Brand first, there will be *less* progressive error affecting that condition than any other. The experiment will be invalidated.

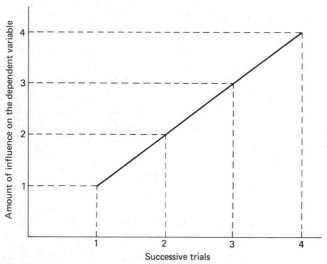

Figure 9.1 The impact of progressive error on responses in an experiment. The later trials (conditions) are affected more than the earlier ones. After Benton J. Underwood, Experimental Psychology (2nd ed.), © 1966, p. 34. By permission of Prentice-Hall, Inc., Englewood Cliffs, New Jersey.

within-subjects
counter-
balancing

Within-Subjects Counterbalancing.   We can control for progressive error through one of two general approaches. First, we can control it by using **within-subjects counterbalancing**. The idea is to divide up the effects of progressive error so that they will be the same for all conditions that each subject completes. How can we do this? Think carefully about what Figure 9.1 is illustrating. The amount of progressive error (that is, the net outcome of fatigue, practice, and so on) in an experiment changes as the experiment continues. We can never expect progressive error to be the same for both conditions as long as we always run one condition first. Progressive error will always be less for the condition we run first. Somehow, we have to set up a procedure to make sure both conditions include some trials when progressive error is relatively low and others when it is relatively high.

If we try different ways of presenting two treatments, we will find one effective way to handle progressive error: present each treatment more than once. We give each subject two glasses of cola, but in a particular order. Let us call New Brand "condition A," and Old Brand "condition B." We can equalize progressive error for these two conditions by presenting them in the order *ABBA*. If you refer to Figure 9.1, you can gain some insight into how the ABBA procedure works. The values of progressive error are given for each of the four successive trials shown. For the first trial, progressive error is equal to 1 unit. For the second trial, 2 units. For the third and fourth trials, 3 and 4 units, respectively. If we run treatment conditions in the ABBA order, progressive error works out to be 5 units for the A condition (1 unit plus 4 units). Progressive error is also 5 units for the B condition (2 plus 3 units). Of course, these numerical quantities are hypothetical, but you can see the logic behind the counterbalancing procedure. Now both conditions contain some trials in which progressive error is relatively high, and others in which it is relatively low. In within-subjects counterbalancing, each subject gets the ABBA sequence. This guarantees that progressive error affects conditions A and B equally for each subject. If there are more than two treatment conditions, we can counterbalance within each subject by continuing the pattern. With three conditions, each subject gets ABCCBA; with four, each subject gets ABCDDCBA; and so on.

between-
subjects
counter-
balancing

Between-Subjects Counterbalancing.   One of the drawbacks of counterbalancing within each subject is that we have to present each condition to each subject more than once. As the number of conditions increases, the length of the sequence also increases. Depending on the experiment, the procedures can become time-consuming, expensive, or just plain boring for the subjects as well as the experimenter. As an alternative, we can often use another set of procedures, **between-subjects counterbalancing**. These procedures serve the same basic purpose as within-subjects counterbalancing. They are used to distribute the effects of progressive error so that they will be the same for all conditions of the experiment. We are not always concerned about the individual subject's responses, but we still want to be sure that progressive error affects the various *treatment conditions* equally. These between-subjects techniques are complete and partial counterbalancing.

complete
counter-
balancing

Complete Counterbalancing.   If we always present treatment conditions in the same order, progressive error will affect some conditions more than others. **Complete counterbalancing** controls for this by using all possible sequences of the conditions, and using every sequence the same number of times. If we had only two treatments, A and B, we would give half the subjects A and then B. We would give the other subjects B first, and then A. You can see that this is very similar to what we did to control order effects within each subject by giving each subject both sequences, AB and BA. When we counterbalance between subjects, we need only to give each subject one sequence. Different subjects are assigned to the different sequences at random. Some subjects go through condition A without any practice; others go through B without any practice. The effects of progressive error should turn out to be about the same for each condition if we pool the data from all subjects.

It is easy to counterbalance when there are only two conditions, but suppose there are more. What if we are testing the hypothesis that people remember happy faces better than sad ones? In the experiment, we have three sets of photographs. One set (A) shows smiling faces. The second set (B) shows frowning faces. The third set (C) is used as a control. It shows faces that appear to be expressionless. We plan to show subjects each set of photographs once. Then we will ask them to go through another much larger set, say 100 in all, and pick out the ones they have seen before. The large set will contain faces of all types so that subjects will not be able to select the right faces simply by picking out all those that are smiling, frowning, or blank. Our dependent variable is the number of faces subjects can recognize in each treatment condition. Clearly we should not show all the "happy" faces first. We know, for instance, that when subjects are asked to remember things, the ones they learn first may interfere with later items. Thus, subjects might recognize the first set of faces more efficiently than later ones. We can control for this kind of error by using complete counterbalancing. We use all the possible sequences of the treatment conditions; we also use each sequence the same number of times.

Table 9.2 shows complete counterbalancing for an experiment with three treatment conditions. There are six possible sequences of the three conditions. For our picture-recognition experiment, we would need sequences like happy, neutral, sad (ACB), and sad, happy, neutral (BAC). To counterbalance completely, we must use all the sequences *and* use each one the same number of times. For six sequences, we will need at least six subjects. Ideally, we should have more than one subject for each sequence, so we need some number of subjects that is a multiple of six. Remember that we have to use all the sequences an equal number of times. We can

TABLE 9.2   THE SIX SEQUENCES OF THREE TREATMENT CONDITIONS

A	B	C		B	A	C
B	C	A		C	B	A
C	A	B		A	C	B

use six, or twelve, or eighteen subjects, but not nine, eleven, or seventeen because these are not multiples of six.

Can we tell in advance how many sequences and how many subjects we will need? How can we be sure we did not miss a sequence? You can find the number of possible sequences by computing n factorial, represented by $n!$ We get $n!$ by computing the following product:

$$n! = 1 \times 2 \times 3 \cdots (n - 1)(n)$$

This may look difficult, but it is really very simple. The n stands for the number we are working with. We begin with 1 and simply multiply each successive number together until we have gone through n. Let us see how it works by computing $4!$:

$$4! = 1 \times 2 \times 3 \times 4 = 24$$

$4!$ is equal to 24. This tells us that when we have 4 treatment conditions, there are 24 possible orders in which to present them.

Earlier we saw that there are six possible sequences if we have only three conditions. You can verify that by the formula too:

$$3! = 1 \times 2 \times 3 = 6$$

The number of possible sequences clearly increases very quickly as the number of treatment conditions rises. To completely counterbalance an experiment, we need at least one subject for each possible sequence. That means we need at least four times as many subjects for a four-condition experiment as we do for a three-condition experiment (24 versus 6 possible sequences). We also need to present each sequence an equal number of times. If we want more than one subject per sequence, we will need multiples of 24 for a four-condition experiment—a minimum of 48 subjects.

Partial Counterbalancing. You can see that it is economical to keep the number of treatments to a minimum. If we double the number of conditions from 3 to 6, we increase the minimum number of subjects needed to completely counterbalance from 6 to 720. Of course it makes sense to omit any condition that is not necessary for a good test of the hypothesis. Still, sometimes six or even more conditions are essential. In those cases, we may use **partial counterbalancing** procedures. The basic idea is still the same. We use these procedures when we cannot do complete counterbalancing but still want to have some control over progressive error. Partial counterbalancing controls progressive error by using some of the available sequences; these sequences are chosen through special procedures.

partial counter-
balancing

The simplest partial counterbalancing procedure is **randomized counterbalancing**: When there are many possible sequences, we randomly select out as many sequences as we have subjects for the experiment. Suppose we have 120 possible sequences (five treatment conditions) and only 30 subjects. We would randomly select 30 sequences, and each subject would get one of those sequences. You can see that this procedure may not control for order effects quite as effectively as

randomized
counter-
balancing

complete counterbalancing, but it is better than simply using the same order for all subjects. If possible, use complete counterbalancing because it is safer. If you must use partial counterbalancing, be realistic about it. If there are 720 possible sequences in the experiment, running three subjects just does not make sense. You will not be able to get good control over order effects. As a rule of thumb, use at least as many randomly selected sequences as there are values of the independent variable.

Carryover Effects

Perry Mason, the great defense attorney, always wins his cases—except one when the client is guilty. He is clever and always finds a way to get to the truth. Imagine him in court, cross-examining a witness. His large, imposing frame commands respect. A witness has just identified the defendant as the woman who passed close by him in the hallway outside the murder victim's apartment. The witness vividly recalls the defendant's rare and expensive perfume. No, he could not be mistaken about it. Mason wants to test the man's ability to identify other scents. He presents the witness with a small vial. Yes, it is essence of lilac. The witness sniffs a second vial and correctly identifies its contents as gasoline. Now, Mason presents the critical test, a vial containing the defendant's perfume. A dismayed and confused witness is unable to identify it. His testimony crumbles. He breaks down and confesses to the crime.

carryover effect

A dramatic and fanciful story indeed—but it illustrates another key problem in the within-subjects design. Mason was using a within-subjects approach when he presented the witness with the vials. What the witness did not know was that Mason was playing with **carryover effects**: the effects of some treatments will persist, or carry over, after they are removed. A few whiffs of gasoline spoiled the witness's ability to identify any other scents for a time. The guilty witness panicked and confessed. On a smaller scale, imagine how carryover effects would sabotage experiments. In the last chapter we saw how some combinations of treatments are impossible to administer to the same subjects. For instance, we cannot both do and not do surgery. Similarly, we do not want to give subjects treatments that will give them clues to what they should do in later conditions. We do not want the effects of early conditions to contaminate later conditions.

We can control for carryover effects to some extent. If treatments affect each other about equally, an experimenter can get reasonably good control by using the same procedures that control for order effects—counterbalancing. Within-subjects counterbalancing and complete counterbalancing will usually control carryover effects adequately. Control is less assured with randomized counterbalancing. Sometimes, though, as we saw with Mason and the gasoline, the effect of one condition is much greater than that of others. Gasoline altered the witness's performance more than lilacs or onions would. When one condition has more impact than the others, we say that the carryover effects are asymmetrical—or more simply, lopsided. When one condition carries over more than the others, control is extremely difficult, if not impossible. In such situations, an experimenter should reconsider the design of the experiment and switch to a between-subjects design if possible.

Choosing among Counterbalancing Procedures.

Every experiment with a within-subjects design will need some form of counterbalancing. Deciding whether to use within- or between-subjects counterbalancing can be a problem in itself. We need to counterbalance within each subject when we expect large differences in the pattern of progressive error from subject to subject. In a weight-lifting experiment we might expect subjects to fatigue at different rates. In that sort of experiment, it makes sense to counterbalance conditions for each person in the study. Counterbalancing within each subject gives the most control over order and carryover effects. In some experiments we do not expect large differences in the way the progressive error affects each subject. To put it another way, if we could graph progressive error for each subject, in some experiments the graphs might look about the same. We do not need to worry about progressive error within each subject when we know the effects will be about the same for everyone.

There are practical things to consider too. You may not have the time to run through all the conditions more than once for each subject. You may not have enough subjects to make between-subjects procedures feasible. The same considerations that come into play as you select a within- or between-subjects design can also limit your choice of controls in the within-subjects experiment. Again, you should look at the procedures that have been used in similar experiments. If prior researchers have had success with between-subjects counterbalancing, it is probably all right to use it. Avoid randomized counterbalancing if you expect carryover effects. When in doubt, counterbalance within-subjects if you can. The worst that can happen is that you may "overcontrol" the experiment. It is always a good idea to use the procedures that give the most control simply because you may not know what the extraneous variables are or whether progressive error really will be the same for all subjects.

SUMMARY

One of the major goals in setting up experiments is to avoid confounding. The independent variable should be the only thing that changes systematically across the conditions of the experiment; extraneous variables must be controlled so that they will not alter the results. Several different control procedures can be used to handle extraneous *physical variables*, aspects of the testing conditions that need to be controlled, such as the nature of the testing room, time of day, the mechanics of running the experiment, and so on.

The three general techniques for dealing with physical variables are *elimination*, *constancy of conditions*, and *balancing*.

Elimination, constancy of conditions, and balancing are essential to all good experiments. However, more complicated control problems occur in experiments with within-subjects designs because each subject takes part in more than one condition of the experiment. In these experiments we have to control for two kinds of extraneous variables, *order effects* and *carryover effects*.

Order effects are the positive and negative changes in performance that occur when a treatment condition falls in different places in a series of treatments. All these effects, both positive and negative, are called *progressive error:* Results are distorted as the experiment *progresses.* We looked at three forms of *counterbalancing,* procedures for controlling order effects. All have the same basic function, to distribute progressive error across the different treatment conditions of the experiment. Within-subjects counterbalancing controls for progressive error within each individual subject and consists of presenting all treatment conditions twice, first in one order, then in reverse order. With two treatment conditions, for example, each subject will get the sequence ABBA. Between-subjects counterbalancing (complete and partial counterbalancing) can accomplish some of the same goals by pooling all subjects' data together to equalize the effects of progressive error for each condition. *Complete counterbalancing* requires using all the possible sequences that can be formed out of the treatment conditions, and using each sequence the same number of times. The number of subjects needed for a completely counterbalanced experiment increases very rapidly as the number of treatment conditions increases. With three conditions, there must be a minimum of six subjects (3!); with six conditions, there must be a minimum of 720 (6!). When complete counterbalancing is not feasible, we may use a *partial counterbalancing* procedure such as *randomized counterbalancing.* This involves selecting a subset of all the available sequences at random.

In addition to order effects, there may also be *carryover effects* in a within-subjects experiment. These occur when the treatment conditions affect each other. Most carryover effects can be controlled adequately by using within-subjects counterbalancing or complete counterbalancing.

Deciding on the particular form of counterbalancing to use may be difficult. Within-subjects counterbalancing offers the most control and should be used whenever possible. If this cannot be done, between-subjects counterbalancing has many practical advantages. Counterbalancing of some form must be used in every experiment that has a within-subjects design. It is always better to err on the side of controlling too much; there is more danger in failing to control something that could affect the results.

REVIEW AND STUDY QUESTIONS

1. What are physical variables in an experiment?

2. How is elimination used as a control procedure? Give two examples of variables that could be controlled by elimination.

3. What is constancy of conditions? Give two examples of variables that can be controlled through constancy of conditions.

4. What is balancing? Give two examples of variables that could be controlled by balancing.

5. Explain the difference between a control group and the control procedures used in an experiment.

6. Suppose a colleague says, "Constancy of conditions does not eliminate extraneous variables from an experiment. So why bother with it?" How would you convince this person that constancy of conditions is an important control procedure?

7. You are doing a study at a local school. Because of the way things are scheduled, you can have one small testing room in the morning and another much larger testing room in the afternoon. If you have two treatment conditions (experimental and control), how can you assign subjects to the testing rooms so that the type of room will not lead to confounding in your experiment?

8. You are planning an experiment on anagrams (jumbled words). You want to test whether different scramble patterns lead to different solution rates. For instance, the letter order 54321 might be easier to solve than 41352 (12345 represents the actual word). You want to use the same words in all conditions so that the type of word will not be a confounding variable. People solve anagrams at different rates, so you are thinking about using a within-subjects design.
   a. If you use a within-subjects design for this experiment, will you have to worry about order effects?
   b. Review the three techniques for handling order effects discussed in this chapter. Which would help you most in this experiment?
   c. What are the carryover effects? Would they be a problem in this experiment? How would you handle them?

9. I have just bought two new pairs of shoes and am wondering which will wear better. Can you design a within-subjects experiment that would answer my question? What extraneous variables would you want to control? Would counterbalancing be useful in this study?

10. A researcher has the hypothesis that subjects will overestimate the speed of a light moving in a circular path, and underestimate the speed of a light moving in a square path. Because of the time it will take to set up the apparatus for each subject, she would like to run the experiment using a within-subjects design.
   a. What problems will arise if she runs all trials with the circular path first?
   b. How would you control for progressive error in this study?

11. A recent television commercial showed people tasting and choosing between two colas. One was labeled "R"; The other was labeled "Q." The majority of people said they liked cola R better than cola Q. Given what you know about experimental design, would you accept the ad's claim that cola R tastes better than cola Q? Why or why not? How might you change the procedures to get more acceptable data?

REFERENCES

Underwood, B. J. *Experimental psychology*. New York: Appleton-Century-Crofts, 1966.

10

Controlling Extraneous Variables: Personality and Social Variables

Personality Variables
    Response Style
    Response Set
Social Variables
    Demand Characteristics
    Experimenter Bias
    Controlling for Social Variables
Summary
Review and Study Questions
References

Key Terms

subject variables	latent content	placebo effect
internal validity	response set	experimenter bias
external validity	demand characteristics	Rosenthal effect
manifest content	social variables	double blind experiment
response style	single blind experiment	

By now you should be feeling more and more optimistic about research. If a researcher plans carefully, keeps the treatment conditions as constant as possible, and uses counterbalancing, he or she is sure to have an airtight experiment. Well, not exactly. Earlier in the text we touched on **subject variables**: all the characteristics of the subjects themselves that might influence the outcome of the experiment. In this chapter, we will look more closely at some important subject variables, response style and response set. We will also consider some of the social factors that affect subjects' responses as well as the experimenter's role in shaping the outcome of the

subject variables

148

experiment. Like physical variables, these personality and social variables must be controlled in order to obtain valid results.

If they are not controlled, we may have experiments that are invalid. A valid experiment measures the true effect of our independent variable. When an experiment has **internal validity**, the changes in the dependent variable across treatment conditions are produced by the experimental manipulations: All the relevant extraneous variables have been controlled so that there is no confounding. However, we are also concerned with **external validity**, whether the findings describe events outside the experiment. Is it possible to extend the results of the experiment to other situations, to other groups of subjects, or to the real world? Both issues can be affected by the experimenter's ability to control for personality and social variables.

internal validity

external validity

PERSONALITY VARIABLES

We can usually control for many subject variables such as intelligence by assigning subjects to treatment conditions at random. Random assignment enables us to form groups of subjects who are about the same on personal characteristics that affect the results of the experiment. When we do not want to rely on randomization (for example, when the number of available subjects is small), we may measure and match subjects on a variable that is known to be related to the dependent variable. Through matching, we can form treatment groups that are roughly the same on critical variables. We use these procedures to be sure the experiment will really tell us what we want to know. Sometimes, however, we can accidentally measure the wrong thing.

Response Style

Take a few moments to look at the statements in Table 10.1. Would you say that each is true or false for you? The items were taken from the Minnesota Multiphasic Personality Inventory (MMPI). The MMPI is made up of a long series of items of this type. The way you answer the items on the test can tell a psychologist various things about your personality—for instance, whether you are anxious or depressed. At first glance, the way people answer such questions seems straightforward. A person who wakes up feeling refreshed ought to answer "true" to the first item. We would expect subjects to respond to the **manifest content** of the questions, the plain meaning of the words that actually appear on the page. If a question asks about poetry, the manifest content of the question is poetry. Subjects should answer each question truthfully based on its manifest content. A subject who never wants to see another poem should say, "I really don't like poetry at all," and answer "False" to item 2.

manifest content

When we give a questionnaire or other paper and pencil test, we are usually interested in the manifest content of the items. "Have you ever visited another country?" means just that; the manifest content of the item is simply foreign travel.

Table 10.1　Sample Items from the Minnesota Multiphasic Personality Inventory

1. I wake up fresh and rested most mornings.
2. I like poetry.
3. I don't seem to care what happens to me.
4. Whenever possible I avoid being in a crowd.
5. Sometimes I have had the same dream over and over.

Source: Copyright 1943, renewed 1970 by the University of Minnesota. Published by the Psychological Corporation, New York, New York. Reprinted by permission of the Psychological Corporation.

Most people would answer based on their actual travel histories. However, researchers have noticed that some interesting things can happen when subjects fill out questionnaires—especially when the questionnaires ask about feelings or attitudes. Some subjects seem to respond to questions in a consistent way: They will answer "Yes" or "True" to most items, or they will say "No" or "False" to most items.

response style　These subjects may have a **response style** (Rorer, 1965), a typical way of answering questions. Some subjects are "yea-sayers"; others are "nay-sayers." Yea-sayers are apt to agree with a question regardless of its manifest content. Nay-sayers tend to disagree no matter what they are asked.

Experiment results can be distorted if we do not guard against response styles. Imagine a simple perception experiment. We have some moving lights on a dark screen. One light moves in a square path; the other moves in a circular path. Both move at the same actual speed. But based on some prior research, we predict that subjects will judge that the light in the circular path moves faster. After subjects watch the lights for a while, we ask them this question: "Did the circular light move faster than the light moving in a square?" By phrasing the question this way, we can expect the yea-sayers to say "Yes," and support our hypothesis. Of course, all the nay-sayers ought to say "No." What is the problem? Some subjects say "Yes" and others say "No." Doesn't it all balance out? Well, the yea-sayers and nay-sayers may be of equal numbers. But now the problem becomes one of validity: Are we really measuring what we set out to measure? We want to know something about how subjects perceive lights that move along paths of different shapes. Instead, we seem to be measuring the way that subjects answer questions.

How can we avoid a problem with response style? In the perception experiment, we can measure the dependent variable (what the subjects saw) in a better way. Instead of just asking whether the circular light moved faster, we might ask this: "Did the circular light move faster, slower, or about the same as the square light?" This question poses its own problems, as we will see in the next section. However, it is a cut above the original question because it cannot be answered with a simple "Yes" or "No." It forces the subject to think more about the answer. This helps to control the effects of yea-saying and nay-saying. Warwick and Lininger (1975) recommend this approach when writing a series of questions. They suggest giving each option some specific content. For instance, think about the difference between these two items:

"Do you agree or disagree that the cost of living has gone up in the last year?"

"In your opinion have prices gone up, gone down, or stayed about the same the past year, or don't you know?" (p. 146)

When we phrase questions to have simple yes/no or agree/disagree answers, we make it easy for subjects to respond based on response style. By building some specific content into the options, we encourage subjects to give more thought to each choice.

If we must use yes/no questions, we can still take some precautions. Table 10.2 shows two versions of the Unfounded Optimism Inventory (UOI). The "optimistic" choice is underlined for each item. We would say that a person who makes many optimistic choices has more unfounded optimism than one who makes few of those choices. Notice that the two versions of our test are quite different. The manifest content of the items is the same for both versions; we are asking about the same things in both sets of questions. The difference is in the way the items are "keyed." To get a high Unfounded Optimism score on version A, a person would have to answer most of the items by saying "Yes." All the items in version A are written so that the "optimistic" response is a "yes" response. Subjects who are yea-sayers would score high on unfounded optimism—even if they happen to be somewhat pessimistic.

TABLE 10.2   THE UNFOUNDED OPTIMISM INVENTORY (UOI)

Version A: No Control for Response Style			Version B: Controlling for Response Style[a]		
1. I know that everything will be all right.	<u>Yes</u>	NO	1. I know that everything will be all right.	<u>Yes</u>	NO
2. I can pick the fastest line at the bank.	<u>Yes</u>	NO	2. I always stand in the slowest line at the bank.	YES	<u>No</u>
3. I often smile at nothing.	<u>Yes</u>	NO	3. I rarely smile, even when provoked.	YES	<u>No</u>
4. If I lose money, I expect it to be returned.	<u>Yes</u>	NO	4. If I lose money I expect it to be returned.	<u>Yes</u>	NO

[a] The Yes/No responses are also counterbalanced to control for order effects.

Now look at version B. Some questions from version A have been rewritten so that the "optimistic" response can be either "Yes" or "No," depending on the question. To get a high Unfounded Optimism score, a subject would have to give both "Yes" and "No" answers. Using a version like this, we would know that subjects who turned up high on Unfounded Optimism are probably not pessimistic yea-sayers. In other words, by controlling for the effects of response style in the questions, we can develop more valid measures. We can come closer to getting the information we are seeking.

Response Set

Someone with a response style will answer questions without paying much attention to the manifest content of each item. The person will answer "Yes" or "No" depending

latent content

response set

on whether he or she is a yea-sayer or a nay-sayer. Other subjects may answer questions based on **latent content**, the meaning behind the question. When we try to "read between the lines," we are looking for latent content. Take a moment to answer the questions in Table 10.3. Can you tell what the latent content of these items is? What are these questions really asking?

The questions are taken from a scale developed to test the idea that subjects may have a **response set**, that some people respond to the latent rather than the manifest content of an item. In other words, they respond based on what they think their answers will show. Crowne and Marlowe (1964) developed this particular set of questions to test whether subjects have the response set called "social desirability." In order to look good on many of the items, you would have to lie. For instance, few of us would find it easy to get along with "loud-mouthed, obnoxious people," although it is socially desirable, or nice, to be able to get along with everyone. Subjects who have the social desirability response set will lie in order to make themselves look better in the eyes of the experimenter. They may not lie on all questions, but they will distort the truth enough to make themselves look better. For instance, Carol C might say "true" to the first question, indicating that she looks into the qualifications of all the candidates running for office. In reality, Carol studies only the qualifications of the major party candidates. She may or may not feel that she is actually lying. She may believe that she is just bending the question a little.

Whether or not the subject feels a sense of guilt or remorse for making a better than true impression is not usually critical to the experiment. What does concern us is the way a response set can alter the data we get. We can never be completely sure that subjects have given us accurate data. In any number of experiments, subjects may distort the truth in order to improve their image. For instance, a subject might report that he is "very confident" about a particular task, whereas he really feels very uneasy about it. If subjects' confidence ratings are the dependent variable, the experiment may lead to some inaccurate conclusions.

What can we do about response sets? A person with a response set will answer based on the latent content of questions. Some subjects may try to give the most socially desirable response; others will try to give a deviant response. To counteract a response set, we can develop alternative questions that have the same latent content. For example, which of the following best describes your attitudes toward pets?

( ) Everyone should have a pet.
( ) I think pets are a waste of time.
    or
( ) Pets are fun but not everyone wants the responsibility.
( ) Pets make good companions.

You can see how the implications of the choices differ. In the first pair, one answer seems to be more socially desirable than the other. John L might feel pressured to pick the first choice so that he will appear to be an animal lover. In the second pair, the choices are about equally acceptable. John L can show that he likes animals

TABLE 10.3 THE MARLOWE-CROWNE SOCIAL DESIRABILITY SCALE PERSONAL REACTION INVENTORY[a]

Listed below are a number of statements concerning personal attitudes and traits. Read each item and decide whether the statement is true or false as it pertains to you personally.

1. Before voting I thoroughly investigate the qualifications of all the candidates. (T)
2. I never hesitate to go out of my way to help someone in trouble. (T)
3. It is sometimes hard for me to go on with my work if I am not encouraged. (F)
4. I have never intensely disliked anyone. (T)
5. On occasion I have had doubts about my ability to succeed in life. (F)
6. I sometimes feel resentful when I don't get my way. (F)
7. I am always careful about my manner of dress. (T)
8. My table manners at home are as good as when I eat out in a restaurant. (T)
9. If I could get into a movie without paying and be sure I was not seen, I would probably do it. (F)
10. On a few occasions, I have given up doing something because I thought too little of my ability. (F)
11. I like to gossip at times. (F)
12. There have been times when I felt like rebelling against people in authority even though I knew they were right. (F)
13. No matter who I'm talking to, I'm always a good listener. (T)
14. I can remember "playing sick" to get out of something. (F)
15. There have been occasions when I took advantage of someone. (F)
16. I'm always willing to admit it when I make a mistake. (T)
17. I always try to practice what I preach. (T)
18. I don't find it particularly difficult to get along with loud-mouthed, obnoxious people. (T)
19. I sometimes try to get even, rather than forgive and forget. (F)
20. When I don't know something, I don't at all mind admitting it. (T)
21. I am always courteous, even to people who are disagreeable. (T)
22. At times I have really insisted on having things my own way. (F)
23. There have been occasions when I felt like smashing things. (F)
24. I would never think of letting someone else be punished for my wrongdoings. (T)
25. I never resent being asked to return a favor. (T)
26. I have never been irked when people expressed ideas very different from my own. (T)
27. I never make a long trip without checking the safety of my car. (T)
28. There have been times when I was quite jealous of the good fortune of others. (F)
29. I have almost never felt the urge to tell someone off. (T)
30. I am sometimes irritated by people who ask favors of me. (F)
31. I have never felt that I was punished without cause. (T)
32. I sometimes think when people have a misfortune they only got what they deserved. (F)
33. I have never deliberately said something that hurt someone's feelings. (T)

[a]The responses shown are the socially desirable ones.

Source: From D. P. Crowne and D. Marlowe, *The approval motive*, pp. 23–24. Reprinted by permission of D. P. Crowne. Copyright 1964 John Wiley & Sons, Inc., New York.

by selecting either item. He can also express his feeling that pets can be a nuisance, but without feeling that his response will stigmatize him in some way. The second set of alternatives is more likely to lead to accurate data.

SOCIAL VARIABLES

social variables

In addition to controlling subject variables that might alter the outcome of the experiment, researchers are concerned about **social variables**, qualities of the relationships between subjects and experimenters that may influence the results. Two principal social variables, demand characteristics and experimenter bias, can be controlled through single and double blind experiments.

Demand Characteristics

demand characteristics

Response set and response style are important in many experiments, especially those in which we obtain data through questionnaires. But there is another more general source of error affecting experiments in which we have human subjects: **demand characteristics**, aspects of the situation itself which *demand* that people behave in a particular way. Have you ever walked along a busy street and noticed someone looking up at the sky or at a building? You may have found yourself turning to look up too. This is a good example of what we mean by demand characteristics. What we do is often shaped by what we think we are expected to do. When you enter a classroom, even on the first day of the term, you probably walk in and take a seat. When the professor begins talking, you listen. Of course you are fulfilling a role you learned in your earliest days at school, the role of the "good student" in the classroom; the cue of being in the classroom leads you to behave in a predictable way. Most research subjects want to be "good" subjects. They want to conform to what they think is the proper role of "subject." They may not even be consciously aware of the ways in which they alter their behavior when they come into an experiment. For example, subjects may assume a very active role. They may try to guess the hypothesis of the experiment, and adjust their responses accordingly.

Let us return to the perception experiment in which two lights move at the same speed but in different paths. We are looking for a difference in the way subjects perceive the movement of these lights. Specifically, we expect subjects to perceive the light in the circular path as moving faster. We ask: "Did the light in the circular path move faster, slower, or about the same as the light in the square path?" If you were a subject in this experiment, what would you think about this question? The experimenter has gone to a lot of trouble to set up these lights and recruit subjects. Suppose you really could not see any difference in the speed of the lights. But why would anyone go to the bother of showing you two lights that move at the same speed, and then ask you whether one moved faster? You might begin to suspect that there really *was* some subtle difference in the speeds, and somehow you did not notice it. But you want to be a good subject. You do not want to tell the experimenter that you were not paying attention, or that you are not very good at judging speed. So, you guess. You say: "Well, maybe the round one really was moving a little faster because it didn't make all those turns. So, I'll say the round one was faster even though I'm not sure that's what I saw."

An experimenter generally wants subjects to be as naive as possible. They should understand the nature and purpose of the experiment, but not the exact hypothesis. The reason for this is simple. If subjects know what we expect to find, they may produce data that will support the hypothesis. On the surface, that may seem like a good thing. Wouldn't it be wonderful if experiments always confirmed their hypotheses? It would—if the experiments were valid. We want to be able to say that the independent variable caused a change in behavior. If behavior changes simply because subjects think the researcher wants an experiment to turn out in a particular way, the experiment has not measured what it was intended to measure.

Subjects often try to guess the hypotheses. This is a problem, especially in experiments that have within-subjects designs. Since the subjects in within-subjects experiments take part in more than one treatment condition, they usually have a better chance to make a stab at guessing the hypothesis. Of course, subjects sometimes guess incorrectly. They may think they are helping by responding in a particular way, but their "help" produces data that make it impossible to confirm the hypothesis. Occasionally subjects will actually try to produce data that conflict with the hypothesis. They may guess the hypothesis, disagree with it, and set out to disprove it. Again they may be wrong; they may actually wind up supporting the predictions. But either way, our problem is that this kind of data is not worth much. We want to set up experiments in which we can test the effect of an independent variable, not the subjects' skill at "psyching out" experiments. Does this sort of thing really happen? Do subjects' experiences and answers change depending on what they think is supposed to happen in the experiment? Can the demand characteristics of an experiment lead to changes in subject behavior? What if subjects simply do what they think they are supposed to do? Orne and Scheibe (1964) devised a clever experiment to evaluate the effects of demand characteristics on research on sensory deprivation.

Traditionally, subjects in sensory deprivation experiments were isolated from sensory experiences of all kinds. They wore translucent goggles so that they could not see shapes. White noise (noise of all frequencies that sounds very much like static on a radio) was played to mask ordinary sounds. Subjects were typically restricted to lying on a soft bed. They wore coverings over their arms to minimize sensations from movement and touch. With these procedures, prolonged sensory deprivation led to emotional upset, disorientation, and even hallucinations. Orne and Scheibe followed a very different procedure. They placed their experimental and control subjects alone in a room that hardly created any deprivation at all. The room was $6 \times 7 \times 8$ feet in size and was furnished with a desk and two chairs. The subjects could easily hear sounds from the hallway and birds chirping outside. They did not wear goggles and so had their normal vision. There was water and a sandwich in case they got hungry. They were given a set of arithmetic problems to work on if they wanted something to do, and they could move around as much as they wanted to within the room.

The difference between the experimental and control groups in this study was the way the experiment was presented to each group. Experimental subjects were interviewed by a man in a white medical coat. A tray of drugs and medical instruments, labeled "Emergency Tray," was in the room. Subjects were told that there was an alarm button in the "deprivation chamber." If they became upset, they were advised to press the alarm button. They were also told that a physician was present. Pulse and blood pressure readings were taken. Everything possible was done to create an atmosphere of seriousness and preparation for a possible crisis. Subjects were also read some instructions for reporting their experiences while in the chamber, including possible visual imagery, unusual feelings, and disorientation—the typical sensory deprivation effects. Control group subjects were told that they were control subjects. The experimenter wore regular business clothes. There was no "Emergency Tray" or alarm button. Subjects were told that if they wanted to leave the chamber, they could simply knock on the window. They were given the same general instructions to report their experiences, but everything was done to create a relaxed impression. When the blood pressure and pulse readings were made, the control subjects were told that the readings were being taken simply because they had been taken for the experimental subjects.

If we compare the two procedures, we see that Orne and Scheibe manipulated demand characteristics in their experiment. All subjects were placed in the same "deprivation" setting. But the experimental subjects were given every reason to expect that something awful, or at least out of the ordinary, might happen to them. The control group was treated in a more casual way that probably communicated something like "You'll be in this room for a while." What would you expect to happen in this experiment? Would subjects show the usual effects of sensory deprivation? If we look just at the physical layout of this experiment, we can see that there is little reason to expect anyone to become disoriented or show any other unusual symptoms in a short period of time. The subjects had full use of all their senses. Their movements were not restricted, they could eat, and they had a task to do if they got bored.

What Orne and Scheibe found implicated demand characteristics as a cause of some of the prior sensory deprivation findings: Their experimental subjects, those led to expect some strange experience, showed significantly more signs of disturbance in the isolation chamber. Compared to the controls, the experimental subjects gave the "impression of almost being tortured" (p. 11). All the subjects in Orne and Scheibe's experiment experienced the same "deprivation," but only the experimental group showed the usual effects of sensory deprivation. For the experimental group, the researchers had created the impression that something unusual would happen to them. The subjects' expectations were confirmed: They experienced a variety of changes that did not occur for the control subjects, who had a different set of expectations. The changes were varied and at times dramatic: "the buzzing of the fluorescent light is growing alternately louder and softer, so that at times it sounds like a jackhammer"; "there are multicolored spots on the wall"; "the numbers on the number sheets are blurring and assuming various inkblot forms." (p. 10) Indeed, one subject hit the panic button and listed "disorganization of senses" as one of his reasons for stopping. These findings do not rule out the possibility that some genuine changes *do* occur when subjects undergo an actual restriction of sensory experience. They do, however, illustrate the importance of demand characteristics in shaping the outcome of such studies.

Controlling Demand Characteristics: Single Blind Experiments.   When we run experiments we try not to give subjects clues to what may happen to them because of the independent variable. We do not want to influence the outcome of the experiment by having subjects know the hypothesis. A good way to control some effects of demand characteristics is through a **single blind experiment**, an experiment in which subjects do not know which treatment they are getting.

single blind
experiment

When we do a single blind experiment we can tell subjects what we expect to happen in the experiment; we can keep them fully informed about the purpose of the study. But we keep them "blind" to one thing: We *do not* tell them what treatment condition they are in. This approach is very common in experiments with drugs. If we give a subject some substance, the subject might react based on what he or she expects the drug to do. For instance, suppose we want to test a new headache remedy. If we give the new drug to several people with headaches, some of them will report that they feel better after taking the medicine. Did the medicine help? Of course, we cannot say; we need a control group of people who do not receive the drug. But researchers know that if you give a person any pill, the person is apt to say the pill helped. We call this the **placebo effect** (pronounced plə–sé–bō).

placebo effect

When we test a drug, we give the control group a placebo—a pill, injection, or other treatment that contains none of the actual medication. We do not tell subjects which treatment they are receiving. The subject is "blind" to that aspect of the experiment. We can eliminate some of the effects of demand characteristics by ensuring that subjects do not know exactly what changes (if any) they should expect. However, as Leavitt (1974) points out, subjects typically know they are getting *a* treatment, and so we may rarely be able to measure the actual effects of a drug *by itself*. Instead, we see the effects of the treatment, plus placebo effects that are shaped by the subjects' expectations. We then compare those effects with the effects of the placebo alone on the control group.

Subjects in a single blind experiment do not know exactly what to expect. They cannot be sure whether they are in the control group or an experimental group. If we see changes in their behavior, those changes are more likely to be caused by the independent variable. Subjects will not be able to report what they think the experimenter wants to hear (for example, that the new medication made them feel better). They will not know what the experimenter expects because they will not know which treatment they are getting.

Figure 10.1 An advertisement for Dr. R. C. Flower's Nerve Pills. The success of some patent medicines can be attributed in part to placebo effects. However, a large measure of alcohol in some preparations may have helped too. National Library of Medicine, Bethesda, Maryland 20014.

Experimenter Bias

Perhaps without realizing it, an experimenter can give subjects cues that tell them how he or she would like them to respond. Subjects will often comply with these subtle requests and give the data the experimenter is seeking. Imagine the experimenter running the perception experiment. She asks, "Does the light in the circular path move faster, slower, or at the same speed as the light in the square path?" As she says "faster" she leans forward slightly, raises her eyebrows, and speaks a little louder. Most of her subjects say that the light in the circular path moved "faster."

experimenter bias   We call this sort of influence **experimenter bias**; the experimenter does something that creates confounding in the experiment. The experimenter may give a cue to respond in a particular way, or he or she may behave differently in different treatment conditions. Dr. R might be warm and friendly in the experimental condition, but indifferent in the control condition. That is all right if the experimenter's demeanor is the independent variable. If it is not, it may confound the results. Subjects might feel more at ease in the experimental condition and so perform better.

So far, it seems that experimenter effects can be a problem only with human subjects. After all, a rat will not notice a smile and then learn faster. Probably not,

Rosenthal
effect

but experimenter effects can be just as important in animal studies as they are in human ones. Experimenters may treat subjects differently depending on what they expect from them. This outcome is called the **Rosenthal effect** after the man who first reported it (Rosenthal, 1976). (It is also called the Pygmalion effect after the legend in which the sculptor Pygmalion fell in love with his own statue of the perfect woman.) Experimenters may handle rats more and handle them more gently if they think they are special. They may give more time to subjects that have gone through a particular treatment. (Box 10.1 summarizes some of Rosenthal's key findings.) The Rosenthal effect can be another source of confounding in an experiment.

The experimenter may also make errors in recording the data from the experiment. He or she may "misread" a scale or score an item incorrectly. Coincidentally, Rosenthal (1978) reported that researchers are more likely to make errors that favor the hypothesis. In a sample of 21 published studies, he found that about 1 percent of all observations made were probably wrong. Of those, two-thirds favored the experimenters' hypotheses. By chance, we would expect only about 50 percent of the errors to support the researchers' hypotheses.

Controlling Experimenter Bias: Double Blind Experiments. How can we eliminate experimenter effects from research? The first step, of course, is to be aware of them. We want to be sure we do not do anything that will contaminate the data. By using written directions, timing all phases of the experiment, and being as consistent as possible, we can avoid some mistakes. But sometimes we just cannot anticipate how bias might creep into an experiment.

Let us say we are doing a study of cartoons and children's art. We want to see whether children who have just watched a cartoon will draw more abstract pictures than children who just watched a filmed version of the same story. The cartoon group sees drawings of people; the film group sees actual people acting out the same story. We show the children the cartoon or film. Then we ask them to draw pictures.

We have developed a way of scoring the children's drawings for abstractness. Our measure includes a number of specific dimensions, such as whether objects are colored in their true-to-life colors. We will score each child's picture on the abstractness scale. If our hypothesis is correct, the drawings of the children who saw the cartoon will be more abstract than the drawings of children who saw the film.

As we sit down to score the pictures, we notice different features. We may also notice that we tend to score somewhat differently depending on which child drew the picture. Sometimes it is not clear how we should score a particular item. Melanie drew what appears to be a green orange. Oranges really *are* green before they get ripe, but they are usually orange in pictures. Should we score this as "abstract" or not? We should have worked out these kinds of issues before running the experiment. But if these questions do arise in scoring, we might find ourselves deciding in favor of the more abstract rating if we were scoring a picture drawn by a child who saw the cartoon. We might distort the scoring a little by being inconsistent. In doing so, we would bias the data so that they would support our own hypothesis. We might do this without even realizing it.

Box 10.1   **The Rosenthal Effect**

In a variety of laboratory and nonlaboratory studies, researchers have documented the self-fulfilling prophecy: Expectations can alter the behavior of others, even animals, as Rosenthal explained:

> Fode and I told a class of 12 students that one could produce a strain of intelligent rats by inbreeding them to increase their ability to run mazes quickly. To demonstrate, we gave each student five rats, which had to learn to run to the darker of two arms of a T-maze. We told half of our student-experimenters that they had the "maze-bright," intelligent rats; we told the rest that they had the stupid rats. Naturally, there was no real difference among any of the animals.
>
> But they certainly behaved differently in their performance. The rats believed to be bright improved daily in running the maze—they ran faster and more accurately—while the apparently dull animals did poorly. The "dumb" rats refused to budge from the starting point 29 percent of the time, while the "smart" rats were recalcitrant only 11 percent of the time.
>
> Then we asked our students to rate the rats and to describe their own attitudes toward them. Those who believed they were working with intelligent animals *liked* them better and found them more pleasant. Such students said they felt more relaxed with the animals; they treated them more gently and were more enthusiastic about the experiment than students who thought they had dull rats to work with. Curiously, the students with "bright" rats said they handled them more but talked to them less. One wonders what students with "dull" rats were saying to those poor creatures. (p. 248)[1]

In a later study, Rosenthal and Jacobson found a similar effect in the classroom. They gave children an IQ test at the start of the school year. Randomly selected children in each class were labeled "intellectual bloomers." "We then gave each teacher the names of these children, who, we explained, could be expected to show remarkable gains during the coming year on the basis of their test scores. In fact, the difference between these experimental children and the control group was solely in the teacher's mind." (p. 248)[1] Eight months later, they found greater gains in the IQ scores of the "bloomers" relative to the other children. Based on this and many other studies, Rosenthal proposed a fourfold explanation for the phenomenon:

> People who have been led to expect good things from their students, children, clients, or what-have-you appear to:
>   —create a warmer social-emotional mood around their "special" students (*climate*);
>   —give more feedback to these students about their performance (*feedback*);
>   —teach more material and more difficult material to their special students (*input*);
>   —give their special students more opportunities to respond and question (*output*). (p. 250)[1]

[1] *Source*: R. Rosenthal. The Pygmalion effect lives. In *Readings in Developmental Psychology Today* (2nd ed.). Edited by Robert E. Schell. New York: Random House, 1977, 247–252. Reprinted from *Psychology Today* magazine. Copyright © 1973 Ziff-Davis Publishing Company.

---

double blind experiment   One of the best ways of controlling for experimenter bias is to run a **double blind experiment**, one in which the subjects do not know which treatment they are in, and the experimenter does not know either. The value of the double blind experiment is this: If the experimenter does not know which treatment the subject is getting, he or she cannot bias the responses in any systematic way. Since the subject is kept in the dark too, the effects of demand characteristics are controlled along with experimenter bias.

If we are running a nutrition experiment and want to use the double blind procedure, we get an assistant to assign subjects to treatment conditions. Experimental subjects receive a dietary supplement (for example, vitamin E). Control subjects receive a placebo. The subjects are not told which treatment they will receive; they only know they are part of an experiment on nutrition and that they may or may not receive a vitamin supplement which is thought to produce various effects. The assistant administers the treatments. When we measure the subjects on the dependent variable (for example, interview them, observe them in a waiting room, or score them on a written test), we also do not know which treatment each received. We are "blind" to that information. After the data have been collected and scored, the assistant lets us know who belonged to each treatment group. We can then go on to evaluate the impact of the independent variable.

In some experiments, the subjects always know what treatment condition they are getting. For instance, in our study of cartoons and children's art, each child would know whether he or she saw a cartoon or a film. The children would not know the exact hypothesis of the study. Still, we could not really say that they are "blind" to the treatment conditions. In these experiments, we may not be able to use a truly double or even single blind procedure. Even so, we can build in some controls for experimenter bias. We can make sure that the person who scores the subjects' responses does not know which treatment each subject received. We might have an independent rater score subjects' drawings. We do not tell the rater which subjects belonged to which group. If we are doing our own scoring, it is more difficult to remain naive. However, with some planning we can skirt the most serious temptations. We standardize the testing and scoring procedures as much as possible. We try to be consistent in the way we handle the experiment from one subject to another. We avoid giving subjects extraneous clues to how to behave. As you design experiments, you will work very hard to control sources of confounding. Do not forget that *you* may be the biggest extraneous variable of all.

Personality and social variables can affect experiments. As you think about an experiment, try to anticipate subjects' reactions. Put yourself in the subject's place. How would you feel about answering your own questions? Would you be inclined to distort your answers because you would be too embarrassed to answer honestly? Would the experimental hypothesis be obvious to you? Think about your own behavior and the design of the experiment. Have you stacked the deck in any way? Do your instructions suggest the changes you expect to observe? Have you taken precautions to keep your own behavior as consistent as possible from one treatment condition to another? Are your instructions written? Are you prepared to introduce yourself and interact with all your subjects in the same way? You may find it useful to make a dry run before you start testing subjects.

This chapter brings us to the close of the method section of the text. We have covered many techniques for designing and running solid experiments. In the next section we will look at results and our next important question: What do we do with our data once we have them?

SUMMARY

An experiment should measure what it is intended to measure: It should be valid. An *internally valid* experiment is one in which the researcher is confident that the changes in behavior across treatments were caused by the independent variable. An experiment is *externally valid* if the results can be applied to other situations. A variety of personality and social variables may lead to invalidity in an experiment: response style, response set, demand characteristics, and experimenter bias.

A subject with a *response style* has a characteristic way of answering questions. Subjects with a response style will answer "Yes" and "True" or "No" and "False" to most items. They do not base their answers on the *manifest content*, the plain, obvious meaning of the words. To control for response style, experimenters write questions in such a way that subjects cannot answer with a simple "Yes" or "No." They try to build specific content into each choice so that subjects will be forced to think about their responses. Experimenters also want to avoid measuring a *response set*. Subjects with a response set respond in terms of *latent content*, the meaning behind the questions. Social desirability is the best known response set. Subjects who have the social desirability response set will lie (or at least distort the truth) in order to look better in the eyes of the experimenter. Social desirability can be controlled to some extent by wording questions so that alternative answers have roughly the same social value. Subjects should then be able to answer the manifest content of the questions.

Demand characteristics can also create problems in experiments. Just being in an experiment can lead to changes in a subject's behavior that may have nothing to do with the experimental manipulation. Subjects may want to be "good" subjects; they may try to provide data that confirm the hypothesis. Their expectations about what will happen to them in the experiment can also shape their responses. One way of controlling demand characteristics is to run a *single blind experiment* in which the experimenter tells subjects everything about the experiment *except* which treatment they will receive. This is a common approach to drug and nutrition experiments. Subjects are told that they may receive a drug or vitamin, or a placebo. The *placebo* is a pill, injection, or other treatment that contains none of the actual substance being tested. Because the subjects in a single blind experiment do not know for sure which treatment condition they are in, they are less likely to provide data that are distorted to conform to their notion of what the researcher expects to find.

The last potential source of error discussed in this chapter is the experimenter. Without realizing it, an experimenter may give subtle cues that tell subjects how they are expected to behave. If an experimenter smiles at subjects every time they give the predicted response, he or she may not be getting an accurate picture of the way the independent variable operates. One way to control for experimenter bias is the *double blind experiment*. In a double blind experiment, the experimenter does not know which treatment the subjects are getting, and the subjects do not know either. This approach enables the experimenter to measure the dependent variable more objectively.

REVIEW AND STUDY QUESTIONS

1. Define each of the following terms:
   a. Manifest content
   b. Latent content
   c. Response style
   d. Response set

2. You are preparing a questionnaire on attitudes toward child-rearing practices: Are parents permissive or strict?
   a. What would you do to control for response style?
   b. Make up a set of four simple questions, controlling for response style.
   c. Would you worry about response set? How might response set affect subjects' responses to the questionnaire?

3. What are demand characteristics? How do they affect our data?

4. What is a single blind experiment?

5. Outline a single blind experiment to test this hypothesis: A new drug, Elate, makes hospital patients less depressed.
   a. What is the independent variable?
   b. What is the dependent variable?
   c. What is a placebo? Will you use one in this experiment? Why?

6. A researcher says, "I want my experiment to be a success. I'm sure my hypothesis is correct. So I'll just give my subjects a couple of hints here and there. You know, maybe a wink now and then if they give a good answer. That way I'll really be able to show that my independent variable had an effect."
   a. How would you convince her that her plan is faulty?
   b. What is a double blind experiment? Would you recommend that she use it? Why or why not?

7. Dr. R is planning a large-scale learning experiment. She would like to have 100 rats in the experimental group and another 100 in the control group. Because she needs so many rats, she says, "Well, I can't test all these animals by myself. I'll ask Dr. G to help me. I'll let her run the animals in the control group while I test the animals in the experimental group."
   a. Knowing what you know about experimenter bias, is Dr. R's solution a good one? What may happen if one experimenter tests all the experimental subjects while another tests all the control subjects?
   b. Given what you know about balancing procedures, can you work out a better plan for Dr. R?

8. Discuss the ways in which response set and response style might influence the validity of an experiment.

REFERENCES

Crowne, D. P., and Marlowe, D. *The approval motive*. New York: Wiley, 1964.

Leavitt, P. *Drugs and behavior*. Philadelphia: Saunders, 1974.

Orne, M. T., and Scheibe, K. E. The contribution of nondeprivation factors in the production of sensory deprivation effects: The psychology of the "panic button." *Journal of Abnormal and Social Psychology*, 1964, 68, 3–12.

Rorer, L. G. The great response-style myth. *Psychological Bulletin*, 1965, 63, 129–156.

Rosenthal, R. *Experimenter effects in behavioral research*. (2nd ed.) New York: Halsted Press, 1976.

Rosenthal, R. The Pygmalion effect lives. In *Readings in Developmental Psychology Today* (2nd ed.) Edited by Robert E. Schell. New York: Random House, 1977, 247–252.

Rosenthal, R. How often are our numbers wrong? *American Psychologist*, 1978, 33, No. 11, 1005–1008.

Warwick, D. P., and Lininger, C. A. *The sample survey: Theory and practice*. New York: McGraw-Hill, 1975.

Part Three

Results: Coping with Data

11

Why We Need Statistics

Key Terms

statistical inference	normal curve	nondirectional hypothesis
variability	significance level	one-tailed test
null hypothesis	Type 1 error	standard normal curve
statistically significant	Type 2 error	inferential statistics
alternative hypothesis	critical region	test statistics
directional hypothesis	two-tailed test	

Somehow the word "statistics" brings terror to the eyes of the most dedicated student. You may be experiencing some of the same symptoms. If you glance through this chapter, however, you will find that there are very few numbers. There are no computations. Instead, the chapter is intended to give you a general understanding of why we use statistics in research. We will also cover some basic terms that you need to understand how statistics are applied. The point of doing statistics is that they enable us to evaluate the data we worked so hard to collect. Let us look at a hypothetical mystery to illustrate the kind of evaluation that takes place.

WEIGHING THE EVIDENCE

Ms. Adams has just been arrested for murder. Detective Katz has found the victim's car keys, footprints, and bifocals in Ms. Adams' apartment. Witnesses say the victim and Ms. Adams were having dinner together at the local coffee shop shortly before the crime was committed. Yes, there is evidence against her. But did she actually commit the crime? Detective Katz knows he must establish her guilt beyond a reasonable doubt. Can he do that? Yes, he has the keys, the footprints, and even the bifocals that were found in Ms. Adams' apartment. He has witnesses who will swear they saw suspect and victim dining calmly on hot pastrami sandwiches shortly before the murder. But is this proof? What Detective Katz has put together is a case based largely on circumstantial evidence. The evidence suggests that Ms. Adams knew the victim well enough to share pastrami sandwiches, and that the victim visited her apartment. The evidence implicates Ms. Adams in the crime, but it does not *prove* that she did it. Other people may have known the victim well enough to share sandwiches too. And other people may have committed the murder. The best Detective Katz can do is establish Ms. Adams' guilt beyond a reasonable doubt. He can show that she, more than anyone else, is likely to be the murderer.

When we carry out a psychological experiment, we find ourselves in a plight similar to the one Detective Katz is in. We have run an experiment. Katz has investigated a case. We have gathered some data. Katz has collected evidence. Katz would like to prove his suspect committed the crime. We would like to prove our independent variable caused the changes we see in our dependent variable.

Given all you have learned about experimentation, you will not be too surprised to learn that we can never actually *prove* an independent variable caused the changes we see in a dependent variable. Proving something means establishing the truth of it by presenting evidence and logical arguments. Do you remember doing proofs in geometry? You began with a premise such as this: In every right triangle, the square of the hypotenuse is equal to the sum of the squares of the legs. You would then use all the facts you knew about geometry to construct a logical argument that would prove the premise true. Your proof would show that the premise is true because there could be no logical alternative. You would come down to a final step that would look something like this: $AB = AB$. Unfortunately, outside of mathematics, proving things is not always so straightforward. Detective Katz would like to prove Ms. Adams is guilty. He believes she is. But can he develop a proof as airtight as AB which is the same as AB? Since his evidence is circumstantial, the best he can do is show that she is *probably* guilty.

When we evaluate the data from a psychological experiment, we do a very similar thing. We carry out statistical tests to determine whether the independent variable *probably* caused changes in the dependent variable from one treatment condition to another. We cannot really prove that it did. Other factors such as subject variables can also lead to differences. However, we can make some statements about how likely it is that the independent variable had an effect. We base those statements on the statistical tests that we do.

STATISTICAL INFERENCE: AN OVERVIEW

As we evaluate the results of an experiment, we naturally want to be able to come to conclusions about the impact of the independent variable. We could just look at our results and see which groups did better. But that would not be very precise. When we run an experiment, we typically do so by using a sample of subjects drawn from a population. Subjects' scores on any dependent variable will differ; scores of individuals in the population will also differ. The question we ask with statistics is this: Are the differences we see between treatments significantly greater than what we would expect to see between *any* samples of subjects drawn from this population? Answering this question involves a **statistical inference**, making a statement about the population and all its samples based on what we see in the samples we have.

statistical
inference

Suppose students in a class are asked to report their weights. The mean or average weight of the 12 students on the window side of the room is 152 pounds. The mean weight of the 12 students on the opposite side of the room is 147 pounds, an absolute difference of 5 pounds. Would you conclude from these measurements that students on the two sides of the room do not belong to the same population? Perhaps they belong to different species. Or perhaps sitting near the windows causes students to gain weight. More likely, you are thinking that it is silly to make anything of a difference of 5 pounds. After all, not everybody has the same weight; any two groups will differ. You have made a statistical inference based on your knowledge of the weight of these groups. You conclude they probably belong to the same population—even though you have not measured everyone in that population.

Defining Variability

When we measure subjects on any variable, we do not expect everyone to come out with exactly the same score. If we measure two or more groups on almost any dimension, we can expect some variability or fluctuation in their scores. Variability is one of the most important concepts you need to understand to analyze the results of experiments. In a commonsense way, **variability** is the amount of fluctuation we see in something. The altitude of Italy varies from places at sea level along the coast to Mt. Rosa, which is 15,203 feet high.[1] We could say there is a lot of variablility in the altitude of places in Italy. There is relatively little variability in the altitude of Brooklyn, New York; all of Brooklyn lies very close to sea level. When we do a

variability

---

1. *Hammond citation world atlas*. Maplewood, N.J.: Hammond, Inc., 1974, p. 35.

statistical test, we are asking whether our pattern of results is significantly different from what we would expect to see because of the usual variability among people in the population. Since we are using the scientific method, we do not want to answer this question in a subjective way. I may wish to argue that my results are obviously significant. You may disagree. Instead of leaving the choice up to the individual, statistical tests have been set up so that we have standards—conventions or guidelines about what is significant so that everyone can agree on whether results are significant or not. In law, we accept the verdict of the jury as our standard of guilt or innocence. In psychology, we accept the outcome of statistical tests to establish whether an independent variable had an effect in a particular experiment. We can summarize the overall process of statistical inference with a few steps. In each experiment, the researcher (1) samples from a population; (2) states a null hypothesis; (3) chooses a significance level; and (4) evaluates the results of the experiment for statistical significance, accepting or rejecting the null hypothesis.

Testing the Null Hypothesis

null hypothesis
In our legal system, a person is presumed innocent until proved guilty. In effect, we assume that the person did not do anything wrong until there is convincing evidence to show otherwise. We make a similar assumption about the independent variable as we set up statistical tests. We do not actually test the research hypothesis of an experiment directly. Instead, we formulate and test the **null hypothesis**, which states that the performance of the treatment groups is so similar that the groups must belong to the same population. In effect, the null hypothesis (H_0) says that any differences we see between treatments amount to nothing. We assume that a suspect is innocent until the evidence leads us to conclude that he or she is guilty. Similarly, when we construct a null hypothesis, we assume that the data of the treatment groups came from the same population. We hold to that assumption until the evidence shows the assumption can be rejected.

At this point you may be feeling a bit confused. "Don't we get our samples from the same population to begin with? Why do we have to *assume* that the data came from the same population?" Actually, the null hypothesis is not as strange as it seems. We do take our subjects from the same population, at least as far as we know. We take random samples and use random assignment to avoid creating treatment groups that differ from each other before the experiment even begins. However, in the experiment we manipulate the independent variable so that the treatment groups are exposed to different conditions. When the experiment is over, we would like to be able to reject the null hypothesis. We would like to show that something in the experiment—the independent variable, we hope—led to differences in the responses of the groups. If we reject the null hypothesis, we are confirming a change between the groups that occurred as a result of the experiment: Our results are **statistically significant**. If we can reject the null hypothesis, we are saying that the data from the treatment groups are now so different that they look as if they came from different populations; the usual variability of scores on the dependent measure is not enough

statistically
significant

to account for our results. When we accept the null hypothesis, we are saying that the groups are still so similar that the experimental manipulation must have had little impact; the pattern can be explained by variability in the population.

alternative hypothesis

There is no way to test the **alternative hypothesis** (H_1), or the research hypothesis, directly. The alternative hypothesis states that the data came from different populations. There is no way to *prove* that this is so, or that the independent variable caused the pattern of results. The best we can do is show it is unlikely that the pattern occurred by chance because of the variation within the population we sampled: We can show that the null hypothesis is probably wrong.

Let us suppose our experiment deals with the effects of background music on job performance. We form two random groups of subjects and place them in identical testing rooms. We give them sets of purchase invoices and instruct them to write a seven-digit account number on each one, separate out the carbon copies, and order them alphabetically. The task is routine and similar to many office jobs. We want to test the hypothesis that background music enhances job performance. We predict that the experimental group which hears background music will process more invoices in a set period of time than a comparable control group. So that we will not create experimenter effects during the testing, we operate our equipment controls from outside the testing rooms. After reading written instructions over an intercom, we turn on the music for the experimental group by flipping a switch on a control panel. The control group performs in an identical but quiet room.

When the testing hour is over, we return to collect our materials. We debrief the subjects, explaining the purpose of the experiment and what we expected to find. To our dismay, subjects in the experimental group become uneasy. They are concerned about their hearing because it seems that they did not hear any music at all. With a little checking, we discover that the control switch is not working. When we thought we turned on the music, nothing happened. The music affected our experimental group as much as the control group—not at all.

What do you think would happen if we went ahead and counted up the number of invoices each group processed anyway? Our treatment groups were randomly selected from the same population and randomly assigned to the two conditions. Thus, we would expect both groups to have processed about the same average number of invoices. Our independent variable had no effect on the experimental group, so there is no reason to expect the performance of the two groups to be very different. We expect their performance will continue to look like the performance of two groups drawn from the same population.

When we do a statistical test, we begin by doing essentially the same thing: We formulate the null hypothesis. The null hypothesis states that the performance of the treatment groups is so similar that the groups must belong to the same population. We reject the null hypothesis when the difference between treatments is so large that chance variations cannot explain it. Figure 11.1 illustrates the general way this process would work in an experiment in which the independent variable has a large effect.

Whether or not we will reject the null hypothesis depends to a large extent on variability. When there is a great deal of variability in the population, large differences

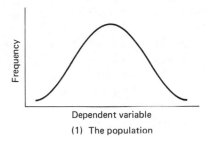

(1) The population

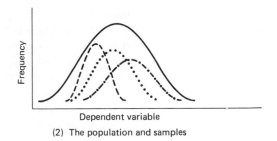

(2) The population and samples

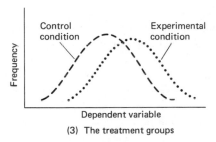

(3) The treatment groups

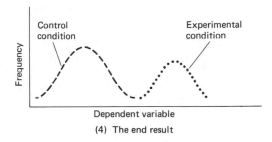

(4) The end result

The researcher's steps

1. Take the population to be sampled: Individual scores on the dependent variable differ.
2. Take samples within the population: Their scores on the dependent variable also differ. Assume the null hypothesis is correct.
3. Apply the treatment conditions to randomly selected, randomly assigned samples.
4. The samples now appear to belong to different populations: Reject the null hypothesis.

Figure 11.1 A schematic representation of statistical inference in an experiment in which the independent variable had a large effect.

between samples will be common. The more variability there is on the dependent measure, the greater the difference between treatment groups has to be before we may say that the data look like they belong to different populations. The more variability, the harder it will be to reject the null hypothesis. In an experiment we want to be precise; we want to know exactly how much variability there is in the data. Then we can estimate the exact odds that we would see such large differences between treatment groups, even if the independent variable had no effect. There is always some chance that the null hypothesis is true; even very large differences can occasionally appear between two samples from the same population.

The reasoning is the same when we evaluate the data from a within-subjects experiment. If the difference in the data from various treatment conditions is large in relation to variability, then we may be able to reject the null hypothesis. We may conclude that the data of subjects under different treatments look like data that probably came from different populations: The odds are that something in the experiment produced a significant change in subjects' behavior from one condition to another. The null hypothesis (H_0) states that the treatment means (averages) come from the same population. Thus, the difference we see between two treatments merely reflects sampling error: We have drawn two samples from a population in which there is variability on the dependent measure. Let us turn to another example so that we can look at these principles in a more concrete way.

APPLYING STATISTICAL INFERENCE: AN EXAMPLE

directional
hypothesis

Imagine we are running another experiment. This is our hypothesis: Time passes quickly when you are having fun. This is a **directional hypothesis**; it predicts the way the difference between groups will go. We are saying that time will go faster for people who are having fun than for people not having fun. We have decided to use a two-group, between-subjects design. We operationally define "having fun" as looking at a collection of cartoons. Our experimental group will be given the cartoons and instructed to examine them to see how funny they are. We will not tell subjects that they will be given 10 minutes for the task. The control group will be given 10 minutes to examine the same cartoons, minus the captions. Control subjects will see the drawings, but they will miss the punch lines and will not have much fun. The independent variable is fun. The dependent variable is subjects' estimates of the amount of time that elapses during the experiment. A small deception is used in this experiment: We do not tell the subjects the true purpose of the experiment beforehand. After they examine the cartoons for 10 minutes, we ask them to estimate the amount of time that has passed since they started. The null hypothesis (H_0) is that the time estimates of the two groups are similar and belong to members of the same population. Note that this is different from the research hypothesis, which says that the fun group will make shorter estimates.

Say we have actually run the experiment. The mean (or average) estimated elapsed time for the control group is 12.5 minutes. The mean estimated elapsed time for the experimental group is 8.4 minutes. On the face of it, it appears that the experimental group really did experience the time as going more quickly than the control group. On average, the members of the experimental group thought that only about 8 minutes had passed. To them it seemed they had been at their task for less time than the actual clock time. The control group on average estimated the elapsed time to be longer than it really was. Can we conclude that fun makes the time pass more quickly?

No. You know that we have to consider the variability of the data before we can draw any conclusions about the differences we find between two treatment groups. We need to evaluate our data with statistical tests. Our first step was to state a null hypothesis: The time estimates came from the same population. Now, if we could

measure the population from which our samples were drawn—say, all college sophomores—we would find that ability to estimate elapsed time varies. Some people
are very accurate; others are inaccurate. Some overestimate time; others underestimate. If we could somehow test all sophomores and ask them to estimate the
length of a 10-minute time interval, we might get a distribution that looks something
normal curve   like the one shown in Figure 11.2. This distribution is a **normal curve**—a symmetrical, bell-shaped curve. The bulk of the scores represented by this distribution
fall close to the center. (Most students' estimates will be fairly accurate.) Many of
the statistical tests you will do include the assumption that the population you have
sampled is normally distributed on the dependent variable. If you could somehow
measure everyone in the population on that variable, the graph of all those measurements would be a normal curve.

Since we are rarely able to measure the whole population we want to study, we
make inferences about what goes on in the population. We base those inferences on
what we see in our samples. Keep in mind that what we want to know about our data
is whether or not the differences we observe between treatment groups are significant.
Can we reject the null hypothesis? The means of different samples of subjects will
vary when they are measured on just about any variable. The question is whether
they vary enough to allow us to conclude that the null hypothesis is *not* a likely
explanation for what we have observed. The null hypothesis says that although the
time estimates of our groups are different, they still come from the same population.
The differences just reflect sampling error. The greater the variability in the data,
the less likely it is that we will be able to reject the null hypothesis. If the variability
is large, then occasionally we would even expect to see very large differences between
samples from that population. Those large differences could occur by chance and
would have nothing to do with the independent variable.

We make our decisions about the null hypothesis on the basis of probabilities.
How likely is it that a difference so large occurred just by chance? What are the odds
that the usual variability in the population led to treatment groups that differ so
much on the dependent variable? We test the null hypothesis (H_0) for two reasons.

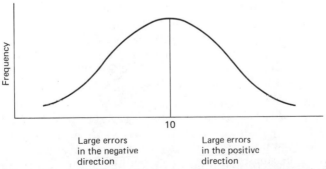

Figure 11.2 Hypothetical distribution of time estimates of all college sophomores estimat-
ing the length of a 10-minute time interval: a normal curve.

First, it is the most likely explanation of what has occurred. When we measure different samples, or even the same sample at different times, we expect some variation between them. It would actually be very unusual to get exactly the same data from different groups. Second, there is no way we can verify the alternative to the null hypothesis directly. The alternative hypothesis (H_1) states that the treatment means are so different that they come from distinct populations. H_1 is actually what we would like to show. We would like to be able to say that the treatment groups differ because of our experimental manipulation. Unfortunately, no matter how different the groups are, there is always some chance that the results were caused by sampling error. Like Detective Katz, the best we can do is show that our explanation for what happened is *probably* true.

Choosing a Significance Level

In order to decide whether the differences between our treatment conditions are significant or important, we need a **significance level**, a criterion for deciding whether to accept or reject the null hypothesis. How much of a difference between treatments do we require? If the differences between treatments are probably caused by the chance variation in the population, we do not have much. You know that there is always a possibility that even extreme differences between treatments occurred by chance.

significance level

Now suppose you knew that by chance, the odds of getting a difference as large as we found are about 2 out of 3. The treatment means were likely to be different—even if the independent variable had no effect at all. Would you be willing to scrap the null hypothesis? If we rejected the null hypothesis against those odds, we would probably be wrong 2 out of 3 times. We would be saying that the means came from different populations when they actually came from the same one.

Naturally we would like to be reasonably sure about our conclusions. If we reject the null hypothesis, we would like to know that our decision is probably correct. How sure we need to be can vary depending on the circumstances: Suppose you are at a sidewalk sale and you find a decent, cheap shirt. However, because it is a sidewalk sale, you cannot try on the shirt, and if you buy it, you cannot return it. You guess there is a 1 in 10 chance that the shirt will not fit. Will you buy it anyway? Your decision will be based on what you stand to lose. If the shirt costs $3, you might risk it. But you might not risk $10. If you are short of cash, you might not be willing to risk anything. Similarly, when we evaluate the results of an experiment, we evaluate the risks involved in making the wrong decision. If we are dealing with life and death research on new drug therapies or suicide prevention, we will be much less willing to risk being wrong. We might be somewhat more relaxed in a taste test of a new beverage. What an experimenter does in a particular experiment depends on what he or she is testing. However, there are conventions for deciding whether to accept or reject the null hypothesis. In psychology, by convention, we can generally reject the null hypothesis if the probability of obtaining this pattern of data is less than 5 percent. Then we say the significance level is $p < .05$ (read "p less than .05").

A significance level of $p < .05$ would be appropriate for our time estimation experiment.

When we choose a significance level of .05, we are saying that we will reject the null hypothesis if we get a pattern of data so unlikely that it could have occurred by chance less than 5 times out of 100. That is actually less than the odds of tossing a coin four times and getting four consecutive heads. It is possible to get four heads in a row—but it just is not likely. If we saw it happen, we would probably ask to see the coin. If we see such unlikely differences between treatment groups, we reject the null hypothesis and say that our results are statistically significant.

In some experiments, we may want a more strict criterion. We may choose a significance level of $p < .01$. That means the odds of getting such large treatment effects are less than 1 in 100—that is a little less than the odds of tossing a coin six times and getting six consecutive heads. Stricter criteria, such as $p < .001$, might be chosen in medical research, or other projects where a strong treatment effect is required.

In order to make a valid test of a hypothesis, think ahead and decide what the significance level will be before running the experiment. It is not legitimate to collect all the data and then pick the significance level depending on how the results turned out. The experiment would yield significant results, but only because we stacked the deck in our favor. For instance, we might find that the difference between performance of two treatment groups is significant at the .20 level. That would mean a difference this large could have occurred by chance about 20 times out of 100. We could accept this as a meaningful difference, but we would not be making a very rigorous test of the hypothesis. Many researchers simply report the likelihood of the results they obtained so that readers can evaluate them on their own. This is frequently done when the results did not reach the significance level the researcher had chosen.

In the time estimation experiment, we are testing the notion that time passes quickly when a person is having fun. Assume we had chosen $p < .05$ as the significance level for this experiment. We would evaluate the results against this criterion. If the results could have occurred by chance more than 5 percent of the time, we would have to accept the null hypothesis: The data are too similar to say that they probably came from different populations, and the results are not statistically significant. On the other hand, if the results could have occurred by chance less than 5 percent of the time, we reject the null hypothesis. The data are statistically significant—they look like they came from different populations. This is just another way of saying that the independent variable apparently had an effect: It altered the behavior of the treatment groups. Our groups started out the same, but their scores on time estimation now look as if they came from different populations.

Figure 11.3 illustrates the way the distributions of sample means from those populations might look. The figure represents what we would find if we were able to test all possible samples from both populations (people who are having fun and people who are not). Of course, there is variability among the samples drawn from both populations; some samples give more accurate estimates than others. However, in this idealized situation you can see that the populations do not overlap. On time

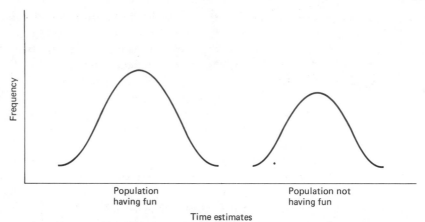

Figure 11.3 Hypothetical distributions of populations having fun and not having fun. The independent variable had a large effect on subjects' time estimates.

estimation, people who are having fun are distinctly different from people who are not. On the average, people who are having fun consistently say that time passes more quickly than it does for the control subjects who are not having fun. If that were really so, we would expect to obtain large differences between treatment groups exposed to the independent variable (fun). We would expect a significant difference between treatment groups if the independent variable had such a large effect on subjects' behavior.

In reality the picture is rarely so perfect. Many extraneous variables can affect the outcome of an experiment, and the data may not be a true reflection of the impact of the independent variable. Also, although the experimental manipulation is effective, its impact may not be as powerful as the one we have drawn here. More typically, we expect some overlap between treatment populations. But we cannot be sure exactly how much overlap there is because we usually cannot measure every possible sample. And because of this overlap, our conclusions about the results may be wrong.

Type 1 and Type 2 Errors

The null hypothesis could be true. It could be that we have somehow obtained treatment means that really do belong to the same population. They seem to be significantly different even though the independent variable had no effect. What are the odds of making that mistake? After all, we reject the null hypothesis only if the treatment groups are very different. Is this really a problem? How serious the error is depends on the actual experiment. If the decision involves a life and death issue, the consequences could be very serious. However, from a practical standpoint, making the wrong decision about the null hypothesis is always serious. Why bother to run a carefully controlled experiment only to draw the wrong conclusions at the end?

Type 1 error   If we reject the null hypothesis when it really is true, we have made a **Type 1 error**: We say that chance differences between treatments were caused by the experiment; the independent variable had little or no effect, but we claim its effect was significant. The odds of making a Type 1 error are exactly equal to the value we choose for the significance level. If we are using a .05 significance level, the probability of a Type 1 error is 5 percent. If our significance level is .05, then 5 times out of 100 we will reject the null hypothesis when we should not. There will be 5 times out of 100 when the extreme differences we see really occurred by chance. If we choose a .01 significance level, the probability of a Type 1 error is .01, or 1 chance in 100.

Could we minimize the odds of a Type 1 error by simply choosing a more extreme significance level? Yes, but there is a tradeoff in that: We can make a second kind of error, a **Type 2 error**: We can accept the null hypothesis even though it is really false. We conclude that the pattern of results was caused by chance variations when it was really caused by the independent variable.

Type 2 error

The more extreme the significance level, the more likely we are to make a Type 2 error. But how does this happen? Won't the differences between treatments be so extreme that we will surely find them? Not necessarily. If the independent variable has a very dramatic effect (and if there is not much variability between subjects on the dependent variable), we might wind up sampling from two completely distinct populations, such as people having fun and people not having fun. There might be no similarity between them at all. More typically, the responses of the populations will overlap. Figure 11.4 illustrates that possibility for the experiment on time estimation.

When data from two populations look the same, there is no sure way we can tell that they come from different populations. These are the cases that lead to a Type 2 error. Because there is overlap between the responses we sample, we are sometimes unable to show a significant difference between the treatments, even though the independent variable had some effect. Instead, we accept the null hypothesis. We say that the differences between the treatment means occurred by chance. The probability of making a Type 2 error is affected by the amount of overlap between the populations being sampled. If the responses of people having fun are very similar to those of people not having fun, it will be hard to show that fun altered

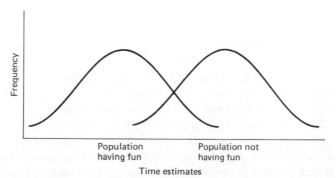

Figure 11.4 Hypothetical distribution of populations having fun and not having fun. The independent variable had a moderate effect on subjects' time estimates.

the responses in any way. The more overlap there is, the harder it is to detect the effect of the independent variable. The probability of making a Type 2 error is represented by the Greek letter β (*beta*). We would be able to find β only if we could measure all possible samples of both populations. But say we knew that the odds of making a Type 2 error were equal to exactly .75 in our experiment. Then the odds of making a correct decision would be equal to $1 - .75$, or .25. If we are likely to be wrong 3 out of 4 times (.75), then we should be right 1 out of 4 times (.25). The odds of correctly rejecting the null hypothesis when it is false are always equal to $1 - \beta$.

Of course, the odds of making a Type 1 error are always equal to the value chosen as the significance level. This is represented by the Greek letter α (alpha). There is some chance (α) that we will reject the null hypothesis when it should have been accepted. There is a $1 - \alpha$ chance that we will accept the null hypothesis when that is the correct decision. Altogether, there are four possible decisions we can make when we evaluate the data from an experiment. These are summarized in Table 11.1.

TABLE 11.1   EVALUATING RESULTS: THE FOUR POSSIBLE OUTCOMES AND THE ODDS THEY WILL OCCUR

		YOUR DECISION	
		Accept the null hypothesis	Reject the null hypothesis
The real story	Null hypothesis is true. (The data came from the same population.)	You are correct $p = 1 - \alpha$	You have made a Type 1 error $p = \alpha$
	Null hypothesis is false. (The data belong to different populations.)	You have made a Type 2 error $p = \beta$	You are correct $p = 1 - \beta$

Note: *p* stands for probability.
    α represents the significance level of the experiment.

When we make a Type 2 error, we accept the null hypothesis. We fail to confirm the research hypothesis of the experiment. The independent variable had an effect, but we are unable to detect it. A Type 2 error is like acquitting a suspect who is guilty: We allow the suspect to go free although he or she really did commit the crime. When we make a Type 1 error, our mistake has greater implications for the suspect. We reject the null hypothesis and conclude that the differences between treatment means are so great that they confirm our predictions. For instance, we may conclude that the time estimates of people having fun are significantly less than the the time estimates of people not having fun. Remember, that does not prove the research hypothesis; it suggests that it is probably true. Of course, we are always pleased to confirm our predictions. We can begin to speculate on all the important consequences of having demonstrated a significant effect. But think about what is happening in this case. When we make a Type 1 error, we explain an effect that does not really exist. A Type 1 error is like putting an innocent person in jail. We attribute a crime to someone who did nothing at all. The possibility of making a Type 1 error makes it especially important that we replicate the findings of experiments.

THE ODDS OF FINDING SIGNIFICANCE

In addition to choosing and applying a significance level, it is important to understand how the odds of finding significance are affected by two factors: the amount of variability in the data, and whether we have a directional or a nondirectional hypothesis. Let us take a closer look at the way these factors influence the outcome of an experiment.

The Importance of Variability

Suppose we could somehow measure all possible samples of college sophomores on time estimation. We would see that the distribution of means of those samples is a normal distribution—a symmetrical, bell-shaped curve. Like individual subjects, some samples perform better than others. Most are about average; but some do well, and some do poorly. Suppose we could take all possible pairs of samples and find the differences between their means. We would get another distribution. The outcome would resemble Figure 11.5. You can see that many of the differences between sample means fall right around zero. Because time estimation is normally distributed, the means of most samples will be close to the mean of the population on that variable. The differences between those means will be very small. However, some differences are very large; they occur at the extremes of the distribution. They represent differences between means of groups that are very far apart on time estimation. As you can see, there are relatively few differences that are so extreme. We find fewer and fewer instances as we move away from zero. There is variability in the differences between means, just as there is variability between samples.[2]

Some differences between means are more likely than others. It is possible to calculate the odds that each difference will occur. The odds of getting very small differences are high. Most sample means fall close to the mean of the population. We should not be too surprised if the groups in our experiment turn out to be very close together on the dependent variable. But the odds of seeing much larger differences are less. The exact odds depend on the amount of variability in the population.

2.   The first statistical tests we will look at are tests used to evaluate differences between treatment means directly. Other characteristics of treatment groups can be compared and evaluated by using different tests.

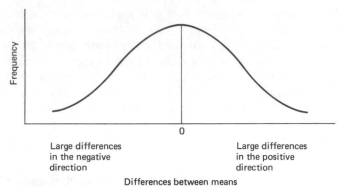

Figure 11.5 Hypothetical distribution of the differences between all possible pairs of means drawn from a distribution.

Large differences are more likely in populations that have high variability on the dependent measure. Figure 11.6 shows you three distributions of differences between sample means. The distributions are similar except for the amount of variability in the populations sampled. The first distribution shows differences between the means of samples from a population in which there was little variability on the variable that was measured. Since the sample means are all relatively close to each other (that is, there was little variability in them), the differences between them also tend to be small. The second distribution is based on a population in which there was a moderate amount of variability on the variable that was measured. You can see that the differences between means of samples from this population tend to be larger than the differences in the first distribution. The third distribution is based on a population in which there was a great deal of variability on the variable that was measured. You can see that this distribution is the widest. The differences between the means of the samples from this population tend to be very large because there is a great deal of variability in the population.

critical region   The shaded areas of these curves are the **critical regions** ($p < .05$), the parts of each distribution that make up the most extreme 5 percent of the differences between means. Differences within these areas will occur by chance less than 5 percent of the time. If our significance level is $p < .05$, we will reject the null hypothesis if the treatment groups differ by amounts that fall within these critical regions. Do you notice anything special about where the cutoffs for the 5 percent levels are? You will find that they fall in a different place for each distribution. Actually, as the amount of variability in the distribution goes up, the critical regions are farther from the center of the distribution. When there is more variability, larger differences are required to reject the null hypothesis.

Ideally, we want our treatment conditions to be the only source of variability in an experiment. We control variables such as testing conditions and practice time that might create differences between subjects' scores. For instance, in the time

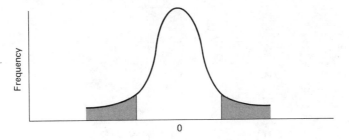

(a) A distribution with low variability

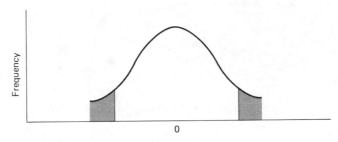

(b) A distribution with moderate variability

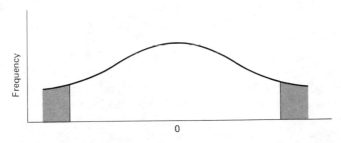

(c) A distribution with high variability

Figure 11.6 Three hypothetical distributions of differences between sample means. Shaded areas represent the most extreme 5 percent of each distribution.

estimation experiment, we must be careful to give everyone exactly 10 minutes to look at the cartoons. Remember, we will be making inferences about the population on the basis of the samples we observe. If our samples produce highly variable data, we must assume that the population is also highly variable on the dependent measure. Any unnecessary sources of variation in an experiment will reduce the chances of rejecting the null hypothesis. They will increase the chances of a Type 2 error. It will be difficult to get significant results if extraneous variables are not carefully controlled.

Figure 11.7   "Darling, you have made a significant difference in my life (p < .01)."

One-Tailed and Two-Tailed Tests

In Figure 11.6 you will also notice that the critical regions of the distributions have been divided up between both ends of the curves. For each curve, the 5 percent critical region includes 2.5 percent on the low end and an additional 2.5 percent on the upper end. These curves have been marked to illustrate a **two-tailed test** of a hypothesis: The critical region of the distribution is divided between its two tails.

two-tailed test

nondirectional hypothesis

  We use a two-tailed test whenever we have a **nondirectional hypothesis**, one that does not predict the exact pattern of results—the direction of the effect we will produce through the experimental manipulation. For example: Cars run on oil A perform differently than cars run on oil B. Notice that the hypothesis predicts there will be a difference between the performance of cars run on two different brands of oil. However, there is no indication of what the pattern of results will be. Will cars run on A perform better than those run on B? The researcher has not made a prediction on that. The hypothesis is nondirectional.

  You can understand why we use a two-tailed test with such a hypothesis if you think about what we mean by significance level and critical region. We want to know if our pattern of results is so unlikely that it was probably not caused by chance variations in the population; we want to know whether differences between treatment groups fall within the critical region. When a researcher states a nondirectional hypothesis, he or she is willing to accept extreme differences that go in either direction. It does not matter whether A is better than B or vice versa; the researcher has only postulated that the independent variable produces a difference. Since differences in either direction are acceptable, the critical region, the most extreme 5 percent of the distribution, has to be split between both tails of the curve. Suppose we did not split it, but instead included 5 percent on each end of the distribution? If we did that, we would be changing the significance level. We would be saying we would reject the null hypothesis if the difference fell in the most extreme 10 percent of the distribution.

Fortunately, we are often able to make a more precise prediction about the effects of the independent variable. These may be based on our own pilot studies, or on prior research we have reviewed. A nondirectional hypothesis can often be transformed into one that is directional: Cars run on oil A perform better than cars run on oil B. Now we are predicting exactly what we will see when we evaluate the performance of cars run on oils A and B; A will fare better than B.

one-tailed test   When we have a directional hypothesis, we make a **one-tailed test**: The critical region is measured in just one tail of the distribution. The hypothesis that time passes quickly when you are having fun is a directional hypothesis. It requires a one-tailed test. Figure 11.8 shows the relative locations of the critical regions of the same distribution using a one-tailed and a two-tailed test.[3] The advantage of using a one-tailed test is obvious. You can see from the figure that the critical level, the value that determines significance, will be smaller when we do a one-tailed test. Treatment effects do not need to be as dramatic when we have a directional hypothesis; we can get significant results more easily when we use a directional hypothesis and a one-tailed test.

You may be thinking that it will be easy to get significance now. We can just state our hypothesis in a directional way. Then if the data go in the other direction, we will change the hypothesis and still have significant results. It is a reasonable idea, but unfortunately we cannot handle things that way. Just as you need to choose a significance level in advance, you need to decide on the hypothesis in advance and stick to it. Otherwise you have not tested anything. If you write a hypothesis to fit results you already have, you are actually describing a set of data after the fact. Of course, there is nothing inherently wrong with offering explanations for observations. That is how we generate new hypotheses. However, we cannot call that experimentation. By definition, when we experiment we make a controlled test of a hypothesis that has already been stated.

So far, we have looked at hypothetical distributions based on the means of all the samples that could be drawn from a population. These make wonderful illustrations of the concepts we are discussing. However, to draw these figures, we had to assume we were somehow able to take huge numbers of samples. In the real world, that is nearly always impossible. We do not have the actual distributions of all sample means when we run an experiment. We rarely even know the average score for the whole population. Instead, we have to draw conclusions on the basis of the few samples of subjects that we do have. To do that, we compute inferential statistics.

standard   3.   The distribution shown is the **standard normal curve**—a distribution standardized so that its
normal curve   mean is equal to 0 and its standard deviation (a measure of variability) is equal to 1. The exact shape of this
distribution is known and so it can be used to evaluate data in a variety of ways. It is especially useful with
information on an entire population, rather than a sample.

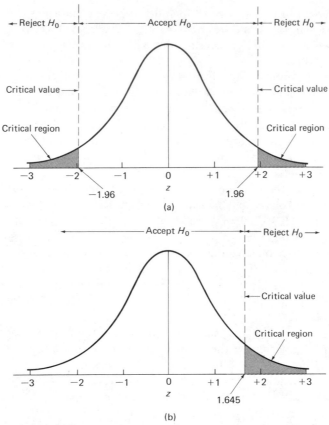

Figure 11.8 The critical region for (a) a nondirectional (two-tailed) test and (b) a directional (one-tailed) test. From Robert B. McCall, *Fundamental Statistics for Psychology*. Copyright © 1970 by Harcourt Brace Jovanovich, Inc. Reprinted by permission of the publisher.

TEST STATISTICS

inferential
statistics

test statistics

Inferential statistics are statistics that can be used as indicators of what is going on in the population. They are also called **test statistics** because they can be used to evaluate results. A test statistic is a numerical summary of what is going on in our data. When we compute a test statistic, we transform the relationship between treatment differences and variability into a simple quantitative measure. Generally speaking, the larger the test statistic, the more likely it is that the independent variable produced a change in subjects' responses. A large test statistic indicates that the differences we see across treatments are large relative to the amount of variability in the data. We are more likely to be able to reject the null hypothesis if we obtain a large test statistic.

You know there is always some chance that the null hypothesis really is true. It is always possible that even a large test statistic is within the range of events that could occur by chance. But think about a throw of the dice. You know that the odds of rolling 7 are greater than the odds of rolling snake eyes. How do you know? Of course, you can calculate the odds of each event. There are more ways to make 7 than there are to make 2. Similarly, researchers have worked hard to calculate just how likely every value of a test statistic would be. Each test statistic has its own distribution of values. For each value, statisticians have calculated the probability that the value could occur just by chance due to random sampling. Those values and probability levels are summarized in tables like the ones you will find at the back of this book.

Although we have anchored our discussion of statistics to examples of particular experiments, we have not dealt with many of the details of doing the actual statistical tests. In the next two chapters, we will look at how we decide which test to use. We will also look closely at the actual procedures used to compute and evaluate test statistics.

SUMMARY

In principle, experimenters would like to prove that the independent variable caused the changes observed in the behavior of subjects under different conditions. However, in practice the best they can do is show that the differences observed were *probably* caused by the experiment. Experimenters carry out statistical tests to determine whether the independent variable probably caused the changes in the dependent variable. They really cannot prove that it did, but they can make statements about how likely it is that the independent variable had an effect.

The first step in a statistical analysis of data is setting up the *null hypothesis*, which states that the differences between treatments amount to nothing. We assume the null hypothesis is true until the evidence shows it can be rejected. The null hypothesis is necessary because we cannot automatically conclude that a difference between treatments is meaningful. Variability in the data is expected. *Variability* is the amount of fluctuation observed. In order to know whether to accept or reject the null hypothesis, an experimenter needs to know how much variability there is on the dependent measure. The more variability there is, the greater the difference between groups has to be before we may say that the data probably came from different populations. Since we cannot actually measure the populations, we make inferences from the samples we do measure.

Some differences between treatments are more likely than others, and it is possible to calculate the odds that each difference will occur. Most sample means (averages) are close to the mean of the population. Thus, the odds of getting treatment means that are fairly similar are high. The odds of seeing much larger differences are less. The exact odds depend on the amount of variability in the population.

We decide whether the differences between treatments are *significant* or important on the basis of probabilities. In psychology, by convention, we usually reject the null hypothesis if the difference between treatments is so extreme that it could have occurred by chance less than 5 times out of 100. This is called a .05 *significance level*. In effect, it says that the probability of getting so large a difference is less than .05 ($p < .05$).

If we have chosen a .05 significance level and the difference between treatments is so large that it could have occurred by chance less than 5 percent of the time, we reject the null hypothesis. When we reject the null hypothesis (H_0), we confirm the alternative hypothesis (H_1). The alternative hypothesis states that the treatment data are sampled from different populations. When we reject the null hypothesis, we are saying that the experiment is the most likely explanation for the differences we have observed.

There are two types of decision errors, Type 1 and Type 2 errors. A Type 1 error means the experimenter has incorrectly rejected the null hypothesis: the conclusion is that the differences between treatment means were probably not caused by chance, although they were. Type 2 errors occur when the independent variable really did have an effect, but the experimenter fails to detect it: The null hypothesis is accepted when the treatment means were actually drawn from different populations. A Type 1 error is more serious because it explains an effect that does not exist.

The decision about the null hypothesis must take variability into account. *Test statistics*, numerical summaries of what is going on in the data, must be computed. For each test statistic, statisticians have calculated the probability of each possible value. Those probabilities are used to judge the significance of the results.

REVIEW AND STUDY QUESTIONS

1. What is variability? Give three examples of dependent measures that you would expect to have high variability.

2. Jack Linden is still looking for a shortcut. After running an experiment, he says: "Oh, wow. The difference between my two treatment means is 60 points. I mean, like, that's such a large difference that I'm sure my independent variable had an effect." What is Jack forgetting? Could you account for his findings without assuming that his independent variable produced the difference between his treatment means?

3. What is a null hypothesis?

4. You have run an experiment to test the effects of noise on motor dexterity. It was a three-group experiment. Your three conditions were a control condition in which there was no noise, a low-noise condition, and a high-noise condition. Your three treatment means are different. State the null hypothesis for your experiment.

5. a. I am going to run an experiment tomorrow in which my significance level will be $p < .05$. What does that mean?

b. If I decide to use p < .01 as my significance level, will it be easier or harder for me to detect the effect of the independent variable? Why?

6. For each of the following examples, explain whether or not the researcher has committed a Type 1 or Type 2 error.
   a. Dr. G rejects the null hypothesis although the independent variable had no effect.
   b. Dr. R correctly accepts the null hypothesis.
   c. Although the independent variable had an effect, Dr. C accepts the null hypothesis.

7. a. What are the odds that you will make a Type 1 error in an experiment?
   b. How could you reduce those odds?

8. Given what you know about Type 1 and Type 2 errors, explain why it is important to replicate the results of an experiment.

9. For each of the following hypotheses, tell whether they are directional or non-directional and whether they would require a one-tailed or two-tailed statistical test:
   a. Adversity builds character.
   b. Television viewing alters children's attention span.
   c. Recall of nonsense syllables improves with repeated presentations.
   d. Newborns behave differently under bright versus dim lights.

10. Mary Malone is a little discouraged. She says: "If we cannot prove that our independent variable had an effect, why bother doing an experiment?" Explain to Mary what we do accomplish when we evaluate the results of an experiment.

12

Analyzing Results: Two-Group Examples

Key Terms

raw data	standard deviation	t test
summary data	level of measurement	robust
descriptive statistics	ratio scale	degrees of freedom
mean	interval scale	t test for independent groups
range	ordinal scale	t test for matched groups
variance	nominal scale	

In the last chapter, we discussed the principles of statistical inference. We focused on the logic behind statistical tests. By now you may be thinking, "Okay, now I have all these principles. But I have some data and I still do not know what to do with them." By the end of this chapter, you will know how to begin your data analysis, and how to carry it through when you have a two-group experiment.

We will begin by looking at the results of an experiment that has two independent groups. We will go through the basic stages of data analysis. We will organize and summarize the data, and trace out the process of selecting a statistical test for them. Then we will actually carry out that test. Finally, we will apply some of the same principles to handle a two-condition experiment that was run within-subjects.

In the last chapter, we considered a hypothetical experiment to compare the time estimates of two groups of subjects, those having fun and those not having fun. One group saw cartoons for 10 minutes. The other group saw the same cartoons with the captions missing. Our assumption was that the incomplete cartoons would not be nearly as much fun for subjects. Compared to subjects who saw the incomplete cartoons, we predicted that subjects who saw the complete cartoons would estimate that less time had passed.

This experiment had a two independent groups design. Subjects were assigned at random to one of the two treatments. The exact hypothesis of the experiment was disguised. Subjects were merely told that they should examine the cartoons carefully and that they would be asked to rate them for "funniness" later. Because there were no strong arguments against it, we chose a $p < .05$ significance level for this experiment.

Suppose we have actually run the experiment and we have the data. What do we do with them? Where do we begin? There are four basic steps in analyzing any set of data: First, we organize the data. Second, we summarize it. Third, we apply a statistical test. Fourth, we interpret the outcome of the test. We will look at each of these steps in detail.

ORGANIZING DATA

We start by organizing the data. The hypothetical data from our time estimation experiment have been organized in Table 12.1. You can see that these data have been laid out in column form. Subjects' responses are divided into two columns, one for each of the two treatment groups. Each subject in each group is listed by number next to his or her datum. Statistical work will go more quickly and be more accurate if you begin by organizing the data and labeling them in a clear and orderly way. Especially with more complex designs, you will avoid a great deal of confusion if you take the time to prepare data tables. Many students find it easiest to use columnar paper, such as bookkeeping paper. At the very least, do your work on lined paper so you will be sure which datum belongs to which subject. You can simplify the task by

Table 12.1   Laying Out Organized Data

| GROUP 1 (INCOMPLETE CARTOONS) | | GROUP 2 (COMPLETE CARTOONS) | |
Subject	Time Estimate (min)	Subject	Time Estimate (min)
1	11.2	6	13.6
2	16.2	7	10.9
3	13.3	8	5.5
4	12.1	9	8.8
5	18.2	10	9.2

planning an orderly data sheet that you can use to record subjects' responses throughout the experiment.

SUMMARIZING DATA: USING DESCRIPTIVE STATISTICS

raw data

Published articles rarely contain the data obtained from every single subject in the experiment. The data we record as we run an experiment is called **raw data**. Raw data are like raw potatoes—they are unprocessed and sometimes hard to swallow.

summary data

Whenever we report the results of an experiment, we report **summary data** rather than raw data. Usually readers are not as interested in the scores of individual subjects, and neither are we. We want to compare treatment effects, and we do that by comparing group data. (The only exception is a small N experiment.) When we have group data, we summarize them with **descriptive statistics,** shorthand ways of describing data. They represent standard procedures for summarizing results. When we want to order a shade, we do not carry the window frame to the hardware store. Instead, we summarize its characteristics using the standard dimensions of length and width. Similarly, we can summarize and describe data by using some of the standard descriptive statistics: the mean, the range, the variance, the standard deviation.

descriptive statistics

The Mean

mean

The **mean** is simply the average of all the scores in a sample. We usually compute the mean for each treatment group in an experiment.[1] To get the mean, add together all the scores of the subjects in a group; then divide that total by the number of subjects in the group. The mean is represented by $\overline{X}$ (read as "X bar").

Every sample of data has a mean, an average that gives us some idea of what the group is like. We hear about average wages, average temperatures, and grade point averages. All these averages are computed in essentially the same way. An

1.   One exception is data measured by categories rather than numbers. For instance, subjects might be asked simply to respond "Yes" or "No." When you have these kinds of data, you may sumarize them by reporting the percentage of subjects' responses that fell in each category.

average is an indicator that provides some description of the total sample. Your grade point average is a quick indication of how you usually perform as a student. Sometimes you do better or worse than your average, but the average is the best overall description of your academic record. We can tell a lot about your record by looking at your average instead of all your grades.

Measuring Variability

We also use descriptive statistics to measure the amount of variability in data. So far, we have talked about variability in a commonsense way; we say that anything which fluctuates has variability. When we do statistical tests, variability has more specific meanings. It is defined numerically by one of several descriptive statistics: the range, the variance, and the standard deviation. By using these statistics, we can compare the variability of one sample with that of another.

range   The simplest measure of variability is the **range**, the difference between the largest and smallest scores in a set of data. If the scores on an exam varied from a high of 100 points to a low of 74, we would say that the range is 26. If the price of a 6 ounce bag of potato chips varies from 39 cents in one store to 53 cents in another, we would say that the price range is 14 cents. The range is often a useful measure. It can be computed quickly, and it gives a straightforward indication of the spread between the high and low scores in a distribution. The problem with using the range is that it does not reflect the amount of variability in all the scores. Figure 12.1 shows you two distributions of test scores that have the same range. However, you can see that the distributions are really very different from each other. Distribution for class 1 indicates that the test scores varied a great deal from student to student. In class 2, however, most students got similar scores: one extreme score accounts for the relatively large size of the range in this case. Knowing that these distributions have the same range tells us very little about them.

Computing the Variance

When we measure variability, we would like to be able to compare different samples in a more meaningful way. Computing the statistic we call the variance enables us to do that. Computing the variance is a way of transforming variability into a standard form that provides a good but simple description of how much individual scores differ from one another. By using the variance, we can talk about the variability of all our scores without having to present an entire set of data each time, just as we can order a shade without carrying a window frame to the shop.

variance   The **variance** is the average squared deviation of scores from their mean. The easiest way to explain this is to show you how we get the variance. Table 12.2 shows the steps we follow to compute the variance of the scores of one group of subjects. The scores are those of the hypothetical group of subjects who estimated the time that passed while they were looking at a series of cartoons with missing captions.

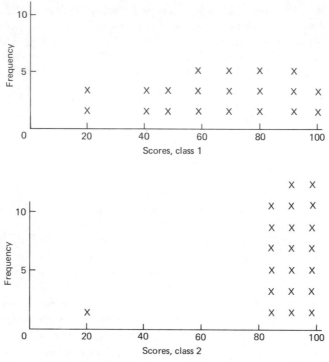

Figure 12.1 Two distributions with the same range (80 points).

The steps are numbered so that you can follow them more easily. One way or another, you will be computing the variance in just about every statistical test that you do, so it is important to master this concept.

Step 1.   We have already listed each subject's score, so step 1 has been completed.

Step 2.   If we have not already done so, we must compute the group mean. The scores of all the subjects in the group are added together. The total is represented in mathematical notation by the Greek letter *sigma* (Σ).

Step 3.   Once you have the total of all the scores in the group, compute the mean. Divide the total of all the scores in the sample by the number of scores you have. The mean is represented by $\overline{X}$. The mean, an average, gives us an idea of what the overall sample is like. The mean time estimate of this sample is 14.2 minutes. You can see that some subjects gave estimates that are above the mean and others gave estimates that are below the mean. In fact, in this sample there are no subjects whose estimates are exactly equal to the mean. The mean is an overall description, but how representative it is of the sample depends on other factors, such as the variance.

TABLE 12.2   COMPUTING THE VARIANCE: TIME ESTIMATES OF SUBJECTS WHO SAW
INCOMPLETE CARTOONS (IN MINUTES)

Step 1. List each subject's score (X_i):

Subject	X_i
1	11.2
2	16.2
3	13.3
4	12.1
5	18.2

Step 2. Add the scores together:
$\Sigma X_i = 71.0$

Step 3. Compute the mean:

$$\bar{X} = \frac{\Sigma X_i}{N}$$

$$\bar{X} = \frac{71.0}{5}$$

$$\bar{X} = 14.2 \text{ min}$$

Step 4. Compute the deviation from the mean for each subject ($X_i - \bar{X}$):

$11.2 - 14.2 = -3.0$
$16.2 - 14.2 = 2.0$
$13.3 - 14.2 = -0.9$
$12.1 - 14.2 = -2.1$
$18.2 - 14.2 = 4.0$

Step 5. Square the deviation from the mean for each subject ($X_i - \bar{X}$)^2:

$(-3.0)(-3.0) = 9.00$
$(2.0)(2.0) = 4.00$
$(-0.9)(-0.9) = 0.81$
$(-2.1)(-2.1) = 4.41$
$(4.0)(4.0) = 16.00$

Step 6. Add the squared deviations together:
$\Sigma(X_i - \bar{X})^2 = 34.22$

Step 7. Compute the variance:

$$s^2 = \frac{\Sigma(X_i - \bar{X})^2}{N - 1}$$

$$s^2 = \frac{34.22}{5 - 1} \text{ or } 8.6 \text{ min}$$

Step 4.   In step 4 of the table we are told to compute the "deviations from the mean" for each subject. Deviations are differences between what we see and what is typical. If someone behaves in an unusual way, we say that his or her behavior deviates, or is deviant from the norm.

A sample of data has a mean, an average that gives us an idea of what the sample is like. The mean of this sample is 14.2 minutes. This tells us that when we added up the estimates of all the subjects in the sample and divided by the number of subjects, we got 14.2 minutes. It does not say that *each* subject estimated 14.2 minutes. Actually, we know that no one in this sample said 14.2 minutes had passed: all the subjects deviated from the group mean. But by how much? We can find out simply by calculating the difference between each subject's estimate and the group mean. We subtract 14.2 ($\bar{X}$) from the actual estimate each subject gave.

Step 5.   Next, we square the deviations from the mean. Remember that when we multiply a negative number (for example, -30) by itself, the result is a positive number. That means that all squared deviations from the mean will be positive numbers even though some of the subjects fell below the mean and so had negative deviations from the mean.

Step 6.   We add all the deviations together to get a total of squared deviations from the mean.

Step 7.   Finally, we compute the variance. You can see that we need the results of steps 1 through 6 before we can do step 7. The formula is just a shorthand way of writing all the operations we perform to get the variance. The variance for a sample is represented by s^2. The s comes from the Greek letter used to represent the variance of a population. The formula tells us that to get the variance of a sample, we have to divide the sum of the squared deviations from the mean by $N - 1$. N is the number of scores.

    The variance formula actually tells us to compute an average—the average of the squared deviations from the mean. That is exactly what we mean by variance. The variance is an indicator of how much variability there is in our data. The more variability, the larger the variance. You may be wondering why the variance formula tells us to divide by $N - 1$: When we computed the mean, we divided by N. When we compute the variance for a sample, we are actually trying to estimate how much variability there is in the population we are sampling. Since we cannot measure the whole population, we draw inferences from samples. We can get a more accurate idea or estimate of how much variability there is in the population if we compute the variance of a sample by dividing by $N - 1$ instead of N.

    Our estimate of the variance would be too small if we divided by N. Because deviations from the mean are squared when we compute the variance, extreme members of the population will enlarge the variance a great deal. A deviation of 4 will add 16 to the total of deviations from the mean; a deviation of 8 will add 64. When we sample, we are likely to miss some of those extreme individuals because there are relatively few of them in the population. Dividing by $N - 1$ gives us a larger variance estimate and corrects for the fact that we miss some of the extremes.

    The variance for the subjects who were shown the incomplete cartoons is 8.6 minutes.[2] If we take the square root of the variance, we have another useful measure of variability, the **standard deviation**, or s. It reflects the average deviation of scores about the mean. We cannot compute that average directly by adding up the deviations; the total of the deviations from the mean is always zero. So we use the square root of the variance to return to the original unsquared units of measurement. The standard deviation of our "no fun" group means that, on average, we can expect each individual subject to deviate from the group mean by 2.93 minutes. We use the same procedures for each treatment group. To save time, let me tell you that those computations yield a group mean of 9.6 minutes and a variance of 8.8 minutes for the "fun group,"

standard deviation

---

2.   We have rounded this off to the nearest tenth. Remember the conventions used for rounding: We round down if the last digit is less than 5. We round up if the last digit is more than 5. If the last digit is 5, we follow this rule: Round up if the digit to be rounded off is an odd number; if the digit to be rounded is an even number, simply drop the 5. Thus, 8.35 becomes 8.4, but 4.65 would be rounded off to 4.6.

subjects who saw cartoons complete with caption. You may want to verify those figures by working through the formulas on your own.

When we report the results of our experiments, we report these summary statistics, usually in place of raw data. We give the mean and the variance of each treatment group. We may also report the range, although the range is often not given in published reports because of its limited use. We have now completed the first two stages of analyzing our results: we have organized and summarized the data. We will use the summary data again when we do the statistical tests.

WHICH TEST DO I USE?

How to choose a statistical test was postponed until now so that the various aspects of data analysis could be presented in one section of the text. However, in practice, it is best to select a test (and a significance level) as you plan the design of the experiment.

When we looked at experimental designs, we developed a set of questions to help us choose the best design for an experiment. We can make decisions about what statistical tests to use in much the same way. The number of independent variables is still important. How many do you have? How many treatment groups? Is the experiment within- or between-subjects? Did you use matching? As you become more familiar with choosing and using statistics, you will not need to go through all these steps one by one. But you will find it much easier to choose the right test if you begin with these questions. In addition to the number of independent variables and treatment conditions, we need to consider the type of data we are analyzing. The way we measured the dependent variable makes a big difference in the way we handle the results. There are different statistical tests for different kinds of data.

Levels of Measurement

level of measurement

The **level of measurement** is the kind of scale used to measure a variable. There are four levels of measurement: ratio, interval, ordinal, and nominal. Height and weight are variables that are measured along **ratio scales**, measures of magnitude or quantitative size. The values of a ratio scale are expressed by numbers such as 3 feet or 18 kilograms. A ratio scale has equal intervals between all its values, and an absolute zero point. These attributes enable us to express relationships between values on these scales as ratios: We can say 2 meters are twice as long as 1 meter.

ratio scale

interval scale

An **interval scale** also measures magnitude or quantitative size and has equal intervals between values. However, it has no absolute zero point. The Fahrenheit and Centigrade temperature scales are interval scales. Although both have zero points, neither has an absolute zero: temperatures below zero are possible on both scales. For that reason, we cannot say that 40° is twice as hot as 20°. But because

ordinal scale

nominal scale

the intervals between values (between degrees) are equal, we can say that the difference between 40° and 20° is the same as the difference between 20° and 0°.

An **ordinal scale** reflects differences only in magnitude, where magnitude is measured in the form of ranks. It does not have equal intervals between values or an absolute zero. Your place in line at the movies may be measured by an ordinal scale. The person who is first in line is closest to getting a ticket. Clearly, your distance from the ticket window could also be measured along a ratio scale of length. Ordinal data can be just as useful, depending on your purposes. If you knew that there were only six tickets left, your rank in line would be enough to tell you whether you should go to a ballgame instead. In a horse race, the first horse wins no matter how large or how small its lead. However, the time of the race (a ratio measurement) would be recorded for comparison with track records.

A **nominal scale** classifies items into distinct categories that have no quantitative relationship to one another. Nominal scaling is sometimes called the lowest order of measurement because it provides the least information. It tells nothing about magnitude, nor does it have equal intervals between values. However, for some variables it·is the only type of scale that can be used. Political affiliation is a commonly used nominal measure. You may be a Democrat, Republican, Independent, or Other. There is no difference in magnitude among these categories; you are not more or less affiliated if you belong to one party rather than another. However, the categories are mutually exclusive—that is, you cannot be both a Republican and a Democrat at the same time.

Variables may be measured by using one of these four different types of scales. It may be possible to measure a variable by more than one of these scales. When this is the case, we prefer the method that provides as much information as we need, and often that means as much information as possible. Thus, ratio and interval scales tend to be preferred over ordinal and nominal measurements. For that reason, we have looked mainly at ratio and interval data in our examples. But remember that different techniques are needed for different types of data.

Selecting a Test for a Two-Group Experiment

To select the right statistical test, first decide which level of measurement is used to measure the dependent variable, and answer the other questions summarized in Table 12.3. You now have all the information you need to select a statistical test.

Let us return to our example. How will we know what statistical test to use? First, we answer the key questions from Table 12.3.

1. There is one independent variable (*fun*).
2. There are two treatment conditions (*fun versus no fun*).
3. The experiment is run between-subjects. (*There are different subjects in each treatment condition.*)
4. The ·subjects are not matched.

TABLE 12.3   THE PARAMETERS OF DATA ANALYSIS

1. How many independent variables are there?
2. How many treatment conditions are there?
3. Is the experiment run between- or within-subjects?
4. Are the subjects matched?
5. What is the level of measurement of the dependent variable?

5. The dependent variable is measured by a ratio scale. (*Time estimates have magnitude, equal intervals, and an absolute zero—there is no way to score below zero.*)

   With this information, we can select a possible test to use for the data. Table 12.4 shows the most common statistical tests, organized by the number of independent variables they can handle, the level of measurement of the dependent variable, and whether the experiment is within- or between-subjects. We will not discuss all the tests in detail; the table note supplies sources to consult for further information.

TABLE 12.4   SELECTING A POSSIBLE STATISTICAL TEST BY NUMBER OF INDEPENDENT VARIABLES AND LEVEL OF MEASUREMENT

| Level of Measurement of Dependent Variable | ONE INDEPENDENT VARIABLE | | | | TWO INDEPENDENT VARIABLES | |
| | Two Treatments | | More Than Two | | Factorial Designs | |
	Two Independent Groups	Two Matched Groups (or Within-Subjects)	Multiple Independent Groups	Multiple Matched Groups (or Within-Subjects)	Independent Groups	Matched Groups (or Within-Subjects)
Interval or ratio	t test for independent groups	t test for matched groups	One-way ANOVA (randomized)	One-way ANOVA (repeated-measures)	Two-way ANOVA	Two-way ANOVA (repeated-measures)
Ordinal	Mann-Whitney U test	Wilcoxon test	Kruskal–Wallis test	Friedman test	—	—
Nominal	Chi square test	—	Chi square test	—	—	—

Note: Shaded boxes list tests not discussed in this text. You can find explanations of them in most standard texts on statistics. A good source is R. B. McCall, *Fundamental statistics for psychology*, New York: Harcourt Brace Jovanovich, 1970. See B. J. Winer, *Statistical principles in experimental design*, New York: McGraw-Hill, 1971, for repeated measures procedures.

There are still other tests that we do not even list, but they are used less often and you may not need them until you take more advanced courses. Here and in the next chapter we will focus on the tests you are most likely to need for your first experiments.

The table indicates "possible" tests; it does not tell you what you will definitely need in all cases. The reason is that it may be possible to use more than one test. Also, before using any test, we must be sure we have the kind of data the test was designed to handle. This goes beyond asking whether our level of measurement is appropriate. As you learn about the tests, you will also learn that each test has its own additional requirements.

THE *t* TEST

For our hypothetical experiment, the test suggested in Table 12.4 is the *t* test for independent groups. When we want to evaluate interval or ratio data from a two-group experiment, we compute the test statistic *t*. The *t* statistic is a computational way of relating differences between treatment means to the amount of variability we would expect to see between any two sets of data drawn from the same population. When we evaluate the likelihood of obtaining a particular value of *t*, we are performing a *t* **test**.

t test

The exact probabilities of each value of *t* have been calculated for us. However, the distribution of these values changes depending on the number of subjects in the samples. Before actually computing *t* for the time estimation example, let us look at the family of *t* distributions and the effects of sample size.

Effects of Sample Size

Size of sample is very important. If we take both small and large samples from the same populations, we will generally find that small samples vary more from the mean of the population than large samples do. You know that test statistics represent a relationship between treatment effects and variability. If sample size affects variability, it also affects the size of the test statistics.

For a test statistic like *t*, sample size is critical because the exact shape of the distribution of *t* changes depending on the size of the samples. The *t* statistic has a whole family of distributions, some of which are shown in Figure 12.2. You can see that the *t* distributions resemble the normal curve we looked at in the last chapter. They are symmetrical, with the greatest concentration of values around the mean. The shape of the *t* distribution becomes more and more like the normal curve as the sample size increases. With small samples, the *t* distribution has a flatter and wider shape.

Sample size is also important because of the assumptions we make whenever we apply *t*. One of the requirements of a *t* test is that the data to be analyzed (interval or ratio) come from populations which are normally distributed. We must be able to assume that if we could somehow measure all the members of the population,

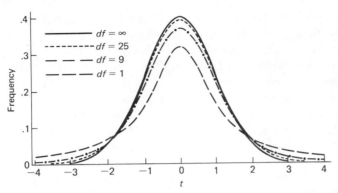

Figure 12.2 Some members of the family of *t* distributions. Adapted from D. Lewis, *Quantitative Methods in Psychology*. New York: McGraw-Hill, 1960.

their scores on the dependent variable would form a normal curve. If the data come from populations that are not normally distributed, we have a problem. The odds of getting each individual *t* value were worked out for populations that are normally distributed. If the data do not come from such populations, the odds that have been worked out for *t* will be wrong for those data. Of course, we can hardly ever measure all the members of a population. We get around this problem by using large samples, so that the correct odds of each *t* value are very close to what they would be if the population were normally distributed. This is rarely a problem because the *t* test **robust** is relatively **robust**—its assumptions can be violated without creating serious errors. If there are at least 10 to 20 subjects in each treatment group, a *t* test is probably safe when the other conditions are met.

Degrees of Freedom

degrees of We select the appropriate *t* distribution based on **degrees of freedom**. [Figure 12.2 **freedom** refers to degrees of freedom (*df*) rather than number of subjects.] The degrees of freedom tell us how many members of a set of data could vary or change value without changing the value of a statistic we already know for those data. Samples that are the same size can have different degrees of freedom depending on the way the experiment is designed, and on the statistic being computed. Let us say we know the mean of the data. Then the degrees of freedom tell us how many members of that set of data could change without altering the value of the mean.

Imagine that my phone number is a set of data. It has seven data. Suppose I tell you that the total of the seven digits in my number is 37, and that the first six digits of the number are 8, 9, 4, 3, 9, and 2. Can you find the last digit? Of course. Since you know the total and six of the digits, you can easily compute the value of the last digit, which is *not free to vary*. Different combinations of the first six digits are possible. But once their values have been set, the value of the last digit is also set if the total must equal 37. If we tried to substitute any other value for the seventh digit, the total, or the known statistic, would no longer be correct. The degrees of freedom for my phone number therefore equal 6. If we included the area code in the data, we would say that my telephone number has 10 digits. It now totals 42. Its degrees of freedom now equal $10 - 1$, or 9. Clearly the degrees of freedom are related to the number of digits, or data, in a sample.

Similarly, the degrees of freedom in the distribution of a statistic vary in a way related to the number of subjects sampled. However, we compute degrees of freedom differently for different test statistics. Sometimes all but one value of a set of data can change; sometimes fewer. The way we compute the degrees of freedom can also be different for different applications of the same statistic. The way we compute the degrees of freedom for t, for instance, changes depending on what we are testing with t. If we are using different statistics or the same statistic applied in different ways, we may have different degrees of freedom even though sample sizes are identical. That is why the critical values of test statistics are always presented and organized by degrees of freedom rather than by number of subjects.

The Critical Value of *t*

Let us look more closely at two distributions of t to get a clearer idea of how degrees of freedom will affect the critical value of t. Figure 12.3 shows distributions of t for 25 degrees of freedom and 9 degrees of freedom. It also shows the cutoffs for the $p < .05$ significance level using a two-tailed test. What is the relationship between these levels?

As the t distribution changes shape, the value of t needed to reject the null hypothesis also changes. Remember that the significance level, or critical level, refers to probabilities. We are looking to see whether the value of t that we compute is

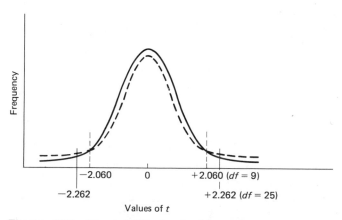

Figure 12.3   The t distribution for 25 and 9 degrees of freedom and critical values at $p < .05$.

more or less likely than our chosen critical value. If the experimental manipulation was effective, the computed value of *t* should be more extreme than the chosen critical value. In terms of probabilities, this may mean, for instance, that the observed value of *t* is so unlikely it could have occurred by chance less than 5 percent of the time.

It is easy to see that the distribution for 9 degrees of freedom is flatter and wider than the other curve shown. In terms of probabilities, you can see that the most extreme 5 percent of this distribution falls relatively far out on the curve. Smaller degrees of freedom mean more variability between samples. That means that more and more cases will be far from the mean of the population; large differences between samples will occur relatively often. Thus, the tails of the *t* distribution will get fatter as sample size (and degrees of freedom) get smaller. With 25 degrees of freedom, the tails of the *t* distribution are thinner: The most extreme 5 percent of the distribution falls closer to the mean.

Can you see what this means for our decision about the null hypothesis? We will reject the null hypothesis if the computed value of *t* is more extreme than the most extreme 5 percent of the distribution. Because the distribution changes shape as the degrees of freedom change, the critical value of *t* also changes. In fact, the critical value of *t* (the value needed to reject the null hypothesis) gets larger as the degrees of freedom get smaller. The fewer the subjects, the less likely it is that we will be able to reject the null hypothesis. And with fewer subjects, we have a greater chance of making a Type 2 error.

Using the *t* Test

Before we can use the *t* test, we have to know how to find the critical values of *t*. Fortunately, they have been worked out for us and organized into tables where we can find them quickly and easily. To use the statistical tables, we need three pieces of information:

1. Will we use a directional or nondirectional test (that is, a one- or a two-tailed test)?
2. What is our significance level?
3. How many degrees of freedom do we have?

In our experiment on fun, we have a directional hypothesis. Our directional hypothesis predicts that the average time estimate of the "no fun" group will be greater than the average time estimate of the "fun" group. That means that we may use a one-tailed test. We chose a $p < .05$ significance level. The degrees of freedom (*df*) for this experiment equal the total number of subjects in both groups, minus the number of groups. Here, $df = 5 + 5 - 2$, or 8. Now, turn to the Appendix in the back of the book and find Table B2. Table B2 shows the critical values of *t* for both one- and two-tailed tests and several degrees of freedom. Find the critical value of *t* for 8 *df*, a one-tailed test, and $p < .05$.

The critical value of t for this experiment is 1.86. If our observed value of t (the value we compute) is less than 1.86, we must accept the null hypothesis. Computed values of t which are less extreme than the critical value indicate that differences between our treatment groups are not large enough to be significant. They were probably caused by chance variations between the samples. If the computed value of t is equal to or greater than 1.86, we reject the null hypothesis. If the computed value of t is more extreme than the table value, it is unlikely that the differences between treatment groups can be explained simply by chance.

The t Test for Independent Groups

t test for independent groups

We cannot just compare raw data or absolute differences between treatment groups; we must evaluate the results by taking variability into account. Treatment groups are likely to differ even if the independent variable had no effect. Computing a test statistic gives a numerical index of this relationship; t is just one of many test statistics we can compute. We use the *t test for independent groups* when we have two different randomly selected samples of subjects, randomly assigned to two treatments, and interval or ratio data. Let us use t to analyze the results of the time estimation experiment. The hypothetical data from that experiment are summarized in Table 12.5.

TABLE 12.5   SUMMARY DATA FOR A HYPOTHETICAL EXPERIMENT ON FUN AND TIME ESTIMATION

No Fun Group (Group 1)	Fun Group (Group 2)
$\overline{X}_1 = 14.2$ min	$\overline{X}_2 = 9.6$ min
$s_1{}^2 = 8.6$ min	$s_2{}^2 = 8.1$ min
$N_1 = 5$	$N_2 = 5$

Note: Since we predicted that the "no fun" group will make larger time estimates, we labeled that group "group 1." Given our prediction, $\overline{X}_1 - \overline{X}_2$ should be a positive number and our computed value of t should be positive. It does not really matter which way the groups are labeled as long as we set up the critical value of t (in a positive or negative direction) consistent with our predictions and our computations of t. We are using hypothetical data here to keep things simple. If you were actually running this experiment, you would want to have more than five subjects in each treatment group.

The table tells us at a glance that the performance of the groups is different. The mean time estimate of subjects in the "no fun" group is 14.2 minutes; that of subjects in the "fun" group is 9.6 minutes. Of course we know that this absolute difference may not be significant. We have to evaluate the difference in terms of the amount of variability we find between any samples drawn from the population. We have to decide whether to accept or reject the null hypothesis. The computation of t for these data is shown in Table 12.6. The formula is just a shorthand way of writing the steps to get t. If you take it slowly and step by step, you should have no trouble.

When we first talked about test statistics in a general way, we said that they

TABLE 12.6 COMPUTATION OF *t* FOR THE DATA PRESENTED IN TABLE 12.5, FUN AND TIME ESTIMATION EXAMPLE

1. Lay out the formula.

$$t_{obs} = \frac{\bar{X}_1 - \bar{X}_2}{\sqrt{\left(\frac{(N_1-1)s_1^2 + (N_2-1)s_2^2}{(N_1+N_2-2)}\right) \cdot \left(\frac{1}{N_1} + \frac{1}{N_2}\right)}}$$

2. Put in all the quantities needed.

$$t_{obs} = \frac{14.2 - 9.6}{\sqrt{\left(\frac{(5-1)8.6 + (5-1)8.1}{(5+5-2)}\right) \cdot \left(\frac{1}{5} + \frac{1}{5}\right)}}$$

3. Calculate the difference between treatment means; begin simplifying the denominator.

$$t_{obs} = \frac{4.6}{\sqrt{\left(\frac{(4)8.6 + (4)8.1}{(8)}\right) \cdot \left(\frac{1}{5} + \frac{1}{5}\right)}}$$

4. Continue simplifying the denominator.

$$t_{obs} = \frac{4.6}{\sqrt{\left(\frac{34.4 + 35.2}{8}\right) \cdot \left(\frac{1}{5} + \frac{1}{5}\right)}}$$

5. Remember to complete all operations inside the parens first.

$$t_{obs} = \frac{4.6}{\sqrt{\left(\frac{69.6}{8}\right) \cdot \left(\frac{2}{5}\right)}}$$

6. Convert all fractions in the denominator to decimals.

$$t_{obs} = \frac{4.6}{\sqrt{(8.7) \cdot (.40)}}$$

7. Complete the multiplication.

$$t_{obs} = \frac{4.6}{\sqrt{3.48}}$$

8. Remember to take the square root of the denominator.

$$t_{obs} = \frac{4.6}{1.86}$$

9. Divide the numerator by the denominator and you have the computed value of *t*. Compare it with the critical value.

$$t_{obs} = 2.47$$

Note: $df = N_1 + N_2 - 2$; $df = 5 + 5 - 2$ or 8.

represent a relationship between treatment effects and variability. If you think about what is shown in the formula for *t*, you will see very clearly how that principle is applied. The numerator (the top) tells us to find the difference between the means of the treatment groups. If the independent variable had a large effect, we would expect this difference to be relatively large. Notice that the denominator of the formula (the bottom) is a collection of terms that represent the variances of the treatment groups and the number of subjects in each. The denominator is an estimate of variability. If the ratio between the two components is relatively large, we may be able to reject the null hypothesis. We will reject it if the computed value of t is more extreme than 1.86. If the observed value of t is more extreme than that, the odds are good that it did not occur by chance.

The computed value of t turns out to be 2.47. Since this is more extreme than the critical value, we reject the null hypothesis: There is a significant difference between the time estimates of subjects who had fun and subjects who did not. How much importance we wish to attach to these findings depends partly on our assessment of the quality of this experiment. Were control procedures adequate? Were variables defined appropriately? These issues will influence our final judgment. The possibility of a Type 1 error must be considered. Before we can draw any sweeping conclusions from the findings, they must be replicated. We will return to these issues when we discuss the interpretation of results.

The t Test for Matched Groups

The procedures we have discussed so far assume that the two samples of subjects are independent, randomly selected groups. We need different procedures when we are looking at the data for matched groups of subjects. If we did statistical tests for these experiments in the same way as for an independent groups experiment, we would overestimate the amount of variability in the populations sampled.

You know that subjects are apt to differ on a dependent variable simply because subjects are not all the same. Even if we are testing rats, we find that some run faster than others. One source of variability is individual differences. Subjects' scores vary because subjects differ from one another. Even the scores of the *same* subjects measured at different times vary, but they usually do not vary quite as much as the responses of different subjects. Neither do the scores of subjects who are matched on a relevant variable. For these reasons, the way that we compute variability changes when we use matched groups or a within-subjects design. You will get a better sense of how these procedures compare by looking at an example of a within-subjects experiment done with two treatment conditions. The research problem is summarized in Box 12.1.

What statistical test would you use for the Yin experiment? This experiment is similar to the time estimation example. We are looking at one independent variable, two treatment conditions, and a ratio scale of measurement (that is, number of errors). However, this experiment is also quite different because it was run with only one group of subjects: it was a within-subjects experiment. (See Table 12.4.) The appropriate statistical test is a t test for matched groups. Obviously, the treatment groups were not matched per se in this experiment; they are simply the same subjects, and there may be no better match than that.

Box 12.1   **A Two-Group Within-Subjects Example**

Robert Yin had already done research which showed that people had trouble recognizing photographs of faces they had seen upside down (Yin, 1969). Now he wanted to test whether inversion would affect recognition of line drawings as well. He showed the same subjects two sets of drawings of faces.[3] After each set, he showed subjects pairs of drawings and asked them to pick out the drawing they had seen before in each pair. Subjects saw one set of drawings and test pairs in the usual upright position; the other set was shown to them upside down (Figure 12.4 shows an upside-down example). The order of presentation of the blocks was counterbalanced across subjects to control for order effects.

Figure 12.4   Do you recognize this person? Reprinted by permission.

---

[3]Yin tested for effects on the memory of costumed figures as well as faces. Since he used the same procedures to handle both kinds of drawings, we will focus only on faces. Yin's results for the costumed figures were similar but less dramatic than the effect of inversion on faces.

---

t test for matched groups

The ***t*** **test for matched groups** uses the same family of *t* distributions you have already seen. It also applies to interval and ratio data, and requires the assumption that the population sampled is normally distributed on the dependent variable. But because it is used to evaluate data from an experiment in which the treatment groups are not independent, the computations are handled differently.

Table 12.7 shows how data and computations from a within-subjects (or matched groups) experiment would look. The data are hypothetical and are presented just to illustrate the procedures simply; Yin used many more subjects. The scores for each subject represent the number of errors each made under each treatment condition. The table also illustrates the computation of t for matched groups: we use the same procedures for within- and matched groups experiments with two treatment conditions.

From the table, you can see that we compute t for these data by looking at differences between each subject's performance under the two treatment conditions.

TABLE 12.7   EVALUATING DATA FROM A WITHIN-SUBJECTS EXPERIMENT ON MEMORY FOR INVERTED FACES.

Subject (or Pair)	Upright Faces (X_1)	Inverted Faces (X_2)	Difference Scores $(X_1 - X_2) = D_i$	D_i^2
1	5	3	$(5 - 3) = 2$	4
2	3	2	$(3 - 2) = 1$	1
3	4	3	$(4 - 3) = 1$	1
4	5	3	$(5 - 3) = 2$	4
5	3	0	$(3 - 0) = 3$	9
			$\Sigma D_i = 7$	$\Sigma D_i^2 = 19$

Computing t

Step 1. This formula for t requires difference scores (D_i). The computation of t is based on differences between pairs of scores rather than group means. (Note how difference scores were computed above.)

$$t_{obs} = \frac{\Sigma D_i}{\sqrt{\dfrac{N \Sigma D_i^2 - (\Sigma D_i)^2}{N - 1}}}$$

Step 2. Put in all the required values. Note that N stands for the number of pairs of data.

$$t_{obs} = \frac{7}{\sqrt{\dfrac{5\,(19) - (7)^2}{5 - 1}}}$$

Step 3. Simplify the denominator. Remember to take the square root.

$$t_{obs} = \frac{7}{\sqrt{\dfrac{(95) - (49)}{4}}} \quad \text{or} \quad \frac{7}{\sqrt{\dfrac{46}{4}}}$$

Step 4. Our computed t. We are now ready to make a decision on the null hypothesis.

$$t_{obs} = 2.06$$

$df = N - 1$, where N is the number of pairs of scores.

Note: A t test for matched groups, to be used for two matched groups or a two-condition within-subjects design, ratio or interval data only. These hypothetical scores represent the number of drawings correctly recognized out of five presented in each condition.

This reflects the logic behind the design we are using. We are evaluating the effect of the independent variable *within* each subject. Similarly, when we have matched pairs of subjects, we want to look at the effects of our independent variable *within* each pair. The observed value of *t* for these data is $t_{obs} = 2.06$. How does that compare to the critical value of *t*? Can we reject the null hypothesis? Who knows? Unfortunately, we never bothered to figure out what the critical value of *t* would be. Of course, we need to look at Table B2 (see Appendix). Assume that the researcher had decided to use a $p < .05$ significance level. Should we use a one- or a two-tailed test? Although he might have made a directional prediction based on prior evidence, Yin was simply testing the notion that inversion would affect line drawings of faces. He did not specify the direction of the effect, so a two-tailed test is appropriate.

Since we computed *t* for this experiment with different procedures, we also have to compute *df* differently. Because we are looking at differences between pairs of scores, our *df* are based on the number of pairs. The *df* for two matched groups are $N - 1$, where *N* is the number of pairs. The degrees of freedom for this experiment are $5 - 1$ or 4. If you look at Appendix Table B2, you will see that the critical value of *t* for 4 *df* and a two-tailed test ($p < .05$) is ± 2.776. Since the computed value of *t* (2.06) is less than the critical value, we accept the null hypothesis, which says that these data were sampled from the same population. (The actual data from Yin's experiment yielded a significant difference: Subjects had significantly more difficulty recognizing drawings presented upside down.)

Notice that using the within-subjects procedures affects the critical value of *t*. In the last example, we had five subjects in each group and 8 *df* ($5 + 5 - 2$). The critical value of *t* was 1.86. Even though we have the same number of actual scores in both examples, we have about half as many degrees of freedom in the within-subjects (or matched groups) experiment. The critical value of *t* for 4 *df* ($p < .05$) is ± 2.776. It takes a more extreme *t* to reach significance in the matched groups or within-subjects experiment.

If we need a larger value of *t* in the matched groups experiment, why bother matching groups at all? It would be easier to find a significant difference with the independent groups design. Actually, it would not. We have not yet discussed all the reasons for variability in data, but one thing should be clear: If we measure the responses of *different* subjects, we are likely to get more variability than we will if we measure the same subjects, or matched subjects. Using the matched groups design lowers the amount of variability in the data. Look at the formulas for *t*: the denominator (the bottom) of each formula reflects variability. When we reduce variability among individual subjects, we make the denominator of the *t* formula smaller. That in turn makes the computed value of *t* larger. To put it more simply, when we use a matched groups or a within-subjects design, we have a tradeoff: We lower the degrees of freedom for the experiment, but we also lower the amount of variability produced by factors other than the independent variable. And, as you already know, that can give us a more precise measure of the effect of the experimental manipulation.

SUMMARY

There are four basic steps in analyzing results: (1) organize the data; (2) summarize them; (3) apply the appropriate statistical test; (4) interpret the outcome of the test. We organize data by making sure that all subjects' responses are labeled clearly and separated by treatment condition. We summarize data by computing *descriptive statistics*, shorthand representations of data. Some commonly used descriptive statistics are the mean, the range, the variance, and the standard deviation.

The *mean* is the average of all scores in a group. We also want to know how much variability there is among subjects' scores, how much they differ from one another. The *range* is the difference between the largest and the smallest scores in a set of data. Two distributions with the same range can look quite different; the range shows only how much the highest and lowest scores differ. The *variance* is a more precise indication of the amount of variability. It reflects the amount of variability among all the scores in a distribution, and so it is a more useful indicator than the range. The larger the variance, the more subjects' scores differ from one another. The *standard deviation* is the square root of the variance. It reflects the average deviation of scores about the mean. Finding the standard deviation converts "squared deviations" back to the original unsquared units of measurement. The larger the standard deviation, the more each individual subject is apt to differ from the group mean.

The level of measurement of the dependent variable is one of the dimensions that determines which statistical test will be used. There are four levels of measurement: ratio, interval, ordinal, and nominal. A *ratio scale* has magnitude, or quantitative size, equal intervals between its values, and an absolute zero point. An *interval scale* has magnitude, equal intervals between values, but no absolute zero point. An *ordinal scale* reflects differences in magnitude as measured by ranks. Ordinal scales do not have equal intervals between values, and they have no absolute zero. A *nominal scale* measures a variable by establishing categories. The categories are not measures of size, and they do not indicate equal intervals. However, they are mutually exclusive: An item cannot belong to more than one nominal category at the same time.

Five basic questions help in choosing an appropriate statistical test: (1) How many independent variables are there? (2) How many treatment conditions are there? (3) Is the experiment run between- or within-subjects? (4) Was matching used? (5) What is the level of measurement of the independent variable?

Two common statistical tests are the *t test for independent groups* and the *t test for matched groups*. We use *t* tests to evaluate interval or ratio data from two-group experiments. The *t* statistic is a computational way of relating differences between treatment means to the amount of variability expected between any two samples of data from the same population. One of the assumptions of the test is that the data come from populations which are normally distributed on the dependent variable. A *t* test is done by computing a *t* statistic for the data. The computed value of *t* is compared to the table or critical value of *t* based on the chosen significance level. If the computed value of *t* is more extreme than the table value, the null hypothesis is rejected; the difference between treatment means is statistically significant.

The t statistic has a whole family of distributions. The appropriate distribution is selected based on the *degrees of freedom* for the experiment. The degrees of freedom indicate how many members of a set of data could vary or change value without changing the value of a statistic already known for that data. With two independent groups, the degrees of freedom for t are equal to the total number of subjects minus 2. As the degrees of freedom of t get larger, the critical value of t will get less extreme. In addition to the degrees of freedom, the critical value of t also depends on whether the hypothesis is directional or nondirectional.

A within-subjects design or matching in a two-group experiment requires different statistical procedures, the t test for matched groups. The same family of t distributions that apply to the independent groups procedures are used. However, t for matched or within-subjects data is computed looking at the differences between each pair of responses. Using the matched groups procedures to compute t reduces the estimate of variability in the data and results in a more precise measure of the effect of the independent variable. However, given the same total number of subjects, the experiment with a matching procedure has roughly half the degrees of freedom as one carried out with independent groups. If the matching was on a variable not highly correlated with the dependent variable, the chances of detecting the effect of the independent variable are reduced.

REVIEW AND STUDY QUESTIONS

1. What are the four basic stages of analyzing the results of an experiment?

2. What are descriptive statistics? Why do we need them in an experiment?

3. Define each of the following and explain what each tells us about a set of data:
   a. The mean
   b. The range
   c. The variance
   d. The standard deviation

4. Two families have the same average income per person. Does this mean that each person in both families earns the same amount of money? Why or why not?

5. Here are two distributions of scores on a memory test. Find the mean, range, variance, and standard deviation of each group.

Group 1	Group 2
5	3
6	1
8	3
3	2
1	5

6. Summarize the characteristics of each of the following levels of measurement and give an example of each:
   a. Nominal
   b. Ordinal
   c. Interval
   d. Ratio

7. What type of scale is being used in each of these instances:
   a. A researcher measures the brand of car purchased by subjects who heard one of three advertising campaigns.
   b. A counselor assesses the divorce rate among couples who had marriage counseling.
   c. A seamstress estimates how much fabric will be needed to make a coat.
   d. Three racks of sweaters are labeled Small, Medium, and Large.
   e. In Murphy's Hardware, all the latex paints are on the top shelf; all the oil base paints are on the bottom shelf.
   f. In Doyle's Hardware, all the quart cans of paint are on the top shelf; all the pints are on the middle shelf; all the gallons are on the bottom shelf.
   g. A researcher asks subjects to reproduce the length of a line they have just seen.

8. What five basic questions do we have to answer before we can select the appropriate statistical test for an experiment?

9. What is a t test? When is it used?

10. Briefly outline the difference between the t test for independent groups and the t test for matched groups.

11. Our computed value of t is more extreme than the table value, or critical value. What does that mean? Do we accept or reject the null hypothesis?

12. Our computed value of t is less extreme than the table value. What does that mean? Do we accept or reject the null hypothesis?

13. Our computed value of t is 3.28. Our critical value of t is ± 2.048. We have 28 degrees of freedom and we are using a two-tailed (nondirectional) test. Draw a simple figure to illustrate the relationship between the critical and the table values of t for this result.

14. Poor Jack is getting more and more confused. He says: "Anyone can see that my group means are different. Why do I have to go through all the trouble of making all these computations of t?" Can you explain to him why these procedures are necessary? What advantage do they have over simply doing the "eye test"?

15. Our computed value of t is -1.07. We have made a directional prediction and our critical value is -1.734. Make a rough illustration of the relationship between the computed and table values of t in this case. Is there a significant difference between the treatment means?

16. A researcher has studied subjects' ability to learn to translate words into Morse code. He has experimented with two treatment conditions: In one condition, the subjects are given massed practice. They spend eight full hours working on the task. In the other condition, subjects are given distributed practice. They also spend eight hours practicing, but their practice time is spread out over four days; they practice two hours each day. After the subjects have completed their practice, they are given a test message to encode. The dependent variable is the number of errors made in encoding the test message. Since intelligence may affect the learning of this new skill, the researcher has matched the subjects on that variable. The results are given below. Decide what statistical test would be appropriate for these data, carry out the test, and evaluate the outcome. Assume that the researcher has chosen a .01 level of significance and that the direction of the outcome has not been predicted.

Massed Practice		Distributed Practice	
S_1	5	S_1	6
S_2	3	S_2	4
S_3	2	S_3	3
S_4	2	S_4	5
S_5	3	S_5	2

17. Assume that the Morse code researcher did not match the subjects.
   a. What statistical test would be appropriate? Carry out that test and evaluate the outcome for $p < .01$, and a nondirectional prediction.
   b. Follow the same procedure as in (a), but assume that the researcher has now predicted that the massed practice group will make *more* errors.

18. Alice has decided that the procedures for finding t for a matched groups design are a little easier to do, so she will just make sure she can match her subjects on some variable. That way she can save a little time on the computations. What is wrong with her approach? What is she forgetting?

REFERENCES

McCall, R. B. *Fundamental statistics for psychology*. New York: Harcourt Brace Jovanovich, 1970.

Winer, B. J. *Statistical principles in experimental design*. (2nd ed.). New York: McGraw-Hill, 1971.

Yin, R. Perception of inverted faces. *Journal of Experimental Psychology*, 1969, *81*, 141–145.

13

Analyzing Results: Multiple-Group and Factorial Experiments

Key Terms

analysis of variance	mean square (**MS**)	random models
within-groups variability	grand mean	mixed models
between-groups variability	post hoc test	main effect
error	fixed models	interaction
F ratio		
sum of squares (**SS**)		

So far we have covered some of the techiques for data from experiments with only two groups. The t tests for matched and independent groups are used when we have interval or ratio data in two-group experiments. However, very often we need to test more than two levels of an independent variable. We may need three or more groups to give an adequate idea of the way that variable operates. We may even want to study more than one independent variable at a time. For those experiments, we need other kinds of statistical procedures.

In this chapter we will look at procedures that can be used for interval or ratio data from multiple-group and factorial experiments. These procedures fall under the general heading of analysis of variance. By the end of this chapter you will know how these procedures work and why they are needed; you will also be ready to carry them out. We will begin by taking a general look at analysis of variance.

ANALYSIS OF VARIANCE

analysis of
variance

The **analysis of variance (ANOVA)** is a statistical procedure used to evaluate differences among two or more treatment means. It is used with interval or ratio data.[1] The name reflects the basic nature of the test—the variance in the data is analyzed into component parts, which are then compared and evaluated for statistical significance. Treatment means are not compared directly. In Chapter 12, the t test was used to evaluate the data from a two-group experiment. You may be wondering why we need another procedure at all. After all, a multiple-group experiment is just a continuation of a two-group design. We could use t tests to compare all the treatment means. We could analyze one pair, and then the next, and just keep doing that until we did all the pairs. But computing several t tests for each experiment is very bothersome. With five treatment levels, you would need ten different t tests to account for all possible pairs of means.

There is also a more serious problem. The more t tests in one experiment, the more apt you are to make a Type 1 error. Remember that when you do a single test, the odds of rejecting the null hypothesis by mistake are equal to your significance level (for example, 5 percent). Doing many t tests in the same experiment distorts those odds and increases the possibility that you will reject a null hypothesis that is true. Although it would be inappropriate to use several t tests in a multiple-group experiment, many of the principles of statistical analysis in the last two chapters still apply. We are still testing a null hypothesis. From the samples we have tested, we draw inferences about the population. We also use distribution curves to evaluate the results according to the significance levels we have chosen.

Still, there are many differences. The analysis of variance does not work like a t test. When we computed t, we calculated differences between treatment groups—differences between treatment means for the independent groups design, and differences between pairs of scores in the matched groups design. We looked at those differences in relation to our estimates of the amount of variability in the populations sampled. The analysis of variance enables us to test the null hypothesis in a slightly different way. It breaks up the variability in the data into component parts. Each

---

1.   Other forms of the basic analysis of variance can be used for noninterval data. However, in this chapter we will talk only about ANOVA in its most common form. We will also assume that we have different subjects in each of our treatment groups.

part represents variability produced by a different combination of factors in the experiment.

In the simplest analysis of variance, all the variability in the data can be divided into two parts: Within-groups variability and between-groups variability. **Within-groups variability** is the degree to which the scores of subjects in the same treatment group differ from one another (that is, how much subjects vary from others in the group). **Between-groups variability** is the degree to which different treatment groups differ from one another (that is, how much difference there is between the scores of subjects under different levels of the independent variable). The proportions of the within-groups and between-groups variability differ from one experiment to another. Sometimes between-groups variability is relatively large; sometimes the two parts are about the same. Their relative proportions vary depending on the impact of the independent variable. When we carry out the analysis of variance, we are actually evaluating the likelihood that the proportions we observe could occur by chance. To understand the way this process works, we need to look more closely at the sources of variability that produce these components.

within-groups variability

between-groups variability

SOURCES OF VARIABILITY

Ideally, when we run an experiment we would like to be able to show that the pattern of data obtained was caused by the experimental manipulation. However, you already know that if we observe changes in the dependent variable across treatment conditions, those changes may not be entirely due to the effects of the independent variable. But what else accounts for changes in the dependent variable? What else might produce variability in the scores of subjects across treatment conditions?

One common source of variability is individual differences. Whether we test children or chimps, we find that some do better than others. Within each treatment group, subjects' scores will differ from one another because subjects are different from one another. We use random assignment or matching in each experiment so that these differences do not confound the results of the experiment. We do not want differences between groups to be produced solely by extraneous subject variables. However, no two groups will be identical in every respect, so individual differences may lead to variability between groups, as well as within the same group.

There are other sources of variability in data. Some differences between scores will be due to things we did not handle well in the experiment. For instance, we may have made small mistakes in measuring lines that subjects drew, or in timing their answers. Extraneous variables of all kinds can produce more variability. They may cause changes in subjects' behavior that we may not detect. One subject is tested when the room is cool, and so does a little better than the others. Like individual differences, these factors can lead to variability within the same group of subjects, as well as between different treatment groups. We can lump all these factors error   together in a single category called **error:** individual differences, undetected mistakes in recording data, and a host of extraneous variables are all aspects of error that produce variability in subjects' data both within and between treatment groups.

Another major source of variability in the data is the experimental manipulation. We test subjects under different treatment conditions (that is, various levels of an independent variable). We predict that these conditions will alter subjects' behavior; we expect subjects under different treatment conditions to behave differently from one another. In other words, we expect our treatment conditions to create variability among the responses of subjects who are tested under different levels of an independent variable.

But the experimental manipulation does not operate like other sources of variability in the experiment. Error leads to variability between different treatment groups; it also produces variability within the same group. Unlike those sources of variability, treatment conditions produce variability only between the responses of different treatment groups. Subjects within the same treatment group are all treated in the same manner. Their scores may differ because of individual differences or error, but not because they were exposed to different levels of the independent variable: Subjects within the same treatment group all receive the *same* level of the independent variable.

When we do an analysis of variance, we break the variability in our data into parts that reflect the sources of variability in the experiment: within-groups variability and between-groups variability. *Within-groups variability is the extent to which subjects' scores differ from one another under the same treatment conditions.* The factors that we call error explain the variability that we see within groups. *Between-groups variability is the extent to which group performance differs from one treatment condition to another.* Between-groups variability is made up of error and the effects of the independent variable. These components are summarized in Table 13.1

We can evaluate the effect of the independent variable by comparing the relative size of these components of variability. The logic behind this is straightforward. The variability within groups comes from error and nothing else. The variability between groups comes from both error and treatment effects. If the independent variable had an effect, the between-groups variability should be larger than the within-groups

TABLE 13.1   SOURCES OF VARIABILITY IN AN EXPERIMENT WITH ONE INDEPENDENT VARIABLE

Variability within Groups	*Variability between Groups*

Error:
   Individual differences
   Extraneous variables
	Error:
	   Individual differences
	   Extraneous variables
	         and
	Treatment Effects

F ratio

variability. We compare the relative sizes of these components by computing a ratio between them called the **F ratio**. Conceptually, it looks like this:

$$F = \frac{\text{Variability from treatment effects} + \text{error}}{\text{Variability from error}}$$

or

$$F = \frac{\text{Variability between groups}}{\text{Variability within groups}}$$

Theoretically, if the independent variable had no effect, the *F* ratio should equal 1. There should be just as much variability within groups as there is between them: the same sources of variability would be operating both within and between treatments. However, the larger the effect of the independent variable, the larger the *F* ratio should be: the independent variable will lead to greater differences between the scores of subjects who receive different levels of the independent variable. Figure 13.1 represents both possibilities graphically.

We use the distribution of *F* to evaluate the significance of the *F* ratio that we compute. *F*, like *t*, is actually a whole family of distributions. The shape of the distribution changes as the size of the samples changes. We will use the degrees of freedom to choose the right distribution and critical value for each experiment. If

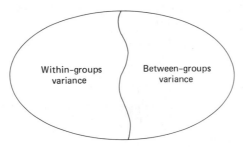

(a) No treatment effects. Within- and between-groups
     variability are about equal.

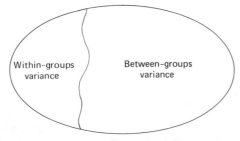

(b) Large treatment effects. Within-groups variability
     is small relative to between-groups variability.

Figure 13.1   The components of variability in an experiment with two possible outcomes.

the F ratio is statistically significant, the amount of between-groups variability is large compared to the amount of within-groups variability. It is so large it is unlikely that all the group means belong to the same population. If F is significant, we reject the null hypothesis that all the treatment means were drawn from the same population: we confirm the existence of differences across the groups that were probably produced by the independent variable.

Now that you have a general idea of how ANOVA works, let us turn to an example of a multiple-group experiment. We will look at some hypothetical data obtained from three groups of subjects who learned high-, medium-, and low-frequency words. We will proceed step by step through the computation of the F ratio. We will test F with a $p < .05$ significance level. Since this experiment has only one independent variable, the statistical test we do is called a one-way analysis of variance.

A ONE-WAY ANALYSIS OF VARIANCE

Assume that we have done a very simple experiment on learning. We have made up three lists of words that have varying frequencies in English. We know that frequency is likely to affect subjects' ability to learn lists of words: Words with greater frequencies are apt to be easier to learn because they are more familiar and also more meaningful to us. We have made up lists of high-, medium-, and low-frequency two-syllable nouns. We defined these categories on the basis of Howes' 1966 count of the frequency of words in spoken English. Our high-frequency words occurred at least 50 times in Howes' sample of 250,000 words. Our medium-frequency words occurred more than once but less than 50 times. The low-frequency items occurred only once in Howes' sample. Words like "hundred," "mother," and "question" are high-frequency words by these criteria. "Coffee" and "paper" are medium-frequency words. "Turtle" and "textbook" are low-frequency words. Our hypothesis is that a list of words which have higher frequency in the spoken language will be recalled with greater accuracy than lists of lower frequency. We have run the experiment using a between-subjects design: Our subjects have been randomly assigned to three different treatment groups, one for each of the three word frequencies. The procedures for presenting the lists and testing recall were identical for all the groups.

This is a three-group experiment. It has one independent variable, the frequency of the words on each list. The dependent variable is the number of items subjects are able to recall, a ratio measure. As in any experiment, we will test the null hypothesis: The means of the three groups were sampled from the same population. Let us use a significance level of $p < .05$ for the data. Table 12.4 indicates that the data from this experiment may be analyzed by using a one-way analysis of variance. Table 13.2 shows some hypothetical data. As you can see, there are three groups. Their scores represent the number of items they recalled from the list of words they were shown. We have already begun our analysis of the data by organizing and summarizing it in table form.

Certain assumptions about our data must be met if we are to use analysis of

TABLE 13.2   HYPOTHETICAL DATA FROM AN EXPERIMENT ON WORD FREQUENCY AND LEARNING

	Group 1 (low frequency)	Group 2 (medium frequency)	Group 3 (high frequency)
S_1	2	1	3
S_2	2	3	4
S_3	1	3	2
S_4	0	3	3
S_5	1	3	4
	$\overline{X}_1 = 1.2$	$\overline{X}_2 = 2.6$	$\overline{X}_3 = 3.2$
	$s_1^2 = .7$	$s_2^2 = .8$	$s_3^2 = .7$

Note: Scores represent the number of words recalled from a list. All subjects saw the same number of items.

variance procedures appropriately. First, the procedures we will use here require that treatment groups are independent from each other and that observations were sampled at random. They also require that the populations from which the groups are sampled are normally distributed on the dependent variable, and that the variances of those populations are roughly equal, or homogeneous. However, the F test is relatively robust. If we have fairly large groups of subjects, the assumptions can be violated without serious errors. The computations shown here are for illustration only. We are looking at very few subjects so that the procedures will be clear. In practice, it would be better to have larger treatment groups because of the assumptions of the ANOVA procedures.

Within-Groups Variance

In order to compute an F ratio for these data, we need two pieces of information: the within-groups variability and the between-groups variability. We begin with the procedures for finding within-groups variability because they are a little simpler.

Think about the definition of within-groups variability—the extent to which subjects' scores vary from the scores of other subjects within the same group. If we had only one group, we could measure its variability by computing the variance. We would use the formula,

$$s^2 = \frac{\Sigma (X - \overline{X})^2}{N - 1}$$

We would begin by finding the sum of squared deviations from the group mean. For each score in the group, we would calculate the difference between that score and the group mean $(X - \overline{X})$. We would square each of those differences $(X - \overline{X})^2$, then add them together (Σ). To get a good estimate of the amount of variability in the population sampled, we would find the variance by dividing the sum of the squared deviations by $N - 1$, the degrees of freedom.

The variance we compute for one group is the average squared deviation from the mean of that group. Of course, when we do an analysis of variance, we are working with several groups at the same time. We need to get an estimate of within-groups variability. That estimate must pool, or combine, the variability in all treatment groups (MS_B). To get MS_B, we divide SS_B by its degrees of freedom. We are now

sum of squares (SS)

working with group means rather than individual subjects' scores. Hence, our degrees of freedom for SS_B (df_B) are equal to $p - 1$, where p is the number of groups. The MS_B gives us a second estimate of the amount of variability in the population. MS_B reflects the amount of variability produced by error *and* treatment effects in the experiment.

$$SS_W = \Sigma \ (X_1 - \overline{X}_1)^2 + \Sigma \ (X_2 - \overline{X}_2)^2 \ldots \ | \ \Sigma \ (X_p - \overline{X}_p)^2$$

The letter p stands for the number of groups in our experiment. In our example we have only three groups, but the analysis of variance procedures can be used with any number of groups. We simply keep adding up the squared deviations of scores from their group means until we have accounted for all the scores in all the groups.

Once we have the sum of squares within groups, we are ready to find the within-groups variance. With only one group, you know that we get a good estimate of the variance in the population if we divide our sum of squared deviations by $N - 1$. $N - 1$ is actually the degrees of freedom for one group. When we compute within-groups variance for several groups, we also need to divide by the degrees of freedom. For one group, the degrees of freedom are $N - 1$. For more than one group, the degrees of freedom are $N - p$. N is the total number of scores; p is the number of groups. We divide through by that number (df_W) to get within-groups variance.

Note that although we are calculating the variance within groups, analysis of variance has its own peculiar terminology. You have learned sum of squares, which is an understandable abbreviation. However, when we finally obtain what we would otherwise call a variance estimate, we change terms rather abruptly. Dividing the SS_W by df_W gives us the mean square. This is actually an abbreviation too, although its origin is not as clear. The mean is an average. The variance is the average squared

mean square

deviation from the mean. So the **mean square** is an average squared deviation. The existence of a plot to confuse students on this point has been suggested many times, but it has never been confirmed. The important point is this: We are still talking about variance in the data. The mean square within groups (MS_W) is one estimate of the amount of variability in the population sampled. It represents one portion of the variability in the data, the portion produced by the combination of sources that we call error. Table 13.3 shows how to compute SS_W and MS_W for our three-group example.

2.   The formulas throughout this chapter are definitional formulas—direct statements of the operations they define. They are presented to clarify the logic behind the ANOVA procedures. Computational formulas are shown in Appendix A. They are derived from the definitional formulas and, although computational formulas are sometimes easier to use, the rationale behind them is less clear.

TABLE 13.3   COMPUTING WITHIN-GROUPS VARIANCE FOR A THREE-GROUP EXAMPLE

Step 1. Compute the deviation of each score from its group mean.	Group 1 (low frequency)	$(X_1 - \bar{X}_1)$	$(X_1 - \bar{X}_1)^2$
	S_1 2	.8	.64
	S_2 2	.8	.64
	S_3 1	− .2	.04
	S_4 0	−1.2	1.44
	S_5 1	− .2	.04
	$\bar{X}_1 = 1.2$		$\Sigma (X_1 - \bar{X}_1)^2 = 2.80$

Step 2. Square the deviation of each score from its group mean.	Group 2 (medium frequency)	$(X_2 - \bar{X}_2)$	$(X_2 - \bar{X}_2)^2$
	S_1 1	−1.6	2.56
	S_2 3	.4	.16
Step 3. Total the squared deviation scores for each group.	S_3 3	.4	.16
	S_4 3	.4	.16
	S_5 3	.4	.16
	$\bar{X}_2 = 2.6$		$\Sigma (X_2 - \bar{X}_2)^2 = 3.20$

Step 4. Add all the group totals together to find SS_w.	Group 3 (high frequency)	$(X_3 - \bar{X}_3)$	$(X_3 - \bar{X}_3)^2$
	S_1 3	− .2	.04
	S_2 4	.8	.64
	S_3 2	−1.2	1.44
	S_4 3	− .2	.04
	S_5 4	.8	.64
	$\bar{X}_3 = 3.2$		$\Sigma (X_3 - \bar{X}_3)^2 = 2.80$

$$SS_w = \Sigma (X_1 - \bar{X}_1)^2 + \Sigma (X_2 - \bar{X}_2)^2 + \Sigma (X_3 - \bar{X}_3)^2 = 8.80$$

Step 5. Find df_w.

$$df_w = N - p$$

N = Number of scores
p = Number of groups

$df_w = 15 - 3$
$df_w = 12$

Step 6. Find MS_w.

$$MS_w = \frac{SS_w}{df_w}$$

$$MS_w = \frac{8.80}{12}$$

$MS_w = .73$

Note: The same procedures apply when the groups are unequal in size.

Between-Groups Variance

Now that we have $\mathbf{MS_W}$, we are ready to calculate the second component of the F ratio, a measure of the variability between groups of subjects. It is a measure that reflects both error and treatment effects: Between-groups variability is the extent to which group performance differs from one treatment condition to another. Let us look a little more closely at the implications of that definition.

  If the independent variable had no effect in this experiment, the subjects in all the groups would have done about equally well. We would not expect to see any dramatic difference in recall from one group to another; the only differences we would see would be due to error. If that were the case, the means of the individual treatment groups would all be about the same. We could compute one overall or **grand mean,** an average of all the treatment means. If our independent variable had no effect, the grand mean would describe the data about as well as three separate means, one for each of the three separate groups. But imagine what would happen if the independent variable really did have an effect on subjects' recall. We could still compute an overall grand mean that would represent the average of all the subjects' scores. However, the means of the individual groups would be quite different from the grand mean. They would also be quite different from one another.

grand mean

  We can measure the amount of variability within groups by finding the total variance of scores from the individual group means. Similarly, we can measure the variability between groups by finding the variance of the group means from their mean, the grand mean of the experiment. Now that you are familiar with the logic behind the procedures, let us compute the between-groups variance. The process is carried out in Table 13.4 for our three-group example. We begin by computing the grand mean, the average of all the treatment means. We then go on to compute deviations of the group means from the grand mean, and next we obtain the squared deviations. Notice, however, that the formula for $\mathbf{SS_B}$ is a little different from the one for $\mathbf{SS_W}$. Instead of simply adding together all the squared deviations, each one is first multiplied by n_j, the number of subjects in each respective treatment group.

  Next, we find the variance about the grand mean, the mean square between groups ($\mathbf{MS_B}$). To get $\mathbf{MS_B}$, we divide $\mathbf{SS_B}$ by its degrees of freedom. We are now working with group means rather than individual subjects' scores. Hence, our degrees of freedom for $\mathbf{SS_B}$ (df_B) are equal to $p - 1$, where p is the number of groups. The $\mathbf{MS_B}$ gives us a second estimate of the amount of variability in the population. $\mathbf{MS_B}$ reflects the amount of variability produced by error *and* treatment effects in the experiment.

Computing and Evaluating the *F* Ratio

We now have both components of variability that we need to compute our F ratio. The F ratio represents this relationship:

$$F = \frac{\text{Variability from treatment effects} + \text{error}}{\text{Variability from error}}$$

TABLE 13.4   FINDING THE BETWEEN-GROUPS VARIANCE FOR OUR THREE-GROUPS EXAMPLE

	Group 1 (low frequency)	Group 2 (medium frequency)	Group 3 (high frequency)	
Step 1. Compute the grand mean, the mean of all the group means.	$\overline{X}_1 = 1.2$	$\overline{X}_2 = 2.6$	$\overline{X}_3 = 3.2$	Grand mean $(\overline{X}_G)$ $$\overline{X}_G = \frac{\Sigma \overline{X}_j}{p}$$ $$\overline{X}_G = \frac{1.2 + 2.6 + 3.2}{3}$$ $$\overline{X}_G = \frac{7}{3}$$ $$\overline{X}_G = 2.3$$
Step 2. Compute the differences between each group and the grand mean.	$\overline{X}_1 - \overline{X}_G =$ $1.2 - 2.3 = -1.1$	$\overline{X}_2 - \overline{X}_G =$ $2.6 - 2.3 = .3$	$\overline{X}_3 - \overline{X}_G =$ $3.2 - 2.3 = .9$	

Step 3. Put those differences in the SS_B formula; n is the number of subjects in each group; j is the number of groups—this general formula can handle any number of groups.

$$\boxed{SS_B = n_1(\overline{X}_1 - \overline{X}_G)^2 + n_2(\overline{X}_2 - \overline{X}_G)^2 + n_3(\overline{X}_3 - \overline{X}_G)^2 \ldots n_j(\overline{X}_j - \overline{X}_G)^2}$$

$$SS_B = 5(-1.1)^2 + 5(.3)^2 + 5(.9)^2$$

Step 4. Square all deviations from the grand mean.

$$SS_B = 5(1.21) + 5(.09) + 5(.81)$$

Step 5. Carry out all multiplications.

$$SS_B = 6.05 + .45 + 4.05$$

Step 6. Obtain the total SS_B.

$$SS_B = 10.55$$

Step 7. Calculate the degrees of freedom; $p =$ number of groups.

$$\boxed{df_B = p - 1}$$

$$df_B = 3 - 1 \text{ or } 2$$

Table 13.4 Finding the Between-Groups Variance for Our Three-Groups Example (cont'd.)

Step 8. Divide SS_B by df_B to find the mean square between groups, the second estimate of population variance.	$MS_B = \dfrac{SS_B}{df_B}$ $MS_B = \dfrac{10.55}{2}$ $MS_B = 5.28$

Note: At this point you can check your work by computing SS_T, which represents the total sum of squares for the data. Since we are simply dividing the variability into two components, $SS_B + SS_W$ should equal SS_T. You can compute SS_T with this formula: $SS_T = \Sigma(X^2) - \dfrac{(\Sigma X)^2}{N}$. N is the number of scores. For this example,

$$SS_T = 101 - \frac{(35)^2}{15}$$

$$SS_T = 101 - \left(\frac{1225}{15}\right)$$

$$SS_T = 101 - 81.67$$

$$SS_T = 19.33$$

Check:

$$SS_T = SS_B + SS_W$$

$$19.33 = 10.55 + 8.80$$

$$19.33 = 19.33$$

We have transformed the components of this formula into the numerical terms, MS_B and MS_W. Thus, the statistical form of the F ratio is as follows:

$$F = \frac{MS_B}{MS_W}$$

If we substitute our computed values into this formula, we find that for our three-group example,

$$F = \frac{5.28}{.73} \text{ or } 7.23$$

To test our F ratio for significance, we need to find the critical value. As you know, F is a whole family of distributions. We use our degrees of freedom to locate the appropriate distribution. But is there a problem? As we computed F, we actually calculated two different degrees of freedom, one to get MS_B and another to get MS_W. Which do we use? Since the F test can be used with any number of groups as well as any number of subjects, we need both. The F distribution changes as the size of treatment groups changes; it also changes as the number of treatment conditions changes.

If you look in the Appendix to this book, you will find that Table B3 lists critical values of F. The table is organized by the degrees of freedom. The values listed across the top refer to the degrees of freedom of the numerator, or top, of the F ratio—here, df_B. Values listed vertically down the side of the table indicate the degrees of freedom of the denominator of the F ratio—here, df_W. To find the appropriate critical value, locate df_B along the top of the table; locate df_W along the side. Then find the place in the table where those two lines meet. We are looking for $df_B = 2$, and $df_W = 12$. (These are simply the df values we computed to get mean squares.) If we look at a portion of the table, we see this:

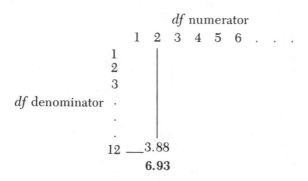

The value in light type, 3.88, is the critical value of F at the .05 level; 6.93, shown in bold face, is the critical value of F at the .01 level. Remember, these values apply only to an F test with 2 and 12 degrees of freedom. We have to look up the critical values for each experiment. Figure 13.2 illustrates the distribution of F with 2 and 12 degrees of freedom. It also shows the distribution of F with 2 and 6 degrees of freedom. As you can see, the critical values change dramatically as the degrees of freedom change.

We chose a significance level of $p < .05$ for our three-group experiment. Our computed value of F was 7.23. The table value of F is 3.88 at the .05 level: Therefore, our computed F is significant. We reject the null hypothesis that the treatment means came from the same population. Our computed F is actually also significant at the .01 level: It is greater than 6.93, the critical value of F at the .01 level.

Preparing a Summary Table.   By now it may seem that we have gone through a thousand steps to evaluate the data from this study. The count is actually slightly less than that, but you can understand why we need to prepare a simple, comprehensive summary of the findings. We would not present all the steps and calculations in an actual report. Instead, we summarize our computations in a summary table. The summary table for our example is shown in Table 13.5. The table includes all the basic information needed to compute F, along with the actual computed value. However, we do not include the table values of F. Since we have given the degrees of freedom, readers can always consult their own tables to get the critical value if

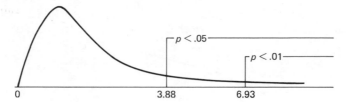

(a) The distribution of F with 2 (numerator) and 12 (denominator) degrees of freedom.

(b) The distribution of F with 2 (numerator) and 6 (denominator) degrees of freedom.

Figure 13.2 The distribution of F with varying degrees of freedom.

they need it. The format of the table is used by convention and you should follow it exactly; list between-groups variance first, and so on.

Graphing the Results.   Another useful way of summarizing the results of an experiment is graphing. We can transform our findings into a picture that shows the reader the overall results at a glance. Look closely at Figure 13.3, which presents the results of our experiment as a graph.

The figure illustrates several general points you should keep in mind. Notice that the figure is well-proportioned; the vertical axis is roughly three-fourths the size of the horizontal axis. Other proportions are not as pleasing to look at. Notice

TABLE 13.5 ANALYSIS OF VARIANCE SUMMARY TABLE

Source	df	SS	MS	F
Between groups	2	10.55	5.28	$\dfrac{MS_B}{MS_W} = 7.23**$
Within groups	12	8.80	.73	
Total	14	19.35		

*$p < .05$.
**$p < .01$.

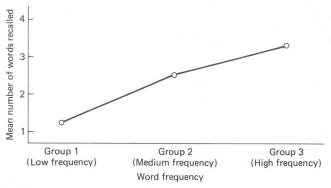

Figure 13.3 Mean number of words recalled as a function of word frequency.

also that the independent variable is plotted on the horizontal axis; the dependent variable is plotted on the vertical axis. Finally, note that the data points represent group means. We usually do not graph the data of individual subjects unless we have a small N design. Of course the axes are labeled clearly so that readers will know exactly what the figure represents.

Interpreting the Results.   We know that the computed F was significant for these data. We will have more to say about interpreting the meaning of that outcome in the next chapter. However, there are some points about the F test that should be made before we go further.

From the graph of our results (Figure 13.3), you can see quite clearly that subjects in different groups performed differently from one another in this experiment. Subjects in the high-frequency group recalled the most items; subjects in the low-frequency group recalled the least. You can also see clearly from the figure that the variation between different groups was not uniform. The high- and low-frequency groups differed more from each other than from the medium group. When we compute F, we test only the overall pattern of treatment means. Our significant F in this example tells us that across all the group means, there is a significant difference. Since the F test does not test the differences between each pair of means, we do not know exactly where the difference is. From the graph, it seems likely that the high and the low groups are significantly different from each other. After all, they differ the most. However, the difference between, say, the low- and the medium-frequency groups may or may not be significant.

post hoc tests

When we need to pinpoint the exact source of the differences across several treatment groups, we need to go beyond the F test. There are several additional tests that are called **post hoc tests**, tests done after the overall analysis indicates a significant difference. We will not go into the details of these tests here, but some of the names you will see include the Tukey and the Scheffé tests. These tests have essentially the same function: They can be used to make pair-by-pair comparisons to pinpoint the source of a significant difference across several treatments.

Let us briefly summarize what we have accomplished in this chapter so far. We took a multiple-group experiment and selected a suitable statistical test on the basis of three dimensions: We considered the number of independent variables, the number of treatment groups, and the level of measurement in making our choice. The experiment had one independent variable (word frequency), and three treatment groups (low, medium, and high frequency). The dependent variable (number of items recalled) was measured by a ratio scale. The data therefore required a one-way analysis of variance, or F test, which we carried out and evaluated. We also prepared a summary table of our analysis and graphed the group means.

The basic principles of the analysis of variance apply in many multiple-group experiments. However, those principles can also be extended to handle more complex research designs. We will carry them further in our next example, an experiment with a factorial design.

ANALYZING DATA FROM A FACTORIAL EXPERIMENT

Factorial experiments are designed to look at the effects of more than one independent variable at a time. They also enable us to look at the interaction between variables. The impact of one independent variable may differ depending on the values of the other independent variables in the experiment. When we analyze the data from a factorial experiment, we evaluate both kinds of effects. We look at the impact of each independent variable; we assess whether there is a main effect of each independent variable. We also measure the size of any interaction between the variables. Let us look at an example of a simple factorial experiment and see what statistical procedures are used to accomplish these goals.

Assume we have set up and run another experiment to explore the relationship between word frequency and recall. Half the subjects saw high-frequency words, and half saw low-frequency words. This time, though, we have run a factorial experiment. In addition to evaluating the effect of frequency, we have manipulated our testing procedures in a 2×2 design. The design is diagrammed in Figure 13.4. Half the subjects have been asked simply to recall the words they saw on the original list. The other half have been given cues to aid them in remembering the words they saw. For instance, suppose subjects saw the word "camel" on the original list. If they were in the "no cue" condition, they were simply asked to recall. If they were in the "cued" condition, we provided the name of the category the word belongs to—animal. Category cues were given for all words on the list.

Our hypothesis, which is based on prior research (for example, Tulving and Pearlstone, 1966), is that cuing will enhance recall. Frequency will also affect recall, with the more frequent words being easier to recall. We have two independent variables in this experiment, word frequency and category cues. Our dependent variable is the number of words correctly recalled from each list, a ratio measure. We will use $p < .05$ as our significance level. If you consult Table 12.4, you will find that the statistical test indicated for these data is a two-way analysis of variance.

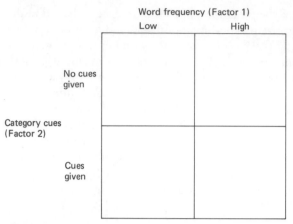

Figure 13.4   Diagram of 2 × 2 factorial experiment on the effects of word frequency and cuing on recall.

You already know how to do the basic, or one-way, ANOVA. The same principles apply to all ANOVA procedures. But when we have a factorial design, additional complexities arise. The procedures for the one-way ANOVA are not designed to give us as much information as we want to get from a factorial experiment. We want to be able to evaluate the effect of each independent variable: we need to know whether the word frequency, as well as the category cues, affects ability to recall words. Of course we also want to know whether there was any interaction between the two variables. We want to assess whether the effects of using different frequencies might differ depending on whether or not cues are given—or perhaps the effect of cues varies depending on whether the word to be recalled is relatively frequent or infrequent.

To answer all these questions with an analysis of variance, we need to break down the variance in the data into more components than we had before. In the one-way ANOVA, we had one independent variable. We divided all the variability in the data into just two parts: within-groups and between-groups variability. Within-groups variability is created by all those sources of error in the experiment: individual differences, the experimenter's mistakes, and other extraneous variables. Between-groups variability is created by all those sources of error plus the effect of the independent variable. The same is true in a factorial experiment. We can separate variability into within-groups and between-groups variance. However, the picture is more complex. Between-groups variability comes from error and treatment effects, but there are several sources of treatment effects in the factorial experiment. Every independent variable may produce its own unique treatment effects; each can produce a portion of the between-groups variability or a main effect. The interaction of the independent variables can produce another portion. This is represented graphically in Figure 13.5, which compares the components of variability for the one-way analysis of variance against a two-way analysis of variance for a two-factor experiment.

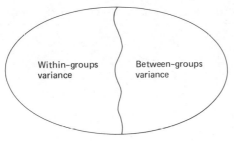

(a) A one-way ANOVA (one independent variable)

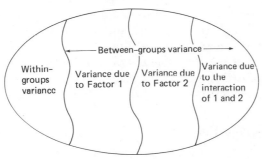

(b) The components of variability for a two-way ANOVA of
a factorial design (two independent variables)

Figure 13.5 The components of variability for (a) a one-way analysis of variance (one independent variable) and (b) a two-way analysis of variance (two independent variables).

We can begin our analysis of variance for the factorial experiment by finding within- and between-groups variability. However, we will also need to break between-groups variability into *its* component parts: the variability associated with *each* of the independent variables, and the variability associated with the *interaction* between them.

When we did the one-way ANOVA, we used a summary table to organize our computations. When we do a two-way ANOVA, it is helpful to plan the summary table in advance. We can use it to keep track of computations as we do them. The outline of the summary table for a two-factor experiment is shown in Table 13.6. You can see that all the sources of variability in the experiment are represented. We must find all these components in order to compute the F ratios needed to judge significance. We will calculate a different F ratio for every source of between-groups variability in the experiment, and use those ratios to decide whether the effects of each independent variable are significant. We will also decide whether there is a significant interaction.

TABLE 13.6 SUMMARIZING THE ANALYSIS OF VARIANCE FOR A TWO-FACTOR EXPERIMENT

Source	df	SS	MS	$F = \dfrac{MS}{MS_w}$
Between groups				
Factor 1				
Factor 2				
Interaction 1 × 2				
Within groups				
Total				

A TWO-WAY ANALYSIS OF VARIANCE

Table 13.7 presents some hypothetical data from our experiment to test the effect of word frequency and category cues on recall. Since this is a 2 × 2 factorial design, the data are divided into four treatment groups. We have already begun the data analysis by computing the mean number of words correctly recalled by each treatment group. Let us take an overall look at the steps required to complete the analysis of variance. The actual computations are shown in Tables 13.8 through 13.11.

Assumptions behind the Two-Way Analysis of Variance

The procedures and formulas for a two-way ANOVA require the same basic assumptions as the one-way ANOVA procedures we examined earlier. They assume that the treatment groups are independent from each other and that the observations

TABLE 13.7 DATA FROM A TWO-FACTOR EXPERIMENT: THE EFFECTS OF WORD FREQUENCY AND CATEGORY CUES ON RECALL IN A LIST-LEARNING TASK

		Word frequency (Factor 1)			
		Low		High	
	No cues given	2 3 1 4 5	$\overline{X}_1 = 3$	4 5 4 6 6	$\overline{X}_2 = 5$
Category cues (Factor 2)					
	Cues given	4 6 5 6 9	$\overline{X}_3 = 6$	12 10 10 9 9	$\overline{X}_4 = 10$

Note: Scores represent number of words correctly recalled from a list.

TABLE 13.8   STEP 1: COMPUTING WITHIN-GROUPS VARIABILITY (MS_W) FOR A 2 × 2 FACTORIAL EXPERIMENT

Word frequency
(Factor 1)

		Low			High		
		X_1	$(X_1 - \bar{X}_1)$	$(X_1 - \bar{X}_1)^2$	X_2	$(X_2 - \bar{X}_2)$	$(X_2 - \bar{X}_2)^2$
No cues given		2	−1	1	4	−1	1
		3	0	0	5	0	0
		1	−2	4	4	−1	1
		4	1	1	6	1	1
		5	2	4	6	1	1
		$\bar{X}_1 = 3$		$\Sigma(X_1 - \bar{X}_1)^2 = 10$	$\bar{X}_2 = 5$		$\Sigma(X_2 - \bar{X}_2)^2 = 4$
		X_3	$(X_3 - \bar{X}_3)$	$(X_3 - \bar{X}_3)^2$	X_4	$(X_4 - \bar{X}_4)$	$(X_4 - \bar{X}_4)^2$
Cues given		4	−2	4	7	−1	1
		6	0	0	6	−2	4
		5	−1	1	9	1	1
		6	0	0	8	0	0
		9	3	9	10	2	4
		$\bar{X}_3 = 6$		$\Sigma(X_3 - \bar{X}_3)^2 = 14$	$\bar{X}_4 = 8$		$\Sigma(X_4 - \bar{X}_4)^2 = 10$

(Row label at far left, spanning vertically: Category Cues (Factor 2))

$$SS_W = \Sigma(X_1 - \bar{X}_1)^2 + \Sigma(X_2 - \bar{X}_2)^2 + \Sigma(X_3 - \bar{X}_3)^2 + \Sigma(X_4 - \bar{X}_4)^2 + \ldots + \Sigma(X_p - \bar{X}_p)^2$$

$SS_W = 10 + 4 + 14 + 10$

$SS_W = 38$

$df_W = N - P$ N = Number of scores; p = Number of groups

$df_W = 20 - 4$ or 16

$$MS_W = \frac{SS_W}{df_W}$$

$MS_W = \dfrac{39}{16}$

$MS_W = 2.44$

were randomly sampled. They also assume that the population from which each treatment group is sampled is normally distributed on the dependent variable. Finally, they assume that the variances of the populations are all about equal (homogeneous). The computations here are done just for the sake of illustration, so we have only five subjects per cell. However, the assumptions behind the ANOVA procedures are more likely to be met with larger groups of subjects. In addition, the

TABLE 13.9   STEP 2: COMPUTING THE BETWEEN-GROUPS VARIABILITY (SS_B) FOR A 2 × 2 FACTORIAL EXPERIMENT

	Group 1	Group 2	Group 3	Group 4	Grand Mean ($\overline{X}_G$)
	$\overline{X}_1 = 3$	$\overline{X}_2 = 5$	$\overline{X}_3 = 6$	$\overline{X}_4 = 8$	Total of all
	$n_1 = 5$	$n_2 = 5$	$n_3 = 5$	$n_4 = 5$	$\overline{X}_G = \dfrac{\text{group means}}{\text{Number of Groups}}$
Step 1. Compute the grand mean, the mean of all the group means.					$\overline{X}_G = \dfrac{3 + 5 + 6 + 8}{4}$ $\overline{X}_G = \dfrac{22}{4}$ $\overline{X}_G = 5.5$
Step 2. Compute the deviation of each group mean from the grand mean.	$\overline{X}_1 - \overline{X}_G =$ $3 - 5.5$ or -2.5	$\overline{X}_2 - \overline{X}_G =$ $5 - 5.5$ or $-.5$	$\overline{X}_3 - \overline{X}_G =$ $6 - 5.5$ or $.5$	$\overline{X}_4 - \overline{X}_G =$ $8 - 5.5$ or 2.5	

$$SS_B = n_1 (\overline{X}_1 - \overline{X}_G)^2 + n_2(\overline{X}_2 - \overline{X}_G)^2 + n_3 (\overline{X}_3 - \overline{X}_G)^2 + \ldots + n_p (\overline{X}_p - \overline{X}_G)^2$$

Step 3. Put the deviations in the SS_B formula; n is the number of subjects in each group.	$SS_B =$ $5(-2.5)^2 +$	$5(-.5)^2 +$	$5(.5)^2 +$	$5(2.5)^2$
Step 4. Square all deviations from the grand mean.	$SS_B =$ $5(6.25) +$	$5(.25) +$	$5(.25) +$	$5(6.25)$
Step 5. Complete all computations.	$SS_B =$ $31.25 +$	$1.25 +$	$1.25 +$	31.25
	$SS_B = 65$			

procedures shown here assume *equal* numbers of subjects in each group and more than one subject per group. If you have unequal Ns, you will need more complicated procedures. The same is true if you have used within-subjects procedures. In either case, consult your instructor, or see Winer's *Statistical Principles in Experimental Design* (1971).

fixed models   Finally, these procedures are set for **fixed models**, experiments in which the values of the independent variables are fixed by the experimenter. In other words,

TABLE 13.10 STEP 3: FINDING THE MAIN EFFECT FOR FACTOR 1 (WORD FREQUENCY) IN A 2 × 2 EXAMPLE

		Word Frequency (Factor 1)	
		Low	High
Step 1. Find the mean at each level of Factor 1: Ignore Factor 2 (rows) and find the mean of each column.	No cues given	$\bar{X}_1 = 3$ $(N = 5)$	$\bar{X}_2 = 5$ $(N = 5)$
	Cues given	$\bar{X}_3 = 6$ $(N = 5)$	$\bar{X}_4 = 8$ $(N = 5)$
	Column means	$\bar{X}_{col\ 1} = 4.5$	$\bar{X}_{col\ 2} = 6.5$
Step 2. Find the difference between each column mean and the grand mean	Column mean − Grand mean $\bar{X}_G = 5.5$	$\bar{X}_{col\ 1} - \bar{X}_G =$ $4.5 - 5.5 = -1.0$	$\bar{X}_{col\ 2} - \bar{X}_G =$ $6.5 - 5.5 = 1.0$

(Category cues (Factor 2))

Step 3.. Put those differences in the **SS₁** formula: n is the number of subjects in each group; p is the number of rows; q is the number of columns. This general formula will handle any number of columns.

$$\mathbf{SS}_1 = np\ \Sigma\ [(\bar{X}_{col\ 1} - \bar{X}_G)^2 + (\bar{X}_{col\ 2} - \bar{X}_G)^2 + \ldots + (\bar{X}_{col\ p} - \bar{X}_G)^2]$$

$$\mathbf{SS}_1 = 5(2)\Sigma[(-1.0)^2 + (1.0)^2]$$

$$\mathbf{SS}_1 = 10[(1) + (1)]$$

$$\mathbf{SS}_1 = 10(2)$$

$$\mathbf{SS}_1 = 20$$

Step 4. To get **MS₁**, divide **SS₁** by df_1.

$$\mathbf{MS}_1 = \frac{\mathbf{SS}_1}{df_1}$$

$df_1 = q - 1$

$df_1 = 2 - 1$ or 1

$$\mathbf{MS}_1 = \frac{20}{1}$$

$$\mathbf{MS}_1 = 20$$

the experimenter chooses to run subjects at certain levels of each independent variable. In our example, the experimenter has chosen to use high and low word frequencies and two levels of the category cue variable—cues versus no cues. However, in experiments with **random models**, the experimenter simply uses randomly selected values of the independent variables. For instance, if the researcher is testing the effects of different brands of cigarettes, he or she might select several brands at random. It is also possible to have experiments that follow a **mixed model** that

random models

mixed model

TABLE 13.11   STEP 3: FINDING THE MAIN EFFECT FOR FACTOR 2 (CATEGORY CUE) IN A 2 × 2 FACTORIAL EXPERIMENT

		Word frequency (Factor 1)			
		Low	High	Row means	Row mean − grand mean
Category cues (Factor 2)	No cues given	$\bar{X}_1 = 3$	$\bar{X}_2 = 5$	$\bar{X}_{row\ 1} = 4$	$\bar{X}_{row\ 1} - \bar{X}_G =$ 4 − 5.5 *or* − 1.5
	Cues given	$\bar{X}_3 = 6$	$\bar{X}_4 = 8$	$\bar{X}_{row\ 2} = 7$	$\bar{X}_{row\ 2} - \bar{X}_G =$ 7 − 5.5 *or* 1.5

Step 1. Find the mean at each level of Factor 2: Ignore Factor 1 (columns) and find the mean of each row.

Step 2. Find the difference between each row mean and the grand mean.

$(\bar{X}_G = 5.5)$

Step 3. Put those differences in the **SS₂** formula; *n* is the number of subjects in each group; *q* is the number of columns; *p* is the number of rows. This general formula will handle any number of rows.

$$\boxed{SS_2 = nq\ \Sigma[(\bar{X}_{row\ 1} - \bar{X}_G)^2 + (\bar{X}_{row\ 2} - \bar{X}_G)^2 + \ldots + (\bar{X}_{row\ p} - \bar{X}_G)^2]}$$

$$SS_2 = 5(2)\ [(-1.5)^2 + (1.5)^2]$$

$$SS = 10\ [2.25 + 2.25]$$

$$SS_2 = 10\ (4.50)\ or\ 45$$

Step 4. To get **MS₂**, divide **SS₂** by df_2.

$$\boxed{MS_2 = \frac{SS_2}{df_2}}$$

$df_2 = p - 1$

$df_2 = 2 - 1\ or\ 1$

$$MS_2 = 45$$

combines some random factors with some fixed factors. Most experiments follow the fixed model, as we do here.

Step 1: Computing Within-Groups Variance.   We begin the ANOVA by filling in the within-groups section of the summary table. We need the degrees of freedom (df), the sum of squares within groups (SS_W), and the mean square within groups (MS_W). To get them, we follow the same basic procedures that we used for the one-way ANOVA. The calculations for our 2 × 2 experiment are shown in Table 13.8. Remember that the mean square within groups represents variability produced by individual differences, extraneous variables, and other sources of error in the experiment. We will use MS_W to evaluate the impact of the independent variables and their interaction in the experiment.

Step 2: Computing Between-Groups Variability. We continue our ANOVA by finding the total sum of squares between groups, SS_B. We need the SS_B because it represents all the variability we have among treatment groups. To complete our ANOVA, we will have to divide the SS_B into its main components: the parts associated with each of the independent variables, and the part associated with the interaction between them. Table 13.9 illustrates the procedures for finding SS_B for our factorial example.

Step 3: Computing Main Effects. As you know, the ANOVA procedures have some special terms associated with them. "Sum of squares" and "mean square" refer to variability in the data. When we want to discuss the variability associated with a single independent variable in a factorial design, we call it a **main effect**, the change in the dependent variable produced by the various levels of one independent variable. In our 2×2 example, we are looking for a main effect of word frequency. We are also looking for a main effect of category cues. The number of main effects to be tested in a factorial experiment is determined by the number of independent variables in the experiment.

main effect

When we carry out our ANOVA, we evaluate whether or not each main effect in the experiment is significant: We compute an F ratio to test the impact of each independent variable. When we test for a significant main effect, we are simply asking again whether subjects' scores on the dependent variable differ depending on the levels of one independent variable that we have manipulated. To measure the total between-groups variability, we calculated the deviation of group means around their grand mean. In effect, we asked how much individual treatment groups differed from the average of all the groups. When we measure a main effect, we want to look only at a particular portion of the total variability. We want to measure how much variability occurs between groups because of the impact of one independent variable.

We can ask a straightforward question: How much do the means of groups under different levels of one variable, say, word frequency, differ from the grand mean of all the groups? This is like the logic we followed in doing the one-way ANOVA: The larger the effect of the independent variable, the larger the differences from the grand mean. In our example, a large main effect of word frequency would mean that subjects' recall varied depending on whether the words to be learned were relatively common or uncommon. When we evaluate the main effect of one independent variable, we treat the data as if that variable is the only one in the experiment. We simply ignore all the other experimental manipulations that were done: we say *we collapse the data across the other conditions of the experiment.* In effect, we pretend that those conditions did not exist. Table 13.10 shows how this is done as we compute SS_1 for our first independent variable, word frequency.

We also need to test for a main effect of the second variable. We know that this second variable may have contributed to the total variability between treatment groups. We can evaluate the main effect of the second variable by using the same basic procedures we followed to get the main effect of word frequency. In effect, we ask whether subjects' recall differed depending on whether they were given category cues or not: Did it differ regardless of whether they were shown high- or low-frequency words? We look at the effects of our second independent variable by simply disregarding the word-frequency manipulation. *We collapse across the word-frequency conditions*. Table 13.11 shows the procedures.

Step 4: Computing the Interaction.   The variability associated with the interaction of the two independent variables is simply what remains after the main effects of the independent variables have been taken into account. The variability between groups that is not explained by either independent variable may be explained by their

interaction   interaction.

Since we have two independent variables, the SS_B must be divided into three parts: the variability associated with the first independent variable (SS_1); the variability associated with the second independent variable (SS_2); and the variability associated with the interaction of the two ($SS_{1 \times 2}$). Once we have computed the total SS_B, SS_1 and SS_2, the simplest way to find $SS_{1 \times 2}$ is by subtracting:

$$SS_{1 \times 2} = SS_B - SS_1 - SS_2$$

The sum of squares for the interaction is entered in the summary table, Table 13.12.

TABLE 13.12   SUMMARY TABLE: ANALYSIS OF VARIANCE FOR A 2 × 2 FACTORIAL EXPERIMENT AND COMPUTED *F* RATIOS (INCLUDES STEP 4)

Source	df	SS	MS	F
Between groups		65^a		
Factor 1 (word frequency)	$p - 1 = 1$	20	20	$F_1 = \dfrac{20}{2.38}$ or 8.40*
Factor 2 (category cues)	$q - 1 = 1$	45	45	$F_2 = \dfrac{45}{2.38}$ or 18.91**
Interaction 1 × 2	$(p - 1)(q - 1) = 1$	0^b	0	$F_{1 \times 2} = \dfrac{0}{2.38}$ or 0
Within groups	$N - p = 16$	38	2.38	
Total	$N - 1 = 19$			

*$p < .05$
**$p < .01$

[a]SS_B is usually not shown in published articles.
[b]We find the sum of squares for the interaction of our two variables by subtracting:

$$SS_{1 \times 2} = SS_B - SS_1 - SS_2$$

The $SS_{1 \times 2}$ represents all the between-groups variability that is not explained by the main effect of either independent variable. Its degrees of freedom depend on the degrees of freedom for the main effects. Here, there is no interaction.

Step 5: Computing the F Ratios. We have now completed nearly all the computations that we need to evaluate the results of our experiment. We summarize our calculations in a summary table, Table 13.12. The table is similar to the one we prepared for the simple ANOVA. The only difference is in the way we represent the sources of variability. Because we have two independent variables in this experiment, we have three sources of variability: Factor 1, Factor 2, and their interaction. The within-groups variability (MS_W) is used as the denominator of all three F ratios required to evaluate the significance of these sources. The three F ratios have been computed and are also shown in the summary table.

Evaluating the F Ratios

To judge whether the computed F ratios are significant, we compare them to the table values of F. We get those values from our table of F values in the Appendix. The procedures are the same as those used for the simple ANOVA. We locate the proper value of F by using the degrees of freedom of the F ratio. We look across the top of Table B3 to find the degrees of freedom that belong to the top, or numerator, of the F ratio. We look along the side of the table to find the degrees of freedom of the denominator of our F ratio. Each F ratio we compute has its own degrees of freedom. That means that each ratio has its own critical value or table value of F. When we evaluate each F ratio, we must be sure we are using the correct degrees of freedom and the correct critical value.

Practice finding the correct critical value by looking up the table values of F for the F ratios we have computed. The F ratio for Factor 1 (word frequency) has 1 degree of freedom for the numerator (MS_1); it has 16 degrees of freedom for the denominator (MS_W). The table value of F (1, 16) is 4.49 at $p < .05$, and 8.53 at $p < .01$. Our computed value of F for Factor 1 is 8.40. Therefore, the effect of Factor 1 is significant at $p < .05$. Our computed value of F is more extreme than the table value. This means the main effect of word frequency is so large that it is probably not due to chance. Whether the lists contained high- or low-frequency words made a significant difference in subjects' recall. We reject the null hypothesis that the means of the high- and low-frequency groups were sampled from the same population.

The F ratio for Factor 2 (category cues) also has 1 degree of freedom for the numerator (MS_2); it has 16 degrees of freedom for the denominator (MS_W). We know that the table value of F (1, 16) is 4.49 at $p < .05$, and 8.53 at $p < .01$. (They turn out to be the same as they were for Factor 1 because we had the same number of treatment levels and subjects for both word frequency and category cues). Our computed value of F for Factor 2 is 18.91. The main effect of Factor 2 is significant at $p < .01$: Our computed value of F for Factor 2 is more extreme (that is, in this case larger) than the table value at $p < .01$. Subjects who received category cues recalled significantly more items than subjects who did not receive cues. We reject the null hypothesis that the means of the groups under the two levels of Factor 2 were sampled from the same population.

The computed F for the interaction is 0. This is clearly not significant. In effect, this tells us that the variability between treatment groups can be explained by the effect of either word frequency or category cues acting separately on subjects' scores. Also, the impact of each independent variable was unrelated to the value of the other independent variable: The effect of word frequency was the same regardless of whether or not subjects received category cues. Similarly, the effect of giving category cues was the same whether subjects saw high- or low-frequency words.

If the interaction had been significant, we would be limited in what we could conclude about the main effects in this experiment. Generally, the existence of a significant interaction makes a discussion of simple main effects unnecesssary. If there is a significant interaction, it is usually more useful to discuss the impact of the independent variables in combination with each other. A significant interaction means that the impact of one independent variable differs depending on the value of the other. We can make accurate predictions about subjects' performance only when we know the subjects' position with respect to both variables. For instance, in this example, a significant interaction would mean that we could accurately predict about how many items the average subject would recall—but only if we knew both that the subject saw high-frequency words, and that the subject received cues. Without the interaction, we can make a reasonably good prediction if we know the subject's position on only one variable. If we know that Carl was given category cues, we automatically also know that he probably did better than the subjects who did not get cues, regardless of whether he saw high- or low-frequency words.

Graphing the Results.   When we had only one independent variable, we had only one line to graph. However, in a factorial experiment we need to do more. The results of our experiment are presented graphically in Figure 13.6. Notice that the vertical axis still represents the dependent variable. The horizontal axis represents the different levels of one independent variable. Each line that is graphed presents the data from a different level of the other independent variable. One line represents the recall of subjects who were given category cues; the other stands for recall under the "no cues" condition. You can see from the location of the lines that there are differences between the scores of subjects under the various conditions of this experiment.

Our example yielded two significant main effects. The distance between the two lines (cues versus no cues) reflects the impact of the category cues variable. If giving category cues had no effect on the number of items subjects recalled, the two lines would fall in the same place on the graph. Similarly, the impact of the word-frequency variable is indicated by the relative position of the data points along the Y axis. If word frequency had no effect on recall, subjects would recall about the same number of items in both the high- and low-frequency conditions. These and other possible outcomes are illustrated in Figure 13.7.

Notice that interactions appear on the graphs as lines which are not parallel. If the lines converge, diverge, or intersect, we may have a significant interaction effect.

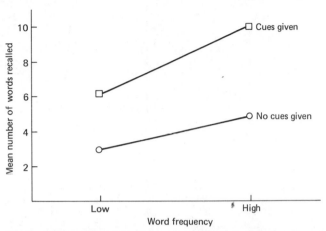

Figure 13.6 Graphing the results of a two-factor experiment: Recall graph of word lists as a function of word frequency and category cues.

Such graphs are useful ways of summarizing the results of an experiment to give an overall view of the findings. They are especially useful in constructing summaries of findings for experimental reports. But they are not substitutes for statistical analysis. Even though the results look impressive, we need to carry out all the statistical procedures before we can make precise statements of whether we will accept them as significant findings.

SUMMARY

The *analysis of variance* procedures are used in experiments having more than two treatment conditions and interval or ratio data. An Analysis of Variance (ANOVA) evaluates the effect of treatment conditions by looking at the variability in data. In the one-way ANOVA, all the variability in the data can be divided into two parts: Within-groups variability and between-groups variability. *Within-groups variability* is the degree to which the scores of subjects in the same treatment group differ from one another; *between-groups variability* is the degree to which different treatment groups differ from one another.

Variability is caused by all the sources of *error* in the experiment: differences between subjects, as well as measurement errors and other extraneous variables. Error also contributes to within-groups and between-groups variability. Between-groups variability, however, reflects variability due to error and treatment conditions. If the independent variable had an effect, there should be more variability between treatment groups than there is within them: Between-groups variability should be large relative to the amount of variability within each group.

The relationship of within- and between-groups variability is evaluated by com-

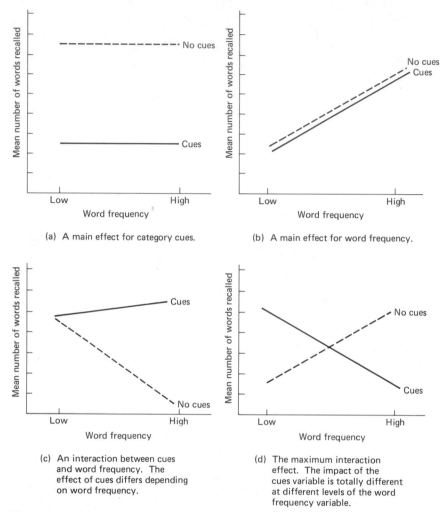

(a) A main effect for category cues.

(b) A main effect for word frequency.

(c) An interaction between cues and word frequency. The effect of cues differs depending on word frequency.

(d) The maximum interaction effect. The impact of the cues variable is totally different at different levels of the word frequency variable.

Figure 13.7   Illustrating other main effects and interactions: Some hypothetical outcomes of an experiment on the effects of word frequency and category cues on list recall.

puting the statistic called *F*. *F* represents the ratio between the variability observed *between* treatment groups and the variability *within* the groups. The larger the *F* ratio, the more likely it is that the variability between groups was caused by the independent variable. *F* is found by computing these quantities: Sum of squares between groups (SS_B) and sum of squares within groups (SS_W). Each of these quantities is divided by its respective degrees of freedom (*df*) to obtain the mean square between groups (MS_B) and mean square within groups (MS_W). The degrees of freedom of the experiment are used to locate the critical values of *F* in standardized tables.

If the computed value of F is more extreme than the table value, the null hypothesis that treatment means were sampled from the same population is rejected.

The basic ANOVA procedures may be extended to handle the data from experiments with more than one independent variable. In factorial experiments, the variability in data may be caused by several sources: It can be produced by error; it may also be produced by each independent variable in the experiment. The effects of each independent variable are called *main effects*. In addition, there may be variability due to the *interaction*, or combination of variables in the experiment. There is an interaction when the effect of one independent variable changes depending on the value of another independent variable in the experiment. In analyzing data from a factorial experiment, an F ratio is computed to evaluate each main effect and each possible interaction. The basic computational procedures for a two-factor experiment (two-way ANOVA) are similar to those for a one-way analysis of variance.

REVIEW AND STUDY QUESTIONS

1. When do we use a one-way analysis of variance?
2. What is within-groups variability?
3. What are the sources of within-groups variance?
4. What is between-groups variance?
5. What are the sources of between-groups variance in an experiment with one independent variable?
6. Explain how the one-way analysis of variance works: How do we use within- and between-groups variance?
7. Briefly explain each of these terms:
   a. Sum of squares within groups ($\mathbf{SS_W}$)
   b. Sum of squares between groups ($\mathbf{SS_B}$)
   c. Mean square within groups ($\mathbf{MS_W}$)
   d. Mean square between groups ($\mathbf{MS_B}$)
   e. the F ratio
8. A researcher computed the F ratio for a four-group experiment. The computed F is 4.86. The degrees of freedom are 3 for the numerator and 16 for the denominator.
   a. Is the computed value of F significant at $p < .05$? Why or why not?
   b. Is it significant at $p < .01$? Why or why not?
9. Suppose we have done a one-way analysis of variance and our computed F is significant. What can we say about the means of the treatment groups of our experiment?
10. Explain why $\mathbf{SS_T} = \mathbf{SS_W} + \mathbf{SS_B}$ in the one-way analysis of variance.

11. In addition to the basic requirements (several treatments, and so on), for using the analysis of variance, what assumptions must we make about our data in order to use the test?

12. Jack is still unconvinced. "I'd rather use a bunch of t tests than try to figure out this analysis of variance." Can you explain to him again why the analysis of variance is more appropriate when we have more than two treatment groups?

13. Some of the ANOVA terminology is different from the terms used in earlier chapters. However, the concepts are similar. Test your understanding of the concepts by matching the following items on the right with the appropriate concept on the left. (Use each term only once.)

		Choice
a. within-groups variance	1. A test statistic.	_____
b. mean square	2. Total of squared deviations.	_____
c. null hypothesis	3. A variance estimate.	_____
d. sum of squares	4. Treatment means are sampled from the same population.	_____
e. between-groups variance		
f. F		
g. critical value	5. The table value of the test statistic at the chosen significance level.	_____
	6. Reflects variability due to error.	_____
	7. Reflects variability due to error *plus* treatment effects.	_____

14. Practice carrying out the one-way ANOVA procedures by calculating the F ratio for these data. The hypothetical scores represent the responses of subjects in four treatment groups who were given four different driver education programs. The dependent variable is the subjects' errors on their state examination for a driver's license:

Group 1	Group 2	Group 3	Group 4
3	1	1	2
3	2	1	3
1	1	3	2
3	4	1	5
1	2	2	1

a. What is the computed value of F for these data?
b. Is F significant at $p < .05$?
c. Prepare a summary table for your data.
d. Graph the results.

15. Take the data from question 14. Add 10 to the score of each subject in group 1.
    a. If you now carried through the ANOVA again, would you expect the computed values of SS_B and SS_W to change? Why or why not?
    b. Would the computed value of F change? If so, how?
    c. Carry out the computations on the new data and see whether your predictions are confirmed.

16. Define these terms:
    a. Main effect
    b. Interaction

17. In the one-way ANOVA, we divide all the variability in our data into just two components. Explain how the ANOVA procedures differ when we are dealing with a factorial experiment.

18. Explain what the components of variability will be in a two-way ANOVA to evaluate the data from a factorial experiment with two independent variables.

19. Identify each of these terms. What does each represent?

    a. SS_1 e. MS_1 i. F_1
    b. SS_2 f. MS_2 j. F_2
    c. $SS_{1 \times 2}$ g. $MS_{1 \times 2}$ k. $F_{1 \times 2}$
    d. SS_W h. MS_W

20. When we carry out the ANOVA for a factorial experiment, we compute an F ratio for each independent variable and for each possible interaction. Explain why we do not compute F_W, an F ratio to evaluate the size of the within-groups variability.

21. An experimenter has studied the effects of cigarette smoking on learning. Two levels of the smoking variable were used: All the subjects are smokers, but half are given cigarettes to smoke during the half hour before the experiment; the other half are not allowed to smoke after they arrive at the laboratory. There are also two levels of the learning variable. Subjects are all given the same materials to study. However, half the subjects are told they will be asked to recall the words they see (intentional learning condition). The remaining subjects are told they will be asked to rate various types of printing for readability. They are *not* told they will be asked to recall the actual words they see (this is the incidental learning condition).
    a. Here are some hypothetical data from a learning and smoking experiment. Practice the two-way ANOVA on these data.

| | Factor 1 (Smoking) | |
	Smoked	Did not smoke
Intentional	4 1 3 5 2	5 3 5 1 2
Incidental	3 5 4 1 2	4 3 2 1 4

Factor 2 (Learning)

    b. Explain what would happen if we added 10 to the score of each subject in the intentional learning groups.

    c. Explain what would happen if we added 10 to the score of each subject in the incidental learning, no-smoking group.

22. Prepare a simple graph to illustrate each of these possible outcomes of this experiment:

    a. There is a main effect for cigarette smoking only: Subjects who smoked remember more. There is no interaction.

    b. There is a main effect for learning: Subjects learned more in the intentional learning condition. There was no main effect for cigarette smoking and no interaction.

    c. There was a strong interaction between smoking and the learning conditions. Illustrate at least two forms this interaction might take.

REFERENCES

Howes, D. A word count of spoken English. *Journal of Verbal Learning and Verbal Behavior*, 1966, 5, 572–604.

Tulving, E., and Pearlstone, Z. Availability versus accessibility of information in memory for words. *Journal of Verbal Learning and Verbal Behavior*, 1966, 5, 381–391.

Winer, B. J. *Statistical principles in experimental design*, 2nd ed. New York: McGraw-Hill, 1971.

Part Four
Discussion

14

Drawing Conclusions: The Search for the Elusive Bottom Line

Evaluating the Experiment from the Inside: Internal Validity
Taking a Broader Perspective: The Problem of External Validity
    Generalizing from the Results
    Generalizing across Subjects
    Generalizing from Procedures to Concepts: Research Significance
    Generalizing beyond the Laboratory
    Increasing External Validity
Handling a Nonsignificant Outcome
    Faulty Procedures
    Faulty Hypothesis
Summary
Review and Study Questions
References

Key Terms

multivariate design
multivariate analysis of variance (MANOVA)
reactivity

unobtrusive measures
field experiment

We have now done all the major steps involved in setting up and running a psychological experiment, and evaluating the results through statistical tests. The goal of an experiment is to establish a cause and effect relationship between an independent and a dependent variable. In this text we have covered a variety of experimental designs and control procedures that enable us to do this in a legitimate way. Once we have analyzed the data through statistics, however, one question remains: What does it all mean? Have we accomplished our goal?

Even when we find a significant treatment effect, we have only established a statistical outcome. We have found that, for the data we collected, there were differences between treatments so large that they could occur by chance just a small percentage of the time. We have not tested the experimental hypothesis directly. Whether or not the results are statistically significant tells us nothing about the quality of the experiment; statistically significant results may or may not have any practical or theoretical implications. You could, in fact, invent data that show significant treatment effects.

Of course, we would like to find statistically significant differences. We would like results to be consistent with predictions. But in addition, we would like findings to be convincing and to have applications in settings outside the particular experiment. As we interpret the results of our experiments, we look beyond the simple question of whether or not they are statistically significant; we evaluate the pros and cons of accepting them at face value. The discussion and evaluation of findings are included in research reports: Besides telling others what we did, we want to tell them what we think it means.

In this chapter we will look at some of the problems of drawing conclusions from the results of an experiment. We will review some of the criteria used to evaluate the worth of an experiment—internal and external validity. We will also focus on some aspects of the generality of particular research findings beyond the context of an experiment. Finally, we will zero in on special problems that arise when our predictions are not confirmed.

EVALUATING THE EXPERIMENT FROM THE INSIDE: INTERNAL VALIDITY

When we evaluate an experiment, we begin by judging it from the inside: Is the experiment methodologically sound? Is it *internally valid*? An experiment is internally valid when there is nothing in the execution of the experiment itself that undermines the value of the results. An internally valid experiment is free of confounding. You will not find many obvious examples of internally invalid experiments in the research literature. All the articles published in major journals (for example, those published by the American Psychological Association) are carefully reviewed before they are accepted. Only the best get published. An experiment that contained an obvious source of confounding probably would not make it into print. However, as you read the literature, be on the lookout for more subtle problems. Perhaps a researcher overlooked something that may be important. Perhaps there is an alternative explanation of the findings if we view them in the context of another theoretical approach. If you can make a good case for your criticism, you may have the beginning of your own study to settle the question.

Of course, the best way to avoid internal invalidity is to plan ahead. As you design experiments, you must be sure that your procedures incorporate the appropriate control techniques. Use standard techniques such as random assignment, constancy of conditions, and counterbalancing throughout your research. But when you are ready to evaluate the outcome of the experiment, do not forget to consider what *actually* happened. The most careful plans may go awry. You may have designed a tight set of procedures before you began testing subjects, but in practice, you may have been forced to deviate from the plan. You may not have accomplished what you intended. Did you find that subjects in your control group did not understand directions? Did they keep asking questions to clarify their task in the experiment? Your instructions may have been confusing under that condition. Can you be sure, then, that those subjects really did what you wanted them to do? Many researchers incorporate an informal interview at the end of the experiment to get at this kind of information. If subjects didn't follow instructions, the experimental manipulation may not be the best explanation of the findings. Similarly, if one group of subjects guessed the hypothesis, their data may be of limited value.

Some of these validity issues are difficult to resolve because of the demand characteristics of the experiment itself. For instance, Orne (1969) suggested that a "pact of ignorance" forms between subjects and experimenter. Subjects are often aware that if they guess the hypothesis of the experiment, their data will be discarded. If you ask them what they understood about the purpose of the experiment, they may not reveal all they know. Similarly, Orne suggests that experimenters may not press subjects for much information either. Most researchers do not want to spend unnecessary time testing additional subjects. They may be tempted to accept subjects' reports at face value instead of requesting additional information that might provide a more objective evaluation.

Always review the experimental procedures *after* the experiment. Did any extraneous variables change along with the independent variable? Did testing conditions change midstream? Were there any other unplanned changes that might have altered subjects' responses? Remember that if something other than the independent variable can explain the results, the experiment is invalid.

TAKING A BROADER PERSPECTIVE: THE PROBLEM OF EXTERNAL VALIDITY

So far we have talked about evaluating an experiment within itself. Did extraneous variables contaminate the results? Is the study free of confounding? In addition, we want to look beyond the experiment to broader questions. We want to know whether the experiment has *external validity*: Do the findings have implications outside the experiment? Can we make any general statements about the impact of the independent variable? An experiment is externally valid if the results can be extended to other situations accurately. However, external validity is not an either/or matter; it is a continuum. Some experiments are more externally valid than others.

Generalizing from the Results

When an experiment has some degree of external validity, we may generalize from the results. One definition of "generalizing" is "making vague." We make our findings more universal than they actually are by ignoring the specific details of the experiment. Instead of speaking in terms of a particular sample (for example, 30 female undergraduates), and a specific set of operational definitions (for example, scores on the Manifest Anxiety Scale), we draw broader inferences from the findings through inductive thinking. When we think inductively, we reason from specific facts to more general principles. Early in the text you saw how we can use induction to formulate research hypotheses. We also use induction when we make generalizations on the basis of a specific set of findings. Whether our generalizations will be accurate depends on a variety of factors that affect the external validity of an experiment.

An externally valid experiment meets two basic requirements. First, the experiment is internally valid; it demonstrates a cause and effect relationship. The results of the experiment were produced by the independent variable. The experiment is free of confounding. Second, findings that are externally valid can be *replicated*. We (or other researchers) can replicate or duplicate the original findings in other experiments. If we get statistically significant results again, we can be more sure that the findings were not just flukes of our sampling procedures, or Type 1 errors. Valid experimental findings appear again and again. Similar effects should reappear in similar studies. Findings that appear once and cannot be replicated have limited scientific importance, and any general conclusions that we draw from such findings may be inaccurate.

Of course, when you complete a single experiment, you do not usually know whether the findings can be replicated, unless you are actually replicating some earlier findings. Partly for that reason, you will often see single articles that contain reports of several experiments. These series of experiments typically extend the findings of one principal study. They provide data on alternative explanations and applications of those findings; they also serve to provide evidence that the findings can be replicated. If a researcher consistently obtains confirmation of a hypothesis throughout a series of experiments, the findings have some degree of external validity.

In addition to the overall requirements of internal validity and replicability, we can also look at external validity as it applies to several important issues: generalizability across subjects, across procedures, and beyond the laboratory.

Generalizing across Subjects

How much can we generalize from one group of subjects to another? How much can we generalize from a sample to the population that interests us? There are no hard and fast answers to these questions. Experiments may have different outcomes when they are run on different samples. For that reason, we try to get samples from the population we want to discuss. If we want to make statements about college students, we ought to sample college students. It makes sense to assume that all college students have some characteristics in common that enable us to speak of them as a group. Nevertheless, we need to be cautious in drawing conclusions about *all* students on the basis of one study. What is true for students in Kansas may not be true of students in New York.

In addition, practical problems prevent us from obtaining truly random samples. There is typically *bias* in the way human subjects are chosen, if only in that they are all volunteers. The student (or homemaker or salesperson) who volunteers may not be typical. As a group, volunteers may be quite different from nonvolunteers. In fact, some researchers have found that volunteers may differ from nonvolunteers on a variety of factors. These include intelligence, education, and attitudes toward psychological testing (see, for instance, Rosenthal and Rosnow, 1975).

The problem becomes even more acute when we try to extend our findings to a larger group, such as "all people." Other writers have commented on the fact that a rather large proportion of research findings in psychology has come from studies of white rats and college students. Of course, many of those findings have been replicated in studies with different species, and with a variety of human subjects too. But the fact remains that the generality of our research is often constrained by practical problems. College students are intrinsically interesting. Perhaps more important, they are also more available for research than the average adult who spends the better part of the day at a regular job. White rats are relatively easy to keep and they cost less than monkeys. These mundane factors shape the research that we do. When we have trouble finding subjects, we will also have trouble getting samples that are typical of the population we are trying to study. Therefore, the external validity of the experiment will be limited.

How far can we go in generalizing from a study? Clearly, the further from the population actually sampled, the shakier our position becomes, at least until we do more testing. As research findings are duplicated in subsequent studies with different types of subjects, their generality is supported. Findings that appeared only with red-headed 19-year-old Stanford University students would not have much generality.

At times, it makes sense to explore some of the questions of generality across subjects *within the same experiment*. For instance, if we suspect that age or social class will alter the impact of an independent variable, we may treat those subject variables as additional independent variables. We might, for example, include several different age groups for testing. When that is not feasible, we may be forced to rely on later studies to clarify the role of those additional variables. On the other hand, we may accept the generality of some findings for ethical reasons. Manufacturers often use laboratory animals to test the safety of new products such as drugs, shampoos, and cosmetics. A product that proved harmful to nonhuman subjects would not be marketed, even though there was no *direct* evidence that it was dangerous to humans.

Generalizing from Procedures to Concepts: Research Significance

Ideally, our findings also illustrate the operation of general principles: they are not unique to the particular procedures used in the experiment. For instance, Hess

(1975) showed that pupil size affected the ratings men gave to photographs. A picture of the same woman received more favorable ratings when she was shown with larger pupils. If this finding has generality across procedures, we would expect to get similar results with different sets of photographs. We would not expect the findings to be peculiar to the photos of one particular person. If the findings also have generality across subjects, we would expect that different types of men would give similar data. We might also expect to see similar responses from women rating photos of men.

Sometimes attempts to generalize across procedures raise theoretical issues that are hard to resolve. These issues arise when we study variables that can have multiple definitions. An operational definition, in principle, defines a variable in terms of observable operations, procedures, and measurements. As we saw in an earlier chapter, some variables, like anxiety, may be defined in various ways. When we generalize from the results of an experiment, we face the problem of going from a specific operational definition of a concept to conclusions about the concept itself. We do not want to talk about the number of errors that subjects made; instead, we want to talk about "learning." We may not be interested in the effects of difficult mazes per se; we want to talk about "frustration." Naturally, it is desirable to view findings from this more abstract perspective; we would like to discover principles that explain behavior *in general*. Ultimately, we would like to use induction to build new theories and to apply our findings to practical problems.

But it is typically risky to generalize from the findings of a single experiment in this way. The reasons are closely related to some of the issues we discussed earlier. We cannot always be certain of how reliable or valid our procedures are. For example, is *my* definition of "learning" tapping into the same phenomenon Dr. D used in his study? Would my findings lead to accurate predictions about learning under other conditions? One experiment may be suggestive, but we go far beyond our data when we expand our findings to explain all possibilities. For these reasons, researchers "hedge" a bit when they discuss results. The discussion sections of research reports are dotted with qualifying statements: "These findings suggest . . .," "it seems reasonable that . . .," "it appears that. . . ." Such statements often distress new researchers who would prefer to be able to say that something occurred with certainty. However, keep these points in mind: First, statistical tests allow us to make probability statements *only*. We never confirm our research hypothesis directly, and we certainly never "prove" it. We are able to say only that the null hypothesis is an unlikely explanation for what we have observed. That restricts the kinds of statements we may make about our findings.

In addition, as we formulate general conclusions, we move further away from the actual observations that we made. We can make some statements with confidence: We can report exactly what we did and what we observed in the experiment. When we begin to interpret results, we go beyond what we actually did and what we actually observed. As we do so, we are on increasingly shaky ground. Researchers qualify the conclusions they draw because there is no way to be certain their generalizations will always be true. Perhaps the findings describe the effects of the independent variable only under a very specific set of circumstances—namely, those defined in one experiment. Perhaps other operational definitions of the variables would lead to other outcomes. As we know, testing different sorts of subjects might do the same.

Still, if our findings have some degree of generality, we expect them to be consistent with the findings of prior researchers who have studied the same variables. Thus as we evaluate the generality of our results, we look at them in the context of the work that has already been done in the field.

We have talked about evaluating statistical significance. But findings also have research significance. As we evaluate them, we ask several pertinent questions. First, are they consistent with prior studies? If so, how do they clarify or extend our knowledge? Do they have any implications for broader theoretical issues? At this stage, we are coming full circle on the research process. We began our experimental plan by reviewing the research literature. We used findings of prior researchers as a guide to the important issues and the most suitable procedures for the area we studied. Now, with our results in hand, we consider the place of our findings in the context of prior work in that area.

If our findings do not mesh with earlier findings, our experiment may be suspect. For instance, we know that newborn babies prefer patterns over solid-colored forms (Fantz, 1963). If we have devised a testing system which leads us to conclude that babies actually prefer unpatterned figures, we have a problem. We must be able to reconcile our findings with what has already been shown. Novel findings are suspicious when the prior findings have been replicated; the burden of explanation usually falls on the researcher who claims the novel findings. The possibility of an undetected flaw in the experiment must be evaluated with special caution.

You will occasionally read reports of findings that appear to be conflicting. Often the apparent contradictions result from subtle differences in the operational definitions, the procedures, and the subjects used in various experiments. These inconsistencies may lead researchers into new studies to discover more general principles.

Generalizing beyond the Laboratory

So far we have talked about using induction to extend the results of specific experiments to other samples, other populations and procedures, and to more general concepts. You know by now that we have some difficulty generalizing from one set of experimental procedures to another with accuracy. As you can imagine, we come up against an even greater problem when we extend the results of a laboratory experiment to what we might observe in the real world. Remember that a laboratory experiment is carried out under specific, controlled conditions. The laboratory researcher tries to eliminate all the extraneous influences that might affect the outcome of the experiment. The laboratory experiment is the most precise tool we have for measuring the effect of an independent variable as it varies under controlled conditions. The problem in extending laboratory findings is simple in principle: The variables we study usually do not occur under the same controlled conditions in real life. All sorts of extraneous factors may affect the influence of any one particular variable.

The degree of control we get in a laboratory experiment gives us a great deal of precision. However, some researchers have argued that it may also provide data that have little relevance to our everyday lives. How safe is it to extend the results of a laboratory experiment to everyday life? There is no clear-cut answer to that question. It is often impossible to know whether the findings of a particular experiment are externally valid until we do additional studies. However, researchers use at least four general approaches to increase and verify the external validity of laboratory findings: multivariate designs, nonreactive measurements, field experiments, and naturalistic observation. Let us look at each in turn.

Increasing External Validity

Multivariate Designs. In this text we have focused on research designs that have one independent and one dependent variable. However, since variables do not usually occur separately, we also looked at factorial designs in which we explore the effects of more than one independent variable at a time. As complicated as those designs may have seemed at first, there are other designs that are even more elaborate.

multivariate designs

They are called **multivariate designs** because they deal with multiple variables. These designs have become increasingly important in psychological research as computer technology has become more widely available. Without computers, they would be impractical.

Multivariate designs enable us to look at many variables in combination. Typically, they are designs in which there is more than one dependent variable.[1] Measurements may be made on one or several samples (Cooley and Lohnes, 1971). The procedures used to evaluate the results of these studies are extensions of the basic techniques you have already learned. Some of the more common multivariate designs are multiple correlation, factor analysis, and multivariate analysis of variance. These procedures are too complicated to go into here, but we will take a brief look at the multivariate analysis of variance so you will have some idea of why these procedures are desirable.

multivariate analysis of variance (MANOVA)

The multivariate analysis of variance is an extension of the analysis of variance described in Chapter 13. We used the ANOVA to study the effect of more than one independent variable in a factorial design. However, those designs had only one dependent variable. By using a **multivariate analysis of variance (MANOVA)**, the researcher can measure the effects of independent variables as they affect sets of dependent variables. He or she can evaluate whether the independent variables influence subjects' scores on the dependent variables as they occur in combination. Through this type of design, a researcher interested in "improvement after psychotherapy" could approach the problem in a more comprehensive way than would be possible through a simpler factorial design.

1. Cooley and Lohnes (1971) point out that a factorial design is also "multivariate" in the sense that it has more than one independent variable. However, it is customary to restrict the term "multivariate" to designs with several dependent measures.

For instance, he or she could explore the effects of several independent variables: type of therapy, type of patient, sex of patient, sex of therapist. He or she could also measure several aspects of improvement instead of just one. The researcher might measure the patients' self-reports, the therapists' reports, and symptoms as rated by objective observers. This would provide a more comprehensive index of "improvement" than any single measure. As with the simpler ANOVA procedures, he or she would also be able to test for interactions among all these variables. Type of therapy and type of patient might interact to affect improvement. Higher-order interactions would be possible too; several variables may operate together to affect improvement. There would also be the option of analyzing differences in trends among the various dependent measures. Perhaps patients' reports show greater improvement than symptom ratings. In short, there is much more information to work with.

The advantage of this and other multivariate procedures is that they allow us to look at combinations of variables that will be more representative of reality. Instead of focusing on one aspect of improvement in therapy, such as self-report, the researcher can evaluate a spectrum of behavior. This provides a perspective on behavior that can have greater external validity than the simpler univariate approach. For that reason, there are now special journals devoted primarily to multivariate research (for example, *Multivariate Behavioral Research*; *Journal of Multivariate Experimental Personality and Clinical Psychology*). We may be able to increase the external validity of some studies by using multivariate rather than univariate approaches. We can also extend earlier findings by applying these new techniques to old questions.

Decreasing Reactivity.   We can also increase external validity by working to min-

reactivity   imize **reactivity** in an experiment. Subjects react to being subjects. They react to being observed. Their responses may not be the same as the responses of others who are not observed. Thus, they may not have external validity.

We dealt with the problem of reactivity implicitly when we discussed the demand characteristics of an experiment. If an experiment has obvious demand characteristics, the results may not have much generality. They may not reflect what we would see outside the laboratory. When a subject comes into an experiment, the subject assumes an active role. The subject has certain expectations about what will happen in the experiment. If the researcher inadvertently gives cues that tell the subject what to do, the problem is even more serious. Subjects may actively try to generate data that support the researcher's predictions. The opposite may also happen: A subject may "guess" the hypothesis, and then try to produce data to refute it.

We try to control demand characteristics and thus reactivity in part by being careful not to give subjects unnecessary cues. However, as Orne (1969) suggested, it may be difficult to get accurate information about our procedures. The "pact of ignorance" that forms between subjects and experimenters can affect external as well as internal validity. We can make better assessments of the impact of experimental manipulations though single- and double-blind experiments, because the results will be less influenced by subjects' reactivity.

Since some subjects react differently from others, we need controls for other social and personality variables as well. An experiment that does not contain the appropriate controls for response set and response style may not have external validity: the subjects in the experiment may have responded in idiosyncratic ways. We have to be especially wary of variables like social desirability. We know, for instance, that subjects in interviews, are apt to present a more favorable picture of themselves, distorting their responses to "look good" in the eyes of the researcher. Results distorted in this way may have little generality; they may not reflect what is true of behavior outside the laboratory.

Developing Unobtrusive Measures.   As long as subjects know they are being observed and measured, their responses may be distorted in some way. If nothing else, they may be a little nervous. For that reason, researchers have also tried to develop specific procedures to measure subjects' behavior without letting them know they

unobtrusive
measures

are being measured. These **unobtrusive measures** are not influenced by subjects' reactions. They have greater external validity because they yield data more similar to what we expect to see outside an experiment.

For example, in Chapter 2 we discussed the Bechtol and Williams (1977) study of littering, which was done partly through unobtrusive measures. They counted up cans on a beach to obtain an index of littering. Many unobtrusive measures depend on *physical* aspects of the environment. We could evaluate the popularity of several attractions in a national park by comparing the condition of the trails leading to those sites; the more popular attractions would have well-worn trails. Similarly, we could judge the seating preferences of patrons of a theater by the condition of the seats.

We can also gather data by observing subjects unobtrusively. For example, Marston, London, Cooper, and Cohen (1977) made unobtrusive observations of obese and thin diners in a restaurant. Without diners' knowledge, they recorded behaviors such as toying with food, size of bites, and rate of biting. They identified a "thin eating" pattern among women: smaller bites, a generally slower rate of eating, and more extraneous behaviors such as putting down the fork now and then. This approach seems to have greater external validity than bringing subjects into a laboratory to observe their eating behavior.

Unobtrusive measures have often been used ingeniously to minimize reactivity. You can find more detailed discussions of nonreactive measures in Webb, Campbell, Schwartz, and Sechrest (1966), and in Willems and Raush (1969).

Field Experiments.   Most unobtrusive measures are used outside the laboratory. Perhaps the most obvious way of dealing with the whole problem of external validity is to simply take the experiment out of the laboratory. If we suspect that subjects will behave differently under more realistic conditions, we can try it and see. Clearly, some experimental problems do not lend themselves to this approach. But those that do can lead us into fruitful new tests of our hypotheses.

field experiment

The **field experiment** meets the basic requirements of an experiment: We manipulate antecedent conditions and observe the outcome on dependent measures of behavior. But instead of studying subjects in the laboratory, we observe them in a natural setting. This approach has greater external validity. For instance, Mann (1977) studied social influence and line-joining behavior. He did his experiment at a bus stop in Jerusalem. Baseline data collected in the control condition showed that people there do not typically form lines to wait for buses. In the experimental condition, confederates of the experimenter took their places at the empty bus stop soon after a bus had stopped there. The experimental manipulations consisted of varying the number of confederates waiting and their positions at the bus stop. Mann found that lines of at least six confederates were required to produce significant levels of line-joining behavior among the first commuters to arrive at the stop.

This approach clearly illustrates the advantages of the field approach. It would be difficult to set up a laboratory situation that would be a credible representation of "waiting for a bus." However, field experiments also have certain limitations. One potential problem is that the researcher often has little control over who participates in the experiment: whoever came to the bus stop during the experiment was included. Thus, samples may not be random. In addition, we may have more difficulty specifying the characteristics of these samples than we do in a laboratory experiment, when we are usually able to get more information about subject variables. Assigning subjects in the field to treatment conditions at random provides some control for subject variables, but we are usually less able to control extraneous variables in a field setting.

Field experiments can be used to validate findings obtained in the laboratory. If results under controlled laboratory conditions have some degree of external validity, we should observe similar outcomes when we study behavior in more realistic settings. Doob and Gross (1968) used this approach to verify data obtained through questionnaires. College students were asked to say whether they would be likely to honk sooner at a stalled new car or a stalled old car in the street. Males predicted they would honk sooner at a newer car. Females predicted they would honk sooner at an older car. In a field experiment, drivers were blocked in traffic by either a new, expensive car, or an old car. Observers recorded the time before honking. They found that in general, subjects in the experiment waited longer before honking at the new, expensive car.

The inconsistencies in the Doob and Gross data highlight the importance of verifying evidence (particularly evidence based on subject reports) in more realistic settings. The logical extension of this process is evaluating findings in the context of ongoing behavior, without experimental intervention. This takes us back to one of the basic methods of gathering psychological data, naturalistic observation.

Confirmation through Naturalistic Observation.   When we first discussed naturalistic observation in Chapter 2, we looked at Miller's (1977) suggestions for the application of naturalistic observation in psychological research. In particular, he suggested that ". . . naturalistic observation can be used *to validate or add substance to previously obtained laboratory findings*" (p. 214). Miller also suggested that the processes of laboratory research and naturalistic observation may be used in a complementary way. We can use naturalistic observation to suggest specific hypotheses about behavior, and then test those hypotheses under the controlled conditions of the laboratory. We can return to the naturalistic setting to verify our findings.

The important implication of Miller's statement is quite simply this: Although we often think of the experiment as a unique, perhaps isolated method of research, we can use it to best advantage when we combine it with other modes of research. Psychologists try to discover principles and applications that will ultimately benefit humanity. Since most of us do not live in laboratories, our research must have some link to everyday life. Psychologists can strengthen that link by using a variety of research methods in combination: they can thus maintain precision without sacrificing relevance.

HANDLING A NONSIGNIFICANT OUTCOME

Up to this point we have approached the problems of interpreting data from a fairly optimistic perspective. We have more or less assumed that the results we are trying to evaluate were statistically significant and that they supported the predictions. But suppose we have run a well-planned experiment that did not work. Our predictions were not confirmed. Our treatment means are embarrassingly similar. Can anything be gained from such an experiment?

Research journals give the impression that all experiments yield significant results. Unfortunately, we do not see all the studies that were carried out and did not make it into print. The occasional negative outcome is there because that outcome has implications for a theoretical position that predicts there *should be* significant differences. In reality, many studies do not turn out exactly the way the researcher expected.

If you ran an experiment and your results were not significant, do not be discouraged; even the best researchers may have an occasional dud. One of the characteristics of a good researcher is that he or she uses nonsignificant findings in a constructive way. A good researcher asks, "*Why* didn't things go as expected?" and uses the answers to generate better studies. If your experiment did not support your predictions, you should evaluate it from two perspectives. First, were the procedures right? Second, was the hypothesis reasonable?

Faulty Procedures

We may not confirm our predictions because our procedures were faulty. Of course, we are always on the lookout for confounding. For instance, we may have inadvertently allowed control subjects a little more practice time, and so compensated for the effects of the special training procedures used in the experimental condition. Review everything you did. Did you apply all the appropriate control procedures? Did you use random assignment? Counterbalancing? Are there problems with demand characteristics or experimenter bias?

Another possibility is that although there were no confounding variables in the experiment, numerous uncontrolled variables increased the amount of variation between individual subjects' scores. Perhaps your reading of the instructions varied from time to time. Some of the subjects were recruited in the laundromat; others came from a factory. Although the effects of these variables tend to "randomize out" across treatment conditions, they still have the net effect of increasing the amount of within-groups or error variance. If we happen to be studying an independent variable that has a relatively weak effect, we may be in trouble. Our experimental manipulation may not be powerful enough to override the effect of all the other sources of variation in the experiment. We may be unable to reject the null hypothesis even though the independent variable had an effect. That is, we may be making a Type 2 error.

Another possibility is that the experimental manipulation is inadequate: the independent variable might have had a powerful effect if we had defined treatment levels in a better way. Our "hungry" rats were deprived of food for only 6 hours. Perhaps 24 hours would be a more effective fast. We instructed our experimental subjects to form mental images of the words on a screen. Perhaps our control subjects did the same even though we told them not to. Better procedures are needed. Of course, the only way to check these possibilities is by running new experiments.

We also look for problems in the way we measured the dependent variable. Did we use a measure that was *valid*? Suppose we are trying to assess the effect of different camera angles on the sexual appeal of photographs. We ask subjects to rate a series of photographs, some of which are mildly erotic. Subjects' ratings may be contaminated by their need to give socially desirable responses. We may end up measuring social desirability rather than the appeal of the photos.

If the experimental procedures are faulty, we have not made a valid test of our hypothesis. The best time to deal with faulty procedures is *before* running the experiment. It seems to be quite easy to formulate after the fact explanations: "I did not get significant results because there were flies in the room when I tested my experimental group." Perhaps.

No one enjoys coming to the end of a data analysis only to find that there are no significant differences between the treatment groups. All that work and so little to show for it. At best, it is disappointing. It is not easy to justify so much effort. Perhaps to save face, we sometimes get caught up in attempts to explain that what we did was fine: we designed sound procedures that are internally valid. Is it our fault that a fire drill was called in the middle of the experiment? Of course not. But few of us like to consider the possibility that the experiment was doomed from the start.

Faulty Hypothesis

When we evaluate the outcome of an experiment, we must look at it from the standpoint of the internal components we have discussed. In addition to procedural aspects, we want to be sure that the experiment represents good thinking. If we have what seems to be a flawless procedure for studying a hypothesis, if we have executed the experiment carefully and the results are not significant, we must at least consider the possibility that the hypothesis was faulty. We need to go back and rethink the problem. Perhaps we overlooked some key feature of prior studies. Perhaps our reasoning was confused. The good researcher uses this evaluation process to decide where to go next.

Be cautious in drawing conclusions from nonsignificant results. They usually are not justified, even if the data are close to being significant. Consider the possibility that the hypothesis needs to be reworked. Use what you learned in this experiment to plan a better one the next time around.

SUMMARY

Some of the problems of evaluating and drawing conclusions from the results of an experiment have to do with whether or not an experiment is valid. An experiment that is *internally valid* is free of confounding. In evaluating the internal validity of an experiment, the researcher considers both the plan for running the experiment and what actually happened. If extraneous variables affected the results, they may not be interpretable. An experiment is *externally valid* if the results can be extended to other situations with accuracy. Inductive thinking can be used to generalize from the results of the particular experiment to broader principles and implications.

To be externally valid, an experiment must first be internally valid. However, external validity is a continuum, not an either/or situation. Some studies have greater external validity than others. Findings that are externally valid can be replicated. They can be extended to different samples of subjects and to the larger population. They can also be extended across different experimental procedures and discussed in terms of general concepts.

A major part of the interpretation of research is placing it in the context of prior work. If findings are not consistent with prior studies, the discrepancy must be explained. These inconsistencies may form the basis of new experiments.

Results can also have implications outside the experimental setting. It is usually difficult to make this determination within the context of a single study. Researchers employ at least four approaches to increase as well as verify the degree of external validity of their findings: multivariate designs, nonreactive measures, field experiments, and naturalistic observation. *Multivariate designs* have more than one dependent variable. Measurements may be made on one or more samples of subjects, and relationships between combinations of variables may be assessed. Researchers also try to decrease *reactivity* in their studies; they measure behavior in such a way that the outcome will not be affected by subjects' reactions to the experiment. Reactivity is reduced by controlling the demand characteristics of the experiment. *Unobtrusive measures* of behavior can also be used to control reactivity. The *field experiment* is another means of increasing external validity. Finally, researchers may confirm the validity of laboratory findings through *naturalistic observation*. Using research methods in combination is another fruitful way to study behavior.

There is also the practical dilemma of dealing with nonsignificant findings. Experimental procedures must always be reviewed for sources of internal invalidity. The thinking that led to the hypothesis should be reviewed to be sure the predictions were reasonable.

REVIEW AND STUDY QUESTIONS

1. Discuss three potential sources of internal invalidity in an experiment. How would you control each one?
2. How does internal validity affect the conclusions that may be drawn from the results of an experiment?
3. What is external validity?
4. An experiment that is not internally valid cannot be externally valid. Why?
5. Why is replicability a requirement for external validity?
6. Explain how we use inductive thinking to extend the findings of an experiment beyond the particular study.
7. What issues affect the decision to generalize the findings of an experiment to (a) other samples of subjects; (b) to other populations?
8. The operational definition of a particular variable may be changed from one experiment to another. Explain how and why this affects the generality of research findings.
9. In writing up a research report, a psychologist concluded by saying: "These results prove my hypothesis. They provide conclusive evidence that working crossword puzzles improves vocabulary." Without knowing the details of the researcher's procedures, what could you say about each of the following:
   a. Assuming that the findings are statistically significant, are the researcher's conclusions justified? Why or why not?
   b. Assume that several researchers have conducted similar experiments. The findings have been inconclusive. What can be said about the conclusion in view of prior research?
   c. Given your answers to (a) and (b), reword the experimenter's conclusions appropriately.
   d. If you chose to conduct a similar study, what extraneous variables might affect the internal validity of the experiment?
10. What are multivariate procedures?
11. How can multivariate procedures be used to increase the external validity of an experiment?
12. How does the reactivity of subjects influence the external validity of an experiment?

13. Discuss three techniques for reducing reactivity.

14. Pick one of the laboratory experiments we have discussed in this text and devise a way to confirm the findings of that experiment either through a field experiment or through naturalistic observation.

15. Alice is not quite sure how to interpret the results of an experiment she did. She found that her data were not quite significant ($p < .07$). What advice would you give her about explaining her findings?

16. Jack is skeptical of this whole chapter: "If we have to put so many limits on what we can say about an experiment, why bother? Let's just talk about what we found and leave it at that." Explain to Jack the purpose of generalizing from our findings. What do we accomplish when we generalize correctly?

REFERENCES

Bechtol, B. E., and Williams, J. R. California litter. *Natural History*, 1977, *86*, No. 6, 62–65.

Cooley, W. W., and Lohnes, P. R. *Multivariate data analysis*. New York: Wiley, 1971.

Doob, A. N., and Gross, A. N. Status of frustrator as an inhibitor of horn-honking responses. *Journal of Social Psychology*, 1968, *76*, No. 2, 213–218.

Fantz, R. L. Pattern vision in newborn infants. *Science*, 1963, *140*, 296–297.

Hess, E. Role of pupil size in communication. *Scientific American*, 1975, *233*, No. 5, 110 ff.

Mann, L. The effect of stimulus queues on queue-joining behavior. *Journal of Personality and Social Psychology*, 1977, *35*, No. 6, 437–442.

Marston, A. R., London, P., Cooper, L., and Cohen, N. In vivo observation of the eating behavior of obese and nonobese subjects. *Journal of Consulting and Clinical Psychology*, 1977, *45*, 335–336.

Miller, D. B. Roles of naturalistic observation in comparative psychology. *American Psychologist*, 1977, *32*, 211–219.

Orne, M. T. Demand characteristics and the concept of quasi-controls. In R. Rosenthal and R. Rosnow (Eds.), *Artifact in behavioral research*. New York: Academic Press, 1969.

Rosenthal, R., and Rosnow, R. L. *The volunteer subject*. New York: Wiley, 1975.

Webb, E. J., Campbell, D. T., Schwartz, R. D., and Sechrest, L. *Unobtrusive measures: Nonreactive research in the behavioral sciences*. Chicago: Rand McNally, 1966.

Willems, E. P., and Raush, H. L. (Eds.) *Naturalistic viewpoints in psychological research*. New York: Holt, Rinehart and Winston, 1969.

15

Writing the Research Report

Report writing is a major part of the research process. For that reason, you may find your instructor shows little sympathy for your reluctance to write up the dullest results. Most likely, you will be required to write a report, whether or not your findings will change the direction of psychology. In this chapter we will discuss the purpose and structure of psychological research reports in detail. As you know, the overall structure of this text parallels the general structure of these reports. We find an introduction, a method section, a section on results, and a discussion in each report. Each report also has an abstract or summary and a list of references. We will begin by reviewing the basic content of each section. Then we will look at an example of an actual research article to see how these ideas are put into practice. We will also focus on some specific aspects of preparing the manuscript of a report, and some points that often cause problems for beginners.

THE WRITTEN REPORT: PURPOSE AND FORMAT

The primary purpose of a written report is communication. Through our report we may tell others what we did and what we found. In addition to reporting findings, a report should also provide enough information to enable other researchers to make a critical evaluation of procedures. We should provide enough information to permit others to make a reasonable judgment about the quality of the experiment. In addition, we want to provide enough information to enable others to replicate and extend the findings.

One of the difficulties people encounter as they write their first reports is that they take too much for granted. After you have worked on a study for some time, what you did may seem quite obvious. The difficulty is that although it is obvious to *you*, your readers will not understand it unless you explain it. Remember that the whole point of writing a report is to communicate information. A reader should be able to understand what you did and why without having to come to you and ask questions about it.

Psychological reports follow the format set up by the American Psychological Association. It is presented in detail in the *Publication Manual* (1974), which was prepared by the APA to make the job of reporting easier for researchers as well as readers. As early as 1928, psychologists and other social scientists recognized the need for standards of presenting research data. The first "manual" was a seven-page article that appeared in the *Psychological Bulletin* in 1929. Now, the manual spans 136 pages and contains material on all aspects of appropriate content, as well as detailed explanations of specific layout and style requirements. Our presentation here will be brief; if you have questions about specific problems, you should refer to the manual.

The need for a standard format for reports becomes clear when you consider the tremendous volume of research going on today. The American Psychological Association alone publishes 17 journals. This means 2,000 articles per year. Many thousands more are reviewed and not accepted for publication. Others are published in numerous non-APA, psychology-related journals. If everyone used a different format for writing reports, it would be difficult for reviewers to evaluate so many articles. It would be difficult for writers to know just how to put together their reports. And it would also be hard for readers to locate the information they need from each article. The format of your report is no place for creativity. Be inventive in designing your experiment. When you report it, you should conform to the APA standards. Although some of the details of format vary from one journal to another, most follow the overall structure outlined here.

MAJOR SECTIONS

Every research report must contain these major components: a descriptive title, an abstract, an introduction, a method section, a results section, a discussion section, and a list of references. We will look at each part in turn so that you will have a clear idea of the basic requirements of each one. For now, we will focus on the *content* of each part. Try to develop a feel for what we accomplish through each section. We will look at layout requirements later.

Descriptive Title

The title of a report should give readers an idea of what the report is about. The simplest way to guarantee this is by naming both the independent and dependent variables of the study in the title, stating the relationship between them. Here are some examples from articles we have discussed in prior chapters: "Effect of initial selling price on subsequent sales" (Doob et al., 1969); "How good news makes us good" (Holloway and Horsstein, 1976); "Social enhancement and impairment of performance in the cockroach" (Zajonc et al., 1969). Titles such as "A psychological experiment" are far too vague to be of much use to a reader who is trying to track down specific information. However, titles should be limited to about 15 words; leave something to be said in the body of the report.

Abstract

An *abstract* is a summary of the report. It should be about 100–175 words long. Write it in the same general style you use in the report. The abstract should be a concise synopsis of the experiment. It should be written so that it makes sense and can stand by itself. It should contain a statement of the problem studied, the method, results, and conclusions. In the abstract you must tell your readers what sorts of subjects you used (for example, 30 adult macaque monkeys). You should describe the design (for example, a 2×2 factorial design). You should summarize the procedures used in the experiment, and the results. Significance levels (for example, $p < .05$) should be included. You should also state the important conclusions you reached.

At this point you may be thinking, "All that in 175 words or less? You must be kidding!" Actually, I'm quite serious. But it may help you to know that abstracts are notoriously difficult to write; they require a technique few of us practice very often. For that reason, many people find it easiest to write the abstract *after* they write the report. You may want to do the same.

The Practical Value of the Abstract.   As you write abstracts, you will have a better appreciation for their content if you understand how and why they are used. With so many journals and articles coming out each year, information can be very hard to track down. It would be quite tedious for a researcher to have to search through the indexes of a dozen different publications, many of which appear monthly. It would also be very time-consuming to read every article. Fortunately, we have another publication, *Psychological Abstracts*, which is a guide to the literature in psychology.

Psychological Abstracts is the major reference source in psychology. You will find it in the Reference section of your library. As the name implies, *Psychological Abstracts* contains the abstracts from journal articles. We can thus locate articles that will help us without having to scan many reports. *Psychological Abstracts* also includes some book listings, as well as references to other kinds of psychology-related documents, such as government reports. You should become familiar with *Psychological Abstracts*. Using it efficiently, however, requires a bit of practice.

Using Psychological Abstracts: Locating Reference Information. *Psychological Abstracts* is made up of several distinct parts. First, monthly issues of the *Abstracts* are self-contained. They include the abstracts and references, an author index, and a brief subject index. A separate author and subject index volume is published twice a year. Index volumes are more efficient to use because they organize the information from six monthly issues into one volume. The actual abstracts are also bound in two separate volumes each year. So, for 1976, for instance, your library has two large, bound volumes of abstracts, and two index volumes—one of each for January–June, 1976, and one of each for July–December, 1976. Every three years, cumulative subject and author indexes are also published.

Unless you are researching a problem of historical interest, it is usually most efficient to start your review of the literature by looking in the most recent *Abstracts* first. Journal articles contain lists of references that can be used to go farther back into a problem if necessary. (Review articles are especially useful for this purpose.) How far you will have to go depends on the problem and your purposes. Usually you will be looking for information related to a particular problem area. Let us say we are planning an experiment on recognition memory and would like to see what other researchers have done in this area.[1] We look in the subject index under the appropriate topic headings. Usually, the more precise we are about what we are seeking, the easier it will be to find. "Recognition" is a fairly specific term. We will have better luck finding research relevant to what we are doing if we look under "recognition" rather than more general terms such as "memory" or "learning." We may also want to look for specific terms that apply to the procedures we have in mind: Recognition for pictures of objects. As you search through the indexes, you will develop a sense of what terms to check out. The indexes also suggest alternative terms to check. The process is simply analogous to what we do when we look in the index of any book, or in the card catalog.

If you were reviewing the work of a particular researcher, you would simply look for that person's name in the author indexes. You can also begin to check the author index as you identify key people in your field of interest. You can quickly check whether they have done anything lately.

Once you have located your subject or author in the index, you will find titles and key words listed there. Figure 15.1 shows a portion of a page from *Abstracts*

---

1. Information on locating reference material is included here to demonstrate the importance of writing good abstracts. The research literature should always be reviewed before designing and conducting a study.

Familiar object pictures viewing with recall vs recognition preparation
strategies, free recall of object names & picture recognition memory,
kindergardners vs 3rd vs 5th graders, 989

Figure 15.1 A sample item from the *Psychological Abstract Index,* 1977, *57.* Copyright 1977, by the American Psychological Association. Reprinted by permission.

Index, 1977, Volume 57, to illustrate what we may find under "recognition." We look through the items listed to see whether any are relevant to our work. We find one on pictures of objects, beside the number 989. It sounds promising, so we would like to read the abstract of the article on that topic. To find it, we look in the *Abstracts* volume that corresponds to this particular *Index* volume, *Abstracts*, Volume 57. However, note that the numbers shown in the *Index* volumes are *not* page numbers. They refer us to the numbers of the references and abstract entries contained in the *Abstracts* volumes. For instance, 989 in *Index* Volume 57 refers to entry 989 in Volume 57 of the *Abstracts*. We look for entry 989 in *Abstracts* Volume 57, and find the entry on page 126 of that volume. A portion of that page is shown in Figure 15.2.

989.   **Tversky, Barbara & Teiffer, Evelyn.** (Hebrew U of Jerusalem, Israel) **Development of strategies for recall and recognition.** . . *Developmental Psychology*, 1976(Sep). Vol 12(5), 406–410. —40 kindergardners, 42 3rd graders, and 40 5th graders (CA's 5 yrs, 5 mo; 8 yrs, 3mo; and 12 yrs, 4 mo, respectively) viewed 30 pictures of familiar objects, and then their free recall of the object names and their recognition of the original pictures were tested. The recognition test included pairing each picture with another similar picture of the same object. Half the Ss in each age group were prepared for recall with a strategy known to improve it in adults, and half were prepared for recognition with a strategy known to improve recognition in adults. Children encoded the stimuli differentially in accordance with the expected memory task and retrieved different stored information for each task. Both free recall and picture recognition memory improved with age. The recall strategy improved free recall performance at all ages, but the recognition strategy improved recognition performance only at the oldest age tested. (16 ref) —*Journal abstract.*

Figure 15.2 A sample item from the *Psychological Abstracts,* 1977, *57.* Copyright 1977, by the American Psychological Association. Reprinted by permission.

As you can see, the entry in the *Abstracts* contains the full journal title of the article. It contains the journal reference so we will be able to locate the article. And it contains the actual journal abstract. We can read the abstract and decide whether the article is relevant to what we are doing. If it is, we can read the article. If it is not, we can simply move on to something else. The abstract is probably the most frequently read part of any article. If the abstract is poor, readers may not go on to read the entire article. That is why it is especially important to include all the pertinent facts of an experiment in the abstract.

Good abstracts make our research more accessible to our readers. Good titles do the same, since the title determines the way that an article will be indexed in the *Psychological Abstracts*. As you use the *Psychological Abstracts* to do your review of the research literature, you are also preparing for the next major section of your research report, the introduction.

Introduction

The introduction sets the stage for what follows. A good introduction tells readers *what* you are doing and *why*. As you write your introduction, think about what readers should get out of it. The focus should be the hypothesis. After reading the introduction, readers should have the following information: What problem are you studying? What does the prior literature in the area say about that problem? What is your hypothesis? Where did that hypothesis come from; what thinking led up to it? What is the overall plan for testing the hypothesis? Do you make any specific predictions about the outcome of the study?

The introduction is the proper place to include the review of the research literature that led to your hypothesis. For instance, you might show how prior findings are inconsistent or ambiguous. Explain how your experiment may clarify the problem. It is not necessary to cite every bit of research that has ever been done in an area; cite just what is most essential to understanding the nature of the problem. Be careful to show how you got to your hypothesis. Readers should be able to follow the thinking that took you there. Do not assume that anything is "obvious."

State your hypothesis explicitly at some point in the introduction. Usually, it should appear toward the end of the introduction, after you have explained the research and thinking that led to it. Identifying independent and dependent variables is appropriate. Then say something about general procedures if that seems warranted. You may want to include a sentence or two about operational definitions to prepare readers for what follows in the report. If you have made predictions about the outcome of the study, by all means say so. Be sure you also say *why* you expect these results; do not expect readers to guess what you are thinking.

Method

The method section tells readers how you went about doing the experiment. It should be detailed enough to allow another researcher to read it and replicate your experiment exactly. It is customary to subdivide the method section into several labeled subsections: subjects, apparatus, procedure; design. You may not need every subsection; you should adjust the format according to the kind of study you are presenting.

Subjects.   The subsection on subjects should tell readers the important characteristics of your sample. It should answer these key questions: How many subjects did you have? What are their relevant characteristics (age, sex, species, weight, and so on)? How were subjects recruited and/or selected? How did you assign the subjects to conditions? Give any additional information that may be important to understanding your experiment. If any subjects dropped out of the study, report that too and explain the circumstances.

Apparatus.   This section is sometimes called the materials section. Use judgment on whether one label is more appropriate than the other for your study. In this subsection, you should provide readers with a description of any equipment used in the study. Standard things like stopwatches and pencils do not have to be described in detail. However, refer to any ready-made specialized equipment by name, manufacturer, and model number. Identify standardized tests by name. If you built your own equipment, or prepared your own stimulus figures or questionnaire, give the details. Sometimes an illustration or sample items need to be included. Be sure to provide all the information essential for replication, including physical dimensions such as length, width, and color if appropriate. Give measurements in metric units.

Procedure.   This section should provide readers with a clear description of all the procedures followed in your experiment. After reading this section, a person should know how to carry out the experiment just as you did it. Any special control procedures you used should be identified here—for instance, "The stimulus words were presented in counterbalanced order to control for order effects." You may want to include the exact instructions you gave to subjects, particularly if the instructions constituted your experimental manipulation. Otherwise simply summarize them.

One easy way to write a procedure section is simply to report everything step by step in chronological order. Use some discretion in reporting commonplace details; the reader does not need to be told obvious things about the procedures. For instance, if you gave subjects a written test, it would be unnecessary to report that they were seated during the test. However, *do* report anything unusual about your procedures. Be sure to identify your experimental manipulations carefully. Spell out the way you measured the dependent variable. Always ask yourself whether someone could replicate your experiment based on what you have said.

Design.   This section is usually optional. If your design is fairly straightforward (for example, two independent groups), it really does not require a separate section. You can easily give all the necessary information elsewhere. However, in your first reports, you may find it helpful to write a design section anyway to keep the plan of your experiment in focus.

You may identify the independent and dependent variables in this section. Indicate the kind of design you have. If it is a complex design, you may want to spell out the treatment labels. For instance, in a $6 \times 4 \times 3$ factorial design, readers might appreciate a reminder that there are 6 levels of reinforcement, 4 levels of food deprivation, and 3 levels of age. As the design becomes more complicated, readers usually need more explicit help in structuring the plan of the experiment. Do what makes the most sense to clarify your study.

Results

The results section of a report should tell readers what you found. Begin it with a brief summary of your principal findings stated *in words*. Then report your summary data (for example, means, standard deviations, or range, as appropriate). Remember that we usually do not report individual scores unless we have a small N design. Tell readers what statistical tests you used to evaluate the data, along with computed values of test statistics. Indicate degrees of freedom and significance levels.

Sometimes results can be summarized most easily through figures or tables, but these should be used sparingly. They should enhance what you have to say about the data. Do not use them to simply repeat what you have already said. If you use figures and tables, they must be referred to first *in words* within the text. They should be an integral part of the presentation, not ornaments dangling in space.

The results section is used only to present the objective data as they appeared in the experiment. Interpretation of the results belongs in the next section.

Discussion

The overall purpose of the discussion section is to evaluate and interpret the results. Your discussion should tie things together for readers. In the introduction, you reviewed the literature and showed readers how you arrived at your hypothesis and predictions. In the method section, you described the details of what you did. In the results section, you presented what you found. Now, in the discussion you need to pull everything together: You need to explain what you have accomplished. How do your findings fit in with the original problem stated in the introduction? How do they fit in with prior research in the area? Are they consistent? If not, can any discrepancies be reconciled?

Begin the discussion section with a clear summary sentence or two restating your results. Any sources of confounding that might influence the interpretation of the data should be reported. Again, though, be reasonable. It is not necessary to mention things that are probably irrelevant: Whether or not all subjects had breakfast probably is not critical, especially if you assigned them to conditions at random. On the other hand, if half the experimental subjects walked out on the experiment halfway through, your readers should know that, as well as how it may have affected the data.

Do not get caught up in offering excuses for why your results were not significant. Rethink both your procedures and your hypothesis if necessary. Do not try to make something out of nonsignificant findings, even if they go in the direction you predicted.

Keep in mind that when your readers finish the discussion section, they should have a sense of closure. They should know where you were going and why. They should know how you got there, what you found, and where it fits in the context of what was already known about the problem.

References

Any articles or books mentioned in the report should be listed among your references at the end. These enable readers to go back and make their own evaluation of the literature. Be sure that the references are accurate, and follow the APA procedures for listing them.

LOOKING AT A JOURNAL ARTICLE

For now, let us turn to a more detailed look at the requirements of a research report by going through an actual journal article. It is the same article we already located through *Psychological Abstracts.* The article will appear on the following right-hand pages with my comments on the left-hand pages, so that you may shift back and forth easily between the two.

General Orientation

Before we launch into our examination of the article, let us review some general concepts you need in order to understand it. The article is a report of an experiment on recall and recognition. On a recall task, a subject is asked to think of the correct answers. When you answer fill-in questions, you are being tested on recall. Recognition requires the subject to pick out the correct items from several options. Multiple-choice questions usually test recognition. Verbal cues seem to be most helpful to recall; visual cues seem more useful for recognition.

Tversky (1974) had shown that adult subjects' performance on recall and recognition tasks could be improved. She did so by providing subjects with appropriate strategies or techniques for handling those tasks. The article we have here is a report of a later experiment to replicate her findings with elementary school children. As you begin to read it, you will find that the authors assume you already know something about recognition and recall. Journal articles are usually written for informed audiences. They are also written with strict constraints on the amount of space that can be devoted to any single topic. That is why you may find some of these articles difficult to follow unless you have already read somewhat extensively in the field.

A Sample Article[2]

Descriptive Title.   Note that the title identifies the main focus of the study. Without reading further, we know that the researchers studied both recall and recognition, and that they studied how the use of strategies for these processes develops.

Names and Affiliation.   The authors' names are given as they would ordinarily be written. Note that titles (Mr., Ms., Dr.) are not given. The university name and location are given.

Developmental Psychology
1976. Vol 12. No. 5. 406–410

Development of Strategies for Recall and Recognition

BARBARA TVERSKY AND EVELYN TEIFFER

Hebrew University of Jerusalem, Jerusalem, Israel

Kindergartners, third graders, and fifth graders viewed 30 pictures of familiar objects, and then their free recall of the object names and their recognition of the original pictures were tested. The recognition test included pairing each picture with another similar picture of the same object. Half the subjects in each age-group were prepared for recall with a strategy known to improve it in adults, and half were prepared for recognition with a strategy known to improve recognition in adults. Children encoded the stimuli differentially in accordance with the expected memory task and retrieved different stored information for each task. Both free recall and picture recognition memory improved with age. The recall strategy improved free recall performance at all ages, but the recognition strategy improved recognition performance only at the oldest age tested.

Investigators of both children's and adults' memory have found different strategies beneficial for different memory tasks (e.g., Flavell, 1970; Paivio, 1971). Strategies are ways of encoding or representing material to facilitate later retrieval. For instance, Paivio and Csapo (1969) found that whereas verbal codes are particularly effective in sequential memory tasks, imaginal or pictorial codes are effective in free recall and paired-associate learning. Moreover, expectations about the type of memory task to be encountered alter the strategies subjects adopt. Frost (1972), for example, has shown that subjects encode visual information in a highly accessible form when anticipating recognition, but they encode verbal information in a highly accessible form when anticipating recall. Even preschool children encode simple pictures or their names verbally when expecting verbal comparison and pictorially when expect-

ing pictorial comparison (Tversky, 1973a). Finally, there is evidence that the cognitive skills underlying various strategies develop at different ages. Rohwer (1970) has argued that children are unable to utilize imaginal codes effectively until they are efficient at verbal encoding; presumably the verbal code allows effective access or retrieval of the image.

Strategies that are effective for adults in improving free recall are those that organize the stimuli on the basis of categories, associations, or subjective relations among the items (Anderson, 1972; Tulving, 1968; Tversky, 1973b). These are skills that develop during the school years, and indeed free recall performance improves during these years (for recent reviews see Hagen, Jongeward, & Kail, 1975; and Jablonski, 1974). There has been less study of strategies in recognition, especially picture recognition, partly because performance is often so high in such tasks that failure is attributable to such trivial factors as momentary inattention at presentation. Also, strategies are typically conceived of in relation to retrieval, and because the items themselves are presented in a recognition test, many researchers have assumed that they need not be retrieved (e.g., Kintsch, 1970). Indeed, the evidence about picture

This research was supported by grants from the Center for Human Development of Hebrew University and from the Batsheva de Rothschild Fund.

We are grateful to Yaakov Wulf and the staff of the Hebrew University Summer Camp for their generous assistance in obtaining subjects.

Requests for reprints should be sent to Barbara Tversky, Department of Psychology, Hebrew University, Jerusalem, Israel.

Abstract.   In the published article, the abstract is usually not labeled. It is set off by smaller type and conspicuous indentation. (Your typed manuscript, of course, will not look like this. Your abstract will be typed on its own page and labeled. We will look at the procedural details of preparing the manuscript a little later.) Notice that the abstract summarizes what was done and what was found; all the main points of the article are presented.

Introduction.   The introduction begins immediately after the abstract. However, notice that it is not labeled. It is never labeled. Notice how carefully the authors present the background research that suggested this study. They tell us the pertinent facts about the field and how these relate to the hypothesis of this experiment. The purpose of the study is stated explicitly at the end of the introduction.

Note the format for citing prior researchers: "Frost (1972), for example, has shown. . . ." Factual statements are references throughout: ". . . (Anderson, 1972; Tulving, 1968; Tversky, 1973*b*)" (1973*b* indicates that this is the second 1973 article by Tversky cited in this report.) Note that the full references for all citations are given in the list of references at the end of the article; we rarely use footnotes to cite references in reports of this type.

Method.   This section gives the details of how the experiment was carried out. Notice that the authors have adapted the format to fit the kind of information they need to present. Each subsection is clearly labeled. In addition to the usual subjects section, we find a special section on stimuli in which the authors describe the slides that were shown to the children. They also explain how they presented the slides under each condition.

In the procedure, section they alert us to some unique features of the testing process. Subjects were tested in groups of threes, by one of three female experimenters. They also included a special detailed subsection on instruction and training. This is an important section, since the conclusions we may draw about children's use of strategies depend heavily on the nature of the strategies and how adequate the training procedures were. Again, enough detail is presented to permit replication. The whole method section is written in the past tense—the experiment is already over.

recognition memory in children is notable for the absence of apparent age trends (e.g., Brown, 1973; Nelson, 1971).

In a procedure used recently (Tversky, 1973b, 1974), adults viewed pictures of familiar objects and were tested on their free recall of the objects' names as well as their ability to recognize each object when paired with another picture of the same object. Typically, recognition is regarded as simply an easier test than free recall, but in this task each test draws on different information that can be encoded from the stimuli. When subjects were prepared for free recall with a strategy appropriate for that task, they encoded the stimulus items differently from when they were prepared for recognition with a strategy appropriate to that task. Recall-set subjects performed considerably better on the recall task than recognition-set subjects, who, in turn, performed far better on the recognition test. Moreover, different information was retrieved to perform each task. The present experiment is a replication on elementary school children of this procedure. The purpose is to assess the ability of children to adapt their encoding strategy to fit the anticipated memory task and to assess the development of performance on these tasks, with and without preparatory strategies.

Method

Subjects

Subjects were 122 middle-class children from a day camp. There were three age-groups: graduates of kindergarten, third grade, and fifth grade. The 20 boys and 20 girls in kindergarten had a mean chronological age (CA) of 5 years 5 months, ranging from 5 years 1 month to 6 years 2 months. The 16 girls and 26 boys in third grade had a mean CA of 8 years 3 months, ranging from 6 years 7 months to 8 years 6 months. The 20 girls and 20 boys in fifth grade had a mean CA of 12 years 4 months, ranging from 11 years 1 month to 12 years 6 months.

Stimuli

The stimuli were 30 slides of line drawings of familiar objects in the following order of presentation: desk, lamp, scissors, camera, binoculars, picture, rug, television, refrigerator, cake, teapot, iron, umbrella, purse, luggage, airplane, submarine, ship, tent, house, fish, cow, butterfly, bird, tree, flowers, tractor, train, truck, car. Pictures were selected so that they could be easily

recognized and given one-word labels by children. The order of presentation was selected to maximize the associations, clusters, and interrelations among items. For the recognition test, each stimulus was presented side by side with another line drawing of the same object which differed from the original in orientation or detail or both. Test order was the same as presentation order, and the original stimulus was presented on the right on half the trials at random.

Procedure

Subjects were tested in groups of three, each attended by one of the three young female experimenters.

After the instructions and training, the 30 stimuli were projected for 4 sec each. This was followed by a free-recall test; each subject whispered his answers to the experimenter assigned to him; the experimenter recorded the answers. The experiment was conducted in a large room, and the subject–experimenter pairs were scattered throughout the room so that the children could not hear each other. When the child stopped naming, the experimenter asked if there were any more items the child could remember. After all the children had completed free recall, a forced-choice recognition test was administered. Pairs of pictures with the same name were projected side by side, and each child indicated which of the pairs he believed he had viewed previously by pointing to one of two rectangles, oriented side by side like the pictures. Each experimenter recorded the responses, and when all the children had responded, the next test pair was presented. Previously it had been shown with adults and similar stimuli that a prior free-recall test did not affect recognition performance (Tversky, 1973b). When the child had completed both tasks, he was told he had done well and was given candy.

Instructions and Training

The children in the recall-set groups, approximately half the subjects of each age and sex, were individually instructed and trained to use a strategy of identifying similarities, relations, and associations among items, and to use these similarities to interrelate items in order to produce higher recall. For instance, they were told,

Imagine that you saw pictures of the following objects: fork, knife, bread, supermarket. Now you can relate the fork to the knife, because they are both used for eating; then you can relate the knife to the bread because the knife cuts the bread, and finally, you can relate the bread to the supermarket because we buy bread at a supermarket.

Then, they were presented with another example and asked to state the connections among the items. The recall task was carefully explained to these subjects before they viewed the test stimuli. The procedure for the recognition test was explained to them after their free recall was assessed and just prior to the recognition test itself.

Children in the recognition-set groups were individually instructed and trained to use a strategy of paying careful attention to the details of objects in order to be

Results.   Again, notice how the authors adapt standard format somewhat to fit their experiment. They begin the results section by immediately referring us to the two figures that summarize the findings clearly and quickly. Notice that the figures do not repeat what is said in the text. Indeed, they are used here to eliminate the need for a wordy presentation of the principal findings. Notice that the figures are well-proportioned. They are pleasing to look at. The lines are clearly labeled by a legend that appears on each figure. The axes are also clearly labeled. We know exactly what we are looking at because the authors have taken the time to indicate the necessary details. Notice that units are marked off on each axis, and the units of measurement (percent and years) are given.

Note the format used to report the test statistics. The statistic (for example, t) is indicated first, in italics. (Indicate italics in your typed manuscript by underlining all test statistics). Degrees of freedom are shown in parens. The computed value and the significance level that applies are given:

$$t\ (36) = 1.13,\ p > .05$$
$$F\ (3,\ 33) = 67.42,\ p < .001$$

(For the F ratio, it is customary to show the df for the numerator first.) Note that we never give the table values—the reader can look them up if necessary. The null hypothesis is not stated either. (However, you should indicate the use of a one-tailed test.)

Here, in addition to the usual analysis of variance, the researchers also used post hoc procedures (Duncan technique) to compare pairs of means. They computed the correlation between recall and recognition scores to verify that the two processes did not interfere with one another. The absence of a correlation indicates that the processes are independent.

able subsequently to discriminate them from similar objects. For instance, they were told,

> Imagine that you saw first a picture of an apple with a leaf. In the second part of the game, you see two pictures of an apple, one with a leaf and one without. Then, you must remember that the picture you saw earlier was of an apple with a leaf.

Then, they were presented with a picture of a cup, taken from the same larger set of pictures from which the 30 stimuli had been selected. Then, the picture of the previous cup was shown next to a picture of a similar cup, and the child was asked to point to the cup viewed previously and to state the differences between the pictures. These children were carefully prepared for the recognition test before viewing the test stimuli, and they were informed about and were administered the recall test after viewing the stimuli and prior to the recognition test.

Results

The average percent recall under recall and recognition instructions as a function of age is illustrated in Figure 1, and the average percent recognition scores are illustrated in Figure 2.

Separate analyses of variance (Winer, 1962) were performed on recall and recognition scores, each with age, instructions and sex as variables. For recall, age, $F(2, 110) = 49.3, p < .001$, instructions, $F(1, 110) = 52.74, p < .001$, and their interaction, $F(2, 110) = 5.12, p < .01$, were significant. No other effects or interactions reached significance. Post hoc comparisons by the Duncan technique showed that the effect of instructions was significant ($p < .01$) at all ages and the effect of age was significant ($p < .01$) under both instruction sets. In order to evaluate the Age × Instructions interaction, t tests were performed on the increment in recall attributable to appropriate instructions. This increment was significantly greater for fifth graders than for third graders, $t(38) = 4.5, p < .01$, and significantly greater for third graders than kindergartners, $t(38) = 6.4, p < .01$. Thus, recall instructions are increasingly effective with age.

The analysis of variance for recognition scores showed a significant improvement in performance with age, $F(2, 110) = 13.9, p < .01$, but no other significant effects or interactions. Moreover, the post hoc comparisons (Duncan technique) showed that although third graders did not significantly outperform kindergartners, the recognition scores of fifth graders were superior to those of third graders ($p < .01$) under each instructional set. Finally, the effect of instructions

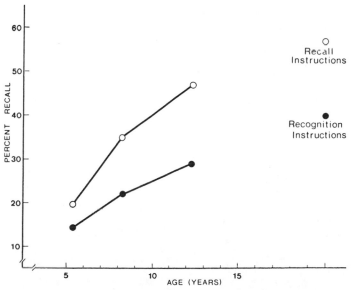

Figure 1.   Percent correct recall as a function of age and instructions.

Discussion.   Note that the authors begin by restating their major findings. Since a variety of effects was observed, this takes relatively more space than it would in a simpler study. The authors go on to offer their explanations for the findings, again referring back to the prior research that formed the basis for their experiment. They also relate their findings to broader theoretical issues regarding the development of mechanisms for encoding information. The researchers end with a clear statement of what they conclude from their results. They do not make vast leaps from their data to grand conclusions about the functioning of the human mind. However, they do place their findings squarely within the context of current thinking on memory and development.

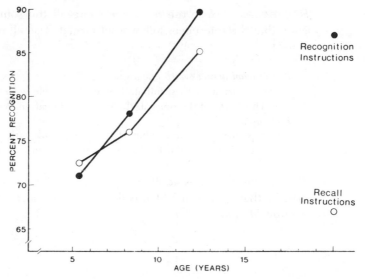

Figure 2. Percent correct recognition as a function of age and instructions.

was tested at each age-group, in spite of the failure to find an overall effect of instructions. Because college students' recognition scores are significantly improved by the recognition strategy, it was expected that only the oldest children could utilize the recognition instructions effectively. This expectation was confirmed, as the only significant comparison was at the oldest age-group, $t(40) = 2.08$, $p < .05$, where recognition-set subjects outperformed recall-set subjects on the recognition test.

Correlations were computed between recall and recognition scores of each subject. High positive correlations would indicate that information stored for recall of an item helped to recognize it and vice versa, that is, that the same stored information was used in performing both tasks. High negative correlations would indicate that storing information for one task was at the expense of storing information for the other. The average correlations both within and across age and instruction groups hovered very close to zero and in no case were significantly different from zero (range = −.17 to +.15). The average overall correlation was +.027, $t(122) = .29$. Thus, information used for recognition was different from information used for recall.

Discussion

Considerable improvements with age in both free recall and picture recognition were observed. Furthermore, children were able to alter their encoding of the same pictorial stimuli in accord with the memory task for which they were prepared. The free-recall strategy was effective at a much earlier age than was the picture recognition strategy. Even the youngest children retrieved different stored information to perform each memory task, attested by the absence of significant relations between recall and recognition of the same items within subjects.

There was steady improvement in recall from kindergarten throughout the elementary school years. Preparation in the strategy of organizing items according to interrelations and associations improved free-recall performance at all ages tested and led to significantly greater improvement as the children grow older. Older children performed better spontaneously in a free-recall task and were better able to use the effective strategy for free recall.

Picture recognition performance improved with age, but that improvement started at a later age—between 8 and 12 years—than did recall improvement.

References.   Here the researchers cite all the sources mentioned in the article. Note that the references follow a set format. Use all underlining and punctuation as shown:

> *For journal articles with one author*:
> Author's surname, First initial. Title of the article with only the first word capitalized.
>   The Name of the Journal, the year of publication, Volume number, page numbers.
> *For books*:
> Author's surname, First initial. Title of the book with only the first word capitalized.
>   City of publication: Publisher's name, year of publication.

The article illustrates additional procedures for sources with multiple authors, and articles that appear in edited collections. For more unusual problems, see the *Publication Manual*.

Moreover, the strategy of paying attention to visual detail was successfully used only by the oldest group of subjects tested, 12-year-olds. Comparison with adults (Tversky, 1973b) indicates that the recognition strategy is even better utilized at ages beyond those tested here. The age trend for recognition is in contrast to the many failures to observe effects of age on picture recognition and suggests that the earlier observations were based on recognition tasks that were too easy or that could be passed by simple verbal labels or codes. This, together with the superior picture recognition of older children supplied with a strategy, should dispel the notions that picture recognition does not develop or is not sensitive to strategies.

It is possible that children in both conditions produced their own encoding strategies appropriate to the expected memory tasks and that these strategies differed from those suggested to them. Regardless of the exact strategies employed, children were able to encode the same stimuli in anticipation of recall differently from when they encoded in anticipation of recognition, and recall encoding was effective at an earlier age than recognition encoding. The finding that a strategy based on verbal encoding or symbolic representation is effective at an earlier age than a strategy based on pictorial encoding or iconic representation casts doubt on theories proposing that children pass through a stage of iconic representation prior to a stage of symbolic representation. Different skills underlie effective performance on different memory tasks and develop at different ages.

REFERENCES

Anderson, J. R. FRAN: A simulation model of free recall. In G. H. Bower (Ed.), *The psychology of learning and motivation* (Vol. 5). New York: Academic Press, 1972.

Brown, A. Judgments of recency for long sequences of pictures: The absence of a developmental trend. *Journal of Experimental Child Psychology*, 1973, *15*, 473–480.

Flavell, J. H. Developmental studies of mediated memory. In H. W. Reese and L. P. Lipsitt (Eds.), *Advances in child development and behavior* (Vol. 5). New York: Academic Press, 1970.

Frost, N. Encoding and retrieval in visual memory tasks. *Journal of Experimental Psychology*, 1972, *95*, 317–326.

Hagen, J. W., Jongeward, R. H., & Kail, R. V., Jr. Cognitive perspectives on the development of memory. In H. Reese (Ed.), *Advances in child development and behavior* (Vol. 10). New York: Academic Press, 1975.

Jablonski, E. Free recall in children. *Psychological Bulletin*, 1974, *81*, 522–539.

Kintsch, W. Models for free recall and recognition. In D. A. Norman (Ed.), *Models of human memory*. New York: Academic Press, 1970.

Nelson, K. E. Memory development in children: Evidence from nonverbal tasks. *Psychonomic Science*, 1971, *25*, 346–348.

Paivio, A. *Imagery and verbal processes*. New York: Holt, Rinehart & Winston, 1971.

Paivio, A., & Csapo, K. Concrete-image and verbal memory codes. *Journal of Experimental Psychology*, 1969, *80*, 279–285.

Rohwer, W. D., Jr. Images and pictures in children's learning: Research results and instructional implications. *Psychological Bulletin*, 1970, *73*, 393–403.

Tulving, E. Theoretical issues in free recall. In T. R. Dixon & D. L. Horton (Eds.), *Verbal behavior and general behavior theory*. Englewood Cliffs, N.J.: Prentice-Hall, 1968.

Tversky, B. Pictorial and verbal encoding in preschool children. *Developmental Psychology*, 1973, *8*, 149–153. (a)

Tversky, B. Encoding processes in recognition and recall. *Cognitive Psychology*, 1973, *5*, 275–287. (b)

Tversky, B. Eye fixations in prediction of recognition and recall. *Memory & Cognition*, 1974, *2*, 275–278.

Winer, B. J. *Statistical principles in experimental design*. New York: McGraw-Hill, 1962.

(Received October 1, 1975)

PREPARING YOUR MANUSCRIPT: PROCEDURAL DETAILS

By now you have a good idea of what we accomplish through a research paper. You have also seen some of the specific techniques used to achieve these goals. Your actual written report will not look exactly like a published article, but your job is to put together a draft that could be turned into the published form. To do that, follow the layout of sections and headings shown in Figure 15.3.

On the first page, give the title, your name, and your affiliation. Also show a "running head" in the bottom half of the page. The running head is a brief version

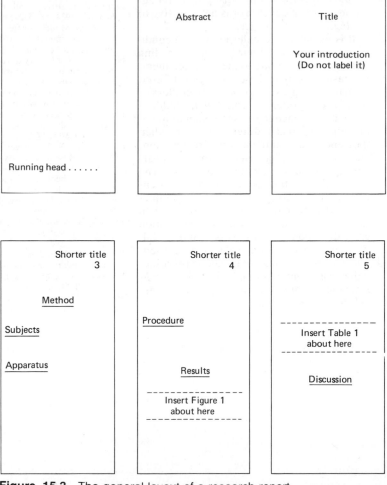

Figure 15.3 The general layout of a research report.

of your title. It should be no more than 60 spaces, including spaces between words. If your complete title is short, your running head may be the same as your full title. The title page is not numbered.

Type the word "Abstract" as a centered heading on the next page. Type the abstract and use double spacing. Type nothing else on this page.

Type the complete title centered at the top of the next page. Then type the introduction. Do not label it; everyone will know what it is. Continue to use double spacing throughout the remainder of the report.

You do not need a new page to start the method section; begin it wherever the

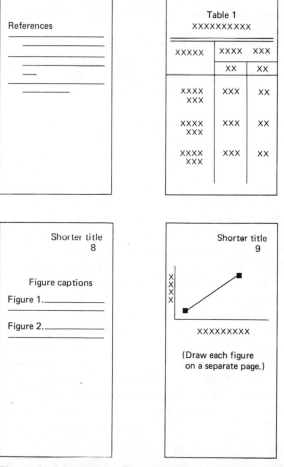

Figure 15.3 (cont'd.) The general layout of a research report. (Note figure pages should not be numbered in manuscripts submitted for publication.)

introduction ends. Type the word "Method" as a centered heading; underline it. Label each subsection of the method section with the appropriate subheading. Start each subheading (such as *Subjects*) flush with the margin of the page. Underline each one.

Your results section may also be started within a page. Start it where the method section ends. Simply type the word "Results" as a centered heading and underline it. Be sure to follow the correct format for reporting statistical data.

Graphs, drawings, or pictures are called "figures." Rows and columns of numbers are called "tables." If you wish to use a figure or a table, be sure to refer to it in words in the text: "Figure 1 illustrates the interaction. . . ." Then, tell the *printer* where the figure would go for publication by showing:

Insert Figure 1 about here

Follow the same procedure for inserting tables. Prepare each table and each figure on a separate page. Write the figure number and article title lightly on the back of each figure; also indicate the top of each figure. Put all the captions to the figures on a separate page. Do not number these pages yet; they will be inserted at the end of the report.

Continue on to the discussion. Type the word "Discussion" as a centered heading. Underline it. Type your discussion.

Put any special reference notes or footnotes on separate pages following the discussion. Put the page of Reference Notes first, and then the page of Footnotes.

On a new page, type the centered heading "References." Underline it. List all your references in alphabetical order by authors' last names. Start each reference flush with the margin of the page. If a reference runs to more than one line, indent additional lines three spaces. Begin the next reference again flush with the margin.

Now put in the pages of tables, in the order they will appear in the text. Put in the page of figure captions. Be sure the captions are in order according to the way they will appear in the text. Last, put in all the figures.

Assign a number to each page, beginning with the Abstract page (the title page is *not* numbered). The Abstract page is page "1." Type the first two or three words of your title at the top of each numbered page, alongside the page number.

We use these procedures so that our reports can be turned into published versions fairly easily. The procedures have become standard because they work. Although they may seem somewhat arbitrary and unnecessarily rigid, the alternative is a chaotic situation in which no one knows what to do or what to expect. The value of these procedures is that in the long run they make our work easier.

MAKING REVISIONS

Now that we have most of the major reporting principles down, we should spend a bit more time looking at the overall picture. The kind of writing that appears in research reports is sometimes rather dry and tedious, but through little fault of the authors. Remember that your task in writing a report is to communicate exactly what you did in the experiment. You must do that as clearly and concisely as possible. There is no space in journals for muddled thoughts and rambling discourses. Authors are often forced to cut articles. You may have to practice doing the same.

Try to say exactly what you mean. That is not as simple as it sounds. One technique some students use is reading aloud. How does it sound? Your own ear can be a guide. Would you be able to understand it if you had not written it? Try to put yourself in your readers' place. Better yet, try to get the opinion of a naive reader. Can your reader follow what you did? Can you make it clearer? Then, *revise your report.*

One of the things that seems to surprise people is that when researchers sit down to write reports, they do not usually stop at a first draft. They may continue to revise and rework the same paper several times before they feel it is acceptable. Somehow, the thought of rewriting seems to unnerve many people. But even the best writers make revisions. They need editors too. Good writing takes work. The first draft of your report should be just that—a first draft. Work on improving it, polishing it, refining it. Put as much care into writing your report as you put into doing the study. A good study merits a good presentation. Evaluate your draft to make sure you have accomplished the goals of each section of the report. Make the necessary changes or additions.

As you work on revisions, be aware of some common errors that can detract from your report. First of all, be sure you understand the difference between "affect" and "effect." "Affect" is a verb: The powerful heat *affected* their thinking. "Effect" is a noun: The *effect* of food deprivation was transient. But, food deprivation *affects* learning. Be careful of other spelling errors too. They detract from the overall quality of your work. Note that the word "data" is a plural noun: "The data *are* convincing."

Try to avoid sexist language as you write. The current APA editorial policies encourage the use of neutral wording. Do not say "A hard-driving businessman" if what you mean to say applies to both sexes; say "Hard-driving business people."

It is inaccurate as well as disappointing to say, "I got no results in this experiment." You *always* get results, although they may not be what you predicted. Conversely, do not make grand statements based on the data of one experiment. Your results may enable you to reject the null hypothesis. However, you have not "proved" anything; you simply confirmed your predictions. If you did not find significant differences, you "failed to reject the null hypothesis." You still have not proved anything—you could be making a Type 2 error. Avoid words like "true" and "absolutely."

Finally, keep in mind that this process is part of a scientific venture. We are looking for observable data that can be evaluated on the basis of objective criteria. This is not the place to talk about personal experiences, popular knowledge, or common sense. Stick to the literature and stick to the facts. Using an occasional "I" now and then to avoid awkward sentences is okay, but do not get too personal. Present and discuss *data.* Pay particular attention to your discussion section. Remember that your discussion should wrap things up; readers should finish your report with an understanding of what the study was about and where it fits. You may offer suggestions for future research, but try to view each report as a document that has a beginning and an end.

SUMMARY

The purpose of a research report is communication. Through a report we tell others what we did and what we found. A report should contain enough information to permit other researchers to evaluate the findings and to replicate them if they choose.

The *Publication Manual of the American Psychological Association* includes detailed information regarding the format, content, and layout of reports. We follow these standards by convention so that writers as well as readers will have a consistent mode for dealing with psychological research.

The psychological research report has these main components: a descriptive title, an abstract, an introduction, a method section, a results section, a discussion, and a list of references.

Abstracts are especially important because they are used in the major reference for psychological information, the *Psychological Abstracts*. *Psychological Abstracts* organizes information from many journals, books, and psychology-related publications into one handy source.

There are many specific procedural details for carrying out the goals of each section of the report. Some of these can be seen in published articles; they are also revealed in a typed manuscript. Reports are written in several stages: the first is a draft which is then revised and polished to give the experiment the best possible presentation.

REVIEW AND STUDY QUESTIONS

1. What is the purpose of a research report?
2. What are the major sections that should be included in each report?
3. A title should be "descriptive." What do we mean by that? What is the importance of using a descriptive title?
4. Practice writing report titles by suggesting a good descriptive title that might be used for a report on each of the following sets of independent and dependent variables:
   a. Food deprivation; the speed of maze running
   b. Practice; time required to solve a word problem
   c. Maturation; fear of strangers
   d. Printer's type; reading rate
5. What is the function of the abstract of a research report?
6. What basic information should be contained in an abstract?

7. What are the *Psychological Abstracts?*

8. Practice using the *Psychological Abstracts* by carrying out each of the following:
   a. Find three references for articles on delayed recall.
   b. Locate an article published in 1977 on the language development of twins.
   c. Obtain references for at least two articles published by Lynne Cooper.
   d. Find an article that would tell us something about the *size* of mental images.

9. What is the *Publication Manual of the American Psychological Association?* Why is it important?

10. What is the function of the introduction of a report? What basic information should you include in an introduction?

11. What is the function of the method section of a report? What basic information should you include in the method section?

12. You want to divide a method section into subsections. What common subsections are often used? What information would you include in each?

13. What information would you include in the results section?

14. The discussion section of a report serves several functions. What are they?

15. Why do we need to include references at the end of a report?

16. Jack is not pleased with this chapter. He says: "If I have to follow all these silly rules for writing up a report, I won't have any chance to be creative." Tell him why a standard format for writing reports is important.

17. How would you show each of the following in a report?:
    a. The results of a *t* test with 38 degrees of freedom, where your computed value of *t* was 1.38.
    b. The results of an *F* test with 1 and 12 degrees of freedom, where your computed value of *F* was 3.78.
    c. The proper placement of a figure within the text.
    d. The proper placement of a table within the text.
    e. The proper reference for this book.
    f. The proper references for the articles located for question 8.

18. Explain the major differences between the manuscript of an article and the printed version we might see in a journal.

REFERENCES

Publication Manual of the American Psychological Association, (2nd ed.). Washington, D.C.: American Psychological Association, 1974.

Tversky, B. Eye fixations in prediction of recognition and recall. *Memory and Cognition*, 1974, *2*, 275–278.

Tversky, B., and Teiffer, E. Development of strategies for recall and recognition. *Developmental Psychology*, 1976, *12*, 406–410.

Appendix A Computational Formulas

TABLE A1. A ONE-WAY ANALYSIS OF VARIANCE FOR A THREE-GROUP EXAMPLE: COMPUTATIONAL FORMULAS[1]

	Group 1	$X_1{}^2$	Group 2	$X_2{}^2$	Group 3	$X_3{}^2$
Step 1. Square each score.	2	4	1	1	3	9
	2	4	3	9	4	16
	1	1	3	9	2	4
Step 2. Total the scores and squared scores of each group.	0	0	3	9	3	9
	1	1	3	9	4	16
	$\Sigma X_1 = 6$	$\Sigma X_1{}^2 = 10$	$\Sigma X_2 = 13$	$\Sigma X_2{}^2 = 37$	$\Sigma X_3 = 16$	$\Sigma X_3{}^2 = 54$
	$N_1 = 5$		$N_2 = 5$		$N_3 = 5$	

Step 3. Total all scores.

$$\Sigma X = 6 + 13 + 16$$
$$= 35$$

Step 4. Total all squared scores.

$$\Sigma X^2 = 10 + 37 + 54$$
$$= 101$$

Step 5. Find sum of squares total. N is the total number of scores.

$$\boxed{SS_T = \Sigma X^2 - \frac{(\Sigma X)^2}{N}}$$

$$= 101 - \frac{(35)^2}{15}$$

$$= 101 - \frac{(1225)}{15}$$

$$= 101 - 81.67$$

$$= 19.33$$

Step 6. Find sum of squares between groups (p is the number of groups).

$$\boxed{SS_B = \frac{(\Sigma X_1)^2}{N_1} + \frac{(\Sigma X_2)^2}{N_2} + \cdots + \frac{(\Sigma X_p)^2}{N_p} - \frac{(\Sigma X)^2}{N}}$$

$$= \frac{(6)^2}{5} + \frac{(13)^2}{5} + \frac{(16)^2}{5} - \frac{(35)^2}{15}$$
$$= 7.20 + 33.80 + 51.20 - 81.67$$
$$= 92.20 - 81.67$$
$$= 10.53$$

Step 7. Find sum of squares within groups.

$$\boxed{SS_W = SS_T - SS_B}$$
$$= 19.33 - 10.53$$
$$= 8.80$$

286

Step 8. Complete the summary table and compute *F*.

Source	df	SS	MS	F
Between groups	$(p - 1) = 2$	10.53	5.26	7.21**
Within groups	$(N - p) = 12$	8.80	.73	
Total	14	19.33		

$^*p < .05$
$^{**}p < .01$

[1]Table 13.3 in this text shows the analysis using definitional formulas. Discrepancies between the computed values found through the two methods are due to rounding errors. The two approaches are mathematically equivalent.

TABLE A2.   A TWO-WAY ANALYSIS OF VARIANCE: COMPUTATIONAL FORMULAS[1]

	Factor 1 (Word frequency)		Row totals	Row means
	Low	High		

Step 1. Total scores in each cell.

Step 2. Find row and column totals and means.

		Low	High	Row totals	Row means
Factor 2 (Category cues)	No cues	$X_1\ X_1^2$ 2 4 $\Sigma X_1 = 15$ 3 9 $\Sigma X_1^2 = 55$ 1 1 $N_1 = 5$ 4 16 5 25	$X_2\ X_2^2$ 4 16 $\Sigma X_2 = 25$ 5 25 $\Sigma X_2^2 = 129$ 4 16 $N_2 = 5$ 6 36 6 36	40	20
	Cues	$X_3\ X_3^2$ 4 16 6 36 $\Sigma X_3 = 30$ 5 25 $\Sigma X_3^2 = 194$ 6 36 $N_3 = 5$ 9 81	$X_4\ X_4^2$ 7 49 6 36 $\Sigma X_4 = 40$ 9 81 $\Sigma X_4^2 = 330$ 8 64 $N_4 = 5$ 10 100	70	35

Step 3. Total all scores and compute grand mean. N is the total number of scores.

	Low	High	
Column totals	45	65	Grand total $\Sigma X = 110$
Column means	22.5	32.5	Grand mean $\dfrac{\Sigma X}{N} = 5.5$

Step 4. Find the total of all squared scores.

$$\Sigma X^2 = 55 + 129 + 194 + 330$$
$$= 708$$

Step 5. Find the sum of squares total.

$$\boxed{SS_T = \Sigma X^2 - \frac{(\Sigma X)^2}{N}}$$

$$= 708 - \frac{(110)^2}{20}$$

$$= 708 - 605$$
$$= 103$$

Step 6. Find sum of squares between groups (p is the number of groups).

$$\boxed{SS_B = \frac{(\Sigma X_1)^2}{N_1} + \frac{(\Sigma X_2)^2}{N_2} + \cdots + \frac{(\Sigma X_p)^2}{N_p} - \frac{(\Sigma X)^2}{N}}$$

$$= \frac{(15)^2}{5} + \frac{(25)^2}{5} + \frac{(30)^2}{5} + \frac{(40)^2}{5} - \frac{(110)^2}{20}$$

$$= 45 + 125 + 180 + 320 - 605$$
$$= 670 - 605$$
$$= 65$$

Step 7. Find sum of squares within groups.

$$\boxed{SS_W = SS_T - SS_B}$$

$$= 103 - 65$$
$$= 38$$

Step 8. Find sum of squares for Factor 1; total (Σ) across all columns.

$$SS_1 = \Sigma \left[\frac{(\text{Total of each column})^2}{(N \text{ in each column})} \right] - \frac{(\Sigma X)^2}{N}$$

$$= \Sigma \left(\frac{(45)^2}{10} + \frac{(65)^2}{10} \right) - \frac{(110)^2}{20}$$

$$= (202.5 + 422.5) - 605$$
$$= 625 - 605$$
$$= 20$$

Step 9. Find sum of squares for Factor 2; total (Σ) across all rows.

$$SS_2 = \Sigma \left[\frac{(\text{Total each row})^2}{(N \text{ in each row})} \right] - \frac{(\Sigma X)^2}{N}$$

$$= \Sigma \left(\frac{(40)^2}{(10)} + \frac{(70)^2}{(10)} \right) - \frac{(110)^2}{20}$$
$$= (160 + 490) - 605$$
$$= 650 - 605$$
$$= 45$$

Step 10. Find sum of squares for the interaction.

$$SS_{1 \times 2} - SS_B - SS_1 - SS_2$$

$$= 65 - 20 - 45$$
$$= 0$$

Step 11. Complete the summary table and compute F. (*p* is the number of levels of Factor 1; *q* is the number of levels of Factor 2.)

Source	df	SS	MS	F
Between groups				
Factor 1	$p - 1 = 1$	20	20	$F_1 = \dfrac{20}{2.38}$ or 8.40*
Factor 2	$q - 1 = 1$	45	45	$F_2 = \dfrac{45}{2.38}$ or 18.91**
Interaction 1×2	$(p - 1)(q - 1) = 1$	0	0	$F_{1 \times 2} = \dfrac{0}{2.38}$ or 0
Within groups	16	38	2.38	
Total	$N - 1 = 19$	65		

*$p \leq .05$
**$p \leq .01$

[1]Tables 13.2 through 13.12 in this text illustrate the definitional formulas for these procedures. The two approaches are mathematically equivalent.

Appendix B Statistical Tables

TABLE B1. RANDOM NUMBERS

03 47 43 73 86	36 96 47 36 61	46 98 63 71 62	33 26 16 80 45	60 11 14 10 95
97 74 24 67 62	42 81 14 57 20	42 53 32 37 32	27 07 36 07 51	24 51 79 89 73
16 76 62 27 66	56 50 26 71 07	32 90 79 78 53	13 55 38 58 59	88 97 54 14 10
12 56 85 99 26	96 96 68 27 31	05 03 72 93 15	57 12 10 14 21	88 26 49 81 76
55 59 56 35 64	38 54 82 46 22	31 62 43 09 90	06 18 44 32 53	23 83 01 30 30
16 22 77 94 39	49 54 43 54 82	17 37 93 23 78	87 35 20 96 43	84 26 34 91 64
84 42 17 53 31	57 24 55 06 88	77 04 74 47 67	21 76 33 50 25	83 92 12 06 76
63 01 63 78 59	16 95 55 67 19	98 10 50 71 75	12 86 73 58 07	44 39 52 38 79
33 21 12 34 29	78 64 56 07 82	52 42 07 44 38	15 51 00 13 42	99 66 02 79 54
57 60 86 32 44	09 47 27 96 54	49 17 46 09 62	90 52 84 77 27	08 02 73 43 28
18 18 07 92 46	44 17 16 58 09	79 83 86 19 62	06 76 50 03 10	55 23 64 05 05
26 62 38 97 75	84 16 07 44 99	83 11 46 32 24	20 14 85 88 45	10 93 72 88 71
23 42 40 64 74	82 97 77 77 81	07 45 32 14 08	32 98 94 07 72	93 85 79 10 75
52 30 28 19 95	50 92 26 11 97	00 56 76 31 38	80 22 02 53 53	86 60 42 04 53
37 45 94 35 12	83 39 50 08 30	42 34 07 96 88	54 42 06 87 98	35 85 29 48 39
70 29 17 12 13	40 33 20 38 26	13 89 51 03 74	17 76 37 13 04	07 74 21 19 30
56 62 18 37 35	96 83 50 87 75	97 12 25 93 47	70 33 24 03 54	97 77 46 44 80
99 49 57 22 77	88 42 95 45 72	16 64 36 16 00	04 43 18 66 79	94 77 24 21 90
16 08 15 04 72	33 27 14 34 09	45 59 34 68 49	12 72 07 34 45	99 27 72 95 14
31 16 93 32 43	50 27 89 87 19	20 15 37 00 49	52 85 66 60 44	38 68 88 11 80
68 34 30 13 70	55 74 30 77 40	44 22 78 84 26	04 33 46 09 52	68 07 97 06 57
74 57 25 65 76	59 29 97 68 60	71 91 38 67 54	13 58 18 24 76	15 54 55 95 52
27 42 37 86 53	48 55 90 65 72	96 57 69 36 10	96 46 92 42 45	97 60 49 04 91
00 39 68 29 61	66 37 32 20 30	77 84 57 03 29	10 45 65 04 26	11 04 96 67 24
29 94 98 94 24	68 49 69 10 82	53 75 91 93 30	34 25 20 57 27	40 48 73 51 92
16 90 82 66 59	83 62 64 11 12	67 19 00 71 74	60 47 21 29 68	02 02 37 03 31
11 27 94 75 06	06 09 19 74 66	02 94 37 34 02	76 70 90 30 66	38 45 94 30 38
35 25 20 16 20	33 32 51 26 38	79 78 45 04 91	16 92 53 56 16	02 76 59 95 98
38 23 16 86 38	42 38 97 01 50	87 75 66 81 41	40 01 74 91 62	48 51 84 08 32
31 96 25 91 47	96 44 33 49 13	34 86 82 53 91	00 52 43 48 85	27 55 26 89 62
66 67 40 67 14	64 05 71 95 86	11 05 65 09 68	76 83 20 37 90	57 16 00 11 66
14 90 84 45 11	75 73 88 05 90	52 27 41 14 86	22 98 12 22 08	07 52 74 95 80
68 05 51 18 00	33 96 02 75 19	07 60 62 93 55	59 33 82 43 90	49 37 38 44 59
20 46 78 73 90	97 51 40 14 02	04 02 33 31 08	39 54 16 49 36	47 95 93 13 30
64 19 58 97 79	15 06 15 93 20	01 90 10 75 06	40 78 78 89 62	02 67 74 17 33

```
05 26 93 70 60    22 35 85 15 13    92 03 51 59 77    59 56 78 06 83    52 91 05 70 74
07 97 10 88 23    09 98 42 99 64    61 71 62 99 15    06 51 29 16 93    58 05 77 09 51
68 71 86 85 85    54 87 66 47 54    73 32 08 11 12    44 95 92 63 16    29 56 24 29 48
26 99 61 65 53    58 37 78 80 70    42 10 50 67 42    32 17 55 85 74    94 44 67 16 94
14 65 52 68 75    87 59 36 22 41    26 78 63 06 55    13 08 27 01 50    15 29 39 39 43

17 53 77 58 71    71 41 61 50 72    12 41 94 96 26    44 95 27 36 99    02 96 74 30 83
90 26 59 21 19    23 52 23 33 12    96 93 02 18 39    07 02 18 36 07    25 99 32 70 23
41 23 52 55 99    31 04 49 69 96    10 47 48 45 88    13 41 43 89 20    97 17 14 49 17
60 20 50 81 69    31 99 73 68 68    35 81 33 03 76    24 30 12 48 60    18 99 10 72 34
91 25 38 05 90    94 58 28 41 36    45 37 59 03 09    90 35 57 29 12    82 62 54 65 60

34 50 57 74 37    98 80 33 00 91    09 77 93 19 82    74 94 80 04 04    45 07 31 66 49
85 22 04 39 43    73 81 53 94 79    33 62 46 86 28    08 31 54 46 31    53 94 13 38 47
09 79 13 77 48    73 82 97 22 21    05 03 27 24 83    72 89 44 05 60    35 80 39 94 88
88 75 80 18 14    22 95 75 42 49    39 32 82 22 49    02 48 07 70 37    16 04 61 67 87
90 96 23 70 00    39 00 03 06 90    55 85 78 38 36    94 37 30 69 32    90 89 00 76 33

53 74 23 99 67    61 32 28 69 84    94 62 67 86 24    98 33 41 19 95    47 53 53 38 09
63 38 06 86 54    99 00 65 26 94    02 82 90 23 07    79 62 67 80 60    75 91 12 81 19
35 30 58 21 46    06 72 17 10 94    25 21 31 75 96    49 28 24 00 49    55 65 79 78 07
63 43 36 82 69    65 51 18 37 88    61 38 44 12 45    32 92 85 88 65    54 34 81 85 35
98 25 37 55 26    01 91 82 81 46    74 71 12 94 97    24 02 71 37 07    03 92 18 66 75

02 63 21 17 69    71 50 80 89 56    38 15 70 11 48    43 40 45 86 98    00 83 26 91 03
64 55 22 21 82    48 22 28 06 00    61 54 13 43 91    82 78 12 23 29    06 66 24 12 27
85 07 26 13 89    01 10 07 82 04    59 63 69 36 03    69 11 15 83 80    13 29 54 19 28
58 54 16 24 15    51 54 44 82 00    62 61 65 04 69    38 18 65 18 97    85 72 13 49 21
34 85 27 84 87    61 48 64 56 26    90 18 48 13 26    37 70 15 42 57    65 65 80 39 07

03 92 18 27 46    57 99 16 96 56    30 33 72 85 22    84 64 38 56 98    99 01 30 98 64
62 95 30 27 59    37 75 41 66 48    86 97 80 61 45    23 53 04 01 63    45 76 08 64 27
08 45 93 15 22    60 21 75 46 91    98 77 27 85 42    28 88 61 08 84    69 62 03 42 73
07 08 55 18 40    45 44 75 13 90    24 94 96 61 02    57 55 66 83 15    73 42 37 11 61
01 85 89 95 66    51 10 19 34 88    15 84 97 19 75    12 76 39 43 78    64 63 91 08 25

72 84 71 14 35    19 11 58 49 26    50 11 17 17 76    86 31 57 20 18    95 60 78 46 75
88 78 28 16 84    13 52 53 94 53    75 45 69 30 96    73 89 65 70 31    99 17 43 48 76
45 17 75 65 57    28 40 19 72 12    25 12 74 75 67    60 40 60 81 19    24 62 01 61 16
96 76 28 12 54    22 01 11 94 25    71 96 16 16 88    68 64 36 74 45    19 59 50 88 92
43 31 67 72 30    24 02 94 08 63    38 32 36 66 02    69 36 38 25 39    48 03 45 15 22

50 44 66 44 21    66 06 58 05 62    68 15 54 35 02    42 35 48 96 32    14 52 41 52 48
22 66 22 15 86    26 63 75 41 99    58 42 36 72 24    58 37 52 18 51    03 37 18 39 11
96 24 40 14 51    23 22 30 88 57    95 67 47 29 83    94 69 40 06 07    18 16 36 78 86
31 73 91 61 19    60 20 72 93 48    98 57 07 23 69    65 95 39 69 58    56 80 30 19 44
78 60 73 99 84    43 89 94 36 45    56 69 47 07 41    90 22 91 07 12    78 35 34 08 72

84 37 90 61 56    70 10 23 98 05    85 11 34 76 60    76 48 45 34 60    01 64 18 39 96
36 67 10 08 23    98 93 35 08 86    99 29 76 29 81    33 34 91 58 93    63 14 52 32 52
07 28 59 07 48    89 64 58 89 75    83 85 62 27 89    30 14 78 56 27    86 63 59 80 02
10 15 83 87 60    79 24 31 66 56    21 48 24 06 93    91 98 94 05 49    01 47 59 38 00
55 19 68 97 65    03 73 52 16 56    00 53 55 90 27    33 42 29 38 87    22 13 88 83 34
```

TABLE B1.   RANDOM NUMBERS (cont.)

53	81	29	13	39	35	01	20	71	34	62	33	74	82	14	53	73	19	09	03	56	54	29	56	93

53 81 29 13 39   35 01 20 71 34   62 33 74 82 14   53 73 19 09 03   56 54 29 56 93
51 86 32 68 92   33 98 74 66 99   40 14 71 94 58   45 94 19 38 81   14 44 99 81 07
35 91 70 29 13   80 03 54 07 27   96 94 78 32 66   50 95 52 74 33   13 80 55 62 54
37 71 67 95 13   20 02 44 95 94   64 85 04 05 72   01 32 90 76 14   53 89 74 60 41
93 66 13 83 27   92 79 64 64 72   28 54 96 53 84   48 14 52 98 94   56 07 93 89 30

02 96 08 45 65   13 05 00 41 84   93 07 54 72 59   21 45 57 09 77   19 48 56 27 44
49 83 43 48 35   82 88 33 69 96   72 36 04 19 76   47 45 15 18 60   82 11 08 95 97
84 60 71 62 46   40 80 81 30 37   34 39 23 05 38   25 15 35 71 30   88 12 57 21 77
18 17 30 88 71   44 91 14 88 47   89 23 30 63 15   56 34 20 47 89   99 82 93 24 98
79 69 10 61 78   71 32 76 95 62   87 00 22 58 40   92 54 01 75 25   43 11 71 99 31

75 93 36 57 83   56 20 14 82 11   74 21 97 90 65   96 42 68 63 86   74 54 13 26 94
38 30 92 29 03   06 28 81 39 38   62 25 06 84 63   61 29 08 93 67   04 32 92 08 00
51 29 50 10 34   31 57 75 95 80   51 97 02 74 77   76 15 48 49 44   18 55 63 77 09
21 31 38 86 24   37 79 81 53 74   73 24 16 10 33   52 83 90 94 76   70 47 14 54 36
29 01 23 87 88   58 02 39 37 67   42 10 14 20 92   16 55 23 42 45   54 96 09 11 06

95 33 95 22 00   18 74 72 00 18   38 79 58 69 32   81 76 80 26 92   82 80 84 25 39
90 84 60 79 80   24 36 59 87 38   82 07 53 89 35   96 35 23 79 18   05 98 90 07 35
46 40 62 98 82   54 97 20 56 95   15 74 80 08 32   16 46 70 50 80   67 72 16 42 79
20 31 89 03 43   38 46 82 68 72   32 14 82 99 70   80 60 47 18 97   63 49 30 21 30
71 59 73 05 50   08 22 23 71 77   91 01 93 20 49   82 96 59 26 94   66 39 67 08 60

Fisher and Yates. From Table XXXIII in *Statistical Tables for Biological, Agricultural and Medical Research,* published by Longman Group Ltd., London. (Previously published by Oliver and Boyd, Edinburgh.) Reprinted by permission of the authors and publishers.

Glossary

ABA design Type of within-subjects design in which A (the control condition) is presented first, followed by B (the experimental condition), followed by a return to the control condition, A.

Alpha level The chosen significance level of an experiment—for instance, $p < .05$; *see also* significance level.

Alternative hypothesis (H_1) Hypothesis which states that data came from different populations and which cannot be tested directly. Also called the *research hypothesis*.

Analysis of variance (ANOVA) Statistical procedure used to evaluate differences among two or more treatment means by breaking the variability in the data into components that reflect the influence of error, and error plus treatment effects; also called the *F test*.

Analytic statement A statement that is always true.

Antecedent conditions All circumstances that occur or exist before the event or behavior to be explained; also called *antecedents*.

ANOVA *See* analysis of variance.

Aristotelian model *See* inductive model.

Balancing Technique used to control the impact of an extraneous variable across treatments by distributing its effect equally across treatment conditions.

Baseline A measure of the dependent variable as it occurs without the experimental manipulation; used to assess the impact of the experimental intervention.

Beta level The odds of making a Type 2 error in an experiment.

Between-groups variability The degree to which treatment groups differ from one another; a measure of the variability produced by treatment effects and error.

Between-subjects counterbalancing Technique for controlling order effects by distributing the effects equally across all conditions of the experiment; unlike within-subjects counterbalancing, no attempt is made to control order effects for each subject.

Between-subjects design Research design in which different subjects take part in each condition of the experiment.

Carryover effect Persistence of the effects of a treatment condition after the condition ends.

Case study Descriptive record of an individual's experiences and/or behaviors that may be used to make inferences about developmental processes, the impact of life events, level of functioning, and the origin of disorders.

TABLE B3. CRITICAL VALUES OF F (.05 LEVEL IN ROMAN TYPE, .01 LEVEL IN **BOLDFACE**) (cont.)

DEGREES OF FREEDOM FOR GREATER MEAN SQUARE [NUMERATOR]

DEGREES OF FREEDOM FOR LESSER MEAN SQUARE [DENOMINATOR]

df	1	2	3	4	5	6	7	8	9	10	11	12	14	16	20	24	30	40	50	75	100	200	500	∞
50	4.03 **7.17**	3.18 **5.06**	2.79 **4.20**	2.56 **3.72**	2.40 **3.41**	2.29 **3.18**	2.20 **3.02**	2.13 **2.88**	2.07 **2.78**	2.02 **2.70**	1.98 **2.62**	1.95 **2.56**	1.90 **2.46**	1.85 **2.39**	1.78 **2.26**	1.74 **2.18**	1.69 **2.10**	1.63 **2.00**	1.60 **1.94**	1.55 **1.86**	1.52 **1.82**	1.48 **1.76**	1.46 **1.71**	1.44 **1.68**
55	4.02 **7.12**	3.17 **5.01**	2.78 **4.16**	2.54 **3.68**	2.38 **3.37**	2.27 **3.15**	2.18 **2.98**	2.11 **2.85**	2.05 **2.75**	2.00 **2.66**	1.97 **2.59**	1.93 **2.53**	1.88 **2.43**	1.83 **2.35**	1.76 **2.23**	1.72 **2.15**	1.67 **2.06**	1.61 **1.96**	1.58 **1.90**	1.52 **1.82**	1.50 **1.78**	1.46 **1.71**	1.43 **1.66**	1.41 **1.64**
60	4.00 **7.08**	3.15 **4.98**	2.76 **4.13**	2.52 **3.65**	2.37 **3.34**	2.25 **3.12**	2.17 **2.95**	2.10 **2.82**	2.04 **2.72**	1.99 **2.63**	1.95 **2.56**	1.92 **2.50**	1.86 **2.40**	1.81 **2.32**	1.75 **2.20**	1.70 **2.12**	1.65 **2.03**	1.59 **1.93**	1.56 **1.87**	1.50 **1.79**	1.48 **1.74**	1.44 **1.68**	1.41 **1.63**	1.39 **1.60**
65	3.99 **7.04**	3.14 **4.95**	2.75 **4.10**	2.51 **3.62**	2.36 **3.31**	2.24 **3.09**	2.15 **2.93**	2.08 **2.79**	2.02 **2.70**	1.98 **2.61**	1.94 **2.54**	1.90 **2.47**	1.85 **2.37**	1.80 **2.30**	1.73 **2.18**	1.68 **2.09**	1.63 **2.00**	1.57 **1.90**	1.54 **1.84**	1.49 **1.76**	1.46 **1.71**	1.42 **1.64**	1.39 **1.60**	1.37 **1.56**
70	3.98 **7.01**	3.13 **4.92**	2.74 **4.08**	2.50 **3.60**	2.35 **3.29**	2.23 **3.07**	2.14 **2.91**	2.07 **2.77**	2.01 **2.67**	1.97 **2.59**	1.93 **2.51**	1.89 **2.45**	1.84 **2.35**	1.79 **2.28**	1.72 **2.15**	1.67 **2.07**	1.62 **1.98**	1.56 **1.88**	1.53 **1.82**	1.47 **1.74**	1.45 **1.69**	1.40 **1.62**	1.37 **1.56**	1.35 **1.53**
80	3.96 **6.96**	3.11 **4.88**	2.72 **4.04**	2.48 **3.56**	2.33 **3.25**	2.21 **3.04**	2.12 **2.87**	2.05 **2.74**	1.99 **2.64**	1.95 **2.55**	1.91 **2.48**	1.88 **2.41**	1.82 **2.32**	1.77 **2.24**	1.70 **2.11**	1.65 **2.03**	1.60 **1.94**	1.54 **1.84**	1.51 **1.78**	1.45 **1.70**	1.42 **1.65**	1.38 **1.57**	1.35 **1.52**	1.32 **1.49**
100	3.94 **6.90**	3.09 **4.82**	2.70 **3.98**	2.46 **3.51**	2.30 **3.20**	2.19 **2.99**	2.10 **2.82**	2.03 **2.69**	1.97 **2.59**	1.92 **2.51**	1.88 **2.43**	1.85 **2.36**	1.79 **2.26**	1.75 **2.19**	1.68 **2.06**	1.63 **1.98**	1.57 **1.89**	1.51 **1.79**	1.48 **1.73**	1.42 **1.64**	1.39 **1.59**	1.34 **1.51**	1.30 **1.46**	1.28 **1.43**
125	3.92 **6.84**	3.07 **4.78**	2.68 **3.94**	2.44 **3.47**	2.29 **3.17**	2.17 **2.95**	2.08 **2.79**	2.01 **2.65**	1.95 **2.56**	1.90 **2.47**	1.86 **2.40**	1.83 **2.33**	1.77 **2.23**	1.72 **2.15**	1.65 **2.03**	1.60 **1.94**	1.55 **1.85**	1.49 **1.75**	1.45 **1.68**	1.39 **1.59**	1.36 **1.54**	1.31 **1.46**	1.27 **1.40**	1.25 **1.37**
150	3.91 **6.81**	3.06 **4.75**	2.67 **3.91**	2.43 **3.44**	2.27 **3.14**	2.16 **2.92**	2.07 **2.76**	2.00 **2.62**	1.94 **2.53**	1.89 **2.44**	1.85 **2.37**	1.82 **2.30**	1.76 **2.20**	1.71 **2.12**	1.64 **2.00**	1.59 **1.91**	1.54 **1.83**	1.47 **1.72**	1.44 **1.66**	1.37 **1.56**	1.34 **1.51**	1.29 **1.43**	1.25 **1.37**	1.22 **1.33**
200	3.89 **6.76**	3.04 **4.71**	2.65 **3.88**	2.41 **3.41**	2.26 **3.11**	2.14 **2.90**	2.05 **2.73**	1.98 **2.60**	1.92 **2.50**	1.87 **2.41**	1.83 **2.34**	1.80 **2.28**	1.74 **2.17**	1.69 **2.09**	1.62 **1.97**	1.57 **1.88**	1.52 **1.79**	1.45 **1.69**	1.42 **1.62**	1.35 **1.53**	1.32 **1.48**	1.26 **1.39**	1.22 **1.33**	1.19 **1.28**
400	3.86 **6.70**	3.02 **4.66**	2.62 **3.83**	2.39 **3.36**	2.23 **3.06**	2.12 **2.85**	2.03 **2.69**	1.96 **2.55**	1.90 **2.46**	1.85 **2.37**	1.81 **2.29**	1.78 **2.23**	1.72 **2.12**	1.67 **2.04**	1.60 **1.92**	1.54 **1.84**	1.49 **1.74**	1.42 **1.64**	1.38 **1.57**	1.32 **1.47**	1.28 **1.42**	1.22 **1.32**	1.16 **1.24**	1.13 **1.19**
1000	3.85 **6.66**	3.00 **4.62**	2.61 **3.80**	2.38 **3.34**	2.22 **3.04**	2.10 **2.82**	2.02 **2.66**	1.95 **2.53**	1.89 **2.43**	1.84 **2.34**	1.80 **2.26**	1.76 **2.20**	1.70 **2.09**	1.65 **2.01**	1.58 **1.89**	1.53 **1.81**	1.47 **1.71**	1.41 **1.61**	1.36 **1.54**	1.30 **1.44**	1.26 **1.38**	1.19 **1.28**	1.13 **1.19**	1.08 **1.11**
∞	3.84 **6.64**	2.99 **4.60**	2.60 **3.78**	2.37 **3.32**	2.21 **3.02**	2.09 **2.80**	2.01 **2.64**	1.94 **2.51**	1.88 **2.41**	1.83 **2.32**	1.79 **2.24**	1.75 **2.18**	1.69 **2.07**	1.64 **1.99**	1.57 **1.87**	1.52 **1.79**	1.46 **1.69**	1.40 **1.59**	1.35 **1.52**	1.28 **1.41**	1.24 **1.36**	1.17 **1.25**	1.11 **1.15**	1.00 **1.00**

George W. Snedecor and William G. Cochran. *Statistical Methods* (c) 1967, Sixth Edition by Iowa State University Press, Ames, Iowa 50010. Reprinted by permisson.

Complete counterbalancing   Technique for controlling progressive error by using all possible sequences of the treatment conditions.

Confounding   Error that occurs when the value of an extraneous variable changes systematically along with the independent variable.

Constancy of conditions   Control procedure used to avoid confounding: keeping all aspects of the treatment conditions identical except for the independent variable that changes across conditions.

Content validity   The degree to which the content of the measure reflects the content of what is measured.

Contradictory statement   A statement that is always false.

Control condition   A condition used to determine the value of the dependent variable without the experimental manipulation. Data from the control condition provide a baseline or standard to compare with behavior under changing levels of the independent variable.

Control group   Subjects in a control condition; subjects not exposed to the experimental manipulation.

Controls   Techniques used to eliminate or hold constant the effects of extraneous variables.

Correlation   The degree of relationship between two measures, determined through statistical procedures.

Correlational study   Study in which two or more traits, behaviors, or events are measured so that the degree of relationship between them may be determined, usually through statistical procedures.

Counterbalancing   Technique for controlling order effects by distributing progressive error across the different treatment conditions of the experiment; may also control carryover effects. *See also* between-subjects and within-subjects counterbalancing.

Critical region   Portion(s) of the distribution of a test statistic extreme enough to satisfy the researcher's criterion for rejecting the null hypothesis—for instance, the most extreme 5 percent of a distribution where $p < .05$ is the chosen significance level. Also called the *region of rejection*.

Deductive model   The process of reasoning from general principles to predictions about specific instances; also called the *Galilean model*.

Degrees of freedom   The number of members of a set of data that can vary or change value without changing the value of a known statistic for those data.

Demand characteristics   Aspects of a situation that demand or elicit particular behaviors; may lead to distorted data by compelling subjects to produce responses that conform to what subjects believe is expected of them in the experiment.

Dependent variable   Variable measured to determine whether the independent variable had an effect.

Descriptive statistics   Standard procedures used to summarize and describe data quickly and clearly; summary statistics reported for an experiment, including mean, range, and standard deviation.

Deviant case analysis   Comparison between histories of typical and atypical individuals used to identify differences that may explain the origin of the deviance in question.

Direct relationship   Positive correlation.

Directional hypothesis   Statement predicting the exact pattern of results that will be observed, such as which treatment group will perform best.

Double blind experiment   Method of controlling experimenter bias by keeping both subjects and experimenters ignorant of the treatment administered to each subject.

Elimination   Technique to control extraneous variables by removing them from an experiment.

Error   Variability within and between treatment groups that is not produced by changes in the independent variable; variability produced by individual differences and other extraneous variables.

Etiology   The origin or cause of a behavior or disorder; also the study of the causes or origins of behaviors and disorders.

Experimental condition   Treatment condition in which subjects are exposed to a non-zero value of the independent variable, a set of antecedent conditions created by the experimenter to test the impact of various levels of the independent variable.

Experimental design   General structure and plan of the experiment, including the number of independent variables, treatment conditions, and whether the same subjects will be in all conditions.

Experimental group   Subjects in an experimental condition.

Experimental hypothesis   Statement of a potential relationship between at least two variables: the antecedent conditions that are manipulated (independent variable), and the behaviors to be measured (dependent variable).

Experimental method   Collecting data through the use of controlled experiments.

Experimental operational definition   Statement of the meaning of the independent variables, and the operations and procedures used to create the various treatment conditions of the experiment.

Experimentation   Process undertaken to discover something new or to demonstrate that events which have already occurred will occur again under a specified set of conditions; one of the five principal tools of the scientific method.

Experimenter bias   Extraneous behaviors of the experimenter that create confounding in the experiment; may include systematic changes in the experimenter's manner across treatment conditions. Sometimes called *experimenter effects*.

Explanation   Specifying the antecedent conditions that produce an event or behavior.

Ex post facto study   Study in which preexisting differences among subjects are treated as independent variables and used to form groups that may be compared on a dependent variable.

External validity   How well the findings of the experiment apply to situations not tested directly (for example, real life).

Extraneous variable   Variable other than the independent and dependent variables; variable that is not the main focus of the experiment and may confound the results if not controlled.

F ratio   Test statistic used in the analysis of variance; the ratio of between- to within-groups variance.

Face validity   The degree to which a measurement technique has self-evident meaning.

Factor   An independent variable.

Factorial design   Experimental design in which more than one independent variable is manipulated.

Field experiment   Experiment conducted outside the laboratory; used to increase external validity, verify earlier laboratory findings, and investigate problems that cannot be studied successfully in the laboratory.

Field study   Research investigation conducted in the field, or real-life setting, typically employing a variety of techniques including naturalistic observation, unobtrusive measures, and interviews.

TABLE B3. CRITICAL VALUES OF F (.05 LEVEL IN ROMAN TYPE, .01 LEVEL IN **BOLDFACE**) (cont.)

DEGREES OF FREEDOM FOR GREATER MEAN SQUARE [NUMERATOR]

DEGREES OF FREEDOM FOR LESSER MEAN SQUARE [DENOMINATOR]

df	1	2	3	4	5	6	7	8	9	10	11	12	14	16	20	24	30	40	50	75	100	200	500	∞
27	4.21 / **7.68**	3.35 / **5.49**	2.96 / **4.60**	2.73 / **4.11**	2.57 / **3.79**	2.46 / **3.56**	2.37 / **3.39**	2.30 / **3.26**	2.25 / **3.14**	2.20 / **3.06**	2.16 / **2.98**	2.13 / **2.93**	2.08 / **2.83**	2.03 / **2.74**	1.97 / **2.63**	1.93 / **2.55**	1.88 / **2.47**	1.84 / **2.38**	1.80 / **2.33**	1.76 / **2.25**	1.74 / **2.21**	1.71 / **2.16**	1.68 / **2.12**	1.67 / **2.10**
28	4.20 / **7.64**	3.34 / **5.45**	2.95 / **4.57**	2.71 / **4.07**	2.56 / **3.76**	2.44 / **3.53**	2.36 / **3.36**	2.29 / **3.23**	2.24 / **3.11**	2.19 / **3.03**	2.15 / **2.95**	2.12 / **2.90**	2.06 / **2.80**	2.02 / **2.71**	1.96 / **2.60**	1.91 / **2.52**	1.87 / **2.44**	1.81 / **2.35**	1.78 / **2.30**	1.75 / **2.22**	1.72 / **2.18**	1.69 / **2.13**	1.67 / **2.09**	1.65 / **2.06**
29	4.18 / **7.60**	3.33 / **5.42**	2.93 / **4.54**	2.70 / **4.04**	2.54 / **3.73**	2.43 / **3.50**	2.35 / **3.33**	2.28 / **3.20**	2.22 / **3.08**	2.18 / **3.00**	2.14 / **2.92**	2.10 / **2.87**	2.05 / **2.77**	2.00 / **2.68**	1.94 / **2.57**	1.90 / **2.49**	1.85 / **2.41**	1.80 / **2.32**	1.77 / **2.27**	1.73 / **2.19**	1.71 / **2.15**	1.68 / **2.10**	1.65 / **2.06**	1.64 / **2.03**
30	4.17 / **7.56**	3.32 / **5.39**	2.92 / **4.51**	2.69 / **4.02**	2.53 / **3.70**	2.42 / **3.47**	2.34 / **3.30**	2.27 / **3.17**	2.21 / **3.06**	2.16 / **2.98**	2.12 / **2.90**	2.09 / **2.84**	2.04 / **2.74**	1.99 / **2.66**	1.93 / **2.55**	1.89 / **2.47**	1.84 / **2.38**	1.79 / **2.29**	1.76 / **2.24**	1.72 / **2.16**	1.69 / **2.13**	1.66 / **2.07**	1.64 / **2.03**	1.62 / **2.01**
32	4.15 / **7.50**	3.30 / **5.34**	2.90 / **4.46**	2.67 / **3.97**	2.51 / **3.66**	2.40 / **3.42**	2.32 / **3.25**	2.25 / **3.12**	2.19 / **3.01**	2.14 / **2.94**	2.10 / **2.86**	2.07 / **2.80**	2.02 / **2.70**	1.97 / **2.62**	1.91 / **2.51**	1.86 / **2.42**	1.82 / **2.34**	1.76 / **2.25**	1.74 / **2.20**	1.69 / **2.12**	1.67 / **2.08**	1.64 / **2.02**	1.61 / **1.98**	1.59 / **1.96**
34	4.13 / **7.44**	3.28 / **5.29**	2.88 / **4.42**	2.65 / **3.93**	2.49 / **3.61**	2.38 / **3.38**	2.30 / **3.21**	2.23 / **3.08**	2.17 / **2.97**	2.12 / **2.89**	2.08 / **2.82**	2.05 / **2.76**	2.00 / **2.66**	1.95 / **2.58**	1.89 / **2.47**	1.84 / **2.38**	1.80 / **2.30**	1.74 / **2.21**	1.71 / **2.15**	1.67 / **2.08**	1.64 / **2.04**	1.61 / **1.98**	1.59 / **1.94**	1.57 / **1.91**
36	4.11 / **7.39**	3.26 / **5.25**	2.86 / **4.38**	2.63 / **3.89**	2.48 / **3.58**	2.36 / **3.35**	2.28 / **3.18**	2.21 / **3.04**	2.15 / **2.94**	2.10 / **2.86**	2.06 / **2.78**	2.03 / **2.72**	1.98 / **2.62**	1.93 / **2.54**	1.87 / **2.43**	1.82 / **2.35**	1.78 / **2.26**	1.72 / **2.17**	1.69 / **2.12**	1.65 / **2.04**	1.62 / **2.00**	1.59 / **1.94**	1.56 / **1.90**	1.55 / **1.87**
38	4.10 / **7.35**	3.25 / **5.21**	2.85 / **4.34**	2.62 / **3.86**	2.46 / **3.54**	2.35 / **3.32**	2.26 / **3.15**	2.19 / **3.02**	2.14 / **2.91**	2.09 / **2.82**	2.05 / **2.75**	2.02 / **2.69**	1.96 / **2.59**	1.92 / **2.51**	1.85 / **2.40**	1.80 / **2.32**	1.76 / **2.22**	1.71 / **2.14**	1.67 / **2.08**	1.63 / **2.00**	1.60 / **1.97**	1.57 / **1.90**	1.54 / **1.86**	1.53 / **1.84**
40	4.08 / **7.31**	3.23 / **5.18**	2.84 / **4.31**	2.61 / **3.83**	2.45 / **3.51**	2.34 / **3.29**	2.25 / **3.12**	2.18 / **2.99**	2.12 / **2.88**	2.07 / **2.80**	2.04 / **2.73**	2.00 / **2.66**	1.95 / **2.56**	1.90 / **2.49**	1.84 / **2.37**	1.79 / **2.29**	1.74 / **2.20**	1.69 / **2.11**	1.66 / **2.05**	1.61 / **1.97**	1.59 / **1.94**	1.55 / **1.88**	1.53 / **1.84**	1.51 / **1.81**
42	4.07 / **7.27**	3.22 / **5.15**	2.83 / **4.29**	2.59 / **3.80**	2.44 / **3.49**	2.32 / **3.26**	2.24 / **3.10**	2.17 / **2.96**	2.11 / **2.86**	2.06 / **2.77**	2.02 / **2.70**	1.99 / **2.64**	1.94 / **2.54**	1.89 / **2.46**	1.82 / **2.35**	1.78 / **2.26**	1.73 / **2.17**	1.68 / **2.08**	1.64 / **2.02**	1.60 / **1.94**	1.57 / **1.91**	1.54 / **1.85**	1.51 / **1.80**	1.49 / **1.78**
44	4.06 / **7.24**	3.21 / **5.12**	2.82 / **4.26**	2.58 / **3.78**	2.43 / **3.46**	2.31 / **3.24**	2.23 / **3.07**	2.16 / **2.94**	2.10 / **2.84**	2.05 / **2.75**	2.01 / **2.68**	1.98 / **2.62**	1.92 / **2.52**	1.88 / **2.44**	1.81 / **2.32**	1.76 / **2.24**	1.72 / **2.15**	1.66 / **2.06**	1.63 / **2.00**	1.58 / **1.92**	1.56 / **1.88**	1.52 / **1.82**	1.50 / **1.78**	1.48 / **1.75**
46	4.05 / **7.21**	3.20 / **5.10**	2.81 / **4.24**	2.57 / **3.76**	2.42 / **3.44**	2.30 / **3.22**	2.22 / **3.05**	2.14 / **2.92**	2.09 / **2.82**	2.04 / **2.73**	2.00 / **2.66**	1.97 / **2.60**	1.91 / **2.50**	1.87 / **2.42**	1.80 / **2.30**	1.75 / **2.22**	1.71 / **2.13**	1.65 / **2.04**	1.62 / **1.98**	1.57 / **1.90**	1.54 / **1.86**	1.51 / **1.80**	1.48 / **1.76**	1.46 / **1.72**
48	4.04 / **7.19**	3.19 / **5.08**	2.80 / **4.22**	2.56 / **3.74**	2.41 / **3.42**	2.30 / **3.20**	2.21 / **3.04**	2.14 / **2.90**	2.08 / **2.80**	2.03 / **2.71**	1.99 / **2.64**	1.96 / **2.58**	1.90 / **2.48**	1.86 / **2.40**	1.79 / **2.28**	1.74 / **2.20**	1.70 / **2.11**	1.64 / **2.02**	1.61 / **1.96**	1.56 / **1.88**	1.53 / **1.84**	1.50 / **1.78**	1.47 / **1.73**	1.45 / **1.70**

TABLE B3. CRITICAL VALUES OF F (.05 LEVEL IN ROMAN TYPE, .01 LEVEL IN **BOLDFACE**) (cont.)

DEGREES OF FREEDOM FOR GREATER MEAN SQUARE [NUMERATOR]

DEGREES OF FREEDOM FOR LESSER MEAN SQUARE [DENOMINATOR]

	1	2	3	4	5	6	7	8	9	10	11	12	14	16	20	24	30	40	50	75	100	200	500	∞
14	4.60 **8.86**	3.74 **6.51**	3.34 **5.56**	3.11 **5.03**	2.96 **4.69**	2.85 **4.46**	2.77 **4.28**	2.70 **4.14**	2.65 **4.03**	2.60 **3.94**	2.56 **3.86**	2.53 **3.80**	2.48 **3.70**	2.44 **3.62**	2.39 **3.51**	2.35 **3.43**	2.31 **3.34**	2.27 **3.26**	2.24 **3.21**	2.21 **3.14**	2.19 **3.11**	2.16 **3.06**	2.14 **3.02**	2.13 **3.00**
15	4.54 **8.68**	3.68 **6.36**	3.29 **5.42**	3.06 **4.89**	2.90 **4.56**	2.79 **4.32**	2.70 **4.14**	2.64 **4.00**	2.59 **3.89**	2.55 **3.80**	2.51 **3.73**	2.48 **3.67**	2.43 **3.56**	2.39 **3.48**	2.33 **3.36**	2.29 **3.29**	2.25 **3.20**	2.21 **3.12**	2.18 **3.07**	2.15 **3.00**	2.12 **2.97**	2.10 **2.92**	2.08 **2.89**	2.07 **2.87**
16	4.49 **8.53**	3.63 **6.23**	3.24 **5.29**	3.01 **4.77**	2.85 **4.44**	2.74 **4.20**	2.66 **4.03**	2.59 **3.89**	2.54 **3.78**	2.49 **3.69**	2.45 **3.61**	2.42 **3.55**	2.37 **3.45**	2.33 **3.37**	2.28 **3.25**	2.24 **3.18**	2.20 **3.10**	2.16 **3.01**	2.13 **2.96**	2.09 **2.89**	2.07 **2.86**	2.04 **2.80**	2.02 **2.77**	2.01 **2.75**
17	4.45 **8.40**	3.59 **6.11**	3.20 **5.18**	2.96 **4.67**	2.81 **4.34**	2.70 **4.10**	2.62 **3.93**	2.55 **3.79**	2.50 **3.68**	2.45 **3.59**	2.41 **3.52**	2.38 **3.45**	2.33 **3.35**	2.29 **3.27**	2.23 **3.16**	2.19 **3.08**	2.15 **3.00**	2.11 **2.92**	2.08 **2.86**	2.04 **2.79**	2.02 **2.76**	1.99 **2.70**	1.97 **2.67**	1.96 **2.65**
18	4.41 **8.28**	3.55 **6.01**	3.16 **5.09**	2.93 **4.58**	2.77 **4.25**	2.66 **4.01**	2.58 **3.85**	2.51 **3.71**	2.46 **3.60**	2.41 **3.51**	2.37 **3.44**	2.34 **3.37**	2.29 **3.27**	2.25 **3.19**	2.19 **3.07**	2.15 **3.00**	2.11 **2.91**	2.07 **2.83**	2.04 **2.78**	2.00 **2.71**	1.98 **2.68**	1.95 **2.62**	1.93 **2.59**	1.92 **2.57**
19	4.38 **8.18**	3.52 **5.93**	3.13 **5.01**	2.90 **4.50**	2.74 **4.17**	2.63 **3.94**	2.55 **3.77**	2.48 **3.63**	2.43 **3.52**	2.38 **3.43**	2.34 **3.36**	2.31 **3.30**	2.26 **3.19**	2.21 **3.12**	2.15 **3.00**	2.11 **2.92**	2.07 **2.84**	2.02 **2.76**	2.00 **2.70**	1.96 **2.63**	1.94 **2.60**	1.91 **2.54**	1.90 **2.51**	1.88 **2.49**
20	4.35 **8.10**	3.49 **5.85**	3.10 **4.94**	2.87 **4.43**	2.71 **4.10**	2.60 **3.87**	2.52 **3.71**	2.45 **3.56**	2.40 **3.45**	2.35 **3.37**	2.31 **3.30**	2.28 **3.23**	2.23 **3.13**	2.18 **3.05**	2.12 **2.94**	2.08 **2.86**	2.04 **2.77**	1.99 **2.69**	1.96 **2.63**	1.92 **2.56**	1.90 **2.53**	1.87 **2.47**	1.85 **2.44**	1.84 **2.42**
21	4.32 **8.02**	3.47 **5.78**	3.07 **4.87**	2.84 **4.37**	2.68 **4.04**	2.57 **3.81**	2.49 **3.65**	2.42 **3.51**	2.37 **3.40**	2.32 **3.31**	2.28 **3.24**	2.25 **3.17**	2.20 **3.07**	2.15 **2.99**	2.09 **2.88**	2.05 **2.80**	2.00 **2.72**	1.96 **2.63**	1.93 **2.58**	1.89 **2.51**	1.87 **2.47**	1.84 **2.42**	1.82 **2.38**	1.81 **2.36**
22	4.30 **7.94**	3.44 **5.72**	3.05 **4.82**	2.82 **4.31**	2.66 **3.99**	2.55 **3.76**	2.47 **3.59**	2.40 **3.45**	2.35 **3.35**	2.30 **3.26**	2.26 **3.18**	2.23 **3.12**	2.18 **3.02**	2.13 **2.94**	2.07 **2.83**	2.03 **2.75**	1.98 **2.67**	1.93 **2.58**	1.91 **2.53**	1.87 **2.46**	1.84 **2.42**	1.81 **2.37**	1.80 **2.33**	1.78 **2.31**
23	4.28 **7.88**	3.42 **5.66**	3.03 **4.76**	2.80 **4.26**	2.64 **3.94**	2.53 **3.71**	2.45 **3.54**	2.38 **3.41**	2.32 **3.30**	2.28 **3.21**	2.24 **3.14**	2.20 **3.07**	2.14 **2.97**	2.10 **2.89**	2.04 **2.78**	2.00 **2.70**	1.96 **2.62**	1.91 **2.53**	1.88 **2.48**	1.84 **2.41**	1.82 **2.37**	1.79 **2.32**	1.77 **2.28**	1.76 **2.26**
24	4.26 **7.82**	3.40 **5.61**	3.01 **4.72**	2.78 **4.22**	2.62 **3.90**	2.51 **3.67**	2.43 **3.50**	2.36 **3.36**	2.30 **3.25**	2.26 **3.17**	2.22 **3.09**	2.18 **3.03**	2.13 **2.93**	2.09 **2.85**	2.02 **2.74**	1.98 **2.66**	1.94 **2.58**	1.89 **2.49**	1.86 **2.44**	1.82 **2.36**	1.80 **2.33**	1.76 **2.27**	1.74 **2.23**	1.73 **2.21**
25	4.24 **7.77**	3.38 **5.57**	2.99 **4.68**	2.76 **4.18**	2.60 **3.86**	2.49 **3.63**	2.41 **3.46**	2.34 **3.32**	2.28 **3.21**	2.24 **3.13**	2.20 **3.05**	2.16 **2.99**	2.11 **2.89**	2.06 **2.81**	2.00 **2.70**	1.96 **2.62**	1.92 **2.54**	1.87 **2.45**	1.84 **2.40**	1.80 **2.32**	1.77 **2.29**	1.74 **2.23**	1.72 **2.19**	1.71 **2.17**
26	4.22 **7.72**	3.37 **5.53**	2.98 **4.64**	2.74 **4.14**	2.59 **3.82**	2.47 **3.59**	2.39 **3.42**	2.32 **3.29**	2.27 **3.17**	2.22 **3.09**	2.18 **3.02**	2.15 **2.96**	2.10 **2.86**	2.05 **2.77**	1.99 **2.66**	1.95 **2.58**	1.90 **2.50**	1.85 **2.41**	1.82 **2.36**	1.78 **2.28**	1.76 **2.25**	1.72 **2.19**	1.70 **2.15**	1.69 **2.13**

Note: The function, $F = e$ with exponent $2z$, is computed in part from Fisher's table VI (7). Additional entries are by interpolation, mostly graphical.

Table B3. Critical Values of F (.05 Level in Roman Type, .01 Level in **Boldface**)

DEGREES OF FREEDOM FOR GREATER MEAN SQUARE [NUMERATOR]

Each cell shows the .05 level value (roman) / .01 level value (**boldface**). Rows = DEGREES OF FREEDOM FOR LESSER MEAN SQUARE [DENOMINATOR].

df	1	2	3	4	5	6	7	8	9	10	11	12	14	16	20	24	30	40	50	75	100	200	500	∞
1	161 / **4,052**	200 / **4,999**	216 / **5,403**	225 / **5,625**	230 / **5,764**	234 / **5,859**	237 / **5,928**	239 / **5,981**	241 / **6,022**	242 / **6,056**	243 / **6,082**	244 / **5,106**	245 / **6,142**	246 / **6,169**	248 / **6,208**	249 / **6,234**	250 / **6,261**	251 / **6,286**	252 / **6,302**	253 / **6,323**	253 / **6,334**	254 / **6,352**	254 / **6,361**	254 / **6,366**
2	18.51 / **98.49**	19.00 / **99.00**	19.16 / **99.17**	19.25 / **99.25**	19.30 / **99.30**	19.33 / **99.33**	19.36 / **99.36**	19.37 / **99.37**	19.38 / **99.39**	19.39 / **99.40**	19.40 / **99.41**	19.41 / **99.42**	19.42 / **99.43**	19.43 / **99.44**	19.44 / **99.45**	19.45 / **99.46**	19.46 / **99.47**	19.47 / **99.48**	19.47 / **99.48**	19.48 / **99.49**	19.49 / **99.49**	19.49 / **99.49**	19.50 / **99.50**	19.50 / **99.50**
3	10.13 / **34.12**	9.55 / **30.82**	9.28 / **29.46**	9.12 / **28.71**	9.01 / **28.24**	8.94 / **27.91**	8.88 / **27.67**	8.84 / **27.49**	8.81 / **27.34**	8.78 / **27.23**	8.76 / **27.13**	8.74 / **27.05**	8.71 / **26.92**	8.69 / **26.83**	8.66 / **26.69**	8.64 / **26.60**	8.62 / **26.50**	8.60 / **26.41**	8.58 / **26.35**	8.57 / **26.27**	8.56 / **26.23**	8.54 / **26.18**	8.54 / **26.14**	8.53 / **26.12**
4	7.71 / **21.20**	6.94 / **18.00**	6.59 / **16.69**	6.39 / **15.98**	6.26 / **15.52**	6.16 / **15.21**	6.09 / **14.98**	6.04 / **14.80**	6.00 / **14.66**	5.96 / **14.54**	5.93 / **14.45**	5.91 / **14.37**	5.87 / **14.24**	5.84 / **14.15**	5.80 / **14.02**	5.77 / **13.93**	5.74 / **13.83**	5.71 / **13.74**	5.70 / **13.69**	5.68 / **13.61**	5.66 / **13.57**	5.65 / **13.52**	5.64 / **13.48**	5.63 / **13.46**
5	6.61 / **16.26**	5.79 / **13.27**	5.41 / **12.06**	5.19 / **11.39**	5.05 / **10.97**	4.95 / **10.67**	4.88 / **10.45**	4.82 / **10.29**	4.78 / **10.15**	4.74 / **10.05**	4.70 / **9.96**	4.68 / **9.89**	4.64 / **9.77**	4.60 / **9.68**	4.56 / **9.55**	4.53 / **9.47**	4.50 / **9.38**	4.46 / **9.29**	4.44 / **9.24**	4.42 / **9.17**	4.40 / **9.13**	4.38 / **9.07**	4.37 / **9.04**	4.36 / **9.02**
6	5.99 / **13.74**	5.14 / **10.92**	4.76 / **9.78**	4.53 / **9.15**	4.39 / **8.75**	4.28 / **8.47**	4.21 / **8.26**	4.15 / **8.10**	4.10 / **7.98**	4.06 / **7.87**	4.03 / **7.79**	4.00 / **7.72**	3.96 / **7.60**	3.92 / **7.52**	3.87 / **7.39**	3.84 / **7.31**	3.81 / **7.23**	3.77 / **7.14**	3.75 / **7.09**	3.72 / **7.02**	3.71 / **6.99**	3.69 / **6.94**	3.68 / **6.90**	3.67 / **6.88**
7	5.59 / **12.25**	4.74 / **9.55**	4.35 / **8.45**	4.12 / **7.85**	3.97 / **7.46**	3.87 / **7.19**	3.79 / **7.00**	3.73 / **6.84**	3.68 / **6.71**	3.63 / **6.62**	3.60 / **6.54**	3.57 / **6.47**	3.52 / **6.35**	3.49 / **6.27**	3.44 / **6.15**	3.41 / **6.07**	3.38 / **5.98**	3.34 / **5.90**	3.32 / **5.85**	3.29 / **5.78**	3.28 / **5.75**	3.25 / **5.70**	3.24 / **5.67**	3.23 / **5.65**
8	5.32 / **11.26**	4.46 / **8.65**	4.07 / **7.59**	3.84 / **7.01**	3.69 / **6.63**	3.58 / **6.37**	3.50 / **6.19**	3.44 / **6.03**	3.39 / **5.91**	3.34 / **5.82**	3.31 / **5.74**	3.28 / **5.67**	3.23 / **5.56**	3.20 / **5.48**	3.15 / **5.36**	3.12 / **5.28**	3.08 / **5.20**	3.05 / **5.11**	3.03 / **5.06**	3.00 / **5.00**	2.98 / **4.96**	2.96 / **4.91**	2.94 / **4.88**	2.93 / **4.86**
9	5.12 / **10.56**	4.26 / **8.02**	3.86 / **6.99**	3.63 / **6.42**	3.48 / **6.06**	3.37 / **5.80**	3.29 / **5.62**	3.23 / **5.47**	3.18 / **5.35**	3.13 / **5.26**	3.10 / **5.18**	3.07 / **5.11**	3.02 / **5.00**	2.98 / **4.92**	2.93 / **4.80**	2.90 / **4.73**	2.86 / **4.64**	2.82 / **4.56**	2.80 / **4.51**	2.77 / **4.45**	2.76 / **4.41**	2.73 / **4.36**	2.72 / **4.33**	2.71 / **4.31**
10	4.96 / **10.04**	4.10 / **7.56**	3.71 / **6.55**	3.48 / **5.99**	3.33 / **5.64**	3.22 / **5.39**	3.14 / **5.21**	3.07 / **5.06**	3.02 / **4.95**	2.97 / **4.85**	2.94 / **4.78**	2.91 / **4.71**	2.86 / **4.60**	2.82 / **4.52**	2.77 / **4.41**	2.74 / **4.33**	2.70 / **4.25**	2.67 / **4.17**	2.64 / **4.12**	2.61 / **4.05**	2.59 / **4.01**	2.56 / **3.96**	2.55 / **3.93**	2.54 / **3.91**
11	4.84 / **9.65**	3.98 / **7.20**	3.59 / **6.22**	3.36 / **5.67**	3.20 / **5.32**	3.09 / **5.07**	3.01 / **4.88**	2.95 / **4.74**	2.90 / **4.63**	2.86 / **4.54**	2.82 / **4.46**	2.79 / **4.40**	2.74 / **4.29**	2.70 / **4.21**	2.65 / **4.10**	2.61 / **4.02**	2.57 / **3.94**	2.53 / **3.86**	2.50 / **3.80**	2.47 / **3.74**	2.45 / **3.70**	2.42 / **3.66**	2.41 / **3.62**	2.40 / **3.60**
12	4.75 / **9.33**	3.88 / **6.93**	3.49 / **5.95**	3.26 / **5.41**	3.11 / **5.06**	3.00 / **4.82**	2.92 / **4.65**	2.85 / **4.50**	2.80 / **4.39**	2.76 / **4.30**	2.72 / **4.22**	2.69 / **4.16**	2.64 / **4.05**	2.60 / **3.98**	2.54 / **3.86**	2.50 / **3.78**	2.46 / **3.70**	2.42 / **3.61**	2.40 / **3.56**	2.36 / **3.49**	2.35 / **3.46**	2.32 / **3.41**	2.31 / **3.38**	2.30 / **3.36**
13	4.67 / **9.07**	3.80 / **6.70**	3.41 / **5.74**	3.18 / **5.20**	3.02 / **4.86**	2.92 / **4.62**	2.84 / **4.44**	2.77 / **4.30**	2.72 / **4.19**	2.67 / **4.10**	2.63 / **4.02**	2.60 / **3.96**	2.55 / **3.85**	2.51 / **3.78**	2.46 / **3.67**	2.42 / **3.59**	2.38 / **3.51**	2.34 / **3.42**	2.32 / **3.37**	2.28 / **3.30**	2.26 / **3.27**	2.24 / **3.21**	2.22 / **3.18**	2.21 / **3.16**

Note: Find the critical value of F for each of your F ratios. Locate the degrees of freedom associated with the numerator of your F ratio along the top of the table. Locate the degrees of freedom associated with the denominator of your F ratio along the side of the table. The place where the correct row and column meet indicates the appropriate critical values. The numbers in light type give you the values at the .05 level; the numbers in dark type give you the values at the .01 level. Reject the null hypothesis when the computed value of F is equal to or greater than the table value.

Table B2. Critical Values of t

	LEVEL OF SIGNIFICANCE FOR ONE-TAILED TEST			
	.05	.025	.01	.005
	LEVEL OF SIGNIFICANCE FOR TWO-TAILED TEST			
df	.10	.05	.02	.01
1	6.314	12.706	31.821	63.657
2	2.920	4.303	6.965	9.925
3	2.353	3.182	4.541	5.841
4	2.132	2.776	3.747	4.604
5	2.015	2.571	3.365	4.032
6	1.943	2.447	3.143	3.707
7	1.895	2.365	2.998	3.499
8	1.860	2.306	2.896	3.355
9	1.833	2.262	2.821	3.250
10	1.812	2.228	2.764	3.169
11	1.796	2.201	2.718	3.106
12	1.782	2.179	2.681	3.055
13	1.771	2.160	2.650	3.012
14	1.761	2.145	2.624	2.977
15	1.753	2.131	2.602	2.947
16	1.746	2.120	2.583	2.921
17	1.740	2.110	2.567	2.898
18	1.734	2.101	2.552	2.878
19	1.729	2.093	2.539	2.861
20	1.725	2.086	2.528	2.845
21	1.721	2.080	2.518	2.831
22	1.717	2.074	2.508	2.819
23	1.714	2.069	2.500	2.807
24	1.711	2.064	2.492	2.797
25	1.708	2.060	2.485	2.787
26	1.706	2.056	2.479	2.779
27	1.703	2.052	2.473	2.771
28	1.701	2.048	2.467	2.763
29	1.699	2.045	2.462	2.756
30	1.697	2.042	2.457	2.750
40	1.684	2.021	2.423	2.704
60	1.671	2.000	2.390	2.660
120	1.658	1.980	2.358	2.617
∞	1.645	1.960	2.326	2.576

Fisher and Yates. From Table III in *Statistical Tables for Biological, Agricultural and Medical Research*, published by Longman Group Ltd., London. (Previously published by Oliver and Boyd, Edinburgh.) Reprinted by permission of the authors and publishers.

Fixed model   Experiment in which the values of the independent variables are fixed (set) by the experimenter.

Galilean model   *See* deductive model.

Generalizing   Process of extending the results of a specific experiment to individuals and situations not directly tested; an inductive process.

Good thinking   Organized and rational thought, including application of the principle of parsimony; one of the five principal tools of the scientific method.

Grand mean   An average of all the treatment means.

H_0   *See* null hypothesis.

H_1   *See* alternative hypothesis.

Higher-order interaction   Interaction effect involving more than two independent variables.

Hypothetical construct   Underlying process, such as hunger and learning, postulated to explain observable behaviors.

Independent variable   Antecedent condition deliberately manipulated by the experimenter to assess its effect on behavior.

Inductive model   Process of reasoning from specific cases to more general principles; also called the *Aristotelian model*.

Inferential statistics   Statistics based on samples but used as indicators of behavior in the population.

Informed consent   Subject's agreement to participate in a research project after the nature and purpose of the study have been explained.

Interaction   Effect occurring when the impact of one independent variable changes depending on the level of another independent variable in the experiment.

Interaction effect   Amount of variability in the dependent measure produced by the combination of two or more independent variables in an experiment, measured by statistical procedures.

Internal validity   Soundness of the procedures within an experiment; how well the experiment measures the impact of the independent variable on the dependent variable.

Internally valid   Experiment in which the results can be successfully attributed to changes in the independent variable; free of confounding.

Interval scale   Measure of magnitude or quantitative size having equal intervals between values, but no absolute zero point.

Intuition   Development of ideas from hunches; knowing directly without reasoning from objective data.

Inverse relationship   Negative correlation.

Large N design   Experiment that requires large groups of subjects, constrasted with small N designs requiring one or two subjects.

Latent content   Implicit meaning; the meaning behind a question.

Laws   Explanatory principles that can be applied (generalized) to all situations.

Level   Value of an independent variable in an experiment.

Level of measurement   Kind of scale used to measure a variable. There are four levels: ratio, interval, ordinal, and nominal.

Main effect   Variability in the dependent variable produced by changes in the level of one independent variable; a treatment effect.

Manifest content   Explicit meaning of a question, sentence, dream, or statement.

MANOVA   *See* multivariate analysis of variance.

Mean   Average of all the scores in a sample; a good estimate of what is typical of the sample.

Mean square (MS)   Average squared deviation; a variance estimate used in ANOVA procedures and found by dividing the sum of squares by the degrees of freedom.

Measured operational definition   A definition of the dependent variable and of the procedures used to measure it.

Measurement   Process of establishing the dimensions of an event or behavior; one of the five principal tools of the scientific method.

Methodology   Scientific techniques used to collect and evaluate psychological data.

Mixed model   Experiment in which some independent variables are fixed factors and others are random factors.

Multiple group design   Research design in which there are more than two treatment conditions and one independent variable.

Multiple independent groups design   Between-subjects design having more than two treatment conditions and having subjects assigned at random to each condition.

Multivariate analysis of variance (MANOVA)   Statistical procedure used to study the impact of an independent variable on two or more dependent variables.

Multivariate design   Research designs and statistical procedures used to evaluate the effects of many variables in combination. Common multivariate designs are multiple correlation, factor analysis, and multivariate analysis of variance.

Naturalistic observation   Technique of observing events as they occur in their natural setting.

Negative correlation   Relationship existing between two variables such that an increase in one measure is associated with a decrease in the other; the value of the computed correlation coefficient is negative. Also called an *inverse relationship.*

Nominal scale   Measure that classifies items into distinct categories having no quantitative relationship to one another.

Nondirectional hypothesis   Hypothesis that predicts a difference without predicting the exact pattern of results.

Normal curve   Symmetrical, bell-shaped curve.

Null hypothesis (H_0)   Statement that the performance of treatment groups is so similar that the groups must belong to the same population; a way of saying the experimental manipulation had no noticeable effect.

Objective   Not influenced by personal feelings or expectations; a characteristic of good scientific data.

Observation   Systematic noting and recording of events; one of the five principal tools of the scientific method.

Occam's razor   *See* principle of parsimony.

Omnibus test   Statistical procedure used to assess whether a statistically significant difference exists among all the treatment means (for example, the F test); post hoc tests must be used to make pair by pair comparisons.

One-tailed test   Statistical procedure used when a directional prediction has been made; the critical region of the distribution of the test statistic (t, for instance) is measured in just one tail of the distribution.

Operational definition   Statement of the precise meaning of a variable within an experiment; defines a variable in terms of observable operations, procedures, and measurements.

Order effects   Changes in performance that occur when a treatment condition falls in different places in a series of treatments.

Ordinal scale   Measure reflecting differences only in magnitude, where magnitude is measured in the form of ranks; has no equal intervals between values and no absolute zero.

Parameter Set of properties whose values determine the characteristics or values of other variables.

Parsimony *See* principle of parsimony.

Partial counterbalancing Technique to control progressive error by using some of the available sequences of the treatment conditions; less effective than complete counterbalancing.

Pearson product moment correlation coefficient (r) Statistical procedure used to determine the degree of relationship between two variables; its values vary between -1.00 and $+1.00$. The absolute (unsigned) value reflects the degree of relationship; the sign (plus or minus) indicates the direction of the relationship.

Phenomenology Nonexperimental method of gathering data by attending to and describing one's immediate experience.

Physical variables Aspect of the testing conditions, such as noise, lighting, and time of day, that need to be controlled.

Pilot study Small-scale study to try out experimental procedures; pretest of the experimental design.

Placebo Pill, injection, or other treatment that contains none of the actual independent variable.

Population All people, animals, or objects with at least one characteristic in common.

Positive correlation Relationship between two measures such that an increase in the value of one measure is associated with an increase in the value of the other; the value of the computed correlation coefficient is positive; also called a *direct relationship*.

Post hoc test Statistical procedure used after the overall data analysis indicates a significant difference among treatments; used to pinpoint which differences are significant.

Practice effects Changes in subjects' performance resulting from practice.

Predictive validity Degree to which a measure, definition, or experiment yields information that enables one to predict what subjects will do in another situation.

Principle of parsimony A criterion for scientific explanations which states that the simplest explanation is preferred until ruled out by conflicting evidence; also known as *Occam's razor*.

Progressive error Fatigue, practice, and other extraneous sequence effects producing changes in subjects' responses during within-subjects experiments.

Psychology experiment Controlled procedure in which at least two different treatment conditions are applied to subjects whose behaviors are then measured and compared to test a hypothesis about the effects of the treatments on behavior.

Psychopathology Disorders involving impairment of personality functioning whose symptoms may include mild to gross disturbances of thought, action, and emotional behavior; the study of such disorders.

Pygmalion effect *See* Rosenthal effect.

Random assignment Technique of assigning subjects to treatments so that each subject has an equal chance of being assigned to each treatment condition.

Random model Experiment in which randomly selected values of the independent variables are used as the treatment levels.

Random number table Computer-generated table of numbers selected so that each number in the set has an equal chance of appearing in each position of the table.

Random selection Unbiased selection process conducted so that all members of the population have an equal chance of being selected to participate in the experiment.

Randomized counterbalancing   Simplest partial counterbalancing procedure in which as many of the available sequences of the treatment conditions as there are subjects for the experiment are randomly selected out.

Range   Difference between highest and lowest scores; a rough indication of the amount of variability in the data.

Ratio scale   Measure of magnitude having equal intervals between values and an absolute zero point.

Raw data   Data recorded as the experiment is run; the responses of individual subjects.

Reactivity   Tendency of subjects to alter responses or behaviors when they are aware of the presence of an observer.

Reliability   Degree of agreement between different observers; degree of consistency from one occasion to another.

Replication   Process of repeating research procedures to verify that the outcome will be the same as before; one of the five principal tools of the scientific method.

Response set   Tendency to respond to the latent meaning of a question rather than its manifest content.

Response style   Tendency to respond in a particular way regardless of the latent or manifest content of the question asked.

Robust   Having the quality that its assumptions can be violated without creating serious errors.

Rosenthal effect   Phenomenon of experimenters treating subjects differently depending on what they expect from them; also called the *Pygmalion effect*.

Sample   Part of something assumed to be representative of the whole.

Sample of subjects   Part of the population of interest chosen to participate in a study, and used to draw inferences about the behavior of the entire population.

Science   Systematic gathering of data to provide descriptions of events taking place under specific conditions, enabling researchers to explain, predict, and control events.

Serendipity   Happy accident; the knack of finding things that are not being sought.

Significance level   Criterion for deciding whether to accept or reject the null hypothesis; also called *alpha level*.

Significant difference   Difference more extreme than the differences one would probably find among *any* groups measured on the dependent variable; meeting a predetermined criterion set by the experimenter, typically $p < .05$.

Single blind experiment   Experiment in which subjects are not told which of the treatment conditions they are getting; procedure used to control demand characteristics.

Small N design   Complete experiment run with only one or two subjects in which baseline data are collected during an initial control condition; the experimental treatment is applied, and the experimenter then reinstates the original control condition to verify that changes observed in behavior were caused by the experimental intervention.

Social facilitation effect   Improvement in performance that occurs when others are present.

Social variables   Qualities of the relationships between subjects and experimenters that may influence the results of an experiment.

Standard deviation   Square root of the variance; measures the average deviation of scores about the mean, thus reflecting the amount of variability in the data.

Standard normal curve   Distribution standardized to have its mean equal to 0, and its standard deviation equal to 1.

Statistical inference   Statement made about a population on the basis of the observed behaviors of samples.

Statistically significant   Meeting the set criterion for significance; the data do not support the null hypothesis, confirming a change between the groups that occurred as a result of the experiment.

Subject variables   All the characteristics of the subjects themselves that might influence the outcome of the experiment.

Sum of squares (SS)   Sum of squared deviations of scores from a mean; an index of variability used in the analysis of variance procedures.

Summary data   Descriptive statistics computed from the raw data of an experiment, including the mean and the standard deviation.

Synthetic statement   Statement that may be either true or false.

Systematic   Following a regular, orderly pattern or plan.

t **test**   Procedure used to evaluate the likelihood of a particular difference between treatment means by computing the test statistic *t*; used to analyze the results of a two-condition experiment with one independent variable and internal or ratio data.

t **test for independent groups**   Procedure used to evaluate the likelihood of a particular difference between treatment means by computing the test statistic *t*; used for two different randomly selected samples of subjects, two treatments, and interval or ratio data.

t **test for matched groups**   Procedure used to evaluate the likelihood of a particular difference between treatment means by computing the test statistic *t*; subjects matched on a variable that is highly related to the dependent variable are assigned to each of two treatment conditions at random.

Test statistics   *See* inferential statistics.

Testable   Capable of being tested, typically used in reference to a hypothesis. Two requirements must be met in order to have a testable hypothesis: procedures for manipulating the setting must exist, and the predicted outcome must be observable.

Theory   Set of general principles that can be used to explain and predict behavior.

Treatment   Specific set of antecedent conditions created by the experimenter and presented to subjects to test its effect on behavior; also called the *treatment condition.*

Two-factor experiment   The simplest factorial design, having two independent variables.

Two-group design   The simplest experimental design, used when only two treatment conditions are needed.

Two independent groups design   Experimental design in which randomly selected subjects are placed in each of two treatment conditions through random assignment.

Two matched groups design   Experimental design having two treatment conditions and subjects matched on a subject variable thought to be highly related to the dependent variable. Subjects are generally first measured on the matching variable, then divided into pairs having the most similar scores; members of each pair are then assigned to treatment conditions at random.

Two-tailed test   Statistical procedure used when a nondirectional prediction has been made; the critical region of the distribution of the test statistic (*t* for instance) is measured in just one tail of the distribution.

Type 1 error   Error made by rejecting the null hypothesis even though it is really true.

Type 2 error   Error made by accepting the null hypothesis even though it is really false.

Unobtrusive measures   Procedures used to assess subjects' behavior without their knowledge; used to obtain more objective data.

Validity   The merit of a statement, or its ability to withstand criticism; the degree to which we are measuring or testing what interests us; whether the procedures can withstand criticism.

Variability   Amount of fluctuation observed in something.

Variance   Average squared deviation from the mean; a more accurate measure of variability than the range.

Within-groups variability   Degree to which the scores of subjects in the same treatment group differ from one another; an index of the degree of fluctuation among scores that is attributable to error.

Within-subjects counterbalancing   Technique for controlling progressive error within each subject by distributing the effects equally across all conditions completed by each subject.

Within-subjects design   Research design in which each subject serves in more than one treatment condition.

Zero value   Level of the independent variable that represents no treatment; a control condition.

Index